The Cost of Racism for People of Color

CULTURAL, RACIAL, AND ETHNIC PSYCHOLOGY BOOK SERIES

Qualitative Strategies for Ethnocultural Research
    Edited by Donna K. Nagata, Laura Kohn-Wood, and Lisa A. Suzuki

Positive Psychology in Racial and Ethnic Groups: Theory, Research, and Practice
    Edited by Edward C. Chang, Christina A. Downey,
    Jameson K. Hirsch, and Natalie J. Lin

The Cost of Racism for People of Color: Contextualizing Experiences of Discrimination
    Edited by Alvin N. Alvarez, Christopher T. H. Liang,
    and Helen A. Neville

The Cost of Racism for People of Color

CONTEXTUALIZING EXPERIENCES
OF DISCRIMINATION

≈

Edited by ALVIN N. ALVAREZ,
CHRISTOPHER T. H. LIANG, and
HELEN A. NEVILLE

AMERICAN PSYCHOLOGICAL ASSOCIATION
WASHINGTON, DC

Copyright © 2016 by the American Psychological Association. All rights reserved. Except as permitted under the United States Copyright Act of 1976, no part of this publication may be reproduced or distributed in any form or by any means, including, but not limited to, the process of scanning and digitization, or stored in a database or retrieval system, without the prior written permission of the publisher.

Published by
American Psychological Association
750 First Street, NE
Washington, DC 20002
www.apa.org

To order
APA Order Department
P.O. Box 92984
Washington, DC 20090-2984
Tel: (800) 374-2721; Direct: (202) 336-5510
Fax: (202) 336-5502; TDD/TTY: (202) 336-6123
Online: www.apa.org/pubs/books
E-mail: order@apa.org

In the U.K., Europe, Africa, and the Middle East, copies may be ordered from
American Psychological Association
3 Henrietta Street
Covent Garden, London
WC2E 8LU England

Typeset in Goudy by Circle Graphics, Inc., Columbia, MD

Printer: United Book Press, Baltimore, MD
Cover Designer: Beth Schlenoff Design, Bethesda, MD

The opinions and statements published are the responsibility of the authors, and such opinions and statements do not necessarily represent the policies of the American Psychological Association.

Library of Congress Cataloging-in-Publication Data
Names: Alvarez, Alvin N. | Liang, Christopher T. H. | Neville, Helen A.
Title: The cost of racism for people of color : contextualizing experiences of discrimination / Alvin N. Alvarez, Christopher T. H. Liang, Helen A. Neville.
Description: Washington, DC : American Psychological Association, 2016. | Series: Cultural, racial, and ethnic psychology book series | Includes bibliographical references and index.
Identifiers: LCCN 2015035793 | ISBN 9781433820953 (alk. paper) | ISBN 1433820951 (alk. paper)
Subjects: LCSH: Race discrimination—United States—Psychological aspects. | Minorities—United States—Psychology.
Classification: LCC E184.A1 A493 2016 | DDC 305.800973—dc23 LC record available at http://lccn.loc.gov/2015035793

British Library Cataloguing-in-Publication Data
A CIP record is available from the British Library.

Printed in the United States of America
First Edition

http://dx.doi.org/10.1037/14852-000

This was fueled and nurtured by the love, patience, and laughter of Grace, Sabrina, and Sophie. And inspired by the resistance and resilience of the many of us who have faced racism yet continue to walk forward.
Salamat kayo!
—*Alvin N. Alvarez*

To all people who are engaged in the fight against racism, may we continue to demonstrate our compassion, strength, creativity, and success. And to Alison, Nate, and Bryce, thank you for giving me the strength to persist in my own fight for racial justice.
—*Christopher T. H. Liang*

To those who have struggled for racial justice. Thank you for providing us hope and showing us that the road to progress is only paved by persistent struggle.
—*Helen A. Neville*

CONTENTS

Contributors xi

Series Foreword xiii
Frederick T. L. Leong

Introduction 3
Alvin N. Alvarez, Christopher T. H. Liang, and Helen A. Neville

I. Theoretical and Methodological Foundations 9

Chapter 1. A Theoretical Overview of the Impact of Racism on People of Color 11
Alex Pieterse and Shantel Powell

Chapter 2. Applying Intersectionality Theory to Research on Perceived Racism 31
Jioni A. Lewis and Patrick R. Grzanka

Chapter 3. Improving the Measurement of Self-Reported Racial Discrimination: Challenges and Opportunities 55
David R. Williams

Chapter 4. Moderators and Mediators of the Experience of Perceived Racism 85
Alvin N. Alvarez, Christopher T. H. Liang, Carin Molenaar, and David Nguyen

II. Context and Costs 107

Chapter 5. Racism and Mental Health: Examining the Link Between Racism and Depression From a Social Cognitive Perspective 109
Elizabeth Brondolo, Wan Ng, Kristy-Lee J. Pierre, and Robert Lane

Chapter 6. Racism and Behavioral Outcomes Over the Life Course 133
Gilbert C. Gee and Angie Denisse Otiniano Verissimo

Chapter 7. Racism and Physical Health Disparities 163
Joseph Keaweʻaimoku Kaholokula

Chapter 8. The Impact of Racism on Education and the Educational Experiences of Students of Color 189
Adrienne D. Dixson, Dominique M. Clayton, Leah Q. Peoples, and Rema Reynolds

Chapter 9. The Costs of Racism on Workforce Entry and Work Adjustment 203
Justin C. Perry and Lela L. Pickett

Chapter 10. The Impact of Racism on Communities of Color: Historical Contexts and Contemporary Issues 229
Azara L. Santiago-Rivera, Hector Y. Adames, Nayeli Y. Chavez-Dueñas, and Gregory Benson-Flórez

III. Interventions and Future Directions 247

Chapter 11. Racial Trauma Recovery: A Race-Informed Therapeutic Approach to Racial Wounds 249
Lillian Comas-Díaz

Chapter 12. Critical Race, Psychology, and Social Policy: Refusing Damage, Cataloging Oppression, and Documenting Desire 273
Michelle Fine and William E. Cross, Jr.

Chapter 13.	Education Interventions for Reducing Racism 295
	Elizabeth Vera, Daniel Camacho, Megan Polanin, and Manuel Salgado
Chapter 14.	Toward a Relevant Psychology of Prejudice, Stereotyping, and Discrimination: Linking Science and Practice to Develop Interventions That Work in Community Settings 317
	Ignacio D. Acevedo-Polakovich, Kara L. Beck, Erin Hawks, and Sarah E. Ogdie

Index 339

About the Editors 355

CONTRIBUTORS

Ignacio D. Acevedo-Polakovich, PhD, Michigan State University, East Lansing
Hector Y. Adames, PsyD, The Chicago School of Professional Psychology, Chicago, IL
Alvin N. Alvarez, PhD, San Francisco State University, San Francisco, CA
Kara L. Beck, MA, Michigan State University, East Lansing
Gregory Benson-Flórez, PhD, The Chicago School of Professional Psychology, Chicago, IL
Elizabeth Brondolo, PhD, St. John's University, Jamaica, NY
Daniel Camacho, MA, Loyola University Chicago, Chicago, IL
Nayeli Y. Chavez-Dueñas, PhD, The Chicago School of Professional Psychology, Chicago, IL
Dominique M. Clayton, PhD, University of Illinois at Urbana–Champaign
Lillian Comas-Díaz, PhD, Transcultural Mental Health Institute, George Washington University, Washington, DC
William E. Cross, Jr., PhD, University of Denver, Denver, CO
Adrienne D. Dixson, PhD, University of Illinois at Urbana–Champaign
Michelle Fine, PhD, City University of New York, New York
Gilbert C. Gee, PhD, University of California, Los Angeles

Patrick R. Grzanka, PhD, University of Tennessee, Knoxville
Erin Hawks, PhD, University of Oklahoma Health Sciences Center, Oklahoma City
Joseph Keaweʻaimoku Kaholokula, PhD, University of Hawaiʻi at Mānoa, Honolulu
Robert Lane, BA, St. John's University, Jamaica, NY
Frederick T. L. Leong, PhD, Michigan State University, East Lansing
Jioni A. Lewis, PhD, University of Tennessee, Knoxville
Christopher T. H. Liang, PhD, Lehigh University, Philadelphia, PA
Carin Molenaar, MEd, Lehigh University, Philadelphia, PA
Helen A. Neville, PhD, University of Illinois at Urbana–Champaign
Wan Ng, MA, St. John's University, Jamaica, NY
David Nguyen, BS, Lehigh University, Philadelphia, PA
Sarah E. Ogdie, MSW, private practice, Community Tampa Bay, Tampa Bay, FL
Angie Denisse Otiniano Verissimo, PhD, California State University, San Bernardino
Leah Q. Peoples, MA, University of Illinois at Urbana–Champaign
Justin C. Perry, PhD, Cleveland State University, Cleveland, OH
Lela L. Pickett, MS, Cleveland State University, Cleveland, OH
Kristy-Lee J. Pierre, MA, St. John's University, Jamaica, NY
Alex Pieterse, PhD, The State University of New York at Albany
Megan Polanin, PhD, Loyola University Chicago, Chicago, IL
Shantel Powell, BS, The State University of New York at Albany
Rema Reynolds, PhD, independent scholar
Manuel Salgado, MsEd, LPC, Loyola University Chicago, Chicago, IL
Azara L. Santiago-Rivera, PhD, The Chicago School of Professional Psychology, Chicago, IL
Elizabeth Vera, PhD, Loyola University Chicago, Chicago, IL
David R. Williams, PhD, Harvard University, Boston, MA

SERIES FOREWORD

As series editor of the American Psychological Association's (APA) Division 45 (Society for the Psychological Study of Culture, Ethnicity, and Race) Cultural, Racial, and Ethnic Psychology book series, it is my pleasure to introduce another volume in the series: *The Cost of Racism for People of Color: Theory, Research, and Practice*, edited by Alvin N. Alvarez, Christopher T. H. Liang, and Helen A. Neville. This volume is particularly timely, given the contemporary focus on the Black Lives Matter movement in reaction to the police killings of African American civilians in our cities. Yet, psychology's interest in racism has a much longer history.

From Kenneth and Mamie Clark's Doll Preference Study in the 1940s to the *Brown vs. Board of Education* ruling, psychologists and other social scientists have been examining the antecedents, manifestation, experiences, and consequences of racism for many decades. From Robert Guthrie's (1976) *Even the Rat Was White: A Historical View of Psychology* to the recent work of Mahzarin R. Banaji and Anthony G. Greenwald on implicit bias as represented in their book *Blindspot: Hidden Biases of Good*

People, the assessment of this central social problem in American society has been ongoing.[1]

The current volume by Alvarez, Liang, and Neville seeks to advance our understanding of this pervasive problem by assembling leading scholars and scientists to share with us their research, critical analysis and perspectives on racism within the current context. The contributors address a wide range of issues from a multitude of perspectives. These include physical and mental health consequences as well as educational and work settings. Perspectives from critical race theory, historical trauma to intersectionality are included. Historical analyses and implications for community interventions are also presented. In many respects, this volume represents a state-of-the-art review of psychological research and theory building related to racism and discrimination.

The impetus for this book series came from my presidential theme for Division 45, which focused on "Strengthening Our Science to Improve Our Practice." Given the increasing attention to racial and ethnic minority issues within the discipline of psychology, I argued that we needed to both generate more research and get the existing research known. From the *Supplement* to the Surgeon General's Report on Mental Health to the *Unequal Treatment* report from the Institute of Medicine—both of which documented extensive racial and ethnic disparities in our health care system—the complex of culture, race, and ethnicity was becoming a major challenge in both research and practice within the field of psychology.[2]

To meet that challenge, Division 45 acquired its own journal devoted to ethnic minority issues in psychology (*Cultural Diversity and Ethnic Minority Psychology*). At the same time, a series of handbooks on the topic were published, including Bernal, Trimble, Burlew, and Leong's (2002) *Handbook of Racial and Ethnic Minority Psychology*.[3] Yet we felt that more coverage of this subdiscipline was imperative—coverage that would match the substantive direction of the handbooks but would come from a variety of research and practice perspectives. Hence, the Division 45 book series was launched.

---

[1]Guthrie, R. (1976). *Even the rat was White: A historical view of psychology*. New York, NY: Pearson.
Banaji, M. R., & Greenwald, A. G. (2013). *Blindspot: Hidden biases of good people*. New York, NY: Delacorte Press.
[2]U.S. Department of Health and Human Services. (2001). *Mental health: Culture, race, and ethnicity, a supplement to* Mental health: A report of the Surgeon General. Washington, DC: Author.
Smedley, B. D., Stith, A. Y., & Nelson, A. R. (Eds.). (2003). *Unequal treatment: Confronting racial and ethnic disparities in health care*. Washington, DC: National Academies Press.
[3]Bernal, G., Trimble, J. E., Burlew, A. K., & Leong, F. T. L. (2002). *Handbook of racial and ethnic minority psychology*. Thousand Oaks, CA: Sage.

The Cultural, Racial, and Ethnic Psychology series was designed to advance theories, research, and practice regarding this increasingly crucial subdiscipline. It will focus on, but not be limited to, the major racial and ethnic groups in the United States (i.e., African Americans, Hispanic Americans, Asian Americans, and American Indians) and will include books that examine a single racial or ethnic group, as well as books that undertake a comparative approach. The series will also address the full spectrum of related methodological, substantive, and theoretical issues, including topics in behavioral neuroscience, cognitive and developmental psychology, and personality and social psychology. Other volumes in the series will be devoted to cross-disciplinary explorations in the applied realms of clinical psychology and counseling as well as educational, community, and industrial–organizational psychology. Our goal is to commission state-of-the art volumes in cultural, racial, and ethnic psychology that will be of interest to both practitioners and researchers. The work of recruiting and reviewing proposals for the book series is carried out by members of the editorial board: Guillermo Bernal, University of Puerto Rico, Rio Piedras Campus; Beth Boyd, University of South Dakota; Lillian Comas-Díaz, private practice, Washington, DC; Sandra Graham, University of California, Los Angeles; Gordon Nagayama Hall, University of Oregon; Helen Neville, University of Illinois at Champaign-Urbana; Teresa LaFromboise, Stanford University; Richard Lee, University of Minnesota; Robert M. Sellers, University of Michigan; Stanley Sue, Palo Alto University; Joseph Trimble, Western Washington University; Michael Zarate, University of Texas at El Paso. They represent the leading scholars in the field.

—Frederick T. L. Leong
Series Editor

The Cost of Racism for People of Color

INTRODUCTION

ALVIN N. ALVAREZ, CHRISTOPHER T. H. LIANG,
AND HELEN A. NEVILLE

Despite long-standing historical evidence that racial discrimination has been and continues to be a chronic and pervasive part of the life experiences of people of color (Jones, 1997), both theoretical developments and empirical investigations into the experiences of people of color as targets of racism have only recently emerged. Until relatively recently, the majority of the scholarship in this area focused on the acquisition and/or the prevention of racist attitudes rather than the experiences of people of color as the target of racism (Burkard, Medler, & Boticki, 2001). Yet, since the late 1990s the literature in this area has rapidly accelerated. For instance, in one study, Paradies (2006) found that of 138 studies on racial discrimination across all racial groups, only six were conducted before 1990. Research on people of color's experiences with racism in the psychology literature has significantly increased. The central purpose of this collection is twofold: (a) to compile the most current and up-to-date literature on the theoretical, empirical, and applied research that examines the racial discrimination experiences of

---

http://dx.doi.org/10.1037/14852-001
The Cost of Racism for People of Color: Contextualizing Experiences of Discrimination, A. N. Alvarez,
C. T. H. Liang, and H. A. Neville (Editors)
Copyright © 2016 by the American Psychological Association. All rights reserved.

people of color and (b) to be a catalyst for innovation and expansion of this rapidly growing area of scholarship.

By assembling the leading scholars on the experience of being a target of racism, we hope that we are able to capture a comprehensive yet concise overview of the major themes and trends in the field. Whereas the majority of empirical research focuses on a single racial ethnic group, each chapter in this collection attempts to capture the experience of racism across various communities of color, whenever possible. This facilitates a comparison of both the shared and unique racial experiences of various racial and ethnic groups. The text integrates perspectives from multiple disciplines to foster further development and refinement of conceptual, methodological, and analytical innovations in psychology. Although the book is designed for individuals within various subfields in psychology (e.g., clinical, counseling, school, community, developmental, industrial–organizational), the content and perspectives also should appeal to scholars and practitioners from a range of disciplines outside of psychology, such as ethnic studies, sociology, public health, and allied health. Throughout the text, the chapter authors provide a concise resource that critically synthesizes the existing literature and they cover methodological innovations and interventions within the literature.

The edited work is organized around three broad sections that capture the state of the field: (a) Theoretical and Methodological Foundations, (b) Contexts and Costs and (c) Interventions and Future Directions. The incorporation of theoretical, empirical, and applied dimensions in the book aligns well with the scientist-practitioner model within applied psychology and is designed to capture the full breadth of the scholarship in this area. Although the material covered in the text is grounded in psychological science, the authors of each chapter integrate literature from multiple disciplines and examine the literature across multiple communities of color to represent the full breadth of the literature in this area. That being said, a caveat is in order. It is beyond the scope of this text to fully describe and do justice to the breadth of experiences with racism—both historical and contemporary—that communities of color face, much less the myriad of outcomes that result from such experiences. That task is best left to a body of literature rather than a single text. Without a doubt, readers will find areas that are not covered as fully as they might prefer. However, as a synopsis that compiles the expertise of leading scholars about broad theoretical and empirical trends, this compilation points readers to insights, resources, and studies that in turn will sharpen their understanding of the impact of racism.

The first section, Theoretical and Methodological Foundations, provides the underlying framework for the entire book by covering current conceptual frameworks that are the impetus for empirical research and also applied interventions. In Chapter 1, Pieterse and Powell provide an essential historical overview of racism and its manifestations, as well as an operational definition grounded in both the ideological and institutional elements. Scholars and practitioners alike will find Chapter 1 to be an invaluable resource as a concise overview of the major theoretical models that attempt to delineate the pathways and mechanisms of the impact of racism and its correlates. More important, however, Pieterse and Powell challenge readers by providing a thoughtful critique of these existing models, with a particular emphasis on the need to incorporate and address the role of resistance and empowerment in responding to racism.

Continuing to challenge readers' understanding of the impact of racism on people of color, Lewis and Grzanka in Chapter 2 call upon scholars to integrate intersectionality theory into their conceptual and methodological frameworks and argue for the need to recognize the multiple social identities that shape one's experience of discrimination. They begin with a historical overview of intersectionality theory and scholarship and the multidisciplinary roots of intersectional critiques, followed by an overview of the intersectional research on perceived racism, gender, social class, and sexual orientation. To facilitate the shift away from single-axis approaches to studying the impact of racism, Lewis and Grzanka conclude their chapter with methodological considerations for researchers in developing intersectional studies that capture the complexities of being the target of racism.

The section then segues into Chapter 3 and Williams's exploration of the major measurement and methodological challenges facing scholars who are attempting to advance the literature on the impact of perceived discrimination. In particular, Williams provides cogent and compelling arguments that for the literature to advance, scholars will need research designs that (a) incorporate a more comprehensive assessment of racism in its various forms, (b) minimize bias, and (c) disentangle the effects of racial stressors from the effects of other psychosocial stressors that confront people of color. Last, to deepen understanding of the intervening variables that influence the impact of racism, the section concludes with Alvarez, Liang, Molenaar, and Nguyen's chapter on selected mediators and moderators of perceived discrimination. Particularly in light of the mounting empirical evidence of racism's adverse impact on people of color, this chapter highlights the imperative to clarify what mitigates this impact. To this end, Alvarez et al. provide an overview of key constructs and issues that refine the understanding of racism's impact.

The outcomes of racism are another main focal point of this volume as evidenced by the largest section of the book—Contexts and Costs. Racism is associated with a number of outcomes. Its negative effects can be observed at the psychological level, behavioral level, physiological level, and community level. Racism also interferes with academic and career well-being. In the chapters in this section (Chapters 5–10), racism's impact is documented and future directions are presented. In Chapter 5, Brondolo, Ng, Pierre, and Lane present a social cognitive perspective to examine the link between racism and depression. In doing so, the authors address multiple cognitive variables (schemas about the self, the world, and others) that are influenced by discrimination and that in turn explain the association found between racism and depression.

In Chapter 6, Gee and Otiniano Verissimo present a life course perspective to explain how racism shapes behavior differently at various life points on the basis of experiences with social stress, institutional barriers encountered, and prevailing social norms. Put differently, Gee and Otiniano Verissimo discuss how racism's impact on behavioral health is in part determined by how people's interaction with social systems change as a function of age and the different social roles available to them at different junctures of their life. In Chapter 7, Kaholokula presents an overview of the growing evidence to support racism's detrimental impact on physiological markers of health and well-being among people of color. Kaholokula provides a detailed review of research on the associations found between racism and adverse birth outcomes, diabetes, cardiovascular diseases, and shorter life expectancies.

In Chapter 8, Dixson, Clayton, Peoples, and Reynolds address how racism is manifest in education settings to shape the academic experiences of people of color. A major focus of their discussion centers on policy and practices that facilitate de jure and de facto segregation in schools in the United States. In Chapter 9, Perry and Pickett address an understudied area of racism outcome research: gaps and present future directions for research on the impacts of racism on career-related processes among people of color. Pulling from literature in sociology, business, psychology, and economics, they present research indicating the negative associations racism has with the job search process, occupational segregation, job retention, job satisfaction, promotion, productivity, and well-being. In Chapter 10, Santiago-Rivera, Adames, Chavez-Dueñas, and Benson-Flórez shift attention away from individual-level outcomes of racism to a discussion of community-level impacts. The authors provide several examples of how racism impacted communities in the past (e.g., mass relocation of indigenous people, segregation) and how those acts continue to shape people of color today. They also offer how contemporary policies and practices are impacting communities today. They focus their discussion on housing practices, delivery of mental health services, education policy and practices, and violence as examples and sites of racism that have disadvantaged people of color.

We conclude the book with the section Interventions and Future Directions. Building on the theoretical and empirical literature reviewed in the first two sections, the authors of the four chapters in this section present implications for healing from experiences of racial discrimination. The chapters draw, in particular, on the emerging research highlighting people of color's sense of resiliency and active resistance against racial oppression as pathways to healing and achieving greater equality. We structured this section to discuss interventions on multiple levels, including on an individual level (i.e., therapy), institutional level (e.g., school), and larger societal level (e.g., laws and polices). Each chapter provides case studies to illuminate intervention strategies, and each outlines future directions for psychologists in terms of research and practice with the goal of creating a more equitable society.

In Chapter 11, Comas-Díaz presents a race-informed therapeutic approach to racial wounds, including the effects of historical racial trauma and current everyday microaggressions. She presents a case study to illustrate the healing process. The model consists of various stages of therapy in which clinicians work with clients to assess and determine the extent of the racial trauma, desensitize or assist in symptom relief, reprocess with a focus on growth, promote psychological decolonization or the normalization of resiliency in the face of historical and contemporary forms of racial trauma, and engage in social action. Comas-Díaz concludes by urging psychologists to get involved in eradicating racism; one step toward this goal is for psychologists to work on public information campaigns against racism.

Fine and Cross provide a hard-hitting critique in Chapter 12 of psychology and its complicity in propagating rationalizations of pathology and dysfunction among people of color. The problem with this traditional approach to research is that it places the blame on people of color to explain inequalities, such as the achievement gap, as opposed to focusing on the system of oppression that produced these inequalities. They describe three community collaborative research projects that counter the dominant discourse by grounding their work within the historical realities of racial oppression and resistance and by collaborating with members of social movements to work toward racial justice. As a way to pay the debt for pathologizing communities of color, Fine and Cross urge psychologists to ensure their research and applied work has direct policy implications, in part by highlighting struggles against and resiliency/strength of people of color and by holding themselves accountable to the communities in which they serve.

The final two chapters underscore the role of antiracism interventions in school and community settings. In Chapter 13, Vera, Camacho, Polanin, and Salgado review antiracism educational interventions in K–12 schools, institutions of higher education, and teacher training. Their review incorporates specific case examples and the empirical research supporting the interventions. They encourage psychologists to serve as advocates by educating the public and politicians about how laws and educational policies can either reinforce racial inequality or promote greater racial equality. In the last chapter, Acevedo-Polakovich, Beck, Hawks, and Ogdie discuss the science–practice gap in general and more specifically as it applies to antiracism interventions.

They posit that one way to address this gap is for scientists to develop partnerships with communities using community-based participatory research. Grounding their discussion in two detailed case studies, the authors illustrate the science-to-practice and the practice-to-science approaches to addressing the science–practice gap. Throughout the chapter, they underscore the importance of rigorous, evidence-based practice.

CONCLUSION

Rather than providing definitive and unambiguous answers, it is our hope that this book raises questions, underscores complexities, and illuminates contradictions about the literature on racism. Simply put, these are precisely the intellectual knots that fuel our collective drive to develop more sophisticated and refined theoretical and methodological approaches to understanding the impact of racism on people of color. It stands to reason that, after studying a centuries-old phenomenon for fewer than 25 years, psychology's research paradigms are in their infancy and the scholarly road forward will be challenging and incremental. Yet, as we survey the road ahead, we are also reminded of the pointed question that Carolyn Payton (1984) posed in the title of her seminal article "Who Must Do the Hard Things?," which wrestled with the role of psychologists as advocates on social issues. Her answer is simple: "Those who can" (p. 397). As scholars, practitioners, and policymakers, we have the privilege of an education that equips us with considerable research and clinical expertise and invaluable publishing and presentation skills. In writing this book, we have hoped and continue to our hope that—in some small measure—the chapters that follow will empower our readers to use that privilege to do the hard things!

REFERENCES

Burkard, A. W., Medler, B. R., & Boticki, M. A. (2001). Prejudice and racism: Challenges and progress in measurement. In J. G. Ponterotto, J. M. Casas, L. A. Suzuki, & C. M. Alexander (Eds.), *Handbook of multicultural counseling* (2nd ed., pp. 457–481). Thousand Oaks, CA: Sage.

Jones, J. M. (1997). *Prejudice and Racism* (2nd ed.). New York, NY: McGraw Hill.

Paradies, Y. (2006). A systematic review of empirical research on self-reported racism and health. *International Journal of Epidemiology, 35,* 888–901. http://dx.doi.org/10.1093/ije/dyl056

Payton, C. R. (1984). Who must do the hard things? *American Psychologist, 39,* 391–397. http://dx.doi.org/10.1037/0003-066X.39.4.391

I
THEORETICAL AND METHODOLOGICAL FOUNDATIONS

I

THEORETICAL AND METHODOLOGICAL FOUNDATIONS

1
A THEORETICAL OVERVIEW OF THE IMPACT OF RACISM ON PEOPLE OF COLOR

ALEX PIETERSE AND SHANTEL POWELL

Among the varied determinants of social structure, race remains an enduring aspect of social categorization within the United States. Yet, as West, Klor de Alva, and Shorris (1996) remind us, "categories are constructed, scars and bruises are felt with human bodies" (p. 58.). Similarly, more than a century ago, Du Bois (1906) highlighted the pernicious effect of racial categorization when stating "The Negro death rate and sickness are largely matters of social and economic condition, and not due to racial traits and tendencies" (p. 276). Through the words of these scholars and social commentators, we are reminded that racism is a real phenomenon that exacts a high and lasting toll on the health and well-being of its targets. As such, we as researchers and theorists have engaged this discussion of the impact of racism on people of color, with a sense of deep humility and respect, first pausing to acknowledge those who have resisted and sacrificed in the fight against racial oppression

(Martinez, Meyer, & Carter, 2012), and whose lives have afforded all of us this present opportunity and responsibility.

Social scientists generally believe that race is a social, not biological construct (A. Smedley & Smedley, 2012); yet, a large body of literature outlines the manner in which race informs social relationships and equitable participation in society (Marger, 2011; B. D. Smedley, 2012). Furthermore, *race*, a system of social categorization based on skin color and physical features, is central to the concept of racism. Within the social and health sciences, racism is now understood to be an ideology of racial superiority with an accompanying set of social structures and interpersonal behaviors that are associated with dominance and oppression (Carter & Pieterse, 2005; Gravlee, 2009; Mays, Ponce, Washington, & Cochran, 2003).

Within American society, the historical record clearly indicates that assumed racial superiority is associated with Caucasian (White) heritage and assigned racial inferiority is applied to individuals of non-Caucasian (non-White) heritage (Frederickson, 1998). Therefore, in the present chapter, we focus on the effects of racism as it pertains to individuals and groups who are not perceived to be White—hereinafter referred to as "people of color." First, we define racism and provide a brief historical context. We then discuss the adverse impacts of racism on people of color and review several theoretical models that outline the influence of racism on human functioning, for example: the race-based traumatic stress model (RBTSM; Carter, 2007), the biopsychosocial model of racism (R. Clark, Anderson, Clark, & Williams, 1999), and the acute racism reactions model (Utsey, Bolden, & Brown, 2001). Finally we draw on both the theoretical and empirical literature to highlight the need to expand theoretical models of racism so that they more greatly emphasize active coping, resistance, and empowerment when seeking to more fully understand the impact of racism on people of color.

HISTORY AND DEFINITION OF RACISM

Racism is viewed as being intricately connected to the construct of race and is understood to incorporate two elements: an ideology of superiority and the practice of inequity (Thompson & Neville, 1999). The construct of race serves as both the justification for, and the cause of, the inequities that exist across racial groups within the United States (Alexander, 2012). A full appreciation of race and racism can be achieved only by adopting a historical context. In that regard, the expansionist and colonial policies of the European powers, the Christianizing of indigenous peoples, the rise of Darwinian ideology, and the growing economic system of capitalism all played vital roles in the invention of race, and to a degree continue to inform the manner in which race and racism is maintained today (Carter & Pieterse, 2005). Beliefs about the abilities and characteristics of various racial groups served as a foundational element in the enslavement and genocide of millions. Armed with an ideology that proclaimed inherent racial superiority, and fueled by a religious fervor that affirmed a sense of superiority, the White power structure within America set out to establish a social system that secured its dominance and engrained the belief of racial superiority for generations to come (A. Smedley & Smedley, 2012). Given this brief historical context, we adopt the following definition of *racism* as an anchor for the present discussion:

> Racism consists of two interlocking dimensions: (a) an institutional [structural] mechanism of domination and (b) a corresponding ideological belief that justifies the oppression of people whose physical features and cultural patterns differ from those of the politically and socially dominated group—Whites. (Thompson & Neville, 1999, p. 163)

PATHWAYS OF RACISM

The description of racism and racial discrimination as comprising three domains—individual, institutional/structural, and cultural (J. M. Jones, 1997)—has been a useful framework in which to understand how racism operates within American society. Briefly, *individual racism* is racism experienced on an interpersonal level. Examples of individual racism include incidents of name calling and aggressive, hostile, or avoidance behavior based on one's racial group membership. *Institutional racism* refers to structures or systems within society that directly and indirectly discriminate against, and limit opportunities for, people of color. Here, examples include the underrepresentation of people of color in professional occupations, such as science, technology, engineering, and mathematics (see Linley & George-Jackson, 2013), and the overrepresentation of individuals of color in the penal system. *Cultural racism* is understood to be the holding of Anglo-American or Eurocentric culture as normative, and the subsequent undervaluing or viewing as inferior cultural norms, beliefs, and lifestyles that stem from a non-Caucasian/European heritage. Examples of cultural racism include the continued stereotypical representations of Native Americans for the purpose of team mascots or emblems (see Feagin, 2014; Miller & Garran, 2008).

Critical race theorists are in agreement that the shift from the Jim Crow era of overt racism, active exclusion, and hostile/aggressive behavior toward people of color has been replaced by color-blind racism that continues to support the ideology of White racial superiority (Bonilla-Silva, 2013). Here, the idea is that although individuals no longer endorse active types of discrimination, they harbor beliefs associated with racial superiority that still results in a prizing and overvaluing of Anglo-American or Eurocentric culture and ideology (Gaertner & Dovidio, 2005). This new type of racism has resulted in resistance to programs such as affirmative action and includes a tendency to blame the targets of racism for not successfully integrating into the dominant culture (Bonilla-Silva, 2013).

An understanding of the different ways in which racism is manifested is important when seeking to appreciate the ongoing effects of racism on people of color. Miller and Garran's (2007) "web of institutional racism" concept provides an elaborate overview of the ubiquitous nature of racism within American society; the concept highlights that individual acts of racism are located within a larger cultural and institutional context. As such, we view racism within the United States as an organizing principle of social structure that carries with it significant disparities in health, education, criminalization, and wealth. Invoking the iceberg metaphor, Gee and Ford (2011) identified structural/institutional racism as being the most damaging of all types of racism. Although individual racism, such as microaggressions (e.g., name calling, distancing), tends to receive more attention in the public media, structural racism tends to be more pernicious and harder to eradicate (Gee & Ford, 2011).

REVIEWING THE ADVERSE IMPACTS OF RACISM ON PEOPLE OF COLOR

J. M. Jones's (1997) tripartite model of racism/racial discrimination provides a useful framework in which to understand the literature as it relates to the effects of racism and the ways that different types of racism are associated with different types of effects. To illustrate, interpersonal racism is more likely to have an individual-level effect, as evidenced in mental health symptoms (e.g., trauma stress, anxiety, depression) and physiological outcomes (e.g., hypertension). Institutional or structural racism is more likely to exhibit structural/social effects of racism, such as health disparities, increased rates of incarceration among people of color, and lower rates of educational achievement. Cultural racism is more likely to be associated with internalized oppression, such as devaluing one's cultural heritage and cultural values or internalizing negative stereotypes associated with one's racial group. Internalized racial oppression has been linked to feelings of shame, hostility, and depressive symptoms (Speight, 2007). It is important to note, however, that racism is a complex phenomenon, with different types of racism being intertwined resulting in complex psychological outcomes with interactive effects (Carter, 2007).

A number of systematic reviews of the literature outline the psychosocial correlates and health-related impact of racism (see Carter, 2007; Gee, Ro, Shariff-Marco, & Chae, 2009; Lee & Ahn, 2011, 2012; Paradies, 2006; Pieterse, Todd, Neville, & Carter, 2012; Priest et al., 2013; D. R. Williams & Mohammed, 2009; Wyatt et al., 2003). In general, the research indicates that for people of color, racism is positively associated with adverse physical and mental health outcomes and is inversely associated with psychological well-being (see Table 1.1). To illustrate, racism has been linked to depression among Blacks and Latinos (Araújo & Borrell, 2006; H. L. Jones, Cross, & DeFour, 2007) and to increased alcohol usage among Native Americans (Beauvais, 1998). Among Black middle-class men, racism is associated with reports of lower psychological well-being (Pieterse & Carter, 2007).

Beyond physical and mental effects, the structure of racism has resulted in significant disparities across racial groups in the areas of health, education, and criminal justice (O. Williams et al., 2010). With regard to educational achievement, Blacks, Latinos, and Native Americans consistently exhibit lower levels of educational achievement, both in school completion and standardized test scores, when compared with their Asians and White counterparts (see Chapter 8, this volume). Furthermore, racism has a

TABLE 1.1
Meta-Analytic Findings: Effects of Racism and Racial Discrimination

Author	Racial group	No. of studies/participants	Findings (R)
Carter & Lau (2013)	Black, Asian, Latino/a	105 studies, $N = 35,435$	Physical health = .13 Mental health = .21
Pieterse, Todd, et al. (2012)	Black/African American	66 studies, $N = 18,160$	Depression/anxiety = .20 Psychiatric symptoms = .27 General distress = .24
Lee & Ahn (2012)	Latino/a American	51 studies, $N = 13,750$	Depression = .29 Anxiety = .37 Psychological distress = .19 Unhealthy behaviors = .15
Lee & Ahn (2012)	Asians	23 studies, $N = 6,731$	Depression = .26 Anxiety = .28 Psychological distress = .17
Lee & Ahn (2011)	Black/African American	27 studies, $N = 5,913$	Psychological distress = .21
K. P. Jones et al. (2013)	All	24 studies, $N = 9,906$	Adverse psychological outcome = .25 Adverse physical outcome = .14
Schmitt et al. (2014)	All	211 studies, N not reported	Psychological well-being = −.21

well-established history in the criminal justice system, with current statistics indicating a stark and disturbing overrepresentation of Blacks and Latinos among individuals who are currently under some form of supervised correction (Alexander, 2012; Pieterse, in press). In the area of health, people of color tend to be disproportionately impacted by such leadings causes of morbidity and mortality as heart disease, cancer, stroke, diabetes, and hypertension, and therefore tend to have higher age-specific mortality rates than compared with Whites (see Chapter 7, this volume). Mechanisms associated with racial health disparities include physiological reactions to racism-related stress and the manner in which these reactions might predispose individuals of color to certain illnesses, the influence of race on the health care provider–patient relationship, lack of cultural competence within the health care system, and disproportionately higher levels of poverty among people of color (Brondolo, Gallo, & Myers, 2009; B. D. Smedley, 2012).

Perhaps the most understudied area when addressing the impact of racism on people of color is that of internalized racial oppression. Speight (2007) emphasized that "the internalization of racism may arguably be the most damaging psychological injury that is due to racism" (p. 130). The act of internalizing a negative or inferior view of one's identity based on one's racial group membership has also been referred to as "colonial mentality" (David & Okazaki, 2006) and as "psychological slavery" (Akbar, 1996). Regardless of the term, the process speaks to a sense of inferiority and evaluation of self from the perspective of the dominant racial majority (see Bulhan, 1985; Fanon, 1967; C. P. Jones, 2000). Pyke (2010) contended that internalized racism has not received sufficient attention in the scholarly literature, partly due to the misperception that internalized racism equates to problematic behavior among oppressed groups. More important, Pyke identified the need to address cultural hegemony and ideologies of White racial superiority as critical to the examination of internalized racial oppression, a project that requires the exposure of the structural and systematic manner in which racism continues to operate within American society. Although limited, empirical findings suggest that internalized racial oppression is also associated with negative physical and psychological outcomes, such depression, alcohol use, low self-esteem, glucose intolerance, and feelings of isolation (Ahmed, Mohammed, & Williams, 2007; Tull & Chambers, 2001).

Historical trauma also remains an underrecognized and understudied area associated with the impact of racism. Brave Heart, Chase, Elkins, and Altschul (2011) defined *historical trauma* as the "cumulative emotional and psychological wounding across generations, including the lifespan, which emanates from massive group trauma" (p. 283). Historical trauma is therefore closely linked to intergenerational trauma (Sotero, 2006). In the context of racism, *intergenerational trauma* is understood to be the traumatic effects of colonization, genocide, force removal, and forced enslavement that is passed from one generation to the next (Ford, 2008). The intergenerational effect of historical trauma has been noted to include loss of cultural identity, experiences of invisibility, lowered self-esteem, feelings of shame, sense of powerless, and hypervigilance (Belcourt-Dittloff & Stewart, 2000; Brave Heart et al., 2011; Quinn, 2007). Some authors have argued that the ongoing effects of historical trauma can be understood as frameworks of suffering; notably, DeGruy (2005) proposed the posttraumatic slave syndrome with regard to the African American experience, and Gone (2007) described Native Americans as being affected by postcolonial anomie, a type of postcolonial stress reaction (Duran & Duran, 1995). Thus, internalized racial oppression and historical trauma are important aspects of racism within the United States and also correlate with adverse health outcomes among people of color. Having briefly outlined the negative influences of racism on the lives of people of color, we now turn to a review of conceptual models that both inform and guide the empirical findings, and we also outline points of possible intervention for practitioners and policy makers.

THEORETICAL MODELS FOR THE IMPACT OF RACISM

Although the study of racism as a sociological phenomenon has received sustained attention in the social science literature for decades, the past 25 years has seen the emergence of important theoretical models used to outline the psychological, physiological, and sociological impact of racism. Most of the earlier models drew on the interactional model of stress (Lazarus & Folkman, 1984) as a framework in which to describe the relationship between racism and various outcomes. More recently, models have explored racism in the context of trauma, and have also started to identify areas of intervention and resistance. A review of the selected theoretical models follows.

Biopsychosocial Model of Racism

The biopsychosocial model (R. Clark et al., 1999) draws on the African American experience and centers on contextual factors that influence the manner in which experiences of racism might lead to various adverse health-related outcomes. The model outlines behavioral, constitutional, and sociodemographic factors that might account for whether an environmental stimulus is perceived as racism and whether this perception, in turn, is viewed as a stressor. The biopsychosocial model suggests that individuals' coping strategies associated with racism and their psychological and/or physiological stress reactions influence health-related outcomes.

Multidimensional Model of Racism-Related Stress

Describing the multidimensional model of racism-related stress, Harrell (2000) explained that "the race-related transactions between individuals or groups and their environment that emerge from the dynamics of racism, and that are perceived to tax or exceed existing individual and collective resources or threaten well-being" (p. 44). To this end, individuals are thought to experience racism-related stress in the following domains: racism-related life events, vicarious racism experiences, daily racism-related microstressors, chronic-contextual stress, collective stress experiences, and transgenerational transmission of racism-related stress. Similar to the R. Clark et al. (1999) model, the extent to which racism-related experiences are associated with adverse health outcomes is mediated by various factors, including internal characteristics (e.g., self-esteem), affective and behavioral responses to stress, sociocultural variables (e.g., coping style, worldview), and external resources (e.g., social support).

Race-Based Traumatic Stress Model

RBTSM (Carter, 2007) is a clinical model that focuses on the types of emotional reactions individuals have in response to racism-related events. This model contends that racism is a form of trauma, however, unlike post-traumatic stress disorder (PTSD), which views the traumatic response as a type of mental illness, the RBTSM views an individual's response to racism-related events as a type of emotional injury. In this regard, Carter (2007) described the model as nonpathological even though a review of the typical emotional reactions include symptoms associated with PTSD (e.g., intrusion, avoidance, hypervigilance, low self-esteem). An important aspect of the RBTSM is the distinction drawn by Carter between racism experiences that are discrimination based and racism experiences that are harassment based. Empirical work using the RBTSM indicates that discrimination-based experiences are associated with reactions such as hypervigilance and arousal and that harassment-based experiences are associated with complex emotional reactions (e.g., depression, extreme emotional distress), and that these reactions tend to be of greater duration (Carter, Forsyth, Mazzula, & Williams, 2005).

Psychosocial Model of Racism and Health

Within the context of health disparities, the psychosocial model of racism and health (Kennedy, 2009) is a framework outlining how racism is associated with attitudes and behaviors that are detrimental to health and wellness. These include a lack of trust in health care providers, increased health risk behaviors, and lower participation in health prevention. Psychological factors, such as depression and increased stress, are viewed as moderators of the relationship between experiences of racism and health-related outcomes and behaviors. Kennedy's (2009) psychosocial model is consistent with emerging work on racism and health outcomes. Scholars suggest three possible pathways associated with experiences of discrimination and corresponding adverse health effects. First, experiences of individual racism are known to be associated with increased stress, which in turn is associated with diseases such as hypertension (Brondolo, Love, Pencille, Schoenthaler, & Ogedegbe, 2011), maladaptive coping mechanisms (e.g., cigarette smoking; Klonoff, 2014), and unhealthy eating (J. D. Clark & Winterowd, 2012). A second pathway is associated with systemic factors, such as disproportionate rates of poverty in communities of color and the manner in which poverty is associated with access to, and availability of effective health care. Third, community location and such factors as segregation also appear to influence health care. A final consideration is that of racialized attitudes and adherence to racial stereotypes among physicians and other medical personal, and the potential negative impact these attitudes have on the quality of health care provided (Klonoff, 2014).

Acute Racism Reactions

The acute racism reaction model focuses on the "psychological and physiological processes associated with the experience of racism and oppression" (Utsey et al., 2001, p. 322). These reactions are drawn from the African American experience; however, they can be applied to other groups of color as well. The six reactions described by Utsey et al. (2001) included race-related trauma, racism-related fatigue (a type of psychological exhaustion), anticipatory racism reaction (a group of defense mechanisms associated with fear and threat), race-related stress/distress (a group of stress-related symptoms, both somatic and psychological, which increase susceptibility to physical illness), racism-related frustration (a sense of powerlessness in the face of chronic exposure to racism, resulting in feelings of anger, aggravation, disappointment, and lowered life satisfaction), and racism-related confusion (a questioning of identity and meaning associated with racist events, which leads to feelings of uncertainty and lowered self-confidence).

Psychosocial Model of Racism and Resistance

More recently, Neville and Pieterse (2009) and Neville, Spanierman, and Lewis (2012) described a model of racism that includes both adverse psychosocial outcomes associated with racism and the manner in which people of color might resist racism and develop a sense of agency. A core feature of the psychosocial model is to emphasize the role of domination and subjugation in the creation and maintenance of racism. To this end, the psychosocial model draws attention to the racial structure within the United States and describes the experience of racism as dynamic and contextual. It is important to note that the psychosocial model integrates resistance and agency among the targets of racism as a central feature of the model.

Rethinking the Impact of Racism on People of Color

The models described above have provided important frameworks in which to understand how racism shapes the lives of people of color. However, in a few areas the models fall short of their explanatory function. Specifically, the models appear to rely heavily on perceptions of racism and, as such, are largely located in the experience of individual racism. Although the models do acknowledge and incorporate other types of racism (e.g., structural, cultural), the primary mechanism through which individuals are impacted still centers on the manner in which the individual makes sense of, or copes with, the experience of racism. As such, the models have less use in explaining those impacts that do not rely on individual perception of understanding of racism. Note that no consistent evidence suggests that people of color tend to experience higher levels of general life stress (see Cohen & Williamson, 1988; Thoits, 2010). An explanation of this finding could be associated with the indirect impact of racism, an impact that at times is not appreciated as racism but is still experienced as a stressor. Therefore, theoretical models and empirical examinations of the impact of racism that centralize the manner in which an individual perceives racism might fail to fully explain or assess how racism shapes the lives of people of color.

The role of internalized racial oppression as both a type of racism and a byproduct of racism has also received insufficient attention in the current theoretical models (C. P. Jones, 2000; Speight, 2007). Internalized racial oppression is an insidious process that, although not within the individual's awareness, exerts a detrimental influence on an individual's heath and sense of well-being (Pyke, 2010). Finally, with the exception of the psychosocial model of racism (Neville & Pieterse, 2009; Neville et al., 2012), none of the models incorporate resisting racism as a central aspect of how racism shapes the lives of people of color. In not centralizing resistance and empowerment, the models therefore present an incomplete picture of the manner in which racism influences the life experiences of people of color.

Unpacking the Impact of Racism

Variability associated with the frequency in which people of color report having experienced racism or discrimination, as well as the extent to which they endorse being negatively impacted by experiences of racism, is well documented (see Pérez, Fortuna, & Alegria, 2008; Scott & House, 2005). To date, numerous moderating or mediating variables associated with the link between perceived racism and health outcomes has been identified (see Chapter 4, this volume). To illustrate, gender has been noted to influence how racism is experienced, especially in relation to the joint effects of racism and sexism, thereby exacerbating the effects of racism for women of color (see Chapter 2, this volume). Residential segregation has been noted as being associated with disparities in health and educational outcomes (Acevedo-Garcia & Lochner, 2003; D. R. Williams & Jackson, 2005; D. R. Williams & Williams-Morris, 2000). Political ideology and activism has been identified as a means of buffering the effects of racism and instilling a sense of agency and empowerment (Watts, 2004). Social class and level of education appear to inform the opportunities and access that people of color might have in a racialized society and also might influence the level of psychological distress associated with perceived racism (Karlsen & Nazroo, 2002; Pieterse & Carter, 2007). Finally, political ideology appears to be associated with the extent to which individuals might engage in acts to resist racism (Watts & Flanagan, 2007; Watts, Williams, & Jagers, 2003), and personality dispositions could inform how individuals respond to or make sense of racism related experiences (Brummett, Wade, Ponterotto, Thombs, & Lewis, 2007).

Emphasizing Empowerment and Resistance

Irrespective of the growing body of literature that seeks to outline and measure the way individuals and groups cope with racism (see Forsyth & Carter, 2012; Wei, Alvarez, Ku, Russell, & Bonett, 2010), psychological models of the impact of racism fail to clearly outline mechanisms associated with the resistance or empowerment strategies for challenging racist ideologies and structures. To illustrate, in a qualitative study of resistance strategies used when confronting racism, Shorter-Gooden (2004) found that only one theme was reflective of direct confrontation. Most of the themes identified by Shorter-Gooden actually spoke to various types of coping, such as spiritual, using social support, and sustaining a positive self-image.

When referencing active resistance in the current discussion, we focus on such efforts as psychoeducational programs to counter internalized racial oppression, antiracism activism directed at police brutality; letter writing or social media campaigns targeting racial profiling, political activism and voter mobilization; acts of civil disobedience or demonstrations; and engaging in structured dialogues focused on deconstructing race (see Griffith et al., 2007). Whether the lack of literature on this specific topic is unintentional in nature or is in fact another form of structural racism is unclear.

Although limited, research does suggest that the act of challenging or confronting racism might be related to positive psychological outcomes (Brown & Tylka, 2011; Pierre & Mahalik, 2005; Watts, Diemer, & Voight, 2011). Krieger and Sidney (1996) found that working class women of color who challenged acts of racial discrimination had lower levels of systolic blood pressure than those who did not. Additionally, laboratory evidence indicates that individuals who actively confront and use assertive responses when encountering discrimination and prejudice report greater levels of life satisfaction (Hyers, 2007). Watts, Williams, and Jagers (2003) described sociopolitical development, a model of antioppression and critical consciousness in which individuals who engage in sociopolitical development (as defined by Watts et al., 2003) report increased self-worth and a greater sense of purpose. Perhaps the psychological benefits of resistance and empowerment is captured by one of their research participants' response:

> I feel [a] strong sense of responsibility, and I like being able to meet my responsibilities as a human being on this planet. The work is grueling and difficult. There are no personal rewards. It's not something that's likeable in that respect as to the actual tasks themselves. But the outcomes and knowing that you are at least in a small way attempting to meet your responsibilities to your community and to the entire community is a feeling that is likeable. (Watts et al., 2003, p. 191)

The historical record does indicate that active resistance of racism has always included a psychological aspect. Steve Biko's (1981) Black consciousness movement was associated with energizing and providing Black South Africans a belief in their self-value and their ability to resist the oppressive apartheid regime. Therefore, given the scholarly findings, historical evidence and participant self-reports do suggest that active resistance of racism might be an important aspect of the manner in which people of color respond to, and are impacted by, experiences of racism. Furthermore, antiracism activism might well have psychological benefits that could counter the more negative psychological outcomes that been noted to be associated with perceived racism (Pieterse, Todd, et al., 2012).

FUTURE DIRECTIONS

In contemplating future directions in both theorizing and empirical investigations of the impact of racism, we believe a most urgently needed area of attention is that of explicating and examining the psychological benefits of resistance and empowerment among people of color. Consciousness raising as a means of countering internalized racial oppression, the extent to which processes such as mature racial identity status and active racial socialization might present a psychological buffer against racism, and strategies associated with collective empowerment/community mobilization or individual acts of resistance all have important implications for psychological health in the face of sustained racial oppression (Brown & Tylka, 2011; Pierre & Mahalik, 2005; Watts et al., 2011). Within psychology, theoretical models are, at best, an approximation of the subjective experiences they attempt to represent and explain. A framework for understanding the impact of racism on people of color, as outlined in Figure 1.1, might lead to a closer approximation of the subjective experiences of those impacted by racism. Furthermore, such a framework encourages scholars to focus on aspects of racism impacts that are understudied and enables clinicians and policymakers to explore further areas for intervention in the ongoing effort to counter and, where possible, eradicate racism as a form of social control (Buhin & Vera, 2009).

Much of the understanding of the impact of racism is located in the African American experience, although more recently this area of examination has been extended to Asian American and Latino/a populations. Of note is the paucity of scholarship focusing on the racism-related experiences of Native Americans. Although we understand that research efforts with Native Americans has been challenging, partly due to a lack of access, we encourage scholars to engage culturally sensitive and appropriate methodologies with Native American communities for the field to further understand the impact

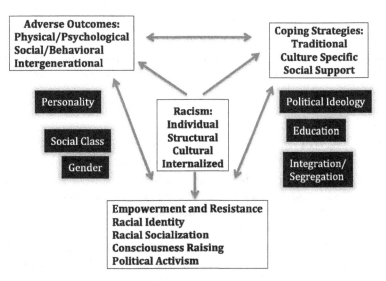

Figure 1.1. Integrated model of effects of racism on people on color. The primary variable (racism and effects) are in the unshaded boxes; the moderating/mediating variables (contextual, demographic, intrapsychic) are in the shaded boxes.

of racism with this population and to collaboratively develop additional tools for coping and resistance. Finally, the intergenerational transmission of race-related trauma needs to be more clearly explicated. Given that theoretical frameworks serve both descriptive and explanatory functions, future scholarship should prize the experiences of all communities of color and seek to provide frameworks in which racism-related experiences are easily identified and an understanding of the ways these experiences continue to shape the lives of individuals and communities of color.

REFERENCES

Acevedo-Garcia, D., & Lochner, K. A. (2003). Residential segregation and health. *Neighborhoods and Health*, 265–287.

Ahmed, A. T., Mohammed, S. A., & Williams, D. R. (2007). Racial discrimination and health: Pathways and evidence. *The Indian Journal of Medical Research, 126*, 318–327.

Akbar, N. (1996). *Breaking the chains of psychological slavery*. Tallahassee, FL: Mind Productions.

Alexander, M. (2012). *The new Jim Crow: Mass incarceration in the age of Colorblindness*. New York, NY: The New Press.

Araújo, B. Y., & Borrell, L. N. (2006). Understanding the link between discrimination, mental health outcomes, and life chances among Latinos. *Hispanic Journal of Behavioral Sciences, 28*, 245–266. http://dx.doi.org/10.1177/0739986305285825

Beauvais, F. (1998). American Indians and alcohol. *Alcohol Health and Research World, 22*, 253–259.

Belcourt-Dittloff, A., & Stewart, J. (2000). Historical racism: Implications for Native Americans. *American Psychologist, 55*, 1166–1167. http://dx.doi.org/10.1037/0003-066X.55.10.1166

Biko, S. (1981). Black consciousness and the quest for a true humanity. *Ufahamu: Journal of African Studies, 11*, 133–142.

Bonilla-Silva, E. (2013). *Racism without racists: Color-blind racism and the persistence of racial inequality in America*. Lanham, MD: Rowman & Littlefield.

Brave Heart, M. Y., Chase, J., Elkins, J., & Altschul, D. B. (2011). Historical trauma among Indigenous Peoples of the Americas: Concepts, research, and clinical considerations. *Journal of Psychoactive Drugs, 43*, 282–290. http://dx.doi.org/10.1080/02791072.2011.628913

Brondolo, E., Gallo, L. C., & Myers, H. F. (2009). Race, racism and health: disparities, mechanisms, and interventions. *Journal of Behavioral Medicine, 32*, 1–8. http://dx.doi.org/10.1007/s10865-008-9190-3

Brondolo, E., Love, E. E., Pencille, M., Schoenthaler, A., & Ogedegbe, G. (2011). Racism and hypertension: A review of the empirical evidence and implications for clinical practice. *American Journal of Hypertension, 24*, 518–529. http://dx.doi.org/10.1038/ajh.2011.9

Brown, D. L., & Tylka, T. L. (2011). Racial discrimination and resilience in African American young adults: Examining racial socialization as a moderator. *The Journal of Black Psychology, 37*, 259–285. http://dx.doi.org/10.1177/0095798410390689

Brummett, B. R., Wade, J. C., Ponterotto, J. G., Thombs, B., & Lewis, C. (2007). Psychosocial well-being and a multicultural personality disposition. *Journal of Counseling & Development, 85*, 73–81. http://dx.doi.org/10.1002/j.1556-6678.2007.tb00446.x

Buhin, L., & Vera, E. M. (2009). Preventing racism and promoting social justice: Person-centered and environment-centered interventions. *The Journal of Primary Prevention, 30*, 43–59. http://dx.doi.org/10.1007/s10935-008-0161-9

Bulhan, H. A. (1985). *Frantz Fanon and the psychology of oppression*. New York, NY: Plenum Press.

Carter, R. T. (2007). Racism and psychological and emotional injury recognizing and assessing race-based traumatic stress. *The Counseling Psychologist, 35*, 13–105. http://dx.doi.org/10.1177/0011000006292033

Carter, R. T., Forsyth, J., Mazzula, S., & Williams, B. (2005). Racial discrimination and race-based traumatic stress. In R. T. Carter (Ed.), *Handbook of racial–cultural psychology and counseling: Vol. 2. Training and practice* (pp. 447–476). New York, NY: Wiley.

Carter, R. T., & Lau, M. (2013). *Racial discrimination and health outcome among racial-ethnic minorities: a meta-analytic review*. Unpublished manuscript, Teachers College, Columbia University.

Carter, R. T., & Pieterse, A. L. (2005). Race: A social and psychological analysis of the term and its meaning. In R. T. Carter (Ed.), *The handbook of racial–cultural psychology and counseling* (pp. 41–65). Hoboken, NJ: Wiley.

Clark, J. D., & Winterowd, C. (2012). Correlates and predictors of binge eating among Native American women. *Journal of Multicultural Counseling and Development, 40*, 117–127. http://dx.doi.org/10.1002/j.2161-1912.2012.00011.x

Clark, R., Anderson, N. B., Clark, V. R., & Williams, D. R. (1999). Racism as a stressor for African Americans. A biopsychosocial model. *American Psychologist, 54*, 805–816. http://dx.doi.org/10.1037/0003-066X.54.10.805

Cohen, S., & Williamson, G. (1988). Perceived stress in a probability sample in the United States. In S. Spacapam & S. Oskampp (Eds.), *The social psychology of health* (pp. 31–67). Newbury Park, CA: Sage.

David, E. J. R., & Okazaki, S. (2006). Colonial mentality: A review and recommendation for Filipino American psychology. *Cultural Diversity and Ethnic Minority Psychology, 12*, 1–16. http://dx.doi.org/10.1037/1099-9809.12.1.1

DeGruy, J. (2005). *Post traumatic slave syndrome: America's legacy of enduring injury and healing*. Portland, OR: Uptone Press.

Du Bois, W. E. B. (1906). *The health and physique of the Negro American*. Atlanta, GA: Atlanta University.

Duran, E., & Duran, B. (1995). *Native American postcolonial psychology*. Albany: State University of New York Press.

Fanon, F. (1967). *Black skin, White masks*. New York, NY: Grove Press.

Feagin, J. (2014). *Racist America: Roots, current realities, and future reparations* (4th ed.). New York, NY: Routledge.

Ford, J. D. (2008). Trauma, posttraumatic stress disorder, and ethnoracial minorities: Toward diversity and cultural competence in principles and practices. *Clinical Psychology: Science and Practice, 15*, 62–67. http://dx.doi.org/10.1111/j.1468-2850.2008.00110.x

Forsyth, J., & Carter, R. T. (2012). The relationship between racial identity status attitudes, racism-related coping, and mental health among Black Americans. *Cultural Diversity and Ethnic Minority Psychology, 18*, 128–140. http://dx.doi.org/10.1037/a0027660

Frederickson, G. M. (1998). *The arrogance of race: Historical perspectives on slavery, racism and social inequity*. Hanover, NH: Wesleyan University Press.

Gaertner, S. L., & Dovidio, J. F. (2005). Understanding and addressing contemporary racism: From aversive racism to the common ingroup identity model. *Journal of Social Issues, 61*, 615–639. http://dx.doi.org/10.1111/j.1540-4560.2005.00424.x

Gee, G. C., & Ford, C. L. (2011). Structural racism and health inequities: Old issues, new directions. *Du Bois Review: Social Science Research on Race, 8*, 115–1132. http://dx.doi.org/10.1017/S1742058X11000130

Gee, G. C., Ro, A., Shariff-Marco, S., & Chae, D. (2009). Racial discrimination and health among Asian Americans: Evidence, assessment, and directions for future research. *Epidemiologic Reviews, 31*, 130–151. http://dx.doi.org/10.1093/epirev/mxp009

Gravlee, C. C. (2009). How race becomes biology: Embodiment of social inequality. *American Journal of Physical Anthropology, 139*, 47–57. http://dx.doi.org/10.1002/ajpa.20983

Griffith, D. M., Mason, M., Yonas, M., Eng, E., Jeffries, V., Plihcik, S., & Parks, B. (2007). Dismantling institutional racism: Theory and action. *American Journal of Community Psychology, 39*, 381–392. http://dx.doi.org/10.1007/s10464-007-9117-0

Gone, J. P. (2007). "We never was happy living like a Whiteman": Mental health disparities and the postcolonial predicament in American Indian communities. *American Journal of Community Psychology, 40*, 290–300. http://dx.doi.org/10.1007/s10464-007-9136-x

Harrell, S. P. (2000). A multidimensional conceptualization of racism-related stress: Implications for the well-being of people of color. *American Journal of Orthopsychiatry, 70*, 42–57. http://dx.doi.org/10.1037/h0087722

Hyers, L. L. (2007). Resisting prejudice every day: Exploring women's assertive responses to anti-Black racism, anti-Semitism, heterosexism, and sexism. *Sex Roles, 56*, 1–12. http://dx.doi.org/10.1007/s11199-006-9142-8

Jones, C. P. (2000). Levels of racism: A theoretic framework and a gardener's tale. *American Journal of Public Health, 90*, 1212–1215. http://dx.doi.org/10.2105/AJPH.90.8.1212

Jones, H. L., Cross, W. E., & DeFour, D. C. (2007). Race-related stress, racial identity attitudes, and mental health among Black women. *The Journal of Black Psychology, 33*, 208–231. http://dx.doi.org/10.1177/0095798407299517

Jones, J. M. (1997). *Prejudice and racism* (2nd ed.). New York, NY: McGraw Hill.

Jones, K. P., Peddie, C. I., Gilrane, V. L., King, E. B., & Gray, A. L. (2013). Not so subtle: a meta-analytic investigation of the correlates of subtle and overt discrimination. *Journal of Management*. Advance online publication. http://dx.doi.org/10.1177/0149206313506466

Karlsen, S., & Nazroo, J. Y. (2002). Relation between racial discrimination, social class, and health among ethnic minority groups. *American Journal of Public Health, 92*, 624–631. http://dx.doi.org/10.2105/AJPH.92.4.624

Kennedy, B. R. (2009). Psychosocial model: Racism as a predictor of adherence and compliance to treatment and health outcomes among African Americans. *Journal of Theory Construction & Testing, 13*, 20–26.

Klonoff, E. A. (2014). Introduction to the special section on discrimination. *Health Psychology, 33*, 1–2. http://dx.doi.org/10.1037/hea0000070

Krieger, N., & Sidney, S. (1996). Racial discrimination and blood pressure: The CARDIA Study of young Black and White adults. *American Journal of Public Health, 86*, 1370–1378. http://dx.doi.org/10.2105/AJPH.86.10.1370

Lazarus, R. S., & Folkman, S. (1984). *Stress, appraisal, and coping*. New York, NY: Springer.

Lee, D. L., & Ahn, S. (2011). Racial discrimination and Asian mental health: A meta-analysis. *The Counseling Psychologist, 39*, 463–489. http://dx.doi.org/10.1177/0011000010381791

Lee, D. L., & Ahn, S. (2012). Discrimination against Latina/os: A meta-analysis of individual-level resources and outcomes. *The Counseling Psychologist, 40*, 28–65. http://dx.doi.org/10.1177/0011000011403326

Linley, J. L., & George-Jackson, C. E. (2013). Addressing underrepresentation in STEM fields through undergraduate interventions. *New Directions for Student Services, 144*, 97–102. http://dx.doi.org/10.1002/ss.20073

Marger, M. (2011). *Race and ethnic relations: American global perspectives* (9th ed.). Belmont, CA: Cengage Learning.

Martinez, E. B., Meyer, M., & Carter, M. (Eds.). (2012). *We have not been moved: Resisting racism and militarism in 21st century America*. Oakland, CA: PM Press.

Mays, V. M., Ponce, N. A., Washington, D. L., & Cochran, S. D. (2003). Classification of race and ethnicity: Implications for public health. *Annual Review of Public Health, 24*, 83–110. http://dx.doi.org/10.1146/annurev.publhealth.24.100901.140927

Miller, J., & Garran, A. M. (2007). The web of institutional racism. *Smith College Studies in Social Work, 77*, 33–67. http://dx.doi.org/10.1300/J497v77n01_03

Miller, J., & Garran, A. M. (2008). *Racism in the United States: Implications for the helping professions*. Belmont, CA: Brooks/Cole.

Neville, H. A., & Pieterse, A. L. (2009). Racism, White supremacy, and resistance. In H. A. Neville, B. M. Tynes, & S. O. Utsey (Eds.), *Handbook of African American psychology* (pp. 159–171). Newbury Park, CA: Sage.

Neville, H. A., Spanierman, L. B., & Lewis, J. A. (2012). The expanded psychosocial model of racism: A new model for understanding and disrupting racism and White privilege. In N. A. Fouad (Ed.), *APA handbook of counseling psychology: Vol. 2. Practice, interventions and applications* (pp. 333–360). Washington, DC: American Psychological Association. http://dx.doi.org/10.1037/13755-014

Paradies, Y. (2006). A systematic review of empirical research on self-reported racism and health. *International Journal of Epidemiology, 35*, 888–901. http://dx.doi.org/10.1093/ije/dyl056

Pérez, D. J., Fortuna, L., & Alegria, M. (2008). Prevalence and correlates of everyday discrimination among U.S. Latinos. *Journal of Community Psychology, 36*, 421–433. http://dx.doi.org/10.1002/jcop.20221

Pierre, M. R., & Mahalik, J. R. (2005). Examining African self-consciousness and Black racial identity as predictors of Black men's psychological well-being. *Cultural Diversity and Ethnic Minority Psychology, 11*, 28–40.

Pieterse, A. L. (in press). Racialized perspectives on the prison industrial complex. In E. L. Short., & L. Wilton (Eds.), *Talking about structural inequalities in everyday life: New politics of race in groups, organizations, and social systems*. New York, NY: Information Age.

Pieterse, A. L., & Carter, R. T. (2007). An examination of the relationship between general life stress, racism-related stress and psychological health among Black men. *Journal of Counseling Psychology, 54*, 101–109. http://dx.doi.org/10.1037/0022-0167.54.1.101

Pieterse, A. L., Todd, N. R., Neville, H. A., & Carter, R. T. (2012). Perceived racism and mental health among Black American adults: A meta-analytic review. *Journal of Counseling Psychology, 59*, 1–9. http://dx.doi.org/10.1037/a0026208

Priest, N., Paradies, Y., Trenerry, B., Truong, M., Karlsen, S., & Kelly, Y. (2013). A systematic review of studies examining the relationship between reported racism and health and well-being for children and young people. *Social Science & Medicine, 95*, 115–127. http://dx.doi.org/10.1016/j.socscimed.2012.11.031

Pyke, K. D. (2010). What is internalized racial oppression and why don't we study it? Acknowledging racisms hidden injuries. *Sociological Perspectives, 53*, 551–572. http://dx.doi.org/10.1525/sop.2010.53.4.551

Quinn, A. (2007). Reflections on intergenerational trauma: Healing as a critical intervention. *First Peoples Child & Family Review, 3*, 72–82.

Schmitt, M. T., Branscombe, N. R., Postmes, T., & Garcia, A. (2014). The consequences of perceived discrimination for psychological well-being: A meta-analytic review. *Psychological Bulletin, 140*, 921–948. http://dx.doi.org/10.1037/a0035754

Scott, L. D., & House, L. E. (2005). Relationship of distress and perceived control to coping with perceived racial discrimination among black youth. *The Journal of Black Psychology, 31,* 254–272. http://dx.doi.org/10.1177/0095798405278494

Shorter-Gooden, K. (2004). Multiple resistance strategies: How African American women cope with racism and sexism. *Journal of Black Psychology, 30,* 406–425. http://dx.doi.org/10.1177/0095798404266050

Smedley, A., & Smedley, B. (2012). *Race in North America: Origin and evolution of a worldview* (4th ed.). Boulder, CO: Westview Press.

Smedley, B. D. (2012). The lived experience of race and its health consequences. *American Journal of Public Health, 102,* 933–935. http://dx.doi.org/10.2105/AJPH.2011.300643

Sotero, M. (2006). A conceptual model of historical trauma: Implications for public health practice and research. *Journal of Health Disparities Research and Practice, 1,* 93–108.

Speight, S. L. (2007). Internalized racism: One more piece of the puzzle. *The Counseling Psychologist, 35,* 126–134. http://dx.doi.org/10.1177/0011000006295119

Thoits, P. A. (2010). Stress and health: Major findings and policy implications. *Journal of Health and Social Behavior, 51,* 41–53. http://dx.doi.org/10.1177/0022146510383499

Thompson, C. E., & Neville, H. A. (1999). Racism, mental health, and mental health practice. *The Counseling Psychologist, 27,* 155–223. http://dx.doi.org/10.1177/0011000099272001

Tull, E. S., & Chambers, E. C. (2001). Internalized racism is associated with glucose intolerance among Black Americans in the U.S. Virgin Islands. *Diabetes Care, 24,* 1498–1498. http://dx.doi.org/10.2337/diacare.24.8.1498

Utsey, S. O., Bolden, M. A., & Brown, A. L. (2001). Visions of revolution from the spirit of Frantz Fanon: A psychology of liberation for counseling African Americans confronting societal racism and oppression. In J. G. Ponterotto, J. M. Casas, L. A. Suzuki, & C. M. Alexander (Eds.), *Handbook of multicultural counseling* (2nd ed., pp. 290–310). Thousand Oaks, CA: Sage.

Watts, R. J. (2004). Integrating social justice and psychology. *The Counseling Psychologist, 32,* 855–865. http://dx.doi.org/10.1177/0011000004269274

Watts, R. J., Diemer, M. A., & Voight, A. M. (2011). Critical consciousness: Current status and future directions. *New Directions for Child and Adolescent Development, 2011,* 43–57. http://dx.doi.org/10.1002/cd.310

Watts, R. J., & Flanagan, C. (2007). Pushing the envelope on youth civic engagement: A developmental and liberation psychology perspective. *Journal of Community Psychology, 35,* 779–792. http://dx.doi.org/10.1002/jcop.20178

Watts, R. J., Williams, N. C., & Jagers, R. J. (2003). Sociopolitical development. *American Journal of Community Psychology, 31,* 185–194. http://dx.doi.org/10.1023/A:1023091024140

Wei, M., Alvarez, A. N., Ku, T. Y., Russell, D. W., & Bonett, D. G. (2010). Development and validation of a Coping with Discrimination Scale: Factor structure, reliability, and validity. *Journal of Counseling Psychology, 57,* 328–344. http://dx.doi.org/10.1037/a0019969

West, C., Klor de Alva, J., & Shorris, E. (1996). Our next race question: The uneasiness between Blacks and Latinos. *Harper's, 292,* 55–63.

Williams, D. R., & Jackson, P. B. (2005). Social sources of racial disparities in health. *Health Affairs, 24,* 325–334. http://dx.doi.org/10.1377/hlthaff.24.2.325

Williams, D. R., & Mohammed, S. A. (2009). Discrimination and racial disparities in health: Evidence and needed research. *Journal of Behavioral Medicine, 32,* 20–47. http://dx.doi.org/10.1007/s10865-008-9185-0

Williams, D. R., & Williams-Morris, R. (2000). Racism and mental health: The African American experience. *Ethnicity & Health, 5,* 243–268. http://dx.doi.org/10.1080/713667453

Williams, O., III, Pieterse, A. L., DeLoach, C., Bolden, M. A., Ball, J., & Awadalla, S. (2010). Beyond health disparities: examining power disparities and industrial complexes from the views of Franz Fanon. *Journal of Pan African Studies, 3,* 151–178.

Wyatt, S. B., Williams, D. R., Calvin, R., Henderson, F. C., Walker, E. R., & Winters, K. (2003). Racism and cardiovascular disease in African Americans. *The American Journal of the Medical Sciences, 325,* 315–331. http://dx.doi.org/10.1097/00000441-200306000-00003

2

APPLYING INTERSECTIONALITY THEORY TO RESEARCH ON PERCEIVED RACISM

JIONI A. LEWIS AND PATRICK R. GRZANKA

Although it may appear to be a new concept in the field of psychology, interdisciplinary research on the intersections of race, gender, sexual orientation, social class, and other aspects of social identity has been in existence for decades. Feminist and critical race theories have conceptualized the term *intersectionality* as an analysis of the systems of oppression and social constructions of race, class, and gender (e.g., Collins, 2000; Crenshaw, 1989). Recently, intersectionality researchers in psychology have challenged the field to explore multiple categories of social group membership (Cole, 2009). However, the majority of research in psychology continues to try to separate and tease apart the experiences of racism from other forms of oppression. To respond to calls from scholars, particularly critical race and feminist scholars in the social sciences, we think it is important to further articulate intersectionality theory and ways to apply an intersectional analysis to research on perceived racism.

http://dx.doi.org/10.1037/14852-003
The Cost of Racism for People of Color: Contextualizing Experiences of Discrimination, A. N. Alvarez, C. T. H. Liang, and H. A. Neville (Editors)
Copyright © 2016 by the American Psychological Association. All rights reserved.

In this chapter, we focus on how intersecting identities shape manifestations of racism and influence how people of color respond to and resist racism. We highlight some of the cutting-edge research in the field of multicultural psychology and seek to advance the discourse on debates, challenges, and future directions in the field. First, we ground our chapter in the theoretical literature by providing a brief history of intersectionality theory and intersectional analysis. We particularly focus on the interdisciplinary research literature on intersectionality because fields such as sociology, women and gender studies, critical race studies, and legal studies have been at the forefront of intersectional research. Next, we review the empirical research literature on perceived racism and intersectional identities, including gender, social class, and sexual orientation. Finally, we discuss the methodological approaches to intersectional analysis, with attention to qualitative, quantitative, and mixed methods research. In addition, we conclude with a checklist as a set of guidelines for researchers attempting to conduct intersectional research on perceived racism.

WHAT IS INTERSECTIONALITY?

Although intersectionality has begun to make a meaningful contribution to psychological theory, research, and practice, its origins stretch far beyond the boundaries of psychology. Indeed, we must look to critical legal studies, sociology, women's studies, and beyond the academy to understand the impetus of the intersectional critique and to chart its contributions to psychological research on racism and intersecting, mutually reinforcing forms of inequality. Black feminist legal scholar Kimberlé Williams Crenshaw (1989) is commonly credited with coining the term in a landmark article about Black women's unique position in the United States' legal system, broadly, and antidiscrimination law, specifically. Responding to the weaknesses of both critical race theory (CRT) and feminist legal studies to adequately comprehend and address the nexus of racism and sexism that shapes Black women's experiences in the United States, Crenshaw developed the analogy of traffic at an intersection to characterize how systems of oppression literally intersect:

> Consider an analogy to traffic in an intersection, coming and going in all four directions. Discrimination, like traffic through an intersection, may flow in one direction, and it may flow in another. If an accident happens in an intersection, it can be caused by cars traveling from any number of directions and, sometimes, from all of them. Similarly, if a Black woman is harmed because she is in the intersection, her injury could result from sex discrimination or race discrimination. (p. 149)

As Crenshaw posited, sometimes Black women experience oppression in ways that are nearly identical to Black men, and other times, their oppression is similar to that of White women; sometimes, they experience the combined effects of race and gender oppression in a kind of double jeopardy. Most important, Crenshaw insisted that Black women often experience discrimination as *Black women*—not the sum of racism and sexism (race + sex) "but as Black women whose identity and social location are not simply derivative of White women's or Black men's lives" (Grzanka, 2014, p. xv). Her point appears relatively simple, and yet implicitly contains a radical critique of "single-axis" approaches to studying inequality that frame race, gender, sexuality, class, and other dimensions of difference as discrete, nonoverlapping variables (Dhamoon, 2011). As Grzanka (2014) described, "Single-axis paradigms generally position racism and sexism as parallel or analogous, as opposed to intersecting or co-constitutive, phenomena. Conversely, in intersectionality . . . racism and sexism are viewed as intimate allies in the production of inequality" (p. xv). Crenshaw's intersectionality can be understood in two significant ways: (a) as a rejection of positivist epistemologies and methodologies that deny the complexity of human experiences and elide the role of subjectivity in producing claims to truth and (b) as an innovative mode of scholarly inquiry and critique that promises more accurate and fair representations of the empirical universe (Ferguson, 2012).

Crenshaw's (1989) framing of interlocking systems of oppression may have used an original term, but hers and other academics' scholarship on the intersections of inequality is indebted to centuries of writing (mostly outside of academia), creative expression (including art, music, and oral history), and activism (in opposition to settler-colonialism, slavery, disenfranchisement, and other forms of social and political violence) by and for African American women (Collins, 2000). Sociologist Patricia Hill Collins's (2000) hugely influential book *Black Feminist Thought* details the ways that African American women's oppression catalyzed potent forms of resistance that have manifest as multifarious forms of activism in and outside of the academy and the formal boundaries of academic disciplines. Collins said that this dialectic of oppression and activism is the foundation of intersectionality as a paradigm because it captures how intersectional theory and methods attempt to both explain *and* transform intersecting systems of inequality, such as sexuality and class or nation and ability. Although artists, writers, and activists, such as Sojourner Truth, Ida B. Wells Barnett, and Anna Julia Cooper, may not have used the term, intersectionality is endemic to Black feminist thought and is derived from Black women's location in what Collins calls the "matrix of domination," that is, the dynamic ways in which forms of oppression are organized to produce and sustain inequality. Intersectional scholarship today retains an investment in listening to marginalized voices and embracing unique, transdisciplinary methods of data collection and analysis because such "alternative" modes of knowledge production tend to expand the understanding of the intersections of inequality that shape the lives of multiply marginalized individuals in the United States and worldwide. The research on perceived racism surveyed here represents a range of approaches to intersectionality that may enliven discourse and inform future projects on the psychosocial consequences of racism, sexism, classism, heterosexism, and other intersecting forms of inequality.

INTERSECTIONAL IDENTITIES AND PERCEIVED RACISM

For the purpose of this brief review of the literature on intersections of perceived racism and other forms of oppression, we highlight the research that explores the relationship between perceived racism broadly defined (which includes racial discrimination, race-related stress, and racial microaggressions) and various health-related outcomes. In addition, we focus on the ways perceived racism has a differential effect on individuals based on gender/sexism, social class/classism, and sexual orientation/heterosexism because the majority of the extant literature using intersectionality has focused on these identities and forms of oppression. Although we do not focus on other intersecting social identities, such as religion, ability, age, or geographic region, we acknowledge that perceived racism affects individuals differentially based on these identities as well.

Intersections of Perceived Racism and Gender

The process of engaging in an intersectional analysis means that the researcher is attempting to complicate her or his understanding of the complexity of studying multiple categories of social group membership, particularly multiple forms of oppression, marginalization, and disadvantage. Scholars have demonstrated a variety of approaches to engaging intersectionality in their research, and no consensus has been reached with regard to executing intersectional analysis (Cho, Crenshaw, & McCall, 2013). Psychologists have recently turned their attention to intersectionality theory as a way to study multiple social categories as more than independent variables that discretely influence mental health and behavior. Drawing on some of these articulations of intersectionality (e.g., Bowleg, 2008; Moradi & Subich, 2003; Shields, 2008; A. J. Thomas, Witherspoon, & Speight, 2008), we argue that researchers have traditionally explored experiences of perceived racism in the field of psychology in five ways: single axis, comparative, additive, interactional, and intersectional. Although these five approaches have been grounded in the research literature on race/racism and gender/sexism, they extend across other dimensions of social inequality reviewed here, including sexual orientation/heterosexism and social class/classism.

The *single-axis approach* has dominated the research literature on racism. This approach assumes that racism is the primary form of oppression that impacts the lives of people of color, and the researcher typically ignores (or controls for) differential experiences based on gender or other social identity groups. This tends to privilege the dominant members within a subordinate group, such as privileging the experiences of men of color over women of color, because single-axis analyses minimize within-group differences and therefore reinforce inequalities within social categories, such as race and gender (Cole, 2009; Crenshaw, 1989).

The second approach is the *comparative approach*, which seeks to explore the differential effects of perceived racism based on gender. Thus, gender is explored as a categorical variable by comparing the differences between men and women in their experiences of perceived racism. For example, Liang, Alvarez, Juang, and Liang (2007) examined whether coping was a mediator in the relationship between perceived racism and race-related stress in a sample of 336 Asian American college students and if these effects differed by gender. Results indicated that coping mediated the relationship between racism and racism-related stress differentially by gender. For men, greater levels of perceived racism were related to greater use of support-seeking coping strategies that were associated with higher levels of racism-related stress. For women, greater levels of perceived racism were related to greater use of active coping strategies that were associated with higher levels of racism-related stress. In a recent exploratory study of the racial microaggression experiences of Latina/o Americans, Nadal, Mazzula, Rivera, and Fujii-Doe (2014) found that men and women experienced different types of microaggressions, such that Latinas experienced greater microaggressions in school or workplace settings. In addition, they also found different experiences based on other demographic characteristics, such as ethnicity, age, and level of education. Although this research is helpful in furthering understanding of the ways that perceived racism operates differently for men and women, the comparative approach does not adequately explore the unique intersections of oppression that men and women of color experience based on both gendered and racialized forms of oppression. In addition, treating gender as a categorical variable oversimplifies the complexity of gender and does little to elucidate why the groups may differ, such as experiences of sexism and patriarchy, male privilege, and gender role socialization (V. G. Thomas, 2004).

Another critique of the comparative approach is that these comparisons can lead to a false dichotomy about a hierarchy of oppressions. For example, a comparative approach to exploring the intersection of racism and sexism continues to assume that researchers need to compare women of color's experiences with men of color's experiences to prove that those of the former are unique and worthy of investigation. Cole (2009) described the process of studying women of color's experiences with discrimination by using a "similar experiences" approach, which compares women of color's oppression with those of either White women or men of color. In this sense, comparative approaches often implicitly reinforce the idea that women of color are not worthy of study on their own and must always be understood in relation to Whiteness and masculinity.

A third approach is the *additive approach*, or the "double-jeopardy" approach. Beal (1970) articulated the concept of double jeopardy to refer to the ways that both racism and sexism affect the lived experiences of women of color (see Bowleg, 2008, for a review). In quantitative research, this approach involves measuring the direct effects of racism and sexism separately and then trying to explore the additive effects. For example, in a sample of African American women, Moradi and Subich (2003) explored whether perceived sexist events and perceived racist events were significantly related to psychological distress, and they found that both variables separately were related to greater psychological distress. This approach still measured experiences of racism and sexism separately and then attempted to see how much each form of oppression contributed to predicting psychological distress. In qualitative research, on the other hand, this approach is typically evidenced by researchers analyzing their data in a way that tries to separate and tease apart the experiences of racism from other forms of oppression by way of thematic coding or a grounded theory approach that privileges the mutual exclusivity of codes (Corbin & Strauss, 2008; Fassinger, 2005).

The fourth approach is the *interactional approach*, which is also known as the "multiplicative approach." This approach is similar to the double-jeopardy approach in that they both share the assumption that multiple forms of oppression can be computed in some way, but the interactional approach assumes that racism and sexism interact in a different way than each variable separately. This approach is often complemented with the additive approach. For example, besides exploring the additive effects of perceived racist and sexist events, Moradi and Subich (2003) also explored whether the interaction of racist and sexist events would significantly predict psychological distress, over and above what could be explained by each variable alone. Thus, the researchers created a statistical interaction term, or moderator effect, which was entered into their statistical model. They found that when each of the variables was included in the model, the interaction of racist and sexist events did not significantly predict psychological distress, yet sexist events alone did. Although this finding adds to the understanding of the interaction of racism and sexism experiences, this approach often still seeks to quantify this interaction in a way that may not meaningfully capture the unique lived experiences of women of color and the ways that the intersection of racism and sexism works in their lives.

The fifth approach to explore the intersection of racism and sexism is the *intersectional approach*, which argues that it is imperative to explore the intersections of racism and sexism jointly because in reality these forms of oppression are experienced simultaneously and cannot be easily teased apart. Because of the history of intersectionality theory as grounded in Black feminist theory, a majority of the research that has explored the intersections of racism and sexism has focused on the experiences of Black women and other women of color in the United States. Philomena Essed (1991), a sociologist, coined the term *gendered racism* to refer to the simultaneous experience of both racism and sexism.

Researchers have recently increased their use of an intersectional perspective to assess gendered racism. For example, A. J. Thomas et al. (2008) explored the construct of gendered racism and its relation to psychological distress and coping styles among a sample of Black women. Findings suggest a significant positive relationship between experiences of gendered racism and psychological distress. In addition, avoidant coping (i.e., trying to avoid thinking about the situation) partially mediated this relationship, such that greater perceived gendered racism was related to greater use of avoidant coping and greater psychological distress. Jones and Shorter-Gooden (2003) conducted a large qualitative interview study of Black women to explore the simultaneous experience of racism and sexism and found that women reported experiencing both race and gender-related stereotypes, particularly in the workplace. However, many women reported that they could not distinguish whether discrimination was based on race, gender, or the intersection of the two. Thus, research that seeks to use categorical race and gender identities as a proxy to explore racism and sexism may miss the intersectional and dynamic nature of these interlocking forms of oppression (see also McCall, 2005, for a review of "intercategorical" approaches to intersectionality).

Lewis and Neville (2015) recently applied an intersectionality framework to the development of a scale to measure Black women's experiences with the intersections of subtle forms of racism and sexism. The Gendered Racial Microaggressions Scale (GRMS) assesses the frequency and stress appraisal of intersecting racial and gender microaggressions. Building on previous qualitative research (Lewis, Mendenhall, Harwood, & Browne Huntt, 2013), the researchers used a mixed methods study design to develop a scale that measures various aspects of gendered racial microaggressions rooted in assumptions and stereotypes of Black womanhood. Their findings indicated that the GRMS was positively related to both racial microaggressions and perceived sexist events. In addition, greater perceived gendered racial microaggressions were related to greater levels of psychological distress. This intersectionality scale is promising because it enables researchers to move beyond additive and interactional approaches to study racism and sexism and toward intersectional approaches that can capture the complexity of interlocking forms of oppression.

Scholars have also used the construct of gendered racism to study the experiences of men of color. Although the concept of gendered racism was originally conceptualized by Essed (1991) as the intersection of racism and sexism experienced by women of color, this term has been applied to the experiences of men of color to refer to their experiences of gendered forms of racism, such as the stereotypes and assumptions of criminality that many Black and Latino men experience (D. W. Sue, 2010). Liang, Rivera, Nathwani, Dang, and Douroux (2010) argued that gendered racism is a construct that can apply to the psychological well-being of men of color, particularly when exploring gender roles, issues of masculinity, and gendered racial stereotypes. For example, Liang, Salcedo, and Miller (2011) explored the ways that race, gender, and cultural values intersect for men of color. Using an additive model, they found that perceived racism significantly moderated the relationship between machismo ideology and gender role conflict in a sample of Latino men. Schwing, Wong, and Fann (2013) used an intersectionality framework to develop a gendered racism stress scale that seeks to measure Black men's experiences with the intersection of racism and masculinity. Specifically, they developed a multidimensional scale to assess the stress associated with stereotypes of Black masculinity, including stereotypes about Black male violence, absent fatherhood, and athletic ability.

With the exception of the single-axis approach, Cole (2009) argued that each of these approaches might represent intersectional analyses; however, we contend that although these approaches can be conceptualized as intersectional in nature from a theoretical perspective, these designs vary in the strength of their adherence to the key tenets of intersectional analysis as articulated in Black feminist thought (cf. Hancock, 2007). Dill and Kohlman (2012) offered a useful distinction between what they called "weak" versus "strong" intersectionality. Weak intersectionality is an approach that merely incorporates and includes multiple identity categories in research design, data collection, and analysis—for example, collecting extensive demographic data and/or recruiting a diverse sample of participants. If identity categories are coded and treated as discrete variables rather than interlocking dimensions of psychosocial experience, such work thereby "explores differences without any true analysis," according to Dill and Kohlman (p. 169). Strong intersectionality, on the other hand, foregrounds the relationships among social categories and analyzes interlocking forms of inequality and oppression.

Thus, building on Dill and Kohlman's (2012) conceptualizations, we argue that these various approaches can be ordered on a continuum from weak intersectionality, where the comparative approach (i.e., inclusion of multiple identities as categorical demographic variables) is located, to strong intersectionality, where the intersectional approach (i.e., consideration of dimensions of difference as interrelated, coconstitutive systems of power and inequality) is. We contend that the optimal approach to advancing understanding of the intersections of multiple forms of social inequality is by intentionally seeking to explore the intersections of racism and other forms of oppression.

Intersections of Perceived Racism and Social Class

Multicultural and feminist scholarship on the intersections of racism and sexism has also paved the way for much of the theory and research on the intersections of race and class, and more specifically, the ways that perceived racism affects individuals differentially by social class. As Cole (2009) noted, "in some academic circles, the phrase *race–class–gender* is invoked so frequently that it has been called a mantra" (p. 171). Thus, the majority of research that focuses on the intersections of racism and class also tends to focus on gender. Scholarship on women of color, in particular, has long established that race and class are gendered and that gender and class are racialized (Baca Zinn & Dill, 1996; Davis, 1983; Smith, 2010).

Social class is understudied in the psychology literature and is typically examined using various proxies for social class. Indirect measures of social class can include income level, occupation, numerical formulas for socioeconomic status, and attitudes and beliefs about social class (Smith & Mao, 2012). Social class researchers argue that it is important to study social class stratification and better understand the ways that social class intersects with other identities to create oppression and disadvantage for some and privilege and advantage for others. Little empirical research explores the intersections of perceived racism and social class, and even fewer studies, the intersections of racism and classism. Smith and Mao (2012) defined *classism* as the "practices, attitudes, assumptions, behaviors, and policies through which social institutions function to perpetuate the deprivation and low status of poor people" (p. 526). Classism also intersects with other forms of oppression, which can contribute to interlocking systems of oppression for people of color and members of other marginalized groups (Smith & Redington, 2010). However, to date, the empirical research on social class has been limited in that it has primarily focused on the negative attitudes, stereotypes, and prejudices that middle- and upper-class people have of poor people from the privileged group's perspective.

The few empirical studies that have explored intersections of race and class have primarily treated race and class as categorical or demographic variables rather than exploring the intersections of race and class oppression. For example, to explore the intersections of ethnicity and class, Lott and Saxon (2002) developed a hypothetical scenario of a woman who was running for office in a parent–teacher organization and asked participants their impressions of the woman on the basis of ethnicity and social class. They found that working-class women were judged more harshly than middle-class women and Latina women were judged more harshly than White women, on the basis of negative stereotypes. Although this research provides interesting information about race and social class, this type of interactional approach has some limitations in the study of race and social class stereotypes. Namely, this approach uses race/ethnicity and social class as categorical variables and the focus of the investigation was on the perpetrators of race and social class stereotypes rather than on the targets of race and class discrimination.

Some social-justice-oriented psychologists (Lott & Bullock, 2007; Smith, 2010) have challenged the field to move beyond studying social class as a categorical variable to conceptualizing and measuring social class in terms of classism experienced by people in poverty and using subjective measures of social class. Smith and Redington (2010) called for increased research on classist microaggressions, which include making comments such as "That's ghetto" and intersecting race and class microaggressions, such as the stereotype of the "welfare queen" (cf. Davis, 1983; Hancock, 2004). The shift in a focus on classism that includes target groups' experiences can fill a gap in the extant literature on social class inequality. For example, Liu (2001) developed the social class worldview model (SCWM) to better understand the subjective experience and worldview of one's social class culture and experience of classism, rather than focusing on "objective" measures of social class, such as income, education, and occupation. A focus on classism has the potential to shift our understanding of social class beyond a categorical variable and toward a more nuanced understanding of the psychosocial impact of classism that differentially affects poor and working-class people, a disproportionate number of which, are also people of color (Smith & Redington, 2010). In addition, a focus on perceived classism rather than merely social class, can lead to more research on the unique experiences of the intersections of classism, racism, and other forms of oppression.

Intersections of Perceived Racism and Sexual Orientation

Much of the research on intersections of the experiences of perceived racism and sexual orientation has focused on lesbian, gay, bisexual, transgender, and queer (LGBTQ) people of color. Some early Black feminist scholarship—particularly that of Barbara Smith and the Combahee River Collective (1977/2007), as well as Audre Lorde (1984)—was situated in an understanding of the intersections of race, gender, and sexual orientation by exploring the lived experiences of Black lesbian women. Beverly Greene (1994), a psychologist, coined the term *triple jeopardy* based on Beal's (1970) conceptualization of double jeopardy and contended that Black lesbian women experience oppression based on the additive or multiplicative effects of their race, gender, and sexual orientation. Growing empirical research has adopted this framework. For example, Bowleg, Brooks, and Ritz (2008) conducted a qualitative study to explore Black lesbian women's experiences with workplace stress and discrimination based on their race, sex/gender, and sexual orientation. They found that Black lesbians experienced four types of workplace stressors related to racism/race, heterosexism/sexual identity, sexism/sex/gender, and intersections of these three forms of oppression. In addition, participants reported various ways they coped with these stressors, including confronting and educating perpetrators, being out and negotiating being out in the workplace, and hiding their sexual orientation. This study adds to the literature regarding the ways sexual minority women of color experience multiple forms of oppression. However, one of the limitations of this study is that the researchers analyzed their data using an additive approach, which tried to separate and tease apart the experiences of multiple marginalized identities, as if sexual minority women of color ever experience their multiple social identities in isolation.

Using an additive framework, DeBlaere et al. (2014) explored the relations between perceived racism, sexism, and heterosexism on the psychological distress of sexual minority women of color. Their findings indicated that when each form of oppression was examined concurrently, perceived heterosexism was the only significant predictor of psychological distress. In addition, collective action (defined as involvement in activities for feminist/women's groups, racial/ethnic minority groups, and sexual minority groups) significantly moderated the relationship between heterosexist experiences and psychological distress, such that lower collective action was more likely to contribute to psychological distress. In another study, Szymanski and Sung (2010) explored the impact of multiple minority stressors as correlates of psychological distress for Asian American LGBTQ individuals. Using an additive approach, they found that heterosexism in communities of color, race-related dating and relationship problems in the LGBTQ community, internalized heterosexism, and outness to the public (level of disclosure of one's sexual orientation) were the only significant predictors of psychological distress among Asian American LGBTQ individuals. The researchers also explored the moderating role of these variables in predicting psychological distress but did not find a significant interaction effect. Although these findings add to the understanding of the additive effects of racism and heterosexism, this approach continues to explore multiple forms of oppression separately, which does not elucidate the intersection of racism and heterosexism in the lives of LGBTQ people of color.

A recent scale to assess racism and heterosexism was created using an intersectional framework to measure the microaggression experiences of LGBTQ people of color. Balsam, Molina, Beadnell, Simoni, and Walters (2011) designed the LGBTQ People of Color Microaggressions Scale, which assesses the intersections of racism and heterosexism. Using a multiphase mixed methods study design, Balsam et al. developed their 18-item scale with the following three subscales: Racism in LGBT Communities, Heterosexism in Racial/Ethnic Minority Communities, and Racism in Dating and Close Relationships. The scale was also significantly related to psychological distress, such that higher scores on the microaggressions scale were positively related to greater distress. Additionally, they found that men reported experiencing greater microaggressions than women; lesbians and gay men reported experiencing greater microaggressions than bisexual men and women; and Asian Americans reported greater microaggressions than African American and Latinas/os. This scale fills a gap in the literature by developing an intersectional measure of microaggressions, which enables researchers to quantitatively examine experiences with multiple marginalized identities using intersectional analysis.

The research literature on the intersections of perceived racism and other social identities and dimensions of social inequality is vast and has evolved over the past few decades. Although the single-axis, comparative, additive, and interactional approaches have existed for quite some time, little research has applied an intersectionality approach to research on perceived racism and gender, sexual orientation, and social class. Many of the recent intersectional studies are promising, particularly the development of intersectional measures of multiple forms of oppression and identity. To encourage researchers to move beyond studying multiple social identities and to begin to more deeply explore intersecting systems of oppression, in the next section we highlight key methodological frameworks to engage in an intersectional analysis.

METHODOLOGICAL FRAMEWORKS FOR INTERSECTIONAL ANALYSIS

Intersectional methodologies fundamentally possess the potential to rethink the very categories, constructs, and key terms of psychological research on race and racism. In the context of psychological research on perceived racism, specifically, intersectionality's focus on the social construction of structural inequalities suggests a rethinking of the central constructs on which such research rests. As Bowleg (2012) elaborated about the strengths of intersectionality in health research, "Privileging a focus on structural-level factors rather than an exclusive focus on the individual is likely to facilitate the development of structural-level interventions more likely to affect the 'fundamental causes' (e.g., poverty, social discrimination) of social inequalities" (pp. 1271–1272). Furthermore, a focus on perceived racism may imply that racism exclusively shapes the experiences of people of color; however, an intersectionality framework encourages researchers to avoid putting multiple forms of oppression on a hierarchy. Intersectionality, therefore, does not examine racism at the expense of other systems of inequality, such as sexism and classism, which cannot be ranked nor understood as mutually independent of race and racism. Based on our review of the literature on perceived racism, specifically, we offer the checklist in Exhibit 2.1 as a guide for scholars negotiating the process of actually developing intersectional research projects, which can be particularly daunting for those of us trained in single-axis and/or additive paradigms. Inspired by similar rubrics offered by

---

EXHIBIT 2.1
Checklist for Intersectional Research on Perceived Racism

Generating the research question

- ✓ **History.** Have I attended to the historical processes that shaped these people's lives and the terms of my research? What are the historical–structural phenomena (e.g., education policy, housing, labor) that have contributed to the research question or problem under investigation?
- ✓ **Literature.** In developing my question(s), have I attended to the foundational literature on intersectionality that will inform my research design? Have I considered interdisciplinary and nonpsychological research and theory that elaborates intersectionality and may enhance my research?
- ✓ **Context.** Have I considered the context-specific factors, including unique cultural practices, beliefs, and ideologies, that influence the lives of the individuals in my research? Where is this psychological problem or issue manifesting, and why does that matter?

Methodology and data collection

- ✓ **Standpoint.** Have I accounted for my own standpoint in relation to the people who are the subject of my research? Where are my own beliefs manifesting in my research design, data collection, and analysis? Can I name and defend these choices?
- ✓ **Methods.** Have I chosen my methods based on my research question, or the other way around? Have I considered nontraditional, mixed methods, and interdisciplinary approaches that might be better suited to my questions?
- ✓ **Measurement/constructs.** How did I arrive at my variables? Are my participants' experiences or the extant research guiding the selection of my variables or constructs under investigation? Have I taken the time to adequately critique the extant research that typically is not intersectional? Do I need to theorize and/or develop new measurement tools to adequately address my research questions?
- ✓ **Sampling.** Have I selected a sample based on convenience or my research questions? Have I considered the multiple identities of my participants and how other samples might be more representative? Do I have theoretical and scientific reasons for choosing to include or not include a "control group"?
- ✓ **Hypotheses.** How might my hypotheses be imposing a single-axis, comparative, additive, or interactional approach on my data? Are hypotheses even necessary or appropriate to my study, given the intersectional nature of the research question? If so, do they enable intersectional dynamics to emerge in data analysis?

(continues)

EXHIBIT 2.1
Checklist for Intersectional Research on Perceived Racism   *(Continued)*

Data analysis

✓ **Power dynamics.** Where is power manifesting in the lives of my participants? Have I considered how power might be operating in ways that are typically "invisible"? What strategies can I use to "see" power at work in my data?

✓ **Analytic strategies.** Why am I using these particular analytic approaches to my data? How might my data be pointing me toward unfamiliar or nontraditional approaches? How might my analytic tools be constraining my potential findings?

✓ **Relationships.** Have I foregrounded the relationships among the social categories and group memberships in my study? Rather than merely include people who occupy multiple positions of subordination, marginality, and/or privilege, have I focused on how these categories co-construct one another and are not discrete aspects of lived experience?

Conclusions and implications

✓ **Action.** What work is my research intended to do in the world? Does my research adequately attend to issues of social justice and the potential for research to catalyze social change, or does my research just generate knowledge for the sake of knowledge? Do the implications of my research extend beyond my own research program?

✓ **Community.** How does my work involve and contribute to the communities or groups under investigation? Have I sufficiently involved them in the development of my conclusion and my steps for future research?

Note. We have grouped these questions across stages of the research process, but that does not mean that issues such as context, standpoint, or action are relevant to consider in only one stage of the research process.

Cole (2009), Hancock (2007), and Morrow (2005), our checklist is intended to help scholars be reflexive through all stages of the research process and is derived from the best practices across qualitative, quantitative, and mixed methods intersectional research. Although some of these questions may strike readers as simply intuitive, these questions reflect best practices and point toward the practical concerns of actually applying intersectionality's insights in psychology.

Given the complexity of exploring intersectional identities, most intersectionality research has used qualitative methodology (Dill, McLaughlin, & Nieves, 2007), and some intersectionality researchers have argued that qualitative methods are better suited to intersectional research (e.g., Bowleg, 2008; Shields, 2008; Stewart & McDermott, 2004). For example, Bowleg (2008) asserted, "The positivist paradigm that undergirds much (but not all) quantitative research appears to be orthogonal to the complexities of intersectionality" (p. 317). Shields (2008), likewise, argued that most quantitative research on intersectionality merely conceptualizes it as a perspective, rather than the theory that drives the research question. Our position is that conducting both qualitative and quantitative intersectionality research is beneficial. Qualitative methods enable researchers to construct questions that seek to explore the complexities of individuals lived experiences and situate their experiences in cultural context. Quantitative methods can enable researchers to explore the ways that intersecting forms of oppression influence different types of outcomes, such as mental and physical health, in ways that are difficult to capture using qualitative and other highly interpretive methods. In addition, we contend that qualitative and quantitative methods can be complementary and helpful in the service of accurately exploring the complexity of intersecting identities and multiple forms of inequality.

We agree with Shields's (2008) position that intersectionality theory should drive the research question (see Generating the research question, Exhibit 2.1), which requires a fundamental shift in thinking about the research process. Engaging in intersectional analysis is an intentional process from the process of study design to the interpretation and dissemination of findings. Researchers should provide an explicit rationale in their research about the variables they plan to explore and how they expect these variables to intersect to shape the outcomes of interest. Next, we discuss some of the methodological challenges and strategies to conducting both qualitative and quantitative intersectional analysis throughout the research process.

The first step in designing a research project is identifying a research topic and formulating the research question (Heppner, Kivlighan, & Wampold, 2008). According to Bowleg (2008), it is important for researchers to be mindful of the way they ask questions because these questions will shape the information researchers obtain. Researchers need to frame their research questions in an intersectional way if they want to engage in intersectional analysis. For example, Bowleg's (2008) work exemplifies how qualitative inquiry has the potential to illuminate meaningful intersectional dynamics—and the potential to obfuscate such dynamics when designed and executed in uncritical or nonreflexive ways. In her study of Black lesbian women's experiences, Bowleg found that her initial interview questions encouraged participants to disaggregate and "rank their identities." For example, Bowleg (2008) asked the following question: "In terms of your life, do you rank these identities, that is by race, sexual orientation, gender or anything else?" (p. 314). In Bowleg's terms, these additive questions—that conceptualized identities in an additive sense that is antithetical to intersectionality—produced additive answers from participants. Although multicultural and feminist psychologists have long argued that culturally biased research produces culturally biased findings (S. Sue, 1999), Bowleg's (2008) insights are particularly useful because she reminds us as researchers that merely including multiple social identities in psychological research does not constitute intersectionality. Psychologists especially run the risk of reproducing and reifying weak intersectionality because of their epistemological and methodological reliance on demographic variables that may inadvertently render experiences of discrimination as parallel, discrete, and nonoverlapping aspects of empirical reality, that is, as racism and not sexism, or as gender first and class second. We encourage researchers to think critically about which questions they want to answer in their research and be intentional about constructing intersectional research questions.

Another important consideration when conducting quantitative research is that researchers tend to develop research questions based on the types of quantitative scales available to measure particular constructs (see Methods in Exhibit 2.1). The choice of which measures to choose that will best answer one's research questions is of upmost importance. However, few quantitative measures explore intersectional identities and forms of inequality. Many of the discrimination measures have been created to focus on separate types of oppression, such as racial, gender, or sexual-orientation discrimination. Although these measures have significantly shaped multicultural and feminist research in positive ways and provided researchers with a host of important measures, we encourage intersectionality researchers to create more intersectional measures to be able to move research beyond exploration and description to better understand the complexity of intersectional identities and forms of social inequality that shape individuals' life experiences and outcomes.

Researchers also need to make decisions about which research design will be best to answer one's research questions. We encourage researchers to avoid constraining themselves by research methodology. Mixed methods research has become more popular in the social sciences broadly (e.g., J. C. Greene, 2007; Tashakkori & Teddlie, 2010), and within the field of multicultural psychology more specifically (Hanson et al., 2005; Stewart & Cole, 2007). We encourage intersectionality researchers to embrace mixed methodology if both quantitative and qualitative methods would be the best methods to answer one's research questions. Often, psychology researchers tend to limit themselves to quantitative research when their research questions might be better answered with a qualitative approach. For example, when exploring new research topics and developing new theoretical constructs, it is often important to conduct qualitative research to explore the complexity of a particular phenomenon and provide an in-depth analysis. It is also helpful when conducting exploratory research questions and helping to determine future research hypotheses (Awad & Cokley, 2010).

Qualitative investigations of perceived racism provide a variety of analytic tools to empirically capture intersectional dynamics, particularly when other methods might obfuscate them. In-depth interviewing is a frequently used method, perhaps most obviously because the interview setting enables the perceiver to articulate her or his perceptions of racism and intersecting social problems (e.g., Shim, 2005). For example, Hall and Fine (2005) used an in-depth interviewing technique known as *narrative analysis* to explore the intersections of race, gender, class, sexual orientation, and age on the lives of two older Black lesbians. Through the lens of positive marginality (i.e., the strengths of living on the margins of the mainstream through multiple marginalized identities), Hall and Fine highlighted four main themes: critical watching and reframing (e.g., countering racial stereotypes), converting obstacles into opportunities, subverting institutions and creating safe spaces, and creating life meaning through activism. Ethnography (Bridges, 2011), focus groups, content analysis, critical discourse analysis of media transcripts (Cole, Avery, Dodson, & Goodman, 2012), critical incident reports, personal reflections, and other texts are also appropriate forms of intersectional qualitative methods. We assert that all qualitative data have the potential to be read intersectionally. Grounded theory (Corbin & Strauss, 2008) and situational analysis (Clarke, 2005) are especially well suited to the interpretation of qualitative data because they emphasize both induction and the power relations immanent to all social interactions. Clarke's cartographic-style "situational," "positional," and "social worlds/arenas" maps, in particular, can help researchers to "see" intersections of oppression where none initially appear in data collection and/or analysis.

In terms of quantitative research, it is also important for researchers to be mindful of the benefits and drawbacks to different research designs, such as experimental, quasi-experimental, and correlational designs. Depending on one's field within the discipline of psychology, one can take any of several different perspectives about which type of research design will best answer the research question. We encourage multicultural intersectionality researchers to consider issues of validity when choosing a research design (see Awad & Cokley, 2010, for a review). According to some multicultural researchers (Awad & Cokley, 2010; S. Sue, 1999), the focus on internal validity, which is typical in experimental designs, at the expense of external validity, tends to ignore issues of culture and the ability to generalize to diverse populations. It is important for researchers to be aware of how their research design will influence the research process and the type of intersectional analysis one will be able to use.

Awad and Cokley (2010) highlighted important considerations when conducting quantitative multicultural research, and we think many of these considerations apply to conducting intersectionality research, particularly quantitative intersectionality research. One important consideration for researchers is choosing study variables (see Methodology and data collection, Exhibit 2.1). Awad and Cokley underscored the importance of distinguishing between distal and proximal variables. *Distal variables* are typically demographic characteristics, whereas *proximal variables* are psychological constructs, such as identity-related variables (e.g., racial, gender, sexual identity). They argued that distal variables lead researchers to explore group differences and interpret the differences they find to demographic characteristics rather than underlying psychological characteristics. This leads to researchers essentializing race, gender, sexual orientation, social class, or other categorical variables rather than exploring psychological constructs, such as racial or gender identity development. Because some demographic characteristics are socially constructed, and the self-identity of particular labels might mean different things to different people, using distal variables can be problematic, particularly when engaging in intersectional analysis (Awad & Cokley, 2010; Bowleg, 2008). We encourage researchers to choose variables that adequately assess the construct of interest rather than using demographic characteristics as a proxy for more complex constructs. Relatedly, researchers also need to select quantitative measures that have been validated on the population of interest to ensure that the psychological construct will be accurately measured. For example, if a researcher plans to explore the impact of perceived racism on symptoms of depression, it would be important for the researcher to know that some research has found that people of color tend to report more somatic symptoms versus cognitive symptoms of depression (Walker & Hunter, 2009). Thus, for researchers exploring depression among people of color, it is important to choose a measure of depression that includes somatic symptoms because a measure with only cognitive symptoms might lead people of color to underreport their symptoms, which would in turn lead to a less accurate measure of the link between perceived racism and symptoms of depression.

The process of intersectional data analysis and interpretation is important to consider. We encourage researchers to consider ways to analyze data that moves beyond single-axis, comparative, and additive approaches (see Data analysis, Exhibit 2.1). Many experimental research designs will lead to the analysis of data using factorial analysis of variance (Awad & Cokley, 2010; Warner, 2008). Although this is one way to analyze the data, we argue that this type of data analysis leads to comparative and additive approaches that do little to explore intersecting forms of oppression. Quasi-experimental designs could be a helpful way to explore psychological constructs in a more experimental design. A survey research design could include some open-ended questions to more fully explore the ways participants make meaning of their identities rather than solely focusing on demographic questionnaires. When demographic variables are used, they can be paired with identity centrality and salience scales, such as Collective Self-Esteem (Luhtanen & Crocker, 1992), to afford participants agency in reflecting on their multiple identities; such fluid and flexible constructs may enable within-group differences to emerge that would otherwise be obscured by traditional analysis of variance. Data can be analyzed in many ways, and we encourage researchers to become more creative and flexible in their use of multiple methods and multiple forms of data analysis to explore intersectional issues.

It is also important for intersectionality researchers to be culturally responsive in the interpretation of their findings (see Conclusions and implications, Exhibit 2.1). This means researchers should avoid oversimplifying their research findings to fit into existing psychological models and frameworks. For example, Harnois and Ifatunji (2011) argued that many of the racial discrimination measures currently developed assume a gender-neutral stance yet actually include items that are more likely to measure the racial discrimination experiences of men of color. For instance, Harnois and Ifatunji highlighted items from Utsey and Ponterotto's (1996) Index of Race-Related Stress that might be more applicable to Black men's experiences, such as "You have observed that white kids who commit violent crimes are portrayed as 'boys being boys', while black kids who commit similar crimes are wild animals" (p. 494). Thus, it is no surprise that when using some of these measures, researchers have found men of color to score higher than women of color on experiences of racial discrimination. This might lead researchers to conclude that men of color simply experience greater racial discrimination without considering that the measurement tools might not adequately assess the gendered racial discrimination experiences that women of color may be more likely to encounter (Harnois & Ifatunji, 2011). It is important for researchers to think about the stereotypes and assumptions certain interpretations of findings will perpetuate with a single-axis approach. Researchers should also contextualize their findings and not overgeneralize the experiences of a group of people, particularly multiply marginalized groups. Finally, researchers should not neglect the activist orientation of intersectionality as developed by Black feminist scholars (Collins, 2000). Intersectionality is not primarily an explanatory theory—it is a critical approach that is expressly geared toward transforming social structures and cultivating social justice. Accordingly, psychologists should pay careful attention to the social implications of their research, including unintended consequences, and should likewise consider how their work might be used to empower structurally disadvantaged groups.

CONCLUSION

In this chapter, we have highlighted intersectionality theory and ways to apply an intersectional analysis to research on perceived racism. We provided a brief historical overview of intersectionality theory with a particular focus on the interdisciplinary research literature. We also reviewed the empirical research literature on perceived racism and intersectional identities, with a focus on gender, social class, and sexual orientation. Building on previous articulations of intersectionality, we highlighted the five approaches that researchers have traditionally used to apply intersectionality theory to perceived racism in the field of psychology: single axis, comparative, additive, interactional, and intersectional. We argued that these five approaches extend across various dimensions of social inequality (e.g., sexism, heterosexism, classism) and can be ordered from weak intersectionality (i.e., single axis) to strong intersectionality (i.e., intersectionality).

We developed our checklist (Exhibit 2.1) to encourage research that reflects the tenets of strong intersectionality and foregrounds the relationships among systems of oppression (Dill & Kohlman, 2012). This list can be framed as a conceptual guidebook for negotiating the perils of challenging extant paradigms and conducting meaningful, social justice research at the intersections of systemic inequalities. Because strong intersectional psychological research on perceived discrimination remains very much in a nascent stage, multicultural and feminist psychologists have both the opportunity and responsibility to follow emergent best practices and create their own pathways for efficacious and innovative intersectional research. We hope that scholars will use and expand this list as they cultivate transformative approaches to the study of perceived racism.

REFERENCES

Awad, G., & Cokley, K. (2010). Designing and interpreting quantitative research in multicultural counseling. In J. Ponterotto, M. Casas, L. Suzuki, & C. Alexander (Eds.), *Handbook of multicultural counseling* (3rd ed., pp. 385–396). Thousands Oak, CA: Sage.

Baca Zinn, M., & Dill, B. T. (1996). Theorizing difference from multiracial feminism. *Feminist Studies, 22*, 321–331. http://dx.doi.org/10.2307/3178416

Balsam, K. F., Molina, Y., Beadnell, B., Simoni, J., & Walters, K. (2011). Measuring multiple minority stress: The LGBT People of Color Microaggressions Scale. *Cultural Diversity and Ethnic Minority Psychology, 17*, 163–174. http://dx.doi.org/10.1037/a0023244

Beal, F. (1970). Double jeopardy: To be Black and female. In T. Cade (Ed.), *The Black woman: An anthology* (pp. 90–100). New York, NY: Signet.

Bowleg, L. (2008). When Black + lesbian + woman ≠ Black lesbian woman: The methodological challenges of qualitative and quantitative intersectionality research. *Sex Roles, 59*, 312–325. http://dx.doi.org/10.1007/s11199-008-9400-z

Bowleg, L. (2012). The problem with the phrase *women and minorities*: Intersectionality—An important theoretical framework for public health. *American Journal of Public Health, 102*, 1267–1273. http://dx.doi.org/10.2105/AJPH.2012.300750

Bowleg, L., Brooks, K., & Ritz, S. F. (2008). "Bringing home more than a paycheck": An exploratory analysis of Black lesbians' experiences of stress and coping in the workplace. *Journal of Lesbian Studies, 12*, 69–84. http://dx.doi.org/10.1300/10894160802174342

Bridges, K. (2011). *Reproducing race: An ethnography of pregnancy as a site of racialization*. Berkeley, CA: University of California Press.

Cho, S., Crenshaw, K. W., & McCall, L. (2013). Toward a field of intersectionality studies: Theory, applications, and praxis. *Signs: Journal of Women in Culture and Society, 38*, 785–810. http://dx.doi.org/10.1086/669608

Clarke, A. E. (2005). *Situational analysis: Grounded theory after the postmodern turn*. Thousand Oaks, CA: Sage.

Cole, E. R. (2009). Intersectionality and research in psychology. *American Psychologist, 64*, 170–180. http://dx.doi.org/10.1037/a0014564

Cole, E. R., Avery, L. R., Dodson, C., & Goodman, K. D. (2012). Against nature: How arguments about the naturalness of marriage privilege heterosexuality. *Journal of Social Issues, 68*, 46–62. http://dx.doi.org/10.1111/j.1540-4560.2012.01735.x

Collins, P. H. (2000). *Black feminist thought: Knowledge, consciousness, and the politics of empowerment* (2nd ed.). New York, NY: Routledge.

Combahee River Collective. (2007). A Black feminist statement. In E. B. Freedman (Ed.), *The essential feminist reader* (pp. 325–330). New York, NY: Modern Library. (Original work published 1977)

Corbin, J., & Strauss, A. (2008). *Basics of qualitative research: Techniques to developing grounded theory* (3rd ed.). Los Angeles, CA: Sage.

Crenshaw, K. W. (1989). Demarginalizing the intersection of race and sex: A Black feminist critique of antidiscrimination doctrine, feminist theory and antiracist politics. *University of Chicago Legal Forum, 140*, 139–167.

Davis, A. Y. (1983). *Women, race, and class*. New York, NY: Vintage.

DeBlaere, C., Brewster, M. E., Bertsch, K. N., DeCarlo, A. L., Kegel, K. A., & Presseau, C. D. (2014). The protective power of collective action for sexual minority women of color: An investigation of multiple discrimination experiences and psychological distress. *Psychology of Women Quarterly, 38*, 20–32. http://dx.doi.org/10.1177/0361684313493252

Dhamoon, R. K. (2011). Considerations on mainstreaming intersectionality. *Political Research Quarterly, 64*, 230–243. http://dx.doi.org/10.1177/1065912910379227

Dill, B. T., & Kohlman, M. H. (2012). Intersectionality: A transformative paradigm in feminist theory and social justice. In S. N. Hesse-Biber (Ed.), *The handbook of feminist research: Theory and praxis* (2nd ed., pp. 154–174). Thousand Oaks, CA: Sage. http://dx.doi.org/10.4135/9781483384740.n8

Dill, B. T., McLaughlin, A. E., & Nieves, A. D. (2007). Future directions of feminist research: Intersectionality. In S. N. Hesse-Biber (Ed.), *Handbook of feminist research: Theory and praxis* (pp. 629–638). Thousand Oaks, CA: Sage.

Essed, P. (1991). *Understanding everyday racism: An interdisciplinary theory*. Thousand Oaks, CA: Sage.

Fassinger, R. E. (2005). Paradigms, praxis, problems, and promise: Grounded theory in counseling psychology research. *Journal of Counseling Psychology, 52*, 156–166. http://dx.doi.org/10.1037/0022-0167.52.2.156

Ferguson, R. A. (2012). Reading intersectionality. *Trans-Scripts, 2*, 91–99.

Greene, B. (1994). Lesbian women of color: Triple jeopardy. In L. Comas-Díaz & B. Greene (Eds.), *Women of color: Integrating ethnic and gender identities in psychotherapy* (pp. 389–427). New York, NY: Guilford.

Greene, J. C. (2007). *Mixed methods in social inquiry*. Hoboken, NJ: Wiley.

Grzanka, P. R. (2014). Intersectional objectivity. In P. R. Grzanka (Ed.), *Intersectionality: A foundations and frontiers reader* (pp. xi–xxvii). Boulder, CO: Westview Press.

Hall, R. L., & Fine, M. (2005). The stories we tell: The lives and friendship of two older Black lesbians. *Psychology of Women Quarterly, 29*, 177–187. http://dx.doi.org/10.1111/j.1471-6402.2005.00180.x

Hancock, A.-M. (2004). *The politics of disgust: The public identity of the "welfare queen."* New York: NYU Press.

Hancock, A.-M. (2007). When multiplication doesn't equal quick addition: Examining intersectionality as a research paradigm. *Perspectives on Politics, 3*, 63–79.

Hanson, W. E., Creswell, J. W., Plano Clark, V. L., Petska, K. P., & Creswell, J. D. (2005). Mixed methods research designs in counseling psychology. *Journal of Counseling Psychology, 52*, 224–235. http://dx.doi.org/10.1037/0022-0167.52.2.224

Harnois, C. E., & Ifatunji, M. (2011). Gendered measures, gendered models: Toward an intersectional analysis of interpersonal racial discrimination. *Ethnic and Racial Studies, 34*, 1006–1028. http://dx.doi.org/10.1080/01419870.2010.516836

Heppner, P. P., Kivlighan, D. M., & Wampold, B. E. (2008). *Research design in counseling* (3rd ed.). Belmont, CA: Brooks/Cole.

Jones, C., & Shorter-Gooden, K. (2003). *Shifting: The double lives of Black women in America*. New York, NY: HarperCollins.

Lewis, J. A., Mendenhall, R., Harwood, S. A., & Browne Huntt, M. (2013). Coping with gendered racial microaggressions among Black women college students. *Journal of African American Studies, 17*, 51–73.

Lewis, J. A., & Neville, H. A. (2015). Construction and initial validation of the Gendered Racial Microaggressions Scale for Black women. *Journal of Counseling Psychology, 62*, 289–302. http://dx.doi.org/10.1037/cou0000062

Liang, C. T. H., Alvarez, A. N., Juang, L. P., & Liang, M. X. (2007). The role of coping in the relationship between perceived racism and racism-related stress for Asian Americans: Gender differences. *Journal of Counseling Psychology, 54*, 132–141. http://dx.doi.org/10.1037/0022-0167.54.2.132

Liang, C. T. H., Rivera, A., Nathwani, A., Dang, P., & Douroux, A. (2010). Dealing with gendered racism and racial identity among Asian American men. In W. M.

Liu, D. Iwamoto, & M. Chae (Eds.), *Culturally responsive counseling with Asian American men* (pp. 63–82). New York, NY: Routledge.

Liang, C. T. H., Salcedo, J., & Miller, H. (2011). Perceived racism, masculinity ideologies, and gender role conflict among Latino men. *Psychology of Men & Masculinity, 12*, 201–215. http://dx.doi.org/10.1037/a0020479

Liu, W. M. (2001). Expanding our understanding of multiculturalism: Developing a social class worldview model. In D. B. Pope-Davis & H. L. K. Coleman (Eds.), *The intersection of race, class, and gender in counseling psychology* (pp. 127–170). Thousand Oaks, CA: Sage. http://dx.doi.org/10.4135/9781452231846.n6

Lorde, A. (1984). *Sister outsider: Essays and speeches.* Trumansburg, NY: Crossing Press.

Lott, B., & Bullock, H. E. (2007). *Psychology and economic injustice.* Washington, DC: American Psychological Association.

Lott, B., & Saxon, S. (2002). The influence of ethnicity, social class, and context on judgments about U.S. women. *The Journal of Social Psychology, 142*, 481–499. http://dx.doi.org/10.1080/00224540209603913

Luhtanen, R., & Crocker, J. (1992). A collective self-esteem scale: Self-evaluation of one's social identity. *Personality and Social Psychology Bulletin, 18*, 302–318. http://dx.doi.org/10.1177/0146167292183006

McCall, L. (2005). The complexity of intersectionality. *Signs: Journal of Women in Culture and Society, 30*, 1771–1800. http://dx.doi.org/10.1086/426800

Moradi, B., & Subich, L. M. (2003). A concomitant examination of the relations of perceived racist and sexist events to psychological distress for African American women. *The Counseling Psychologist, 31*, 451–469. http://dx.doi.org/10.1177/0011000003031004007

Morrow, S. (2005). Quality and trustworthiness in qualitative research in counseling psychology. *Journal of Counseling Psychology, 52*, 250–260. http://dx.doi.org/10.1037/0022-0167.52.2.250

Nadal, K. L., Mazzula, S. L., Rivera, D. P., & Fujii-Doe, W. (2014). Microaggressions and Latina/o Americans: An analysis of nativity, gender, and ethnicity. *Journal of Latina/o Psychology.* Advance online publication. http://dx.doi.org/10.1037/lat0000013

Schwing, A. E., Wong, Y. J., & Fann, M. (2013). Development and validation of the African American Men's Gendered Racism Stress Inventory. *Psychology of Men & Masculinity, 14*, 16–24. http://dx.doi.org/10.1037/a0028272

Shields, S. A. (2008). Gender: An intersectionality perspective. *Sex Roles, 59*, 301–311. http://dx.doi.org/10.1007/s11199-008-9501-8

Shim, J. K. (2005). Constructing 'race' across the science-lay divide: Racial formation in the epidemiology and experience of cardiovascular disease. *Social Studies of Science, 35*, 405–436. http://dx.doi.org/10.1177/0306312705052105

Smith, L. (2010). *Psychology, poverty, and the end of social exclusion: Putting our practice to work.* New York, NY: Teachers College Press.

Smith, L., & Mao, S. (2012). Social class and psychology. In N. A. Fouad, J. A. Carter, & L. M. Subich (Eds.), *APA handbook of counseling psychology: Vol. 1. Theories, research, and methods* (pp. 523–540). Washington, DC: American Psychological Association.

Smith, L., & Redington, R. M. (2010). Class dismissed: Making the case for the study of classist microaggressions. In D. W. Sue (Ed.), *Microaggressions and marginality: Manifestation, dynamics, and impact* (pp. 269–285). Hoboken, NJ: Wiley.

Stewart, A. J., & Cole, E. R. (2007). Narratives and numbers: Feminist multiple methods research. In S. N. Hesse-Biber (Ed.), *The handbook of feminist research* (pp. 327–344). Thousand Oaks, CA: Sage.

Stewart, A. J., & McDermott, C. (2004). Gender in psychology. *Annual Review of Psychology, 55*, 519–544. http://dx.doi.org/10.1146/annurev.psych.55.090902.141537

Sue, D. W. (2010). *Microaggressions in everyday life: Race, gender, and sexual orientation*. Hoboken, NJ: Wiley.

Sue, S. (1999). Science, ethnicity, and bias: Where have we gone wrong? *American Psychologist, 54*, 1070–1077. http://dx.doi.org/10.1037/0003-066X.54.12.1070

Szymanski, D. M., & Sung, M. R. (2010). Minority stress and psychological distress among Asian American sexual minority persons. *The Counseling Psychologist, 38*, 848–872. http://dx.doi.org/10.1177/0011000010366167

Tashakkori, A., & Teddlie, C. (2010). *Sage handbook of mixed methods in social and behavioral research* (2nd ed.). Thousand Oaks, CA: Sage.

Thomas, A. J., Witherspoon, K. M., & Speight, S. L. (2008). Gendered racism, psychological distress, and coping styles of African American women. *Cultural Diversity and Ethnic Minority Psychology, 14*, 307–314. http://dx.doi.org/10.1037/1099-9809.14.4.307

Thomas, V. G. (2004). The psychology of Black women: Studying lives in context. *Journal of Black Psychology, 30*, 286–306. http://dx.doi.org/10.1177/0095798404266044

Utsey, S. O., & Ponterotto, J. G. (1996). Development and initial validation of the index of race-related stress. *Journal of Counseling Psychology, 43*, 490–501. http://dx.doi.org/10.1037/0022-0167.43.4.490

Walker, R. L., & Hunter, L. R. (2009). From anxiety and depression to suicide and self-harm. In H. A. Neville, B. M. Tynes, & S. O. Utsey (Eds.), *Handbook of African American Psychology* (pp. 401–415). Thousand Oaks: Sage.

Warner, L. R. (2008). A best practices guide to intersectional approaches in psychological research. *Sex Roles, 59*, 454–463. http://dx.doi.org/10.1007/s11199-008-9504-5

3

IMPROVING THE MEASUREMENT OF SELF-REPORTED RACIAL DISCRIMINATION: CHALLENGES AND OPPORTUNITIES

DAVID R. WILLIAMS

In the United States, as in other racialized countries in the world, racially nondominant and stigmatized groups have higher rates of disease and death than the dominant groups within their societies (Williams, 2012). In U.S. data, these patterns are evident for African Americans (or Blacks), American Indians and Alaskan Natives (or Native Americans), Native Hawaiians and other Pacific Islanders, Hispanic (or Latino) immigrants with long-term residence in the United States and for economically disadvantaged Asian Americans (Williams, 2012). These striking disparities are persistent over time, although slightly less now than in the past, and are evident at every level of income and education (Braveman, Cubbin, Egerter, Williams, & Pamuk, 2010; Williams, 2012). In recent years, increased attention has been given to the role of racism as a determinant of these patterns of racial inequality in health and as a contributor to the residual effects of race after socioeconomic status (SES) is controlled.

This chapter focuses on one aspect of racism: subjective reports of experiences of discrimination. The terms *self-reported discrimination*, *perceived discrimination*, and *interpersonal discrimination* are used to describe this phenomenon in the literature, and I use them interchangeably here. These types of reports have been categorized as stressful life experiences, on the basis of their psychological appraisal and physiological and psychological responses, and they have been neglected in the traditional assessment of stressors (Clark, Anderson, Clark, & Williams, 1999). A limitation of measuring discrimination at the individual level in this way is that such measures capture only incidents that individuals are willing or able to report, as I discuss further in the section Measuring Vigilance and Anticipatory Stress.

Research reveals that perceived discrimination is adversely related to a broad range of health outcomes and health risk behaviors (Pascoe & Smart Richman, 2009; Williams & Mohammed, 2009). For example, Lewis and colleagues have shown that chronic everyday discrimination is positively associated with coronary artery calcification (Lewis et al., 2006), C-reactive protein (Lewis, Aiello, Leurgans, Kelly, & Barnes, 2010), blood pressure (Lewis et al., 2009), giving birth to lower weight infants (Earnshaw et al., 2013), cognitive impairment (Barnes et al., 2012), subjective and objective indicators of poor sleep (Lewis et al., 2013), visceral fat (Lewis, Kravitz, Janssen, & Powell, 2011), and mortality (Barnes et al., 2008). Research on discrimination has also found that exposure to racial bias is associated with lower levels of health care seeking and adherence behaviors among racial minorities. Further, research in the United States, South Africa, Australia, and New Zealand documents that discrimination makes an incremental contribution over and above SES in accounting for racial disparities in health (Williams et al., 2008; Williams & Mohammed, 2009).

In this chapter, I provide an overview of measurement challenges related to perceived discrimination and the research needed to advance the field. I attend to measurement challenges in the recent research on perceived discrimination and health. Perceived discrimination is a psychosocial stressor, and much can be learned from the research literature on stress and survey that can advance the study of discrimination and health (Williams & Mohammed, 2009). Enhancing the understanding of perceived discrimination and health will require more systematic attention to comprehensively capturing measuring all relevant aspects of discrimination, capturing vigilance and anticipatory stress, minimizing multiple forms of potential bias, and enhancing understanding of how discrimination combines with other forms of bias and stress to affect health.

CAPTURING ALL RELEVANT TYPES OF PERCEIVED DISCRIMINATION

The current conceptualization and assessment of perceived discrimination is limited and does not capture all types of race-related stressful experiences. The stress literature classifies stressors into multiple subtypes: life events, traumas, chronic stressors, and macrostressors (Cohen, Kessler, & Gordon, 1995). Prior research has shown that failure to assess stress comprehensively underestimates the effects of stress on health (Thoits, 2010). Thus, it is likely that the available scientific evidence on perceived discrimination and health, as impressive as it is, still understates the full impact of interpersonal discrimination on health.

Major life events are acute, observable defined experiences, such as death of a loved one, divorce, or job loss. The majority of commonly used measures of discrimination in recent studies capture discriminatory experiences that are analogous to life events in the stress literature (Bastos, Celeste, Faerstein, & Barros, 2010). These include the Experiences of Discrimination scale (Krieger, 1990), the Schedule of Racist Events (Landrine & Klonoff, 1996), the Major Experiences of Discrimination scale (Kessler, Mickelson, & Williams, 1999), the Racism and Life Experiences Scale (Harrell, 1997), and the Index of Race-Related Stress (Utsey & Ponterotto, 1996). *Traumas* are life events that are extreme and overwhelming. They are a type of stressful experiences (e.g., having been in a life-threatening accident, kidnapped, sexually assaulted, tortured) that can have long-term adverse effects on health (Pearlin, Schieman, Fazio, & Meersman, 2005; Stam, 2007). They are different from life events in that they capture experiences that are extreme, overwhelming, and often horrific in impact. Traumas have not received much attention in the discrimination literature, although it is likely that traumatic experiences are reported on some of the life events-like measures of discrimination but with inadequate detail collected to distinguish them from less severe experiences. Carter (2007) emphasized the need to assess race-related traumatic experiences as distinct from major experiences of racial discrimination. He indicated that emotional reaction to these severe, life-threatening, or dangerous experiences will likely be intense and that these experiences thus have great potential for psychological injury.

Chronic stressors refers to experiences that are ongoing or recurrent. They can occur in major domains of life, such as problems in marriage relationships and difficulties at work, or they can be more minor every day hassles—like rush-hour traffic or long workdays. These experiences provide persistent negative exposure to threat or excessive demand (Baum, Cohen, & Hall, 1993) so that although they are difficult to measure, they are stronger predictors of the onset and course of the illness than acute life events (Cohen et al., 1995). Studies of discrimination have given inadequate attention to assessing all relevant types of chronic exposure to discrimination, with the exception of the recent fairly widespread use of the Everyday Discrimination Scale (Williams, Yu, Jackson, & Anderson, 1997). The scale attempts to capture aspects of interpersonal discrimination that are chronic or episodic but generally minor, somewhat analogous to the assessment of daily hassles in the stress literature. Items include being "treated with less courtesy than others," receiving "poorer service than others at restaurants or stores," or "people act as if they think you are not smart" or "as if they are afraid of you." The scale has several attractive features, including its brevity, good psychometric properties (Krieger, Smith, Naishadham, Hartman, & Barbeau, 2005), use in multiple racial/ethnic populations in the United States, and increasing use in international contexts (e.g., South Africa; Williams et al., 2008).

However, the current assessment of racial bias gives only limited attention to the measurement of chronic race-related stressors in major domains of life such as work, school, or the criminal justice system (Bastos et al., 2010). As noted, it is instructive that some of the striking associations linking chronic discrimination to subclinical disease are found in analyses with the Everyday Discrimination Scale. An important limitation of the use of the Everyday Discrimination Scale is that it is typically used as the only measure of perceived discrimination and psychosocial stress. This scale captures an important, but nonetheless limited aspect of the phenomenon of discrimination and cumulative exposure to acute and chronic stressors. The Perceived Racism Scale (McNeilly et al., 1996) also captures some aspects of chronic discrimination, but more effort is needed to comprehensively assess chronic and ongoing experiences of discrimination, especially those in the domain of work, a major context of discriminatory experiences in contemporary society.

Macrostressors are large-scale stressors, such as economic recessions or natural disasters. Research has found that events such as earthquakes, terrorist attacks, and the onset of war are associated with increased hospital admissions and acute symptoms of heart disease and heart disease mortality (Bhattacharyya & Steptoe, 2007). Highly publicized race-related traumatic events, such as examples of police brutality, are likely to have similar effects. An example of such an event is the 2006 Duke University lacrosse team incident in which a Black woman accused White male members of the sports team of racial derogation, rape, and violence (Smart Richman & Jonassaint, 2008). Racially divisive media coverage and rhetoric followed this incident, and Black students at Duke University were stressed and had concerns about their safety. An experimental study that was being conducted at Duke at that time found that compared with students who participated in the experiment before the lacrosse team incident, Black students, especially females, who participated after media attention to the incident had higher levels of cortisol and were unresponsive to the experimental task (Smart Richman & Jonassaint, 2008). Similarly, Lauderdale (2006) documented the adverse health consequences of the well-documented increase in discrimination and harassment of Arab Americans in the six months after the terrorist attacks of September 11, 2001. She found that Arab American women in California had an increase in the rate of low birth weight and preterm birth in the 6 months after September 11 compared with the 6 months before. Other women in California did not experience a change in birth outcome risk post-September 11.

Future research is needed to identify the extent to which major race-related stressors can initiate new disease processes or exacerbate existing disease. Some of the items on the Index of Race-Related Stress capture aspects of macrostressors (Utsey & Ponterotto, 1996), but comprehensively assessing the potential contribution of large-scale race-related traumatic events will require researchers to capitalize on emergent opportunities to assess the health consequences of macrostressors. Such efforts could use some of the strategies used in the larger stress literature, such as creatively using hospital admissions and vital statistics data. It is also noteworthy that although some of the psychological and physiological responses to macrostressors may be immediate, others may unfold over time. For example, research indicates that cardiac mortality tends to be elevated for at least 6 months postbereavement (Bhattacharyya & Steptoe, 2007).

Assessing exposure to racial discrimination in its full complexity necessitates attention to capturing potential intergenerational effects of racism. *Historical trauma* is one example of an intergenerational effect. This term refers to the cumulative psychological wounding of an individual and his/her group due to the history of genocide and other atrocities that, for example, American Indians and other indigenous people experienced from European colonizers. The explicit attempt of much research on this dimension of racism is to capture such exposure over the life span of the individual and across generations, such as research on the effects of historical trauma on the health of American Indians (Walters et al., 2011). Assessment instruments with good psychometric properties have been developed to assess historical trauma and have found, for example, that 50% of American Indians think regularly about these historical losses (Whitbeck, Adams, Hoyt, & Chen, 2004). Empirical studies have also linked exposure to historical trauma to multiple health outcomes (Walters et al., 2011). This research is similar to studies of other generational group traumas, including those on the health consequences of the Jewish Holocaust on survivors and their descendants. More generally, this research highlights the importance of assessing not only stressful life experiences but also the role that traumatic reminders of these experiences can play (Stam, 2007).

The comprehensive assessment of discrimination also requires attending to all of the contexts in which it may occur, such as employment, education, obtaining housing, medical care, and other goods and services. Recent research on discrimination in online contexts illustrates this point. A study of 264 adolescents found that 20% of Whites, 29% of Blacks, and 42% of people of multiracial/other races reported that they had experience discrimination in some online context (Tynes, Giang, Williams, & Thompson, 2008). In addition, 71% of Blacks and Whites and 67% of multiracial/other had witnessed racial discrimination that was not targeted at them personally (vicarious discrimination). It is important to note that after adjustment for age, gender, ethnicity, other adolescent stress, and offline discrimination, online individual racial discrimination was positively related to depressive symptoms and anxiety symptoms. Online vicarious discrimination was unrelated to mental health.

Measuring discrimination comprehensively will also require researchers to not only capture the multiple domains of discrimination but also ensure that adequate questions are asked in each domain. Some studies still use a single question to assess discrimination. In the assessment of multiple phenomena, survey methodologists find that multiple questions about components of a phenomenon will provide a more accurate level than a few global questions (Casswell, Huckle, & Pledger, 2002; Schaeffer & Presser, 2003). Multiple questions are more likely to clearly convey what is being asked and to yield a more thorough search of memory. For each class of discriminatory experiences, adequate attention should be given to ensuring that questions are asked about all of the various types of discriminatory experiences in all of the relevant contexts in which they might occur.

IMPROVING MEASUREMENT OF THE STRESSFUL DIMENSIONS OF DISCRIMINATION

Research on stress and health reveals that exposure to most stressful experiences do not lead to illness. The majority of people exposed to even the most severe stressors have transient symptoms in response to these challenges (Baum et al., 1993; Yehuda, Bryant, Marmar, & Zohar, 2005). Emotional reactions and symptoms in response to traumas and other severe stressors are commonplace, but most of them are resolved in the following weeks or months. For example, research has found that only 5% to 10% of those exposed to traumatic life experiences go on to develop posttraumatic stress disorder (PTSD; Bryant, 2003; Carter, 2007) and about 20% to 25% of people who experience major stressful life events developing major depression (Cohen, Janicki-Deverts, & Miller, 2007).

A key challenge in the measurement of interpersonal discrimination is to assess the role of discriminatory experiences that are likely to have long-term negative effects. Research on stress indicates that multiple characteristics of stressors are important predictors of the long-term negative effects of stress. Stressors or difficulties that make continuing demands or pose ongoing threats (e.g., domestic violence, severe chronic illness, ongoing poverty) tend to have adverse effects (Dohrenwend, 2006). Thus, the frequency and duration of stressor exposure are key determinants of the impact of stress, with chronic or repeated stressors or prolonged exposure being particularly pathogenic. Stressors that are ambiguous, negative, unpredictable, and uncontrollable also tend to have negative effects on health (Carter, 2007; Dougall, Craig, & Baum, 1999). The intensity of the stressor also matters, including how disturbing and upsetting it is (Dougall et al., 1999). Stressors that have major negative impact on one's environment and social functioning because they occur in central role areas of an individual's life, adversely affect multiple areas, trigger loss of resources, disrupt normal activities, and cause a lot of change or readjustment are likely to be very consequential (Carter, 2007; Dohrenwend, 2006). Limited evidence from the discrimination literature suggests that characteristics of the perpetrator may also predict the degree of adverse impact with the effects being more negative when the perpetrator belongs to the same racial group as the target (Mays, Cochran, & Barnes, 2007).

More systematic attention to identifying and assessing the markers of the stressfulness of discriminatory experiences is an important priority for future research. The ambiguity surrounding an experience of discrimination could be a determinant of the stressfulness of the encounter, and greater attention should be given to assessing attributional ambiguity (Carter, 2007). Bennett, Wolin, Robinson, Fowler, and Edwards (2005) found stronger, more negative effects from subtle or ambiguous racial encounters than from blatant ones. An indirect and crude indicator of severity is the assessment of the number, intensity, and duration of experiences (Carter, 2007). Obtaining subjective ratings from the respondent regarding the severity and negative impact of the stressful experience is a more direct strategy (Cohen et al., 2007). In the PTSD literature, for example, respondents are often asked after reporting a stressful event to indicate how much they had been affected by it and how upset they had been by it (Carter, 2007). Similarly, a study relating caregiver stress to mortality had respondents indicate "how much of a mental or emotional strain" each reported caregiving task had been (Schulz & Beach, 1999). Such approaches lead to stronger associations between life events and mental health in the general stress literature (Dohrenwend, 2006), but inadequate attention has been given to this issue in research on discrimination and health.

In the discrimination literature, a few have assessed the severity of exposure. Camara Jones's Reactions to Race module used in the Behavioral Risk

Factor Surveys includes questions that ask about emotional and physical symptoms as a result of exposure to discriminatory experiences (Centers for Disease Control and Prevention, 2013). The discrimination module in the national Midlife in the United States (MIDUS) study also included two items that captured the burden of discrimination over the life course (Kessler et al., 1999). After reporting their levels of everyday and major experiences of discrimination, respondents were asked to indicate how much discrimination had interfered with their lives and how much harder their lives had been because of discrimination. A recent study summed these items into a global measure of the perceived stressfulness of discrimination (Grollman, 2014) and found that persons who experienced multiple forms of discrimination reported greater stressfulness of discrimination. The Jackson Heart Study included three questions to capture the burden of lifetime discrimination (Sims et al., 2012). In addition to the two questions from the MIDUS study, a third assessed the extent to which experiences of discrimination over the respondent's lifetime had been very stressful, moderately stressful, or not stressful. This study found that these measures of stressfulness and burden were associated with a small elevated risk of hypertension. Another study of discrimination and hypertension found no association overall but a positive association among a subset of respondents who reported high levels of stress because of discrimination (Din-Dzietham, Nembhard, Collins, & Davis, 2004). One limitation of this strategy is that for studies of self-reported measures of physical or mental health, respondents' reports of stressfulness can lead to confounding between the measure of stress and the self-reported outcome (Dohrenwend, 2006).

An alternative strategy is to explicitly denote the inclusion or exclusion criteria for which stressful experiences should be included in a category (Dohrenwend, 2006). For example, in the Traumatic Life Events Questionnaire (Kubany et al., 2000), a typical question of having been in a motor vehicle accident is replaced by "Were you involved in a motor vehicle accident for which you received medical attention or that badly injured or killed someone?" This strategy could usefully be applied to questions about racial discrimination in which behaviorally descriptive language that avoided global and emotionally charged words could specify the experiences that should be included. This approach can improve assessment but may miss stressors that did not fall into the narrow criteria (Dohrenwend, 2006).

MEASURING VIGILANCE AND ANTICIPATORY STRESS

Understanding the full impact of the stress generated by discrimination will require attention to capturing vigilance related to the threat of discrimination. The negative physiological effects of stress can begin with the initial perception of threat, which often occurs before the actual exposure to the stressor. Research indicates that anticipatory coping and anxiety, heightened vigilance, and intrusive thoughts or images can often trigger negative effects of potential stressors on health (Baum et al., 1993; Carter, 2007; Dougall et al., 1999; Pearlin et al., 2005; Yehuda et al., 2005). Brosschot, Gerin, and Thayer's (2006) review indicated that repeated or chronic activation of the cognitive imagery of one or more psychosocial stressors can prolong the stress and exacerbate its negative effects on health. It is important to note that this anticipatory stress, reflected in chronic or sustained vigilance, can lead to dysregulation of both emotional and physiological functioning that can increase risks for multiple diseases.

Carter (2007) used the term *cultural paranoia* to refer to the high level of vigilance that many minority group members maintain. Growing evidence indicates that heightened vigilance related to the threat of discrimination has pathogenic effects on health. Two decades ago, Williams, Lavizzo-Mourey, and Warren (1994) suggested that the finding of elevated nocturnal blood pressure levels of African Americans during sleep could reflect a heightened vigilance and a failure to ever completely relax because of the constant threat of discrimination and other dangers linked to residence in hostile residential contexts. Recent studies document that exposure to discrimination directly contributes to the elevated levels of nocturnal blood pressure among Blacks (Brondolo et al., 2008; Tomfohr, Cooper, Mills, Nelesen, & Dimsdale, 2010). Similarly, Lindström (2008) found that a single-item indicator of anticipatory ethnic discrimination was associated with lower levels of psychological health in a national sample of adults in Sweden. A study of Latino college students found that the anticipation of being discriminated against led to greater concern and threat emotions before an encounter with the potential perpetrator and more stress and greater cardiovascular responses after the encounter (Sawyer, Major, Casad, Townsend, & Mendes, 2012).

In the 1995 Detroit Area Study (DAS), Williams and colleagues developed the Everyday Discrimination Scale and a six-item scale to capture heightened vigilance (Clark, Benkert, & Flack, 2006; Williams et al., 1997). *Heightened vigilance* refers to living in a state of psychological arousal to actively cope and attempt to protect oneself from threats linked to discrimination and other dangers in one's immediate environment (Williams et al., 1994). In the DAS, after respondents reported experiences of everyday discrimination, they were asked,

> In dealing with the experiences that you just told me about, how often do you (a) Think in advance about the kind of problems that you are likely to experience? (b) Try to prepare for possible insults before leaving home? (c) Feel that you always have to be careful about your appearance (to get good service or avoid being harassed)? (d) Carefully watch what

you say and how you say it? (e) Carefully observe what happens around you? and (f) Try to avoid certain social situations and places? (Clark et al., 2006, p. 568)

Recent studies with this scale or abbreviated versions of it highlight the importance of assessing the health consequences of race-related vigilance. In a study of African American youth (M age = 12 years old), Clark et al. (2006) showed that vigilance was inversely related to large arterial elasticity (a preclinical index of cardiovascular function) for boys but not for girls. A study of adults in Baltimore found that Blacks have higher levels of vigilance than Whites and that vigilance was positively associated with depressive symptoms and contributed to the Black–White disparity in depression (LaVeist, Thorpe, Pierre, Mance, & Williams, 2014). Similarly, a study of 3,105 adults in Chicago found vigilance predicts elevated risk of sleep difficulties, independent of income and education, and racial differences in sleep difficulty were completely attenuated when adjusted for vigilance (Hicken, Lee, Morenoff, House, & Williams, 2014). Another analysis with this same sample found that vigilance was associated with increased odds of hypertension for Blacks and Hispanics but not Whites (Hicken et al., 2014). At low levels of vigilance, racial disparities in hypertension are small, but as vigilance increased, the racial/ethnic gap in hypertension widened for Blacks and Hispanics. Moreover, vigilance remained predictive of hypertension when adjusted for hypertension risk factors and discrimination.

MINIMIZING BIAS IN THE ASSESSMENT OF DISCRIMINATION

Problems of unreliability of recall, recall bias, criterion validity, and construct validity have all been documented for life event measures of stress (Dohrenwend, 2006) and are applicable to measures of discrimination. It is important to capture exposure to discrimination over the life course (Gee, Walsemann, & Brondolo, 2012), and many scales of discrimination assess lifetime occurrence of discriminatory events. However, problems linked to recall are more severe when the recall period of stressors is longer and when the data is gathered from retrospective reports. The stress literature documents that multiple factors affect recall processes in complex ways. For example, a study of motor vehicle accident victims who provided symptoms 1 month after the incident and were asked to recall those symptoms 2 years later found that the severity of the stress and injury and the trajectory of recovery can lead to overreporting or underreporting of symptoms (Harvey & Bryant, 2002). Although most individuals correctly recalled the majority of the symptom clusters, persons with few symptoms 2 years later tended to omit symptoms that they had reported in the acute phase of the disease, and persons with high levels of symptoms at the 2-year interview were more likely to recall the presence of acute symptoms that they had not reported in the initial assessment. Experience sampling is one approach to reduce some of the biases that might exist in reporting discrimination due to impaired memory (Kaiser & Major, 2006). The experience sampling method is a daily diary approach that asks participants to stop at certain times and make notes of their experience in real time; the point is for them to record temporal things like feelings while in the moment.

Self-reports of discrimination depend, in part, on the motivation and the willingness of research participants to report discrimination. An individual's willingness and motivation can lead to two types of perception bias (Kaiser & Major, 2006). First, some individuals may perceive more discrimination than actually exists (a *vigilance bias*) or, second, some may perceive less discrimination than actually exists (a *minimization bias*).

Bias Linked to Minimization

Researchers have documented that some people who have objectively experienced discrimination minimize it by failure to pay attention to it, underestimating it, or even denying being a target (Kaiser & Major, 2006). Acknowledging being a victim of discrimination may be psychologically costly for some, and discrimination is often not readily visible and perpetrators often denying that it had occurred. Thus, disadvantaged social groups that have been the targets of discrimination often fail to recognize and report it (Kaiser & Major, 2006). Some evidence suggests that coping with stress by denying its occurrence is evident for several stressors (Vos & de Haes, 2007). Related constructs include avoidance, distancing, suppression, and repressive coping. Denial can reflect conscious or unconscious efforts to minimize the pain of negative experiences. It has been argued that the emotional pain of racism can render some individuals unable to recall specific events (Carter, 2007). Some have also suggested that denial should be viewed not as a one-time event but as a process or continuum from facts to ambiguous events (Vos & de Haes, 2007). Thus, denial can range from being a passive escape strategy linked to poorer psychological function to being a part of a series of active distractive strategies that are adaptive and lead to lower levels of psychological distress. Getting a clearer sense of the levels and consequences of denial in research on discrimination should be a priority for future research. Denial should be understood within the context of a broad range of strategies used for responding to discrimination (Brondolo, Brady Ver Halen, Pencille, Beatty, & Contrada, 2009; Noh & Kaspar, 2003).

An important recent development is the emergence of efforts to assess discrimination using measurement tools that do not rely on self-report. A novel application of the Implicit Association Test (IAT) is its use to capture the extent to which individuals see themselves and their racial/ethnic group as a perpetrator versus a target of discrimination (Krieger et al., 2011). This measure seeks to minimize the limitations of self-reported data by capturing experiences of racial bias that respondents are unwilling or unable to report. So far, implicit measures of discrimination show weak or modest associations with health outcomes (Krieger et al., 2010, 2011). Nevertheless, the IAT offers a glimpse of the health effects of racial bias that might otherwise be hidden. At the same time, this work is still in its infancy, and it is not currently clear exactly what it is about discrimination these measures capture (Williams & Mohammed, 2013). Researchers do not know whether unconscious processes related to race captured by these novel measures reflect actual prior exposure to racial discrimination, heightened vigilance regarding discrimination, the threat or fear of discrimination, the burden of past experiences of racial bias, or the severity of prior exposure. These concerns are reinforced by the very low correlations (.10 or smaller) between the implicit measures attempting to capture racial discrimination and validated explicit measures of discrimination (Krieger et al., 2011). In contrast, in the study of racial prejudice, correlations between explicit measures of prejudice and implicit ones are about .25 (Hofmann, Gawronski, Gschwendner, Le, & Schmitt, 2005; Nosek et al., 2007). Thus, the very low correlations for the measures of discrimination raise the possibility that the two types of measures may not be capturing different phenomena related to race. Another question regarding implicit measures attempting to capture racial discrimination is whether they assess psychological stress appraisal processes due to the perception of an environmental stressor that explicit measures of psychosocial stressors (including discrimination) are presumed to capture (Williams & Mohammed, 2013). Research is needed to provide a clearer picture of what the discrimination IAT measure is capturing and how it can enhance understanding of the role of discrimination in health.

Bias Linked to Vigilance

The prior history of an individual and/or his/her group experiences with discrimination can lead to attributing ambiguous experiences to discrimination. Such vigilance can protect the individual from physical harm and can foster feelings of self-worth when faced with negative evaluations since the individual can attribute these experiences to external reasons instead of personal failure. We do not have a clear picture of all of the social contextual triggers of perceptions of bias. For example, some limited evidence indicates that vigilance for discrimination increases with the threat of discrimination

(Kaiser & Major, 2006). Other data suggest that larger cultural worldviews affect the likelihood of reporting experiences of discrimination with persons who belong to low-status social groups but who endorse a meritocratic worldview being less likely to report that they had personally been a victim of discrimination (Kaiser & Major, 2006). That is, they are more likely to blame negative outcomes on themselves than on discrimination. At the same time, members of high-status groups who endorse individual mobility beliefs (the view that advancement is possible for all people in America) are more likely to report that they had personally been a victim of discrimination, resulting in a positive association between individual mobility beliefs and reporting reverse discrimination among Whites.

Reports of discrimination are also positively associated with SES and with a greater sense of racial consciousness, and researchers need to better understand these complex patterns (Smith, 2002). Nondominant group members with higher education are more likely to interact with dominant racial group members as equals and more likely to be aware of their legal rights with regards to discrimination. Those with stronger racial identity are more likely to have greater sensitivity to the persistence of discrimination. Alternatively, reports of discrimination by these groups could reflect overreporting, with these individuals perceiving discrimination that did not exist or twisting the perception of their experiences to be consistent with their worldview or ideology. It is important to note that even if the reports of the more educated and racially conscious are viewed as accurate—it could mean that the true level of discrimination is being underreported by the less educated and less racially conscious (Smith, 2002). Accordingly, it highlights an important measurement challenge that needs to be addressed.

More systematic evaluation is needed of the extent to which answers about questions regarding discrimination could be subject to systematic biases linked to culture, nationality, age, and other social and psychological factors. A review of this literature indicates that the current evidence is unclear with regard to whether vigilance or minimization biases might predominate (Kaiser & Major, 2006). Some experimental data have compared perceptions of discrimination among subordinate groups versus dominant groups in response to the same event and found that women (compared with men) and Blacks (compared with Whites) were more likely to interpret critical feedback as discriminatory. However, the review also indicates that other experimental evidence found no differences in the perceptions of rejections as bias among nondominant versus dominant group members.

The use of anchoring vignettes is a potentially useful approach that could be used across a broad range of contexts to identify and address subgroup differences in the understanding and interpretation of questions about racial discrimination (Hopkins & King, 2010). Anchor vignettes are a strategy used to enhance the validity of questionnaire measures across social groups and contexts. In this approach, researchers use anchor vignettes (identical hypothetical scenarios) to gauge respondents' perceptions and evaluation of the behavior in the vignettes. This enables for the identification of group differences in evaluation and the use of these differences in the evaluations of the anchor to convert the answers of one group to make them comparable to the answers of another group. Dowd and Todd (2011) showed, for example, using anchoring vignettes to showcase reporting differences for self-reported health status by race, ethnicity, and SES. For example, compared with Whites, Blacks and Hispanics are more optimistic in their ratings of multiple domains of health, possibly because they may be using their less healthy counterparts as the relevant reference group. It is important to note that these reporting differences lead to an underestimation of racial/ethnic disparities in health. Strikingly, in domains such as pain, shortness of breath, and depression, racial/ethnic inequalities that were not evident in ordered probit models emerged after accounting for reporting differences (Dowd & Todd, 2011).

Biases Linked to the Data Collection Context

Research is needed to assess the effects of the mode (personal interview, phone, internet, mail questionnaire) used in the assessment of discrimination. Some research suggests that a survey's mode can have an important impact on both responses to the questions and which population subgroups are represented in the study. For example, Dolan and Kavetsos (2012) compared interview-administered with telephone-administered responses to health questions in the Annual Population Survey (UK) and found large differences by survey mode. Another UK study found that persons in a telephone interview were less likely (3–7 percentage points) to rate several dimensions of identity (national, religion, racial, ethnic background; political beliefs; sexual orientation) as important compared with persons in a face-to-face interview (Nandi & Platt, 2011). An Australian study found markedly higher levels of financial stress in a self-completed interview than in a computer-assisted face-to-face interview (Breunig & McKibbin, 2011). Future research should assess the extent to which survey mode affects the levels and effects of reported discrimination.

The very topic of racial discrimination may be sufficiently sensitive that researchers may need to take steps to minimize bias. Research on race-of-interviewer effects has found that Blacks are often reticent to reveal their true racial beliefs on race sensitive questions when talking to White interviewers. It is important to note that one carefully executed study found that the strongest effect of Blacks being deferent to a White interviewer was for reporting experiences of racial discrimination (Krysan & Couper, 2003). The effects for racial discrimination were larger than for attitudes on four other categories of race-related questions regarding racial and race-associated policies, Black politics and the pace of civil rights. On the other hand, opposite to what would be expected based on the race of interviewer effects literature, Suh (2000) found that reports of racial discrimination among Black women were higher when the interviewer was a woman of another race. More generally, research on asking sensitive questions in survey research reveals that to the extent that respondents perceive questions regarding discrimination to be socially unacceptable or undesirable, they are likely to underreport those experiences (Tourangeau & Yan, 2007). Research has also shown that the mode of administration of sensitive questions influences responses—In particular, the presence of others in the interview context adversely affects accurately collecting complete data. Thus, eliminating the presence of an interviewer by using a self-administered instrument and using forgiving, or normalizing, wording for sensitive questions can be helpful in addressing this issue (Tourangeau & Yan, 2007).

Little attention has been given in the research on discrimination and health to biases that could be induced by question context or order. The extant research indicates that the order of questions and the context of questions that precede a specific battery of items can introduce random error or even bias in the assessment of psychosocial phenomenon, including questions about race and racial phenomenon (Schwarz, 1999; Wilson, 2010). Research also reveals that careful survey design that uses a buffer, or transition question can minimize context effects (Schwarz & Schuman, 1997) and that using these questions in the assessment of discrimination differs markedly. For example, in the in-person, interviewer-administered National Survey of American Life and the South African Stress and Health study, the major experiences of discrimination questions were introduced with, "In the following questions, we are interested in the way other people have treated you or your *beliefs* about how other people have treated you. Can you tell me if *any* of the following has ever happened to you?" (Williams et al., 2004, 2008). In contrast, using a self-administered paper-and-pencil questionnaire, the national MIDUS study introduces the same questions with,

> How many times in your life have you been discriminated against in each of the following ways because of such things as your race, ethnicity, gender, age, religion, physical appearance, sexual orientation, or other characteristics? (If the experience happened to you, but for some reason other than discrimination, enter "0"). (Kessler et al., 1999, p. 311)

Some evidence suggests that reports of discrimination are higher if respondents are asked if they "felt" discriminated than if they were asked if discrimination occurred (Smith, 2002). Future research should also identify the effects, if any, of the transition questions that precede discrimination question modules, and the most effective content and phrasing of these questions.

What Question Wording Should Be Used?

A major debate in the literature has to do with whether it is better to make race salient in the assessment of racial discrimination or to opt for the use of neutral terminology. Many questions that are used to assess discrimination use what has been termed the *one-stage approach*: They explicitly ask respondents to report on "racial discrimination" or experiences of discrimination "because of your race." A potential limitation of questions explicitly framed about race is the possibility of interviewer effects in which participants are motivated to please the interviewer by reporting the kind of information that s/he believes the interviewer is interested in (Smith, 2002). Repeated questions about discrimination "because of your race" could trigger higher reports of racial discrimination. An alternative, two-stage approach, closely associated with the work of Williams and his colleagues (Kessler et al., 1999; Williams et al., 1997) frames the questions about discrimination in terms of unfair treatment and asks about attribution only after a generic experience has been endorsed. This approach appears reasonable, given that the most frequently used term in the social science assessment of discrimination is "unfair" treatment (Smith, 2002). In addition, some qualitative research suggests that respondents interpret questions about unfair treatment in terms of discrimination (Williams et al., 2012). The two-stage approach seeks to address not only the problem about the sensitivity of questions about discrimination but also concerns about attributional ambiguity. Respondents are often uncertain of the reason (or attribution) for a specific interpersonal incident. Thus, building attribution into the question is likely to underestimate discriminatory encounters for which the attribution is uncertain (Williams, Neighbors, & Jackson, 2003). In contrast, asking questions about both racial and nonracial discrimination may capture more of the potential pathogenic phenomenon of perceived unfairness, and also reduce some of the measurement error that can occur if questions are asked only of racial discrimination.

On the other hand are concerns about the ability of such questions to capture racial discrimination accurately. Some evidence suggests that one-stage approach leads to higher reports of discrimination. One study compared Blacks' reports of discrimination using a single-item question assessing whether the respondent had "ever been treated unfairly or badly because of your race or ethnicity" to the responses to six items about unfair treatment (at work, by the police, in education and housing) that were followed by a question asking for the main reason for unfair treatment (Brown, 2001). He found that 67% reported racial discrimination with the one-stage question compared with 50% with the two-stage approach. Similarly, Chae et al. (2008) studied the relationship between discrimination and smoking in a sample of 2,073 Asian Americans in the National Latino and Asian American Study. They compared results for analyses of the nine-item Everyday Discrimination Scale (assessed with no attribution) to the results for a three-item scale that consisted of two items that measured how often respondents felt that they were disliked or treated unfairly because of their race or ethnicity and a third item capturing how often respondents had seen friends of their racial/ethnic background treated unfairly. The study found that 74% of Asians reported everyday discrimination, 62% reported racial/ethnic discrimination, and the correlation between the two measures was .43. The study found that both measures of discrimination predict smoking even after controlling for the other and the authors concluded "that racial/ethnic discrimination is distinct from the experience of unfair treatment." Some have concluded that higher reports of discrimination with the one-stage approach reflects more valid assessments of racial discrimination (Brown, 2001; Chae et al., 2008; Krieger, 2012). However, these studies comparing the one-stage versus two-stage approaches have not used experimental designs, and it is important to note, the items compared (as described above) differ in ways besides the explicit reference to race and ethnicity (Brown, 2001; Chae et al., 2008).

Experimental evidence tells a similar story. Gomez and Trierweiler (2001) found higher reports of both racial and gender discrimination among Black male and female students and White women, respectively, when asked explicitly about "racism and race discrimination" or "sexism and gender discrimination" than if first asked about their college experiences and subsequently asked a follow-up question that ascertained the reasons for mistreatment. This finding has been interpreted by some to mean that making race salient in the assessment of discrimination leads to response bias compared with the use of neutral terminology (Gomez & Trierweiler, 2001; Williams & Mohammed, 2009). In the California Health Interview Survey, 7,505 adults were randomly assigned to a one-stage or two-stage version of an eight-item modified version of the Everyday Discrimination scale (Shariff-Marco et al., 2011). The study found that 21% of respondents reported racial/ethnic discrimination with the two-stage approach compared with 49% with the one-stage approach (for Blacks, the levels were 53% vs. 83%).

Careful experimental designs are needed in future research in multiple contexts with multiple racial/ethnic groups in which these alternative approaches are directly compared (Smith, 2002). If reliable differences emerge from these tests, research would need to identify why the levels of reported discrimination differ and which approach yields more valid data. Panel surveys using bounded and aided recall techniques to assess the extent to which processes of forgetting and telescoping affect cross-sectional reports of discrimination are a critical priority in this area (Smith, 2002). Open-ended follow-up questions after reports of perceived unfair treatment provide evidence supportive of the validity of these self-reports capturing experiences that would reasonably be considered discrimination (Williams et al., 2012). At the same time, Bobo and Suh (2000) found that some initial reports of racial discrimination did not appear to be racially motivated in the details provide by follow-up open-ended question. Clearly, more in-depth cognitive interviewing that explores what respondents understand the terms *discrimination* and *unfair treatment* to mean would also be useful.

Adding open-ended follow-up questions to both the one-stage and two-stage approaches to the assessment of discrimination could provide rich qualitative detail about these experiences that could help to elucidate the extent to which different wording is eliciting reports of different phenomena. Smith (2002) also suggested using a factorial vignette approach in which vignettes describing individuals experiencing discrimination would vary the race and other sociodemographic characteristics of the targets of discrimination to examine the extent to which race and other social characteristics affect the evaluation of the respondents.

In addition, validation studies of racial discrimination are needed to identify which approach to the assessment of self-reported discrimination provides the greatest accuracy. Validation studies are challenging, but options include aggregate cross-validation studies of victims of discrimination and perpetrators of discrimination and using multiple methods in a single study, such as surveys, institutional records, and ethnographic research (Smith, 2002).

RACIAL DISCRIMINATION SHOULD BE STUDIED IN RELATIONSHIP TO OTHER STRESSORS

The impact of racial discrimination on health needs to be understood in the context of other forms of discrimination in society. An unresolved issue is the extent to which racial bias has effects that are distinctive from other forms of unfair treatment. Because of the centrality of race in society, the salience of racial identity can affect the appraisal processes of some individuals in ways that could lead race-attributed experiences to be more impactful because they are especially threatening to an individual's sense of rights and opportunities (Pearlin et al., 2005). Some studies have found that perceptions of racial and nonracial discrimination are similarly related to health (Williams & Mohammed, 2009). Neuroimaging research suggests that the perception of unfairness is associated with negative emotional responses and can activate regions of the brain involved with emotional regulation, suggesting that seeking justice and fairness may be a basic human impulse and its violation can trigger physiological consequences (Tabibnia, Satpute, & Lieberman, 2008). Some evidence suggests that irrespective of attribution, the perception of unfair treatment may generate negative psychological and physiological reactions. A study analyzing data from participants in the Whitehall Study in the United Kingdom found that a generic measure of perceived unfairness was inversely related to social class and was an independent predictor of incident coronary events (De Vogli, Ferrie, Chandola, Kivimäki, & Marmot, 2007). Lewis et al. (2006) also found that although perceived everyday discrimination attributed to race was unrelated to coronary calcification for Black women, a combined measure capturing perceived racial and nonracial discrimination was positively associated with coronary calcification. However, one study found that Black women who attributed chronic discrimination to race demonstrated greater blood pressure reactivity than those who attributed them to other social status categories (Guyll, Matthews, & Bromberger, 2001). Future research is needed to more systematically assess the extent to which the racial discrimination differs in its causes and consequences from other types of discrimination and the extent to which the approach to capturing attribution affects understanding of the levels and health consequences of racial discrimination. Research also should assess how multiple types of discrimination combine to affect health.

The experience of self-reported discrimination is an important and neglected psychosocial stressor. However, it does not capture all of the health-relevant aspects of racism, nor all of the psychosocial stressors necessary to estimate the contribution of racism-generated stressors to disparities in health. The inclusion of a scale of perceived discrimination in a study does not reflect the assessment of all of the relevant psychosocial stressors that respondents face. The stress of perceived discrimination should be measured and analyzed in the context of larger societal forces, including institutional racism, that initiate and sustain differential exposure to a broad range of stressors. Taking institutional discrimination seriously will require renewed focus on racial differences in traditional stressors: violence, criminal victimization, neighborhood conditions, financial stress, and relationship stress. Pearlin et al. (2005) emphasized that the stressors that are patterned by social disadvantage are the "serious stressors" that capture major hardships, conflicts, and disruptions in life, especially those that are chronic and recurring and that occur in major social domains. Financial stressors, especially those that are characterized by continuity and repetitiveness over the life course, are among the most powerful of stressful life experiences (Pearlin et al., 2005).

An example of the comprehensive assessment of stressors comes from the Chicago Community Adult Health Study. Based on prior research, this study measured stress in eight domains that reflect key arenas in which people operate (e.g., home, job, neighborhood) and major roles/statuses they assume. These included acute life events, work stressors, financial stress, life discrimination (everyday discrimination, major experiences of discrimination), work discrimination, relationship stress, childhood adversity, and neighborhood stress, with multiple indicators in each stress domain (Sternthal, Slopen, & Williams, 2011). This study found a graded association between the number of stressors and poor health, with each additional stressor associated with worse health. Moreover, for Blacks and U.S.-born Hispanics, stress exposure explained a substantial portion of the health gap, even after adjusting for SES. Additional analyses of this same sample found that discrimination made a unique contribution to accounting for racial differences in sleep even after adjustment for other stressors and income and education (Slopen & Williams, 2014).

Understanding how experiences of racial discrimination combine with other mechanisms of racism, such as the internalization of stereotypes (Carter, 2007), and with other sources of stigmatization, such as discrimination because of one's weight, is also important. Given the elevated rates of obesity in minority populations and the persisting stigma and discrimination of overweight individuals (Carr & Friedman, 2005), exploring the elevated risks at multiple intersections of stigmatization is important. A recent study found an interaction between racial discrimination and implicit anti-Black bias (internalized racism) in predicting shorter telomere length among Black men (Chae et al., 2014). This study found that racial discrimination was associated with shorter telomere length only among Blacks with implicit anti-Black bias.

CONCLUSION

The research on self-reported discrimination and health is continues to grow at a rapid pace. In this chapter, I outlined several limitations of the current approaches to the assessment of discrimination and described needed research in multiple areas. Already, impressive research documents the role of discrimination in physical and mental health. Greater attention to the appropriate conceptualization and measurement of racial discrimination can strengthen scientific understanding of the conditions under which exposure to discrimination can lead to adverse changes in health status and provide greater impetus for renewed attention to dismantling the structures that support discrimination in society.

REFERENCES

Barnes, L. L., de Leon, C. F. M., Lewis, T. T., Bienias, J. L., Wilson, R. S., & Evans, D. A. (2008). Perceived discrimination and mortality in a population-based study of older adults. *American Journal of Public Health, 98*, 1241–1247. http://dx.doi.org/10.2105/AJPH.2007.114397

Barnes, L. L., Lewis, T. T., Begeny, C. T., Yu, L., Bennett, D. A., & Wilson, R. S. (2012). Perceived discrimination and cognition in older African Americans. *Journal of the International Neuropsychological Society, 18*, 856–865. http://dx.doi.org/10.1017/S1355617712000628

Bastos, J. L., Celeste, R. K., Faerstein, E., & Barros, A. J. D. (2010). Racial discrimination and health: A systematic review of scales with a focus on their psychometric properties. *Social Science & Medicine, 70*, 1091–1099. http://dx.doi.org/10.1016/j.socscimed.2009.12.020

Baum, A., Cohen, L., & Hall, M. (1993). Control and intrusive memories as possible determinants of chronic stress. *Psychosomatic Medicine, 55*, 274–286. http://dx.doi.org/10.1097/00006842-199305000-00005

Bennett, G. G., Wolin, K. Y., Robinson, E. L., Fowler, S., & Edwards, C. L. (2005). Perceived racial/ethnic harassment and tobacco use among African American young adults. *American Journal of Public Health, 95*, 238–240. http://dx.doi.org/10.2105/AJPH.2004.037812

Bhattacharyya, M. R., & Steptoe, A. (2007). Emotional triggers of acute coronary syndromes: Strength of evidence, biological processes, and clinical implications. *Progress in Cardiovascular Diseases, 49*, 353–365. http://dx.doi.org/10.1016/j.pcad.2006.11.002

Bobo, L. D., & Suh, S. A. (2000). Surveying racial discrimination: Analyses from a multiethnic labor market. In L. D. Bobo, M. L. Oliver, J. H. Johnson, Jr., & A. Valenzuela (Eds.), *Prismatic metropolis: Inequality in Los Angeles* (pp. 527–564). New York, NY: Russell Sage Foundation.

Braveman, P. A., Cubbin, C., Egerter, S., Williams, D. R., & Pamuk, E. (2010). Socioeconomic disparities in health in the United States: What the patterns tell us. *American Journal of Public Health, 100*, 186–196. http://dx.doi.org/10.2105/AJPH.2009.166082

Breunig, R., & McKibbin, R. (2011). The effect of survey design on household reporting of financial difficulty. *Journal of the Royal Statistical Society, 174A*, 991–1005. http://dx.doi.org/10.1111/j.1467-985X.2011.00696.x

Brondolo, E., Brady, N., Thompson, S., Tobin, J. N., Cassells, A., Sweeney, M., . . . Contrada, R. J. (2008). Perceived racism and negative affect: Analyses of trait and state measures of affect in a community sample. *Journal of Social and Clinical Psychology, 27*, 150–173. http://dx.doi.org/10.1521/jscp.2008.27.2.150

Brondolo, E., Brady Ver Halen, N., Pencille, M., Beatty, D., & Contrada, R. J. (2009). Coping with racism: A selective review of the literature and a theoretical and methodological critique. *Journal of Behavioral Medicine, 32*, 64–88. http://dx.doi.org/10.1007/s10865-008-9193-0

Brosschot, J. F., Gerin, W., & Thayer, J. F. (2006). The perseverative cognition hypothesis: A review of worry, prolonged stress-related physiological activation, and health. *Journal of Psychosomatic Research, 60,* 113–124. http://dx.doi.org/10.1016/j.jpsychores.2005.06.074

Brown, T. N. (2001). Measuring self-perceived racial and ethnic discrimination in social surveys. *Sociological Spectrum, 21,* 377–392. http://dx.doi.org/10.1080/027321701300202046

Bryant, R. A. (2003). Early predictors of posttraumatic stress disorder. *Society of Biological Psychiatry, 53,* 789–795. http://dx.doi.org/10.1016/S0006-3223(02)01895-4

Carr, D., & Friedman, M. A. (2005). Is obesity stigmatizing? Body weight, perceived discrimination, and psychological well-being in the United States. *Journal of Health and Social Behavior, 46,* 244–259. http://dx.doi.org/10.1177/002214650504600303

Carter, R. T. (2007). Racism and psychological and emotional injury: Recognizing and assessing race-based traumatic stress. *The Counseling Psychiatrist, 35.*

Casswell, S., Huckle, T., & Pledger, M. (2002). Survey data need not underestimate alcohol consumption. *Alcoholism, Clinical and Experimental Research, 26,* 1561–1567. http://dx.doi.org/10.1111/j.1530-0277.2002.tb02456.x

Centers for Disease Control and Prevention. (2013). *Behavioral risk factor surveillance system survey questionnaire.* Retrieved from http://www.cdc.gov/brfss/questionnaires/pdf-ques/2013%20brfss_english.pdf

Chae, D. H., Nuru-Jeter, A. M., Adler, N. E., Brody, G. H., Lin, J., Blackburn, E. H., & Epel, E. S. (2014). Discrimination, racial bias, and telomere length in African-American men. *American Journal of Preventive Medicine, 46,* 103–111. http://dx.doi.org/10.1016/j.amepre.2013.10.020

Chae, D. H., Takeuchi, D. T., Barbeau, E. M., Bennett, G. G., Lindsey, J., & Krieger, N. (2008). Unfair treatment, racial/ethnic discrimination, ethnic identification, and smoking among Asian Americans in the National Latino and Asian American Study. *American Journal of Public Health, 98,* 485–492. http://dx.doi.org/10.2105/AJPH.2006.102012

Clark, R., Anderson, N. B., Clark, V. R., & Williams, D. R. (1999). Racism as a stressor for African Americans. A biopsychosocial model. *American Psychologist, 54,* 805–816. http://dx.doi.org/10.1037/0003-066X.54.10.805

Clark, R., Benkert, R. A., & Flack, J. M. (2006). Large arterial elasticity varies as a function of gender and racism-related vigilance in Black youth. *The Journal of Adolescent Health, 39,* 562–569. http://dx.doi.org/10.1016/j.jadohealth.2006.02.012

Cohen, S., Janicki-Deverts, D., & Miller, G. E. (2007). Psychological stress and disease. *JAMA, 298,* 1685–1687. http://dx.doi.org/10.1001/jama.298.14.1685

Cohen, S., Kessler, R. C., & Gordon, L. U. (1995). *Measuring stress: A guide for health and social scientists.* New York, NY: Oxford University Press.

De Vogli, R., Ferrie, J. E., Chandola, T., Kivimäki, M., & Marmot, M. G. (2007). Unfairness and health: Evidence from the Whitehall II Study. *Journal of Epidemiology and Community Health, 61,* 513–518. http://dx.doi.org/10.1136/jech.2006.052563

Din-Dzietham, R., Nembhard, W. N., Collins, R., & Davis, S. K. (2004). Perceived stress following race-based discrimination at work is associated with hypertension in African-Americans. The metro Atlanta heart disease study, 1999–2001. *Social Science & Medicine, 58,* 449–461. http://dx.doi.org/10.1016/S0277-9536(03)00211-9

Dohrenwend, B. P. (2006). Inventorying stressful life events as risk factors for psychopathology: Toward resolution of the problem of intracategory variability. *Psychological Bulletin, 132,* 477–495. http://dx.doi.org/10.1037/0033-2909.132.3.477

Dolan, P., & Kavetsos, G. (2012). *Happy talk: Mode of administration effects on subjective well-being* (CEP Working Paper No. 1159). London, England: London School of Economics and Political Science.

Dougall, A. L., Craig, K. J., & Baum, A. (1999). Assessment of characteristics of intrusive thoughts and their impact on distress among victims of traumatic events. *Psychosomatic Medicine, 61,* 38–48. http://dx.doi.org/10.1097/00006842-199901000-00008

Dowd, J. B., & Todd, M. (2011). Does self-reported health bias the measurement of health inequalities in U.S. adults? Evidence using anchoring vignettes from the Health and Retirement Study. *The Journals of Gerontology. Series B. Psychological Sciences and Social Sciences, 66,* 478–489. http://dx.doi.org/10.1093/geronb/gbr050

Earnshaw, V. A., Rosenthal, L., Lewis, J. B., Stasko, E. C., Tobin, J. N., Lewis, T. T., . . . Ickovics, J. R. (2013). Maternal experiences with everyday discrimination and infant birth weight: A test of mediators and moderators among young, urban women of color. *Annals of Behavioral Medicine, 45,* 13–23. http://dx.doi.org/10.1007/s12160-012-9404-3

Gee, G. C., Walsemann, K. M., & Brondolo, E. (2012). A life course perspective on how racism may be related to health inequities. *American Journal of Public Health, 102,* 967–974. http://dx.doi.org/10.2105/AJPH.2012.300666

Gomez, J. P., & Trierweiler, S. (2001). Does discrimination terminology create response bias in questionnaire studies of discrimination? *Personality and Social Psychology Bulletin, 27,* 630–638. http://dx.doi.org/10.1177/0146167201275011

Grollman, E. A. (2014). Multiple disadvantaged statuses and health: The role of multiple forms of discrimination. *Journal of Health and Social Behavior, 55,* 3–19. http://dx.doi.org/10.1177/0022146514521215

Guyll, M., Matthews, K. A., & Bromberger, J. T. (2001). Discrimination and unfair treatment: Relationship to cardiovascular reactivity among African American and European American women. *Health Psychology, 20,* 315–325. http://dx.doi.org/10.1037/0278-6133.20.5.315

Harrell, S. P. (1997). *The Racism and Life Experience Scales (RaLES): Self-administration version*. Los Angeles: California School of Professional Psychology.

Harvey, A. G., & Bryant, R. A. (2002). Acute stress disorder: A synthesis and critique. *Psychological Bulletin, 128*, 886–902.

Hicken, M. T., Lee, H., Morenoff, J., House, J. S., & Williams, D. R. (2014). Racial/ethnic disparities in hypertension prevalence: Reconsidering the role of chronic stress. *American Journal of Public Health, 104*, 117–123. http://dx.doi.org/10.2105/AJPH.2013.301395

Hofmann, W., Gawronski, B., Gschwendner, T., Le, H., & Schmitt, M. (2005). A meta-analysis on the correlation between the implicit association test and explicit self-report measures. *Personality and Social Psychology Bulletin, 31*, 1369–1385. http://dx.doi.org/10.1177/0146167205275613

Hopkins, D. J., & King, G. (2010). Improving anchoring vignettes: Designing surveys to correct interpersonal incomparability. *Public Opinion Quarterly, 74*, 201–222. http://dx.doi.org/10.1093/poq/nfq011

Kaiser, C. R., & Major, B. (2006). A social psychological perspective on perceiving and reporting discrimination. *Law & Social Inquiry, 31*, 801–830. http://dx.doi.org/10.1111/j.1747-4469.2006.00036.x

Kessler, R. C., Mickelson, K. D., & Williams, D. R. (1999). The prevalence, distribution, and mental health correlates of perceived discrimination in the United States. *Journal of Health and Social Behavior, 40*, 208–230. http://dx.doi.org/10.2307/2676349

Krieger, N. (1990). Racial and gender discrimination: Risk factors for high blood pressure? *Social Science & Medicine, 30*, 1273–1281. http://dx.doi.org/10.1016/0277-9536(90)90307-E

Krieger, N. (2012). Methods for the scientific study of discrimination and health: An ecosocial approach. *American Journal of Public Health, 102*, 936–944. http://dx.doi.org/10.2105/AJPH.2011.300544

Krieger, N., Carney, D., Lancaster, K., Waterman, P. D., Kosheleva, A., & Banaji, M. (2010). Combining explicit and implicit measures of racial discrimination in health research. *American Journal of Public Health, 100*, 1485–1492. http://dx.doi.org/10.2105/AJPH.2009.159517

Krieger, N., Smith, K., Naishadham, D., Hartman, C., & Barbeau, E. M. (2005). Experiences of discrimination: Validity and reliability of a self-report measure for population health research on racism and health. *Social Science & Medicine, 61*, 1576–1596. http://dx.doi.org/10.1016/j.socscimed.2005.03.006

Krieger, N., Waterman, P. D., Kosheleva, A., Chen, J. T., Carney, D. R., Smith, K. W., . . . Samuel, L. (2011). Exposing racial discrimination: Implicit & explicit measures—the My Body, My Story study of 1005 U.S.-born Black and White community health center members. *PLoS ONE, 6*, e27636. http://dx.doi.org/10.1371/journal.pone.0027636

Krysan, M., & Couper, M. P. (2003). Race in the live and virtual interview: Racial deference, social desirability, and activation effects in attitude surveys. *Social Psychology Quarterly, 66,* 364–383. http://dx.doi.org/10.2307/1519835

Kubany, E. S., Haynes, S. N., Leisen, M. B., Kaplan, A. S., Watson, S. B., Burns, K., & Owens, J. A. (2000). Development and preliminary validation of a brief broad-spectrum measure of trauma exposure: The Traumatic Life Events Questionnaire. *Psychological Assessment, 12,* 210–224. http://dx.doi.org/10.1037/1040-3590.12.2.210

Landrine, H., & Klonoff, E. A. (1996). The schedule of racist events: A measure of racial discrimination and a study of its negative physical and mental health consequences. *The Journal of Black Psychology, 22,* 144–168. http://dx.doi.org/10.1177/00957984960222002

Lauderdale, D. S. (2006). Birth outcomes for Arabic-named women in California before and after September 11. *Demography, 43,* 185–201. http://dx.doi.org/10.1353/dem.2006.0008

LaVeist, T. A., Thorpe, R. J., Jr., Pierre, G., Mance, G. A., & Williams, D. R. (2014). The relationships among vigilant coping style, race, and depression. *Journal of Social Issues, 70,* 241–255. http://dx.doi.org/10.1111/josi.12058

Lewis, T. T., Aiello, A. E., Leurgans, S., Kelly, J., & Barnes, L. L. (2010). Self-reported experiences of everyday discrimination are associated with elevated C-reactive protein levels in older African-American adults. *Brain, Behavior, and Immunity, 24,* 438–443. http://dx.doi.org/10.1016/j.bbi.2009.11.011

Lewis, T. T., Barnes, L. L., Bienias, J. L., Lackland, D. T., Evans, D. A., & Mendes de Leon, C. F. (2009). Perceived discrimination and blood pressure in older African American and White adults. *The Journals of Gerontology: Series A. Biological Sciences and Medical Sciences, 64A,* 1002–1008. http://dx.doi.org/10.1093/gerona/glp062

Lewis, T. T., Everson-Rose, S. A., Powell, L. H., Matthews, K. A., Brown, C., Karavolos, K., . . . Wesley, D. (2006). Chronic exposure to everyday discrimination and coronary artery calcification in African-American women: The SWAN Heart Study. *Psychosomatic Medicine, 68,* 362–368. http://dx.doi.org/10.1097/01.psy.0000221360.94700.16

Lewis, T. T., Kravitz, H. M., Janssen, I., & Powell, L. H. (2011). Self-reported experiences of discrimination and visceral fat in middle-aged African-American and Caucasian women. *American Journal of Epidemiology, 173,* 1223–1231. http://dx.doi.org/10.1093/aje/kwq466

Lewis, T. T., Troxel, W. M., Kravitz, H. M., Bromberger, J. T., Matthews, K. A., & Hall, M. H. (2013). Chronic exposure to everyday discrimination and sleep in a multiethnic sample of middle-aged women. *Health Psychology, 32,* 810–819. http://dx.doi.org/10.1186/1471-2458-13-1084

Lindström, M. (2008). Social capital, anticipated ethnic discrimination and self-reported psychological health: A population-based study. *Social Science & Medicine, 66,* 1–13. http://dx.doi.org/10.1016/j.socscimed.2007.07.023

Mays, V. M., Cochran, S. D., & Barnes, N. W. (2007). Race, race-based discrimination, and health outcomes among African Americans. *Annual Review of Psychology, 58*, 201–225. http://dx.doi.org/10.1146/annurev.psych.57.102904.190212

McNeilly, M. D., Anderson, N. B., Armstead, C. A., Clark, R., Corbett, M., Robinson, E. L., . . . Lepisto, E. M. (1996). The Perceived Racism Scale: A multidimensional assessment of the experience of White racism among African Americans. *Ethnicity and Disease, 6*, 154–166.

Nandi, A., & Platt, L. (2011, March). *Effect of interview modes on measurement of identity* (Working Paper No. 2011-02). Retrieved from https://www.understandingsociety.ac.uk/research/publications/working-paper/understanding-society/2011-02.pdf

Noh, S., & Kaspar, V. (2003). Perceived discrimination and depression: Moderating effects of coping, acculturation, and ethnic support. *American Journal of Public Health, 93*, 232–238. http://dx.doi.org/10.2105/AJPH.93.2.232

Nosek, B. A., Smyth, F. L., Hansen, J. J., Devos, T., Lindner, N. M., Ranganath, K. A., . . . Banaji, M. R. (2007). Pervasiveness and correlates of implicit attitudes and stereotypes. *European Review of Social Psychology, 18*, 36–88. http://dx.doi.org/10.1080/10463280701489053

Pascoe, E. A., & Smart Richman, L. (2009). Perceived discrimination and health: A meta-analytic review. *Psychological Bulletin, 135*, 531–554. http://dx.doi.org/10.1037/a0016059

Pearlin, L. I., Schieman, S., Fazio, E. M., & Meersman, S. C. (2005). Stress, health, and the life course: Some conceptual perspectives. *Journal of Health and Social Behavior, 46*, 205–219. http://dx.doi.org/10.1177/002214650504600206

Sawyer, P. J., Major, B., Casad, B. J., Townsend, S. S., & Mendes, W. B. (2012). Discrimination and the stress response: Psychological and physiological consequences of anticipating prejudice in interethnic interactions. *American Journal of Public Health, 102*, 1020–1026. http://dx.doi.org/10.2105/AJPH.2011.300620

Schaeffer, N. C., & Presser, S. (2003). The science of asking questions. *Annual Review of Sociology, 29*, 65–88. http://dx.doi.org/10.1146/annurev.soc.29.110702.110112

Schulz, R., & Beach, S. R. (1999). Caregiving as a risk factor for mortality: The Caregiver Health Effects Study. *JAMA, 282*, 2215–2219. http://dx.doi.org/10.1001/jama.282.23.2215

Schwarz, N. (1999). Self-reports: How the questions shape the answers. *American Psychologist, 54*, 93–105. http://dx.doi.org/10.1037/0003-066X.54.2.93

Schwarz, N., & Schuman, H. (1997). Political knowledge, attribution and inferred interest in politics: The operation of buffer items. *International Journal of Public Opinion Research, 9*, 191–195. http://dx.doi.org/10.1093/ijpor/9.2.191

Shariff-Marco, S., Breen, N., Landrine, H., Reeve, B. B., Krieger, N., Gee, G. C., . . . Johnson, T. P. (2011). Measuring everyday racial/ethnic discrimination in health surveys. *Du Bois Review, 8*, 159–177. http://dx.doi.org/10.1017/S1742058X11000129

Sims, M., Diez-Roux, A. V., Dudley, A., Gebreab, S., Wyatt, S. B., Bruce, M. A., . . . Taylor, H. A. (2012). Perceived discrimination and hypertension among African Americans in the Jackson Heart Study. *American Journal of Public Health, 102*, 258–265. http://dx.doi.org/10.2105/AJPH.2011.300523

Slopen, N., & Williams, D. R. (2014). Discrimination, other psychosocial stressors, and self-reported sleep duration and difficulties. *Sleep, 37*, 147–156.

Smart Richman, L., & Jonassaint, C. (2008). The effects of race-related stress on cortisol reactivity in the laboratory: Implications of the Duke lacrosse scandal. *Annals of Behavioral Medicine, 35*, 105–110. http://dx.doi.org/10.1007/s12160-007-9013-8

Smith, T. W. (2002). *Measuring racial and ethnic discrimination* (General Social Survey Methodological Report No. 96). Chicago, IL: National Opinion Research Center, University of Chicago. Retrieved from http://gss.norc.org/Documents/reports/methodological-reports/MR096.pdf

Stam, R. (2007). PTSD and stress sensitisation: A tale of brain and body. Part 1: Human studies. *Neuroscience and Biobehavioral Reviews, 31*, 530–557. http://dx.doi.org/10.1016/j.neubiorev.2006.11.010

Sternthal, M. J., Slopen, N., & Williams, D. R. (2011). Racial disparities in health: How much does stress really matter? *Du Bois Review, 8*, 95–113. http://dx.doi.org/10.1017/S1742058X11000087

Suh, S. A. (2000). Women's perceptions of workplace discrimination: Impacts of racial group, gender, and class. In L. D. Bobo, M. L. Oliver, J. H. Johnson, Jr., & A. Valenzuela (Eds.), *Prismatic metropolis: Inequality in Los Angeles* (pp. 561–596). New York, NY: Russell Sage Foundation.

Tabibnia, G., Satpute, A. B., & Lieberman, M. D. (2008). The sunny side of fairness: Preference for fairness activates reward circuitry (and disregarding unfairness activates self-control circuitry). *Psychological Science, 19*, 339–347. http://dx.doi.org/10.1111/j.1467-9280.2008.02091.x

Thoits, P. A. (2010). Stress and health: Major findings and policy implications. *Journal of Health and Social Behavior, 51*, 41–53. http://dx.doi.org/10.1177/0022146510383499

Tomfohr, L., Cooper, D. C., Mills, P. J., Nelesen, R. A., & Dimsdale, J. E. (2010). Everyday discrimination and nocturnal blood pressure dipping in Black and White Americans. *Psychosomatic Medicine, 72*, 266–272. http://dx.doi.org/10.1097/PSY.0b013e3181d0d8b2

Tourangeau, R., & Yan, T. (2007). Sensitive questions in surveys. *Psychological Bulletin, 133*, 859–883. http://dx.doi.org/10.1037/0033-2909.133.5.859

Tynes, B. M., Giang, M. T., Williams, D. R., & Thompson, G. N. (2008). Online racial discrimination and psychological adjustment among adolescents. *Journal of Adolescent Health, 43,* 565–569. http://dx.doi.org/10.1016/j.jadohealth.2008.08.021

Utsey, S. O., & Ponterotto, J. G. (1996). Development and validation of the index of race-related stress (IRRS). *Journal of Counseling Psychology, 43,* 490–501. http://dx.doi.org/10.1037/0022-0167.43.4.490

Vos, M. S., & de Haes, J. C. J. M. (2007). Denial in cancer patients, an explorative review. *Psycho-Oncology, 16,* 12–25. http://dx.doi.org/10.1002/pon.1051

Walters, K. L., Mohammed, S. A., Evans-Campbell, T., Beltrán, R. E., Chae, D. H., & Duran, B. (2011). Bodies don't just tell stories, they tell histories: Embodiment of historical trauma among American Indians and Alaska Natives. *Du Bois Review: Social Science Research on Race, 8,* 179–189. http://dx.doi.org/10.1017/S1742058X1100018X

Whitbeck, L. B., Adams, G. W., Hoyt, D. R., & Chen, X. (2004). Conceptualizing and measuring historical trauma among American Indian people. *American Journal of Community Psychology, 33,* 119–130. http://dx.doi.org/10.1023/B:AJCP.0000027000.77357.31

Williams, D. R. (2012). Miles to go before we sleep: Racial inequities in health. *Journal of Health and Social Behavior, 53,* 279–295. http://dx.doi.org/10.1177/0022146512455804

Williams, D. R., Gonzalez, H. M., Williams, S., Mohammed, S. A., Moomal, H., & Stein, D. J. (2008). Perceived discrimination, race and health in South Africa: Findings from the South Africa Stress and Health Study. *Social Science & Medicine, 67,* 441–452. http://dx.doi.org/10.1016/j.socscimed.2008.03.021

Williams, D. R., Herman, A., Kessler, R. C., Sonnega, J., Seedat, S., Stein, D. J., Moomal, H., Wilson, C. M. (2004). *The South Africa Stress and Health Study: Questionnaire.* Unpublished manuscript, Department of Social and Behavioral Sciences, Harvard T. H. Chan School of Public Health, Boston, MA.

Williams, D. R., John, D. A., Oyserman, D., Sonnega, J., Mohammed, S. A., & Jackson, J. S. (2012). Research on discrimination and health: An exploratory study of unresolved conceptual and measurement issues. *American Journal of Public Health, 102,* 975–978. http://dx.doi.org/10.2105/AJPH.2012.300702

Williams, D. R., Lavizzo-Mourey, R., & Warren, R. C. (1994). The concept of race and health status in America. *Public Health Reports, 109,* 26–41.

Williams, D. R., & Mohammed, S. A. (2009). Discrimination and racial disparities in health: Evidence and needed research. *Journal of Behavioral Medicine, 32,* 20–47. http://dx.doi.org/10.1007/s10865-008-9185-0

Williams, D. R., & Mohammed, S. A. (2013). Racism and health: I. Pathways and scientific evidence. *American Behavioral Scientist, 57,* 1152–1173. http://dx.doi.org/10.1177/0002764213487340

Williams, D. R., Neighbors, H. W., & Jackson, J. S. (2003). Racial/ethnic discrimination and health: Findings from community studies. *American Journal of Public Health, 93*, 200–208. http://dx.doi.org/10.2105/AJPH.93.2.200

Williams, D. R., Yu, Y., Jackson, J. S., & Anderson, N. B. (1997). Racial differences in physical and mental health: Socioeconomic status, stress, and discrimination. *Journal of Health Psychology, 2*, 335–351. http://dx.doi.org/10.1177/135910539700200305

Wilson, D. C. (2010). Perceptions about the amount of interracial prejudice depend on racial group membership and question order. *Public Opinion Quarterly, 74*, 344–356. http://dx.doi.org/10.1093/poq/nfp092

Yehuda, R., Bryant, R., Marmar, C., & Zohar, J. (2005). Pathological responses to terrorism. *Neuropsychopharmacology, 30*, 1793–1805. http://dx.doi.org/10.1038/sj.npp.1300816

4

MODERATORS AND MEDIATORS OF THE EXPERIENCE OF PERCEIVED RACISM

ALVIN N. ALVAREZ, CHRISTOPHER T. H. LIANG,
CARIN MOLENAAR, AND DAVID NGUYEN

Perceived racism has been demonstrated to be negatively associated with poor outcomes in behavioral health (e.g., alcohol abuse), mental health (e.g., depression), physical health (e.g., cardiovascular reactivity), academic well-being (e.g., lower self-efficacy), and problematic health behaviors (e.g., suicidal attempts; Williams & Mohammed, 2009). Yet, the factors that influence these outcomes are less clear. As a relatively new area of scholarship, critical questions remain empirically unanswered. For instance, what are effective ways of coping with one's experiences with racism? What role do friends and family play in helping to ameliorate the effects of perceived racism? Is it effective to prepare our children to encounter racism? Although such questions have intuitive appeal to scholars, practitioners, and lay persons alike, empirical answers to these questions are needed to better understand the factors that mitigate the impact of racism on people of color. To this end, the

http://dx.doi.org/10.1037/14852-005
The Cost of Racism for People of Color: Contextualizing Experiences of Discrimination, A. N. Alvarez, C. T. H. Liang, and H. A. Neville (Editors)
Copyright © 2016 by the American Psychological Association. All rights reserved.

purpose of the current chapter is to examine the literature on those factors that mediate and/or moderate the impact of perceived racism. In light of the breadth of variables that could influence these relationships, the focus of the current chapter is on a select set of variables that have direct clinical application for practitioners: coping, social support, cognitive processes, and ethnic/racial socialization that influence the outcomes of perceived racism. For a more extensive discussion of how demographic variables (e.g., age, gender, sexual orientation) influence perceived racism, readers are referred to Chapters 2 and 6 (this volume).

To provide a basic conceptual foundation for the current chapter, we provide a brief overview of mediators and moderators (for a more extensive discussion, see Frazier, Tix, & Barron, 2004; Holmbeck, 2003). *Mediators* describe the mechanism by which a predictor variable influences a criterion variable, that is, the predictor influences the mediator that in turn influences the criterion. As such, the mediator accounts for some portion of the variance in the relationship between the predictor and criterion, and by the directionality of this influence, the model is inherently causal. Although the design of a cross-sectional study may not permit causal interpretations, the underlying theoretical assumptions of meditational models may still be causal in nature (Rose, Holmbeck, Coakley, & Franks, 2004). In contrast, *moderators* affect the direction or strength of the relationship between predictor and criterion. As such, the predictor variable interacts with different levels or values of the moderator to influence the criterion variable. Thus, the key distinction here is that in moderation models, this interaction is not causal in nature; rather, these models outline the different conditions under which the predictor influences the criterion. Frazier et al. (2004) distinguished between the two by noting that "whereas moderators address 'when' or 'for whom' a predictor is more strongly related to an outcome, mediators establish 'how' or 'why' one variable predicts or causes an outcome variable" (p. 116). Despite such distinctions, in practice, variables can be treated as moderators or mediators—depending upon the underlying theory (Frazier et al., 2004).

COPING

Of the intervening variables that have a direct clinical impact, coping is certainly a variable whose relevance is self-evident. Indeed, the question of what are the effective ways to cope with perceived discrimination is fundamental for both clinicians and clients alike. Yet, despite both the clarity and simplicity of this question, the empirical findings to date have yielded far more questions than definitive answers, and coping has been studied as both a mediator and a moderator, depending on the study. According to Lazarus and

Folkman (1984) *coping* can be defined as "constantly changing cognitive and behavioral efforts to manage specific external and/or internal demands that are appraised as taxing or exceeding the resources of the person" (p. 141). In general, coping has been conceptualized as a mediator, that is, coping is a response elicited by racism that in turn directly influences its outcomes (see Lazarus & Folkman's, 1984, transactional stress model and Clark, Anderson, Clark, & Williams's, 1999, biopsychosocial model of racism). However, it is important to note that coping has also been analyzed as a moderator in a number of studies (Noh, Beiser, Kaspar, Hou & Rummens, 1999; Wei, Ku, Russell, Mallinckrodt, & Liao, 2008), albeit without a theoretical rationale.

To date, coping has been associated with a number of negative outcomes related to perceived discrimination—higher psychological distress (Alvarez & Juang, 2010; Forsyth & Carter, 2012), higher blood pressure (Clark & Gochett, 2006), increased cortisol secretion (Tull, Sheu, Butler, & Cornelious, 2005), and lower life satisfaction (Barnes & Lightsey, 2005)—as well as positive outcomes, such as increased activism (Szymanski, 2012). In general, the findings in this area have been mixed, with no definitive answer as to what is a universally effective strategy for coping with racism. Instead, the mixed findings underscore the complexity and nuances of coping and challenge us as researchers and psychologists to reexamine our clinical and cultural assumptions about what constitutes effective coping. For instance, although some studies have found support for the role of proactive styles of coping (e.g., confrontation, problem solving) in reducing adverse outcomes (Alvarez & Juang, 2010; Choi, Han, Paul, & Ayala, 2011; Noh & Kaspar, 2003), other studies have found that seemingly "passive" strategies, such as forbearance, acceptance, and distraction, may also be effective in reducing adverse outcomes (Noh et al., 1999; Vera et al., 2011). Thus, in light of these complexities, rather than asking the global question of what are the effective strategies for coping with racism, the more pertinent questions for clinicians and scholars may be to ask more refined questions regarding the idiosyncrasies of the incidents and individuals involved rather than coping per se: What characteristics of the racial incident influence how individuals cope? What personal and cultural characteristics of the targeted individual(s) affect coping? and Which strategies are effective for whom?

One of the main challenges in addressing these questions is that perceived racism by its nature is idiosyncratic and multifaceted. Indeed, various scholars (e.g., Williams & Mohammed, 2009) have argued for the need to study the full range of experiences that constitute racism—many of which have been inadequately studied (e.g., vicarious racism, transgenerational racism, institutional racism). Given the range of different types of racism, both the coping strategies and outcomes associated with these different forms of racism may be equally complex. As Brondolo, Brady ver Halen, Pencille,

Beatty, and Contrada (2009) observed, the path or mechanisms that link a particular form of racism to a particular form of coping and its related outcomes may be highly contextual and dependent on the idiosyncrasies of the specific incident. For instance, the manner in which an individual copes with a racial epithet or verbal harassment may differ if the perpetrator is a little child on a playground, a friend on the same football team, or a boss. Contextual variables, such as severity of the incident, chronicity, relationship to the perpetrator, power relative to the perpetrator, setting, and so forth, may all influence the manner in which an individual copes with such a situation. For instance, Foster (2009) found that acceptance is a more likely coping mechanism when people regard discrimination as being an isolated event, and that active styles of coping are more likely when people regard discrimination as both chronic and pervasive.

Likewise, the feasibility and availability of certain coping strategies may be directly related to characteristics of the individual or community being targeted. Factors such as gender, generational status, identity centrality, acculturation, and educational or social capital may all shape the manner in which individuals cope with racism (David & Knight, 2008; Noh & Kaspar, 2003). In terms of demographic characteristics, although racism is often the focus of this area of the literature, scholars should be mindful of how the intersectionality and multiplicity of one's identities shapes both the experience of discrimination and the manner in which individuals cope (see Chapter 2, this volume). As illustrated in David and Knight's (2008) study, older Black gay men's use of more disengaged styles of coping was attributed to their multiple minority statuses and their coming of age in a period of greater hostility to racial, ethnic, and queer communities.

Coping may be influenced not only by individual traits and identities but also by the social and historical context in which racism occurs. Nagata and Cheng (2003) described the "conspiracy of silence" among Japanese American internees in response to their illegal incarceration in the 1940s and that it stands in stark contrast to the highly visible political activism of subsequent generations of Japanese Americans who agitated for reparations in the 1970s and 1980s. In effect, the ability to respond to racism with such active coping styles may be a function of cultural values and a community's social, economic, and political capital. For instance, forbearance was an effective buffer against discrimination for Southeast Asian refugees (Noh et al., 1999), whereas for a group of Korean Canadians, a problem-focused style of coping was the significant moderator (Noh & Kaspar, 2003). Noh and Kaspar (2003) attributed this difference to the fact that with higher educational attainment, socioeconomic status, and acculturation levels after living in Canada for 20 years or more, a proactive style of coping was more feasible for Korean Canadians than recently arrived Southeast Asian refugees. In short, a clear understanding of *how* people of color cope with racism can only be obtained when researchers are equally clear about who they are studying and the unique characteristics, identities, life experiences and sociocultural contexts that shape the manner in which they cope.

Although the situational complexities of racist incidents and the targeted individuals are intuitively understandable, aligning research designs and instruments to measure this complexity is equally challenging. In general, many of the quantitative studies that have examined coping have typically used measures that average across the type of coping that one uses in response to a discriminatory incident. For instance, on the COPE Inventory (Carver, Scheier, & Weintraub, 1989), participants are asked to respond to what they generally do when they experience a stressful event. Yet, if each racial incident is highly contextualized, an accurate understanding of how individuals cope with specific incidents of racism becomes obscured with aggregate measures of coping.

Moreover, in studies of perceived racism, coping has often been measured with generic instruments designed to measure how individuals cope with stress in general, rather than perceived racism in particular. As a result, the extent to which individuals use discrimination-specific (e.g., contacting a civil rights group, filing a discrimination grievance) or race-specific/ethnicity-specific (e.g., faith in ancestors, support from an ethnic/racial group or organization) forms of coping is unclear. Yet, evidence indicates that the manner in which people of color cope with race-related stress is distinct from how they respond to general stress. T. L. Brown, Phillips, Abdullah, Vinson, and Robertson (2011), for example, found that African Americans were significantly more likely to use religion and venting in dealing with race-related stressors versus generic stressors. However, the limited number of race-specific/ethnicity-specific measures (e.g., Africultural Coping Styles Inventory; Utsey, Adams & Bolden, 2000) or discrimination-specific measures (e.g., Racism-Related Coping Scale [Forsyth & Carter, 2012], Coping With Discrimination Scale [Wei, Alvarez, Ku, Russell, & Bonett, 2010]) points to an area of the literature in need of further investigation. Moreover, even when key race-specific/ethnicity-specific coping mechanisms are included in measures, the manner in which these constructs are often operationalized oversimplifies highly complex responses that people have to racism. For instance, although religion is sometimes included in measures of coping, it is often reduced to two or three items that assess the degree to which individuals turn to their faith or to God. However, the simplicity of these items obscures the understanding of the healing mechanisms of religion—from the healing power of prayer, to the social support of a congregation sharing their coping strategies to protect one another, to the role models of resiliency and resistance that are found in Biblical narratives, to the restorative power of gospel music, to the sense of empowerment and self-efficacy that individuals feel from being Christian (Abrums, 2004). In effect, the challenge for scholars and clinicians alike is not only to understand what coping mechanisms people of color use in response to racism but also to understand how these coping mechanisms operate and mitigate race-related stress.

SOCIAL SUPPORT

Social support is a specific form of coping that has been studied in the association between perceived racism and various outcomes (Brondolo et al., 2009). Lin (1986) defined *social support* as "the perceived or actual instrumental and/or expressive provisions supplied by the community, social networks, and confiding patterns" (p. 18). It can come from a number of different sources, including intimate relationships, interactions with the community, or with individuals who people interact with in passing (Sarason & Sarason, 2009). Social support can consist of emotional support (i.e., expressing emotions while a provider shows empathy, care, and reassurance), informational support (i.e., advice to cope with problems), instrumental support (i.e., aid in the form of materials, such as money), and appraisal support (i.e., affirmation and feedback; Cohen, 2004; Zhu, Woo, Porter, & Brzezinski, 2013). Authors also have distinguished the perception of support from the enactment of support. *Perceived support*, which is defined as "support believed to be available should a stressor occur" (Birditt, Antonucci, & Tighe, 2012, p. 728), may reduce the anxiety of possible failure and danger by providing to an individual the perception of an available secure base from which he or she may explore and attend to new situations with reasonable risk (Sarason & Sarason, 2009). Researchers have further differentiated perception of availability of support from support-seeking behaviors. These distinctions have resulted in social support being conceptualized as both a moderator and a mediator in the association between stress and health outcomes. Unfortunately, whether researchers are studying the perception of available social support or the social-support-seeking behavior, it may be difficult to differentiate the constructs. Researchers themselves also may not consider the differences and may use measures of support seeking to test the moderator hypotheses.

The perception of the availability of social support, as well as its enactment, has been argued to serve as a protective factor for a number of stressors, such as perceived racism (Brondolo et al., 2009). From this perspective, the belief that a network can provide the emotional, informational, or tangible support will serve to mitigate the negative influence of the stressor. However, a recent meta-analysis (Schmitt, Branscombe, Postmes, & Garcia, 2014) indicated that 73% of all tests failed to demonstrate support for this moderator hypothesis. In fact, nearly as many findings show that social support exacerbated the effect of racism as those showing it is a buffer (Schmitt et al., 2014). The strength and direction of effect of social support in these associations is likely contingent upon the type of and context in which the support is sought and provided or in how the construct was operationalized within a study. Below, we provide a select review of studies that demonstrate the specificity with which social support must be tested as a moderator variable.

Recent studies suggest that level of exposure to racism, as well as the type of social support, is critical to examine in research. As an example, although perceived emotional support did not appear to be protective against depression for African American women, Ajrouch, Reisine, Lim, Sohn, and Ismail (2010) found that women with lower perceived levels of availability of instrumental support who experienced moderate levels of discrimination reported higher levels of depressive symptomatology than women with higher levels of perceived instrumental support. However, the protective value of social support diminished for individuals who experienced higher levels of discrimination.

Examining how social support interacts with other individual difference variables is necessary to understand when and for whom social support is useful. Several authors have examined three-way interaction effects. In one study, Brittian, Toomey, Gonzales, and Dumka (2013) found a positive association between perceived racism and externalizing behaviors for youth who were not oriented to their Mexican heritage and who reported low social-support-seeking behavior but a negative association for those with high levels of self-reported social-support-seeking behavior. The buffering effect was not found for adolescents who were highly oriented to their Mexican roots. In a related study, Wei, Yeh, Chao, Carrera, and Su (2013) found that individuals who reported using family support less had a significant positive association between perceived racism and psychological distress among those with low levels of self-reported self-esteem and that those with high self-esteem had a negative perceived-racism–distress association. These two studies indicate that using social support for people of color may depend on individual difference variables. Research examining the role of other individual difference variables is needed before the protective role of social support is discounted.

It appears that the location and source of social support, perceived or enacted, also is important to consider. For instance, Jasinskaja-Lahti, Liebkind, Jaakkola, and Reuter (2006) found that *enacted* support from relatives as well as from friends in the host culture and in the country of origin mitigated the effect of discrimination on well-being for those experiencing high levels of discrimination. Perception of *availability* of support, however, was not protective. In another study, Bowleg et al. (2013) reported that both social support from friends as well as social support from a significant other moderated the relationship between racism and sexual risk behaviors for Black men. Their findings provide evidence that social support can be protective at high levels of discrimination.

Although minimal support for using social support as a way to cope with perceived racism has been indicated (Schmitt et al., 2014), the current review shows the potential role of social support. It appears that the use of social support is contingent upon the source of support, perception of and availability of support, self-esteem, and cultural orientation, which all may interact to dictate the use of social support as a buffer against the deleterious effects of racism. In examining social support in the context of other variables, researchers are heeding Pearlin's (1989) recommendation that the examination of social support is incomplete without looking the context of an individual's social network. Future studies should continue to examine the protective qualities of the different forms and sources of social support.

Research also is needed to determine whether seeking social support can help to explain some of the negative outcomes associated with experiences of racism. From this vantage point, seeking social support after an experience with a stressor is viewed as a type of coping strategy that is, in turn, associated with outcomes. In several studies, seeking social support was found to exert a mediating effect in the association between perceived racism and racism-related stress (Liang, Alvarez, Juang, & Liang, 2007), as well as in the relationship between perceived racism and depressive symptoms (Kim, 2014). In these studies, perceived racism was associated with higher levels of social-support-seeking behavior. Whereas seeking social support was indicated to be associated with an increase in levels of racism-related stress, it was found to be correlated with fewer depressive symptoms. Differences in these findings may be a function of measurement or of sampling issues. Continued examination of seeking social support as a mediator would help to further elucidate its role for people of color who experience racism.

COGNITIVE PROCESSES

Drawing from social cognitive theory, researchers have primarily examined the role of cognitive variables as a mediator in the racism–outcome association (see Chapter 5, this volume). According social cognitive models, social processes activate cognitive schemas that can negatively affect psychological functioning. In the following section, we provide an overview of several cognitive strategies that have been explored in the racism-outcome association. We focus on research exploring control, psychological rumination, and belief systems.

Wallston, Wallston, Smith, and Dobbins (1987) defined *perceptions of control* as "the belief that one can determine one's own internal states and behavior, influence one's environment, and/or, bring about desired outcomes" (p. 5). An individual's sense of lacking personal control is associated with more distress and less overall well-being for economically disadvantaged persons (Lachman & Weaver, 1998). In regard to psychological well-being, personal control has been found to partially mediate the association between perceived racism and psychological distress and to partially mediate the association between perceived racism and self-esteem for Latino/a individuals (Moradi & Risco, 2006), whereas both of these associations were fully mediated by personal control for Arab Americans (Moradi & Hasan, 2004). Sense of control also was found to mediate the relationship between perceived racism and depressive symptoms and academic performance of Latino/a adolescents (Chithambo, Huey, & Cespedes-Knadle, 2014). Chithambo et al. (2014) surmised that individuals who perceive less control plan passively instead of exerting agency over their social environment or planning academically.

The importance of control is particularly problematic for individuals who face repeated instances of racial discrimination, as their sense of personal control is repeatedly challenged by experiences of racism (Ruggiero & Taylor, 1995). In one longitudinal study, Gibbons et al. (2012) found that perceived racism was associated with increased anger, which appeared to diminish self-control among African American adolescents. This loss of sense of self-control was then associated with increased substance use and/or thoughts about using substances. Thus, it may be that repeated exposure to racism requires individuals to use personal resources that are needed to maintain self-control. More longitudinal research in this area is needed to further clarify the pathway of perceived racism to loss of control to negative psychological or academic problems of youth and adults.

Psychological rumination is conceptualized as the preservation of negative events and mood states. Individuals that ruminate tend to relive the experience. Psychological rumination is associated with the development and maintenance of depressive symptoms (Nolen-Hoeksema, Parker, & Larson, 1994) and has been indicated to partially mediate the relationship between discrimination and increased depressive symptoms, hostility, aggression, and anger among people of color. Treynor, Gonzalez, and Nolen-Hoeksema (2003) distinguished between two different subtypes of rumination: *brooding* (focusing on dysphoric mood) and *reflective pondering* (efforts to understand causes of dysphoric mood; Miranda, Polanco-Roman, Tsypes, & Valderrama, 2013; Treynor et al., 2003). Furthermore, Miranda et al. (2013) found that irrespective of ethnic identity, brooding but not reflective pondering, mediated the relationship between experiences of discrimination and increased depressive symptoms for people of color.

Overall, psychological rumination and brooding appear to represent a maladaptive cognitive response for people of color who experience racism (Borders & Liang, 2011). This cognitive response may be particularly damaging for individuals who experience covert acts of racism, as the encounter may result in replaying the event in an effort to find meaning. In so doing, these individuals prolong the negative outcomes of the original stressor. Further research may examine whether rumination mediates the associations differently on the basis of racial identity centrality or racial identity, whether the experience of racism is overt or covert, the context of the event, or if the experiences are time-limited or chronic.

Belief in an unjust world (BUW) was conceptualized by Lench and Chang (2007) as cognitive schemas that frame the world as unfair and in which injustice occurs to people who deserve otherwise. They suggested that BUW may mediate the associations between an unjust event and outcomes. Specifically, they viewed BUW as a defensive and protective response to an individual's repeated experience of perceived injustice. In their research, they found that participants who endorsed BUW were more likely to report anger, and to attribute negative, unjust, perceptions to their experiences. They also suggested the potential for individuals, who endorse BUW, to avoid seeking out help from others. Liang and Borders (2012) also found that BUW helped explain the association between perceived racism and higher levels of aggression and anxiety as well decreased social connectedness among people of color. However, Liang and Borders (2012) cautioned against simply attributing blame for an individual's expression of aggression, anxiety, and decreased social connectedness on the victim. Instead, they argued that focus must be placed on validating an individual's experiences of racism while also tempering the BUW. Furthermore, they contended that inequities that are embedded in systems and policies that facilitate environments in which racial discrimination is accepted need to be addressed.

In contrast to BUW, as well as other cognitive schemas reviewed here, belief in a just world (BJW) has been considered a buffer in the association between injustice and outcomes. BJW refers to the hypothesis that individuals have an inherent desire to view their social and physical environments as predictable, stable, orderly, and just. Lerner and Miller (1978) believed that each person possesses BJW and that these beliefs encourage people to persist in their pursuit of life goals despite injustices. Considering the theoretical protective elements of endorsing BJW, as well as findings that it buffers the negative effects of sex-based discrimination (Choma, Hafer, Crosby, & Foster, 2012), religious discrimination, and age-based discrimination (Lipkus & Siegler, 1993), one may come to conclusion that BJW may be beneficial for reducing some negative outcomes associated with racism.

Future examinations are needed to determine whether BJW is protective or harmful in regard to the short- and long-term well-being of people of color. For instance, although BJW may protect against the harmful effects of racism in the short-term, unmitigated and high levels of acceptance in this belief may compromise an individual's ability to acknowledge injustices and may result in higher levels of internalized racism.

Both BJW and BUW could have protective and harmful implications for individuals who encounter racism. Because these two belief systems have not been studied enough to determine their utility or role, more work is necessary to understand whether and how these beliefs may contribute to the well-being of people of color who experience racism. Future research should consider how beliefs that the world is fair to the self may differ in their protective value from beliefs that the world is fair to others (Lipkus, Dalbert, & Siegler, 1996; Sutton & Douglas, 2005). Furthermore, researchers may consider testing whether different levels of BJW may confer protective or exacerbating effects depending on racial attitudes. For instance, it may be that low levels of BJW may be detrimental to people of color who experience racism but have less well-developed understanding of racism. These individuals may internalize racism and place blame on themselves or people of color for injustices they experience. On the other hand, high levels of BJW may also be detrimental for the same individuals. For example, these individuals may believe the directed racism is deserved and that they have no right to defend themselves. Moderate levels of BJW for individuals with deep knowledge of race-relations may be protective. That is, understanding how racism operates enables individuals to attribute injustice externally while a moderate level of BJW contributes to the maintenance of hope that one's efforts will be rewarded. Future research also may be conducted to determine whether BUW is a temporary reaction to racism or whether chronic exposure to racism results in trait-like BUW.

On the basis of the literature at the time of this review, cognitive variables, such as BJW, BUW, perceptions of control, and rumination, can serve as both protective and maladaptive responses against negative outcomes, depending on how individuals use them. Further research regarding the development of cognitive responses may help increase understanding of how to better support individuals and how to help individuals protect against outcomes that can threaten their overall wellbeing. Researchers may consider how multiple cognitive processes may interact and influence outcomes. For instance, researchers may consider the effect of Perceived Racism × Locus of Control × BJW on depressive symptomatology. Alternatively, researchers may study a multiple mediation model involving psychological rumination and BUW on psychological distress.

ETHNIC/RACIAL SOCIALIZATION

We now shift our focus from internal psychological processes (i.e., coping and cognitive processes) to ethnic/racial socialization. In this section, we review the literature on parental ethnic/racial socialization in the aforementioned associations. We focus on ethnic/racial socialization because of our belief that these are facets of a client's life that a mental health professional may be able to address in the context of traditional psychotherapy or through prevention workshops in their communities. However, we also recognize the mental health professional's role in addressing social injustices at the systemic level (see Chapter 12, this volume).

Ethnic/racial socialization is the process by which parents communicate to their children the meaning of their membership in an ethnic or racial group. Authors have proposed various multidimensional conceptualizations of ethnic/racial socialization. In a review of the empirical literature on ethnic/racial socialization, Hughes et al. (2006) categorized the methodology, measurement, and samples of more than 50 studies. These dimensions of ethnic/racial socialization were (a) cultural socialization, (b) racial bias preparation, (c) egalitarianism, and (d) promotion of mistrust (Hughes & Chen, 1997). *Cultural socialization* reflects parental practices that convey messages of cultural pride, with an emphasis on the cultural group's history and traditions. *Racial bias preparation* refers to parents promoting within their children an understanding and awareness of racial prejudice and discrimination, and appropriate responses to racism events. *Egalitarianism* reflects parent behaviors that instill in the child an appreciation and knowledge of diverse racial and ethnic groups and the importance of equality. The *promotion of mistrust* refers to parents teaching their children the need to be cautious of other ethnic and racial groups, particularly non-Hispanic White individuals in the United States. In their review, Hughes et al. (2006) found that cultural socialization and racial bias preparation were the two most studied forms of ethnic/racial socialization practices. However, the lack of conceptual clarity and common terminology may hamper efforts to fully understand the influence of ethnic/racial socialization for people of color (Hughes et al., 2006).

Ethnic/racial socialization practices of parents are thought to exert a protective influence on individuals through their effect on the identity development and self-esteem of children of color (Evans et al., 2012; Neblett, Rivas-Drake, & Umaña-Taylor, 2012; Stevenson, Reed, & Bodison, 1996). Findings indicate ethnic/racial socialization's influence as a precursor to healthy self-esteem and group-level identity (C. M. Brown & Ling, 2012; Murry, Berkel, Brody, Miller, & Chen, 2009) and point to a complex interplay of identity and cognitive (i.e., pessimism, optimism) variables (Liu & Lau, 2013). That is, parent socialization efforts or subsequent exposure to ethnic/racial socialization may lead to a positive ethnic or racial identity, hopefulness, and higher expectations for self.

This cascade of effects is not uniform for different forms of ethnic/racial socialization. For instance, although Liu and Lau (2013) reported that cultural socialization practices were protective, they also found that preparation for racial bias and promotion of cultural mistrust were both associated with higher levels of trait pessimism and lower levels of optimism. Although the research findings on ethnic/racial socialization have been inconsistent (Hughes et al., 2006), the positive associations found between ethnic/racial socialization, ethnic identity (e.g., Hughes, Hagelskamp, Way, & Foust, 2009; Stevenson, 1995), and self-esteem (e.g., Constantine & Sha'Kema, 2002) has led some researchers to test moderator and mediator models.

Although ethnic/racial socialization was initially theorized to buffer the effects of perceived racism on negative outcomes, the empirical evidence suggests that different forms of ethnic/racial socialization appear to influence the perceived racism–outcomes association differently. Wang and Huguley (2012) found that parent cultural socialization practices buffered the negative effect of perception of teacher and peer discrimination on the grade point average, educational aspirations of urban African American adolescents. However, ethnic/racial socialization may not always be protective. For instance, racial bias preparation exacerbated the negative effects of high levels of discrimination from adults on adolescents' public regard (Rivas-Drake, Hughes, & Way, 2009) and high proactive racial socialization (i.e., cultural pride, racial bias preparation) and high reactive racial socialization (i.e., racial bias preparation without empowering component) heightened the negative association found between high own-group conformity pressures and anxiety, as well as behavioral and emotional control (Chávez & French, 2007).

Racial socialization has not consistently exerted a significant interaction effect on the perceived racism–outcome association. For instance, whereas Chávez and French (2007) found that both proactive and reactive racial socialization exacerbated the effect of own-group conformity pressures, they did not find any effect of it on perceived discrimination. In another study, racial bias preparation exerted a negative effect on the perceived teacher-discrimination–public-regard association but not for the perceived teacher-discrimination–private-regard association (Rivas-Drake et al., 2009). The null findings were dependent on not only the outcome but also on the perpetrator of discrimination—no interaction effects involved discrimination from peers.

As a whole, the mixed findings could be an indication that different agents and types of racism, the ethnic background of the person of color, and the outcome must all be considered. The mixed findings also can be a function of nonlinear associations. For instance, in a sample of African American youth, Harris-Britt, Valrie, Kurtz-Costes, and Rowley (2007) found that preparation for racial bias moderated the association between perceived racism and self-esteem, such that a moderate level of preparation for bias socialization was protective but that high and low levels were not. In short, high and low levels of this form of racial socialization may be maladaptive. Individuals who experience high levels of preparation for racial bias may become hypervigilant, believe the world is unjust, or experience a lack of personal mastery over their environment. Individuals who experience low levels may not be prepared for racism and may instead internalize messages of racism. Similar nonlinear associations may be found for other types of racial socialization practices and should be examined in future studies of the moderating role of the different types of ethnic/racial socialization practices.

Researchers have also examined mediational models. The models are grounded in the belief that cultural socialization practices instill racial and cultural pride or a positive ethnic identity within an individual. Stevenson and Arrington (2009), for instance, found that some forms of ethnic/racial socialization, namely coping with antagonism and cultural legacy appreciation, mediated the association between racism and racial identity. In these results, perceived racism was positively associated with both forms of ethnic/racial socialization, which were in turn positively related to private regard, racial centrality, and nationalist identity, respectively. They also reported that mainstream fit socialization appeared to either partially or fully mediate these same associations, such that mainstream fit socialization was negatively associated with private racial regard, racial centrality, and nationalist identity.

The research evidence points to a high level of complexity that has yet to be synthesized theoretically or tested empirically. The differential effects exerted by each component necessitate more specificity when studying the moderating or mediating role of racial socialization. As an example, the study of ethnic/racial socialization would benefit from researcher's consistent use of measures of specific types of socialization efforts (e.g., racial bias preparation, cultural pride) over global measures of ethnic/racial socialization. Failure to do so may result in findings that are falsely suggestive of the lack of buffering or indirect effects of ethnic/racial socialization (Hughes et al., 2006; Stevenson & Arrington, 2009). Furthermore, research may move beyond the study of racial bias preparation and cultural pride to examine role of cultural mistrust socialization, as well as egalitarianism. Research may address whether cultural mistrust or egalitarianism socialization buffers or exacerbates the influence of perceived racism on mental health. Examining a three-way interaction involving perceived discrimination, egalitarianism socialization, and racial bias preparation or cultural pride may further unpack the role of ethnic/racial socialization on the academic, behavioral, and psychological well-being of youth and adults. For instance, Spencer (1983) argued that socialization to egalitarianism absent racial bias preparation may put African American youth at risk.

Given that the vast majority of the empirical literature has focused on the role of ethnic/racial socialization among African Americans experiencing racism, testing the model fit for other racial/ethnic groups is needed. For instance, by virtue of the varying immigration trajectories, recently immigrated Asian Americans, both within and across different Asian ethnic groups, may have different experiences of ethnic/racial socialization than other Asian Americans with longer residence and family histories in the United States. Newly immigrated parents may not focus their efforts on racial bias preparation but instead on cultural pride. More research is needed to understand if and how parents prepare their children for racism and whether or not this practice (or lack of socialization) has any influence on psychological outcomes of children from other ethnic minority groups. Generalizing findings focused on African Americans to other groups may not be appropriate. Further empirical examination of models will help to determine if ethnic/racial socialization exerts a similar influence across different groups of people of color.

Although ethnic/racial socialization is typically construed as a childhood or adolescent experience, it may be better to understand it as a lifetime process whereby the development of new understandings of race is born from one's own ongoing ethnic/racial group and cross-racial group encounters. These practices may set a foundation for a child to understand how race and racism plays a role in their experience of their world. However, it is important to study specific forms of ethnic/racial socialization practices, as the type of ethnic/racial socialization experience (e.g., cultural pride, preparation for racial bias) may shape the degree to which an individual is aware of, or vigilant to, the many forms of racism. Perceptions of racism also may result in further socialization practices from adolescents, teachers, or adult peers as one gets older. These subsequent socialization experiences may further influence how an individual may view his or her race-based experiences and may shape his or her coping responses to racism. Given this transactional experience, further work is needed to delineate how, why, and for whom ethnic/racial socialization is associated with perceived racism and its outcomes. Longitudinal designs would be required to tease out which forms and ways socialization shape perceptions of racism and how those may, in turn, influence subsequent socialization experiences.

CONCLUSION

In this chapter, we sought to provide an overview of some constructs that have been studied for their moderating or mediating roles. Our review points to the need for more research to study these variables with more complexity. Use of longitudinal designs with sophisticated quantitative analyses, or qualitative and mixed-method approaches, may help to unravel how these factors operate in isolation and in tandem. No matter the methodology, this review points clearly to the need to study and understand the influence of multiple individual and socio-environmental processes and the association between perceived racism and negative outcomes. We recognize that several other variables are not addressed in this chapter (e.g., structures and policies that support racism) that also must be a focal point for change efforts. This discussion, however, was outside the scope of this chapter. Instead, we selected these particular individual-level and socio-environmental constructs because we believe that these may be potential areas for continued research and which are amenable to clinical interventions. It is important to note that our approach to this chapter is grounded in our belief that basic racism research must serve a clinical purpose for people of color.

REFERENCES

Abrums, M. (2004). Faith and feminism: How African American women from a storefront church resist oppression in healthcare. *Advances in Nursing Science, 27*, 187–201. http://dx.doi.org/10.1097/00012272-200407000-00004

Ajrouch, K. J., Reisine, S., Lim, S., Sohn, W., & Ismail, A. (2010). Perceived everyday discrimination and psychological distress: Does social support matter? *Ethnicity & Health, 15*, 417–434. http://dx.doi.org/10.1080/13557858.2010.484050

Alvarez, A. N., & Juang, L. P. (2010). Filipino Americans and racism: A multiple mediation model of coping. *Journal of Counseling Psychology, 57*, 167–178. http://dx.doi.org/10.1037/a0019091

Barnes, P. W., & Lightsey, O. R., Jr. (2005). Perceived racist discrimination, coping, stress, and life satisfaction. *Journal of Multicultural Counseling and Development, 33*, 48–61. http://dx.doi.org/10.1002/j.2161-1912.2005.tb00004.x

Birditt, K. S., Antonucci, T. C., & Tighe, L. (2012). Enacted support during stressful life events in middle and older adulthood: An examination of the interpersonal context. *Psychology and Aging, 27*, 728–741. http://dx.doi.org/10.1037/a0026967

Borders, A., & Liang, C. T. H. (2011). Rumination partially mediates the associations between perceived ethnic discrimination, emotional distress, and aggression. *Cultural Diversity and Ethnic Minority Psychology, 17*, 125–133. http://dx.doi.org/10.1037/a0023357

Bowleg, L., Burkholder, G. J., Massie, J. S., Wahome, R., Teti, M., Malebranche, D. J., & Tschann, J. M. (2013). Racial discrimination, social support, and sexual HIV risk among Black heterosexual men. *AIDS and Behavior, 17*, 407–418. http://dx.doi.org/10.1007/s10461-012-0179-0

Brittian, A. S., Toomey, R. B., Gonzales, N. A., & Dumka, L. E. (2013). Perceived discrimination, coping strategies, and Mexican origin adolescents' internalizing and externalizing behaviors: Examining the moderating role of gender and cultural orientation. *Applied Developmental Science, 17*, 4–19. http://dx.doi.org/10.1080/10888691.2013.748417

Brondolo, E., Brady ver Halen, N., Pencille, M., Beatty, D., & Contrada, R. J. (2009). Coping with racism: A selective review of the literature and a theoretical and methodological critique. *Journal of Behavioral Medicine, 32*, 64–88. http://dx.doi.org/10.1007/s10865-008-9193-0

Brown, C. M., & Ling, W. (2012). Ethnic/racial socialization has an indirect effect on self-esteem for Asian American emerging adults. *Psychology, 3*, 78–81. http://dx.doi.org/10.4236/psych.2012.31013

Brown, T. L., Phillips, C. M., Abdullah, T., Vinson, E., & Robertson, J. (2011). Dispositional versus situational coping: Are the coping strategies African Americans use different for general versus racism-related stressors? *The Journal of Black Psychology, 37*, 311–335. http://dx.doi.org/10.1177/0095798410390688

Carver, C. S., Scheier, M. F., & Weintraub, J. K. (1989). Assessing coping strategies: A theoretically based approach. *Journal of Personality and Social Psychology, 56*, 267–283. http://dx.doi.org/10.1037/0022-3514.56.2.267

Chávez, N. R., & French, S. B. (2007). Ethnicity-related stressors and mental health in Latino Americans: The moderating role of parental racial socialization. *Journal of Applied Social Psychology, 37*, 1974–1998. http://dx.doi.org/10.1111/j.1559-1816.2007.00246.x

Chithambo, T. P., Huey, S. J., Jr., & Cespedes-Knadle, Y. (2014). Perceived discrimination and Latino youth adjustment: Examining the role of relinquished control and sociocultural influences. *Journal of Latina/o Psychology, 2*, 54–66. http://dx.doi.org/10.1037/lat0000012

Choi, K. H., Han, C. S., Paul, J., & Ayala, G. (2011). Strategies for managing racism and homophobia among U.S. ethnic and racial minority men who have sex with men. *AIDS Education and Prevention, 23*, 145–158. http://dx.doi.org/10.1521/aeap.2011.23.2.145

Choma, B., Hafer, C., Crosby, F., & Foster, M. (2012). Perceptions of personal sex discrimination: The role of belief in a just world and situational ambiguity. *The Journal of Social Psychology, 152*, 568–585. http://dx.doi.org/10.1080/00224545.2012.667459

Clark, R., Anderson, N. B., Clark, V. R., & Williams, D. R. (1999). Racism as a stressor for African Americans. A biopsychosocial model. *American Psychologist, 54*, 805–816. http://dx.doi.org/10.1037/0003-066X.54.10.805

Clark, R., & Gochett, P. (2006). Interactive effects of perceived racism and coping responses predict a school-based assessment of blood pressure in black youth. *Annals of Behavioral Medicine, 32*, 1–9. http://dx.doi.org/10.1207/s15324796abm3201_1

Cohen, S. (2004). Social relationships and health. *American Psychologist, 59,* 676–684. http://dx.doi.org/10.1037/0003-066X.59.8.676

Constantine, M. G., & Sha'Kema, M. B. (2002). Black adolescents' racial socialization experiences their relations to home, school, and peer self-esteem. *Journal of Black Studies, 32,* 322–335. http://dx.doi.org/10.1177/002193470203200303

David, S., & Knight, B. G. (2008). Stress and coping among gay men: Age and ethnic differences. *Psychology and Aging, 23,* 62–69. http://dx.doi.org/10.1037/0882-7974.23.1.62

Evans, A. B., Banerjee, M., Meyer, R., Aldana, A., Foust, M., & Rowley, S. (2012). Racial socialization as a mechanism for positive development among African American youth. *Child Development Perspectives, 6,* 251–257. http://dx.doi.org/10.1111/j.1750-8606.2011.00226.x

Forsyth, J., & Carter, R. T. (2012). The relationship between racial identity status attitudes, racism-related coping, and mental health among Black Americans. *Cultural Diversity and Ethnic Minority Psychology, 18,* 128–140. http://dx.doi.org/10.1037/a0027660

Foster, M. D. (2009). Perceiving pervasive discrimination over time: Implications for coping. *Psychology of Women Quarterly, 33,* 172–182. http://dx.doi.org/10.1111/j.1471-6402.2009.01487.x

Frazier, P. A., Tix, A. P., & Barron, K. E. (2004). Testing moderator and mediator effects in counseling psychology research. *Journal of Counseling Psychology, 51,* 115–134. http://dx.doi.org/10.1037/0022-0167.51.1.115

Gibbons, F. X., O'Hara, R. E., Stock, M. L., Gerrard, M., Weng, C.-Y., & Wills, T. A. (2012). The erosive effects of racism: Reduced self-control mediates the relation between perceived racial discrimination and substance use in African American adolescents. *Journal of Personality and Social Psychology, 102,* 1089–1104. http://dx.doi.org/10.1037/a0027404

Harris-Britt, A., Valrie, C. R., Kurtz-Costes, B., & Rowley, S. J. (2007). Perceived racial discrimination and self-esteem in African American youth: Racial socialization as a protective factor. *Journal of Research on Adolescence, 17,* 669–682. http://dx.doi.org/10.1111/j.1532-7795.2007.00540.x

Holmbeck, G. N. (2003). Toward terminological, conceptual, and statistical clarity in the study of mediators and moderators: Examples from the child-clinical and pediatric psychology literatures. In A. E. Kazdin (Ed.), *Methodological issues & strategies in clinical research* (3rd ed., pp. 77–105). Washington, DC: American Psychological Association.

Hughes, D., & Chen, L. (1997). When and what parents tell children about race: An examination of race-related socialization among African American families. *Applied Developmental Science, 1,* 200–214. http://dx.doi.org/10.1207/s1532480xads04104_4

Hughes, D., Hagelskamp, C., Way, N., & Foust, M. D. (2009). The role of mothers' and adolescents' perceptions of ethnic–racial socialization in shaping ethnic–

racial identity among early adolescent boys and girls. *Journal of Youth and Adolescence, 38,* 605–626. http://dx.doi.org/10.1007/s10964-009-9399-7

Hughes, D., Rodriguez, J., Smith, E. P., Johnson, D. J., Stevenson, H. C., & Spicer, P. (2006). Parents' ethnic/racial socialization practices: A review of research and directions for future study. *Developmental Psychology, 42,* 747–770. http://dx.doi.org/10.1037/0012-1649.42.5.747

Jasinskaja-Lahti, I., Liebkind, K., Jaakkola, M., & Reuter, A. (2006). Perceived discrimination, social support networks, and psychological well-being among three immigrant groups. *Journal of Cross-Cultural Psychology, 37,* 293–311. http://dx.doi.org/10.1177/0022022106286925

Kim, I. (2014). The role of critical ethnic awareness and social support in the discrimination-depression relationship among Asian Americans: Path analysis. *Cultural Diversity and Ethnic Minority Psychology, 20,* 52–60. http://dx.doi.org/10.1037/a0034529

Lachman, M. E., & Weaver, S. L. (1998). The sense of control as a moderator of social class differences in health and well-being. *Journal of Personality and Social Psychology, 74,* 763–773. http://dx.doi.org/10.1037/0022-3514.74.3.763

Lazarus, R. S., & Folkman, S. (1984). *Stress, appraisal, and coping.* New York, NY: Springer.

Lench, H. C., & Chang, E. S. (2007). Belief in an unjust world: When beliefs in a just world fail. *Journal of Personality Assessment, 89,* 126–135. http://dx.doi.org/10.1080/00223890701468477

Lerner, M. J., & Miller, D. T. (1978). Just world research and the attribution process: Looking back and looking ahead. *Psychological Bulletin, 85,* 1030–1051. http://dx.doi.org/10.1037/0033-2909.85.5.1030

Liang, C. T. H., Alvarez, A. N., Juang, L. P., & Liang, M. X. (2007). The role of coping in the relationship between perceived racism and racism-related stress for Asian Americans: Gender differences. *Journal of Counseling Psychology, 54,* 132–141.

Liang, C. T. H., & Borders, A. (2012). Beliefs in an unjust world mediate the associations between perceived ethnic discrimination and psychological functioning. *Personality and Individual Differences, 53,* 528–533. http://dx.doi.org/10.1016/j.paid.2012.04.022

Lin, N. (1986). Conceptualizing social support. In N. Lin, A., Dean, & W. M. Ensel (Eds.), *Social support, life events and depression* (pp. 17–30). London, England: Academic Press. http://dx.doi.org/10.1016/B978-0-12-450660-2.50008-2

Lipkus, I. M., Dalbert, C., & Siegler, I. C. (1996). The importance of distinguishing the belief in a just world for self versus for others: Implications for psychological well-being. *Personality and Social Psychology Bulletin, 22,* 666–677. http://dx.doi.org/10.1177/0146167296227002

Lipkus, I. M., & Siegler, I. C. (1993). The belief in a just world and perceptions of discrimination. *The Journal of Psychology: Interdisciplinary and Applied, 127,* 465–474. http://dx.doi.org/10.1080/00223980.1993.9915583

Liu, L. L., & Lau, A. S. (2013). Teaching about race/ethnicity and racism matters: An examination of how perceived ethnic racial socialization processes are associated with depression symptoms. *Cultural Diversity and Ethnic Minority Psychology, 19*, 383–394. http://dx.doi.org/10.1037/a0033447

Miranda, R., Polanco-Roman, L., Tsypes, A., & Valderrama, J. (2013). Perceived discrimination, ruminative subtypes, and risk for depressive symptoms in emerging adulthood. *Cultural Diversity and Ethnic Minority Psychology, 19*, 395–403. http://dx.doi.org/10.1037/a0033504

Moradi, B., & Hasan, N. T. (2004). Arab American persons' reported experiences of discrimination and mental health: The mediating role of personal control. *Journal of Counseling Psychology, 51*, 418–428. http://dx.doi.org/10.1037/0022-0167.51.4.418

Moradi, B., & Risco, C. (2006). Perceived discrimination experiences and mental health of Latino/a American Persons. *Journal of Counseling Psychology, 53*, 411–421. http://dx.doi.org/10.1037/0022-0167.53.4.411

Murry, V. M., Berkel, C., Brody, G. H., Miller, S. J., & Chen, Y. F. (2009). Linking parental socialization to interpersonal protective processes, academic self-presentation, and expectations among rural African American youth. *Cultural Diversity and Ethnic Minority Psychology, 15*, 1–10. http://dx.doi.org/10.1037/a0013180

Nagata, D. K., & Cheng, W. J. (2003). Intergenerational communication of race-related trauma by Japanese American former internees. *American Journal of Orthopsychiatry, 73*, 266–278. http://dx.doi.org/10.1037/0002-9432.73.3.266

Neblett, E. W., Rivas-Drake, D., & Umaña-Taylor, A. J. (2012). The promise of racial and ethnic protective factors in promoting ethnic minority youth development. *Child development perspectives, 6*, 295–303. http://dx.doi.org/10.1111/j.1750-8606.2012.00239.x

Noh, S., Beiser, M., Kaspar, V., Hou, F., & Rummens, A. (1999). Perceived racial discrimination, coping: A study of Southeast Asian refugees in Canada. *Journal of Health and Social Behavior, 40*, 193–207. http://dx.doi.org/10.2307/2676348

Noh, S., & Kaspar, V. (2003). Perceived discrimination and depression: Moderating effects of coping, acculturation, and ethnic support. *American Journal of Public Health, 93*, 232–238. http://dx.doi.org/10.2105/AJPH.93.2.232

Nolen-Hoeksema, S., Parker, L. E., & Larson, J. (1994). Ruminative coping with depressed mood following loss. *Journal of Personality and Social Psychology, 67*, 92–104. http://dx.doi.org/10.1037/0022-3514.67.1.92

Pearlin, L. I. (1989). The sociological study of stress. *Journal of Health and Social Behavior, 30*, 241–256. http://dx.doi.org/10.2307/2136956

Rivas-Drake, D., Hughes, D., & Way, N. (2009). A preliminary analysis of associations among ethnic/racial socialization, ethnic discrimination, and ethnic identity among urban sixth graders. *Journal of Research on Adolescence, 19*, 558–584. http://dx.doi.org/10.1111/j.1532-7795.2009.00607.x

Rose, B. M., Holmbeck, G. N., Coakley, R. M., & Franks, E. A. (2004). Mediator and moderator effects in developmental and behavioral pediatric research. *Journal of Developmental and Behavioral Pediatrics, 25,* 58–67. http://dx.doi.org/10.1097/00004703-200402000-00013

Ruggiero, K. M., & Taylor, D. M. (1995). Coping with discrimination: How disadvantaged group members perceive the discrimination that confronts them. *Journal of Personality and Social Psychology, 68,* 826–838. http://dx.doi.org/10.1037/0022-3514.68.5.826

Sarason, I. G., & Sarason, B. R. (2009). Social support: Mapping the construct. *Journal of Social and Personal Relationships, 26,* 113–120. http://dx.doi.org/10.1177/0265407509105526

Schmitt, M. T., Branscombe, N. R., Postmes, T., & Garcia, A. (2014). The consequences of perceived discrimination for psychological well-being: A meta-analytic review. *Psychological Bulletin, 140,* 921–948. http://dx.doi.org/10.1037/a0035754

Spencer, M. B. (1983). Children's cultural values and parental child rearing strategies. *Developmental Review, 3,* 351–370. http://dx.doi.org/10.1016/0273-2297(83)90020-5

Stevenson, H. C. (1995). Relationship of adolescent perceptions of racial socialization to racial identity. *Journal of Black Psychology, 21,* 49–70. http://dx.doi.org/10.1177/00957984950211005

Stevenson, H. C., & Arrington, E. G. (2009). Racial/ethnic socialization mediates perceived racism and the racial identity of African American adolescents. *Cultural Diversity and Ethnic Minority Psychology, 15,* 125–136. http://dx.doi.org/10.1037/a0015510

Stevenson, H. C., Reed, J., & Bodison, P. (1996). Kinship social support and adolescent racial socialization beliefs: Extending the self to family. *The Journal of Black Psychology, 22,* 498–508. http://dx.doi.org/10.1177/00957984960224006

Sutton, R. M., & Douglas, K. M. (2005). Justice for all, or just for me? More evidence of the importance of the self-other distinction in just-world beliefs. *Personality and Individual Differences, 39,* 637–645. http://dx.doi.org/10.1016/j.paid.2005.02.010

Szymanski, D. M. (2012). Racist events and individual coping styles as predictors of African American activism. *The Journal of Black Psychology, 38,* 342–367. http://dx.doi.org/10.1177/0095798411424744

Treynor, W., Gonzalez, R., & Nolen-Hoeksema, S. (2003). Rumination reconsidered: A psychometric analysis. *Cognitive Therapy and Research, 27,* 247–259. http://dx.doi.org/10.1023/A:1023910315561

Tull, E. S., Sheu, Y. T., Butler, C., & Cornelious, K. (2005). Relationships between perceived stress, coping behavior and cortisol secretion in women with high and low levels of internalized racism. *Journal of the National Medical Association, 97,* 206–212.

Utsey, S. O., Adams, E. P., & Bolden, M. (2000). Development and initial validation of the Africultural Coping Systems Inventory. *The Journal of Black Psychology, 26*, 194–215. http://dx.doi.org/10.1177/00957984000026002005

Vera, E. M., Vacek, K., Coyle, L. D., Stinson, J., Mull, M., Doud, K., . . . Langrehr, K. J. (2011). An examination of culturally relevant stressors, coping, ethnic identity, and subjective well-being in urban, ethnic minority adolescents. *Professional School Counseling, 15*, 55–66. http://dx.doi.org/10.5330/PSC.n.2011-15.55

Wallston, K. A., Wallston, B. S., Smith, S., & Dobbins, C. J. (1987). Perceived control and health. *Current Psychological Research & Reviews, 6*, 5–25. http://dx.doi.org/10.1007/BF02686633

Wang, M. T., & Huguley, J. P. (2012). Parental racial socialization as a moderator of the effects of racial discrimination on educational success among African American adolescents. *Child Development, 83*, 1716–1731. http://dx.doi.org/10.1111/j.1467-8624.2012.01808.x

Wei, M., Alvarez, A. N., Ku, T. Y., Russell, D. W., & Bonett, D. G. (2010). Development and validation of a Coping with Discrimination Scale: Factor structure, reliability, and validity. *Journal of Counseling Psychology, 57*, 328–344. http://dx.doi.org/10.1037/a0019969

Wei, M., Ku, T. Y., Russell, D. W., Mallinckrodt, B., & Liao, K. Y. (2008). Moderating effects of three coping strategies and self-esteem on perceived discrimination and depressive symptoms: A minority stress model for Asian international students. *Journal of Counseling Psychology, 55*, 451–462. http://dx.doi.org/10.1037/a0012511

Wei, M., Yeh, C. J., Chao, R. C., Carrera, S., & Su, J. C. (2013). Family support, self-esteem, and perceived racial discrimination among Asian American male college students. *Journal of Counseling Psychology, 60*, 453–461. http://dx.doi.org/10.1037/a0032344

Williams, D. R., & Mohammed, S. A. (2009). Discrimination and racial disparities in health: Evidence and needed research. *Journal of Behavioral Medicine, 32*, 20–47. http://dx.doi.org/10.1007/s10865-008-9185-0

Zhu, X., Woo, S. E., Porter, C., & Brzezinski, M. (2013). Pathways to happiness: From personality to social networks and perceived support. *Social Networks, 35*, 382–393. http://dx.doi.org/10.1016/j.socnet.2013.04.005

II
CONTEXT AND COSTS

5

RACISM AND MENTAL HEALTH: EXAMINING THE LINK BETWEEN RACISM AND DEPRESSION FROM A SOCIAL COGNITIVE PERSPECTIVE

ELIZABETH BRONDOLO, WAN NG,
KRISTY-LEE J. PIERRE, AND ROBERT LANE

Racism and *ethnic discrimination* have been defined as "the processes, norms, ideologies, and behaviors that perpetuate racial inequality" (Gee, Ro, Shariff-Marco, & Chae, 2009, p. 130) Racism places a substantial strain on the mental health of targeted individuals, and the evidence indicates a consistent relationship of racism to a variety of mental health outcomes (Paradies, 2006; Pascoe & Smart Richman, 2009; Priest et al., 2013). Despite substantial growth in the research in this area, the specific pathways linking racism to mental health outcomes are still not well understood.

The underlying psychobiological pathways driving the development of mental health impairments share common features, but the disorders also have distinct psychobiological determinants and distinct neuropsychological profiles (Joormann & Vanderlind, 2014). The effects of racism, a salient and noxious psychosocial stressor, may vary depending on the biopsychosocial processes involved in the initiation and maintenance of the

http://dx.doi.org/10.1037/14852-006
The Cost of Racism for People of Color: Contextualizing Experiences of Discrimination, A. N. Alvarez,
C. T. H. Liang, and H. A. Neville (Editors)
Copyright © 2016 by the American Psychological Association. All rights reserved.

disorder. Therefore, to provide a mechanistic understanding of the ways in which racism can affect psychological processes within the individual, we focus on a single outcome: depression.

The evidence linking racism to both depressive symptoms and diagnosis of major depressive disorder is consistent, with effects seen across ages and across racial and ethnic groups (Kwok et al., 2011; Paradies, 2006; Priest et al., 2013). To develop an understanding of the mechanisms linking racism to depression, our review and discussion are guided by social cognitive models of the development and maintenance of depression (Beck, 1987; Hammen, Krantz, & Cochran, 1981; Joormann & Gotlib, 2010; Young, Klosko, & Weishaar, 2003). Our aim is to provide a framework for conceptualizing the specific social cognitive processes by which racial and ethnic discrimination lead to depression (see Figure 5.1). Some of these processes may be pertinent to other disorders as well.

Social cognitive models suggest that depression is a function of cognitive vulnerabilities within the individual, stress exposure, and their interaction (Beck, 1987). Considered broadly, these cognitive vulnerabilities can include negative schemas (i.e., underlying constellations of thoughts, attitudes, and affect) about the self, the world, and others (Beck, 2005; Halvorsen et al., 2009). Cognitive vulnerabilities also include impairments in cognitive control as a function of variations in attention, memory, and other cognitive processes involved in the regulation of affect and behavior (Joormann & Gotlib, 2010). These cognitive vulnerabilities can undermine effective responses to stress exposure and lead to the generation of new stressors, particularly interpersonal stressors (Liu & Alloy, 2010). A substantial body of research suggests that a wide range of cognitive vulnerabilities, as well as exposure to interpersonal stressors, contributes to the development and the maintenance of depressive symptoms (Eberhart, Auerbach, Bigda-Peyton, & Abela, 2011; Joormann & Vanderlind, 2014).

Initial models of social cognition and depression focused on cognitive vulnerabilities as they related to individual-level disadvantages or stressors (Beck, 1987, 2005). More recent investigations document the ways in which social and economic disadvantages in the broader environment contribute to the development of cognitive vulnerabilities (Miller, Chen, & Cole, 2009). One source of social and economic disadvantage stems from racial/ethnic prejudice.

Racial/ethnic prejudice reflects cultural, institutional- and individual-level assumptions (or stereotypes) about the characteristics associated with members of targeted groups. These assumptions drive biased beliefs about the relative rights and protections that should be afforded to members of these groups. When this prejudice is enacted in subtle and overt discriminatory behaviors, targeted individuals can experience threats to social inclusion, achievement, and safety (Brondolo, Ver Halen, Libby, & Pencille, 2010;

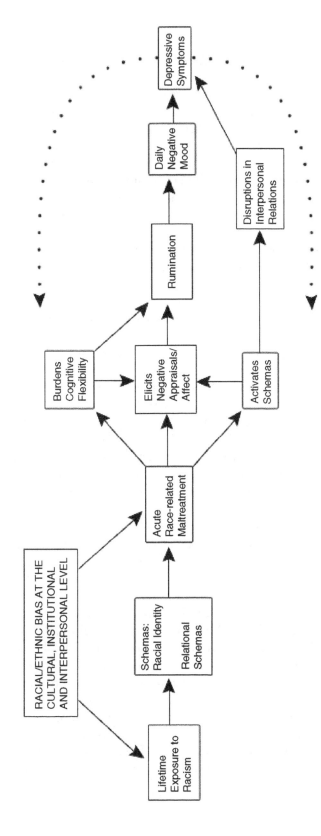

Figure 5.1. A model of the social-cognitive pathways leading from racism to depression.

Contrada et al., 2000; Harrell, 2000). These threats directly and indirectly limit access to social, economic, and political capital, affecting a wide range of interpersonal relationships and opportunities for development (Brondolo, Libretti, Rivera, & Walsemann, 2012; Brondolo et al., 2010).

Consistent with work by Cohen, Garcia, Purdie-Vaughns, Apfel, and Brzustoski (2009) on the drivers of racial disparities in educational achievement, we propose that exposure to racial and ethnic discrimination creates a recursive cycle precipitating and maintaining depressive symptoms (see Figure 5.1). As we review, the evidence suggests that exposure to racial and ethnic discrimination is associated with the development of negative schemas and cognitions about the self, others, and the world. These schemas may become activated when targeted group members experience race-related maltreatment directly or vicariously, when they recall past events, and across a wide variety of circumstances when their race holds heightened salience (e.g., when they are the only minority group member) or when they are exposed to race-related stereotypes (e.g., through the media; Dovidio, 2009).

Activation of these racism-related negative schemas may affect stress reactivity and stress recovery across a wide range of situations. Negative schemas about the self and the world can potentiate concerns about failure and fairness. These concerns can intensify appraisals of threat and harm in situations relevant to achievement or resource allocation (Brondolo, Ver Halen, Pencille, Beatty, & Contrada, 2009). Negative schemas about relations with others can potentiate concerns about exclusion and rejection. These concerns may undermine the quality of the relationships and reduce the effectiveness of these relationships at buffering the effects of race-related and other stressors (Liu & Alloy, 2010).

The effects of these schemas on stress reactivity and stress recovery are compounded by the effects of racism on cognitive flexibility. Acute exposure to race-related stress imposes cognitive demands, as individuals must first evaluate the intentions of the perpetrator and determine an appropriate course of action (Brondolo, Ver Halen, et al., 2009; Operario & Fiske, 2001). These demands can burden cognitive processing capacity, reducing cognitive flexibility (Murphy, Richeson, Shelton, Rheinschmidt, & Bergsieker, 2013). In turn, limitations in cognitive flexibility prolong exposure to negative thoughts and feelings and sustain rumination, a repetitive focus on negative information inherent to depression (Nolen-Hoeksema, 1991).

The transactional nature of the relationships among cognitive vulnerabilities, interpersonal stress, and negative mood may create a recursive cycle maintaining depressive symptoms (Calvete, Orue, & Hankin, 2013). Activation of one component of this cycle may exacerbate the effects of the others. Depressed mood undermines the motivation and energy required to break the cycle.

The effects of racism on identity may also contribute to the recursive nature of the relationships among cognitive processes, stress, and mood. Research suggests that racism increases the importance of race in personal and group identity (i.e., increases racial centrality; Quintana, 2007). But threats may become more painful and more difficult to resolve, the more they endanger core aspects of self and/or group identity (Thoits, 2013).

In this chapter, we identify sources of race-related stress and examine their effects on elements of this cycle, including cognitive vulnerabilities, interpersonal stress, identity, and depressive symptoms. Each section details what is currently known and delineates areas in need of further research. Our goal is to provide direction for research and intervention efforts designed to prevent discrimination and reduce its effects on mental health.

POTENTIAL MEDIATORS OF THE EFFECTS OF RACISM TO DEPRESSION: THE ROLE OF SCHEMAS

Potential mediators of the racism–depression relation can be examined within the context of social cognitive theories of depression (e.g., Cassidy, O'Connor, Howe, & Warden, 2004). Cognitive schemas, that is, the mental structures formed of beliefs, affect, and attitudes attained in past experiences (Mor & Inbar, 2009; Stein & Corte, 2008), are a central focus of these theories. They influence how people evaluate themselves and others, shape appraisals of current social interactions, and drive expectations of outcomes in future interactions (Mor & Inbar, 2009).

Schemas have a bidirectional relationship with the underlying cognitive processes involved in cognitive control and flexibility. Specifically, they govern the degree to which individuals attend to and remember negative information. In turn, underlying impairments in processes associated with attention or working memory are likely to influence the development and rigidity of underlying schemas (Joormann & Vanderlind, 2014).

As we discuss, studies of the mediators of the racism–depression relationship have evaluated the effects of racism on schemas about the self (e.g., self-esteem, personal control), schemas about the world at large (e.g., hostility, unjust world beliefs), and schemas about other people (e.g., race-based rejection sensitivity, stereotype confirmation concern), as well as schemas related to group identity (e.g., racial centrality). In the next section, we examine the evidence linking racism to these schemas and to underlying processes of cognitive control.

SCHEMAS ABOUT THE SELF

Self-schemas reflect consistent ideas about the self that are acquired during life experiences, including interactions with others (Markus, 1977). They can be organized along two primary dimensions: getting along (i.e., the ability to develop and maintain social connections), and getting ahead (i.e., the ability to advance our interests and protect our safety; Smith, 2014). Put another way, they reflect appraisals of personal social desirability or warmth, and competence and status. When self-schemas reflect negative evaluations (e.g., low social desirability, low ability), they can trigger the development of depressive symptoms (Beck, 1987).

Racial bias is likely to shape the development of self-schemas through communications about the social desirability, competence, and status associated with membership in different ethnic and racial groups (Brondolo et al., 2012). Racial bias both creates and reflects stereotyped beliefs about the characteristics associated with members of these groups. Communications about ethnic/racial stereotypes are likely to exert effects on targeted individual's schemas about themselves and others, because the content associated with racial and ethnic stereotypes maps easily onto the cognitive structure of these schemas (Cuddy, Fiske, & Glick, 2008; Smith, 2014).

When these stereotypes are widely disseminated (e.g., through the media, in institutional priorities, policies), they become part of the collective representations of the targeted groups shared by individuals both in and outside of the group (Crocker & Major, 1989). The cultural communication of stereotypes associated with a targeted groups' relative warmth and competence is likely to drive the expression of discriminatory behavior in interpersonal contexts (Blair, 2002; Brondolo et al., 2012; Krieger, 1999). For example, one diary study of African Americans revealed that among the most common exposures to discrimination in an interpersonal context were negative communications about competence (e.g., "Your ideas or opinions were minimized or ignored"; Burrow & Ong, 2010).

The persistence and pervasiveness of race-related maltreatment may make it difficult to avoid internalizing some of the negative evaluative messages into one's schemas about the self and one's racial/ethnic group. In fact, evidence from implicit association tests reveals that a substantial proportion of Black Americans show preference for images of Europeans versus African Americans (Ashburn-Nardo, Monteith, Arthur, & Bain, 2007; Jost, Banaji, & Nosek, 2004). *Intragroup racism* (i.e., discrimination by members of a targeted group to other members of the group) may also reflect the internalization of these negative stereotypes (Coard, Breland, & Raskin, 2001). Researchers hypothesized that persistent negative messages about one's racial or ethnic group would damage not only group esteem but also self-esteem, as social components of self-esteem reflect appraisals of (presumably discriminatory) attitudes from others (Gray-Little & Hafdahl, 2000; Twenge & Crocker, 2002).

Racism may also influence self-esteem though self-stereotyping. In self-stereotyping, stereotype-related information about one's racial or ethnic group is infused in an individual's identity as both a group member and individual. For example, when members of an ethnic group are stereotyped as "lazy," they may come to view their group and themselves as "lazy" as well.

The threat of race-based maltreatment may partly drive this self-stereotyping (Latrofa, Vaes, & Cadinu, 2012). When individuals belong to low-status groups and are threatened by members of a higher status group, they are more likely to describe themselves as possessing both the positive and negative characteristics associated with the collective representations of their ingroup. Endorsing stereotyped characteristics of one's racial/ethnic group as self-relevant may strengthen the ingroup connection and may consequently offset some of the negative emotional impact of race-related maltreatment (Latrofa et al., 2012).

But this connection may come at a price. Ingroup characteristics may become embedded into schemas related to personal identity, because minority group members may have closer relationships between their ethnic group identity and their personal identity (Latrofa et al., 2012). When group stereotypes reflect negative traits, endorsing them may undermine self-esteem.

The data on the relationship of racism to explicit measures of self-esteem have been evaluated in two systematic reviews (Paradies, 2006; Priest et al., 2013). In the review of 26 studies of adults, Paradies (2006) reported that 35% ($n = 9$) found a negative relationship of racism to self-esteem, whereas half ($n = 13$) found no association. In the review of studies of children, 62% ($n = 58/93$) reported a negative relationship between racism and self-esteem, although an additional study found a positive relationship between racism and negative self-esteem.

Self-esteem may also mediate the relationship of racism to depression, although the effects are not fully consistent. Specifically, self-esteem was a significant mediator of the association of racism to depression among men (but not women) of Chinese, Indian, and Pakistani descent, living in Scotland, (Cassidy et al., 2004); among Latino adolescents, particularly those who were highly acculturated (Umaña-Taylor & Updegraff, 2007); and among participants in a large population-based sample of mixed-race individuals in the United States (Branscombe, Schmitt, & Harvey, 1999; Hunte, King, Hicken, Lee, & Lewis, 2013). Moradi and Risco (2006) additionally reported that self-esteem mediates the relationship of discrimination to distress among Latino/as, but only when perceived control is added to the model.

Another component of self-schemas that has been investigated in the context of racism includes personal control (i.e., beliefs in one's ability to determine the outcome of personally salient events). Racism is negatively related to perceived control in some studies (Moradi & Hasan, 2004; Moradi & Risco, 2006). Evidence from some (Moradi & Hasan, 2004; Moradi & Risco, 2006) but not all (Lambert, Herman, Bynum, & Ialongo, 2009) studies suggests that perceived control mediates at least a portion of the relationship of racism to depression.

In sum, racism appears to be negatively associated with schemas about the self, including self-esteem and personal control. However, the effects are inconsistent, as a substantial proportion of studies failed to find these relationships (Paradies, 2006; Priest et al., 2013). Some studies suggest that self-esteem (Cassidy et al., 2004; Umaña-Taylor & Updegraff, 2007) and, to a lesser degree, personal control, mediate the relationship of racism to depressive symptoms (Moradi & Hasan, 2004; Moradi & Risco, 2006).

Further research is needed in a number of areas. The inconsistent findings in studies of the association of racism to self-esteem suggest that there may be important moderators or buffers of the effects of racism. One experimental study suggests that the framing of the race-related stress may matter. When individuals viewed exposure to racism as part of their group's historic and ongoing struggle against oppression, the effects of race-related maltreatment on self-esteem were mitigated (Tawa, Suyemoto, & Roemer, 2012).

Linked to this notion, cultural orientation (i.e., individualistic vs. collectivistic orientation) may support Black Americans' self-esteem (Twenge & Crocker, 2002). Black Americans report higher levels of individualism than any other group, with a specific focus on individual uniqueness and social equality (Vargas & Kemmelmeier, 2013). Twenge and Crocker (2002) suggested that individualism may render external threats to self-esteem less relevant. Research identifying other individual-, family-, and community-level buffers is needed.

Racial socialization efforts focused on racial pride and self-respect may help minority individuals buffer some of the effects of discrimination on explicit self-esteem (Brondolo, Ver Halen, et al., 2009; Rivas-Drake et al., 2014). However, it is unclear if efforts to increase explicit racial pride protect against racism-related decreases in nonconscious or implicit self-esteem. Implicit self-esteem has been linked to depression in longitudinal studies (Sowislo & Orth, 2013).

Discrepancies between explicit and implicit self-esteem (i.e., fragile self-esteem) have been associated with depression and with increased interpersonal stress (Borton, Crimmins, Ashby, & Ruddiman, 2012). It would be valuable to investigate whether racism may foster similar discrepancies between explicit and implicit group esteem. For example, Black individuals who believe others have a negative view of their group (i.e., are aware of racial prejudice) demonstrated less implicit preference for Blacks versus Europeans on implicit association tests, even when their explicit attitudes towards their group were highly positive (Livingston, 2002). Among Black Americans, implicit preferences for Europeans have been associated with depressive symptoms (Ashburn-Nardo et al., 2007). Similar relationships of implicit antigay bias to depressive symptoms have been seen in studies of gay adults (Hatzenbuehler, Dovidio, Nolen-Hoeksema, & Phills, 2009).

SCHEMAS ABOUT THE WORLD

Schemas about the world reflect underlying beliefs about the predictability and controllability of the environment, and may contribute to depressive symptoms when they reflect beliefs that the individual will not be treated in a fair or just way (Beck, 1987). Discriminatory behavior may permit some groups to gain access to resources and privileges at the expense of others. Perceiving unfair treatment might reasonably result in the development of negative cognitions about fairness and justice in one's dealings with the world at large.

Studies of racism's effects on negative cognitions about the world have measured cynical hostility, cultural mistrust, and unjust world beliefs. Exposure to racism has been consistently positively associated with hostility (Branscombe et al., 1999; Brondolo, Libby, et al., 2008; Brondolo et al., 2011; Broudy et al., 2007; Hunte et al., 2013; Krieger et al., 2011), cultural mistrust (Benkert, Peters, Clark, & Keves-Foster, 2006), and beliefs in an unjust world. Hostility significantly mediated the relation of interpersonal racism to depression in a large population-based sample (Hunte et al., 2013). Beliefs in an unjust world (e.g., believing effort is not fairly rewarded and bad acts may go unpunished) mediated the relation of racism to anxiety and social connectedness but not depressive symptoms (Liang & Borders, 2012).

In sum, the data linking racism to different types of negative schemas about the world are more consistent and clear than the data on the relation of racism to cognitions about the self. Some negative world schemas, such as hostility, are also related to depressive symptoms. Negative schemas linked to hostility appear to mediate the effect of racism on depression.

Further research is needed to understand the specific characteristics of negative schemas about the world, which mediate the relationship of racism to depression. Consistent with theories of hopelessness (Abramson, Metalsky, & Alloy, 1989), the data suggest that schemas are likely to be depressogenic when their content reflects the notion that individuals cannot personally exert effective control over the outcomes of their efforts. It will be important to identify the types of cognitions that reflect a realistic assessment of potential hazards, limitations, and opportunities without undermining hope and self-efficacy.

Institutional racism is likely to drive negative schemas about the world. For example, inadequate representation of minority group members in important social and political functions may prevent the growth of trust and engagement (Vargas & Kemmelmeier, 2013). However, such hypotheses have yet to be adequately tested. Information on the degree to which the relation of racism to negative cognitions about the world varies with membership in other vulnerable groups (e.g., low socioeconomic status, sexual minority) is insufficient. Exposure to multiple hazards may shape the meaning and effects of negative world cognitions (Cole, 2009).

SCHEMAS ABOUT OTHERS AND THEIR EFFECTS ON RELATIONSHIPS WITH OTHERS

Relational schemas are schemas about others and their effects on relationships with others (Baldwin, 1992). They reflect one's point of view when thinking about other people (i.e., mental representations of others, including one's view of their relative warmth and status). They also reflect beliefs about the degree to which others view us with warmth and acceptance. When activated, relational schemas can drive people's expectations about and appraisals of the costs, benefits, and course of social interactions (Miranda, Andersen, & Edwards, 2013).

Relational schemas develop from one's social experiences. When interpersonal, institutional, and cultural racism shapes social experiences, effects on relational schemas are likely as well (Brondolo et al., 2012). Consistent with the recognition of the effects of racism on interpersonal relationships, much of the research on the psychological sequelae of racism has focused on constructs that can be considered within the domain of relational schemas.

Racism has been positively associated with beliefs about the influence of racial bias on health care providers' warmth and responsiveness (e.g., provider mistrust; Benkert et al., 2006), as well as with schemas reflecting other peoples' attitudes towards one's racial or ethnic group (e.g., public regard; Sellers, Smith, Shelton, Rowley, & Chavous, 1998) and collective group esteem (Crocker, Luhtanen, Blaine, & Broadnax, 1994). Furthermore, racism has been positively associated with the anticipation of social judgment or rejection because of another's racial/ethnic bias, as assessed in constructs such as stereotype confirmation concern (Contrada et al., 2000,

2001; Schmader & Croft, 2011), race-based rejection sensitivity (Mendoza-Denton, Downey, Purdie, Davis, & Pietrzak, 2002), and stigma consciousness (Pinel, 1999).

These constructs serve as racism-related relational schemas, because they reflect concerns about the way the racial/ethnic bias of others may affect interpersonal interactions. These relational schemas, like all schemas, can increase cognitive vulnerability, because of their effects on attention, memory, and mood. Specifically, some relational schemas are associated with increased focus on other people's approval. In the presence of social threat, a heightened need to avoid negative evaluations (or gain approval) from others has been documented to increase risk for depression (Miranda, Andersen, & Edwards, 2013). Other relational schemas, including stereotype confirmation concern, can increase self-focused attention, as individuals try to evaluate their risk for confirming negative stereotypes. Increases in vigilant self-focused attention are also likely to increase negative mood (Mor & Winquist, 2002).

Race-based relational schemas appear to increase risk for negative psychosocial outcomes. For example, prior research reports positive associations of stereotype confirmation concern with depressive symptoms (French & Chavez, 2010), and of both race-based rejection sensitivity and stigma consciousness with psychological distress (Mendoza-Denton et al., 2002). Public regard has been negatively associated with psychological distress (Lee & Ahn, 2013).

RELATIONAL SCHEMAS AND THE GENERATION OF INTERPERSONAL STRESS

Social cognitive theories of depression suggest relational schemas increase the risk for depression in the presence of interpersonal stress (Calvete et al., 2013). Racism increases the risk for exposure to interpersonal stress (Brondolo et al., 2012). Studies assessing race-related maltreatment on a daily and weekly basis suggest some members of racial and ethnic minority groups endure episodes of interpersonal race-/ethnicity-related maltreatment several times per week (Burrow & Ong, 2010; Mallett & Swim, 2009). Relational schemas may arise in response to such ongoing race-related interpersonal stressors. Stress generation theories suggest negative relational schemas activate in response to interpersonal stress and potentiate depression by increasing the degree to which these episodes elicit distress (Liu & Alloy, 2010).

Racism-based relational schemas also may be activated when individuals anticipate prejudicial attitudes or discriminatory behavior (Nuru-Jeter et al.,

2014). Individuals may feel compelled to be vigilant, both to avoid a direct race-related threat and to avoid confirming negative views of their in-group and themselves (Ruiz, 2014). Consequently, relational schemas may contribute to new interpersonal stressors. Consistent with these ideas, race-based rejection sensitivity (Mendoza-Denton et al., 2002) and low public regard (Liang & Fassinger, 2008) have been associated with self-reported difficulty in interpersonal relationships.

In sum, racism appears to foster a wide range of race-based negative relational schemas. Race-based relational schemas are associated with indices of psychological distress, including depressive symptoms. Relational schemas may be associated with increased risk for depression, at least in part through their effects on responses to interpersonal stress. The effects of racism on interpersonal relationships may explain, in part, how the link between racism and depression can become self-perpetuating. Racism may undermine a broad range of interpersonal relationships that could help buffer the effects of other stressors on depression.

More research is needed on the relations between racism, relational schemas and interpersonal stress, and depression. Researchers have begun exploring these pathways in studies of the effects of racism on marriage (Simons, Simons, Lei, & Landor, 2012) and on interactions between health care providers and patients (Blair et al., 2013). More work is needed on the effects of racism on relational schemas in other contexts (i.e., at work or school; Brondolo & Jean-Pierre, 2014). Research is required to develop interventions to mitigate the effects of racism on negative relational schemas that drive interpersonal stress, particularly in interracial contexts.

Not all negative relational schemas are depressogenic. Some research indicates that certain relational schemas may buffer the effects of racism on depression, although the outcomes vary depending on the context and tone of the messages. Specifically, studies suggest that preparation for bias (as reflected in low public regard), may attenuate the effects of racism on psychological distress (Sellers, Caldwell, Schmeelk-Cone, & Zimmerman, 2003; Sellers & Shelton, 2003), but the context in which these messages are delivered moderates their effects. For example, a recent study indicates that low public regard is positively associated with depression among individuals living in a racially segregated area and is inversely associated with depression among individuals who live in a more integrated area (Hurd, Sellers, Cogburn, Butler-Barnes, & Zimmerman, 2013). In a highly integrated area, low public regard may serve to prepare individuals for potentially negative encounters. More work is needed to explicitly identify contextual variables, including neighborhood characteristics and the nature of personal relationships that affect the development of these relational schemas and depression.

THE ROLE OF IDENTITY

A review of the effects of racial identity on depression is outside this chapter's scope (but see Brondolo, Ver Halen, et al., 2009; Lee & Ahn, 2013). Here, we focus on how the effects of racism on the development of racial identity may contribute to the recursive nature of the relationships among schemas, stress, and depressive symptoms.

Events that are related to personal identity are more likely to be perceived as stressful, and consequently may have greater effects on self-esteem or negative mood (Thoits, 2013). Evidence from longitudinal studies suggests that exposure to racism appears to increase racial centrality (i.e., the importance of race to one's personal identity; Quintana, 2007). Given the widespread communication of stereotypes about racial and ethnic groups, an increase in racial centrality may also increase the relevance of a wide range of stereotyped characteristics to personal and group identity (Latrofa et al., 2012).

The greater the number of stereotypes, the more situations may be capable of activating identity-related schemas and evoking stereotype threat effects. For example, if a targeted racial group is exposed to negative stereotypes about intellectual ability, then tasks needing intellectual effort may activate identity-related concerns, especially if race is made salient at the same time. If a group is stereotyped as low in warmth, then a wide range of interpersonal situation may evoke stereotype threats.

Processes related to stereotype threat are well understood to contribute to impairments in achievement (Schmader & Croft, 2011; Steele & Aronson, 1995). These processes may confer increased risk of depression as well. Although the evidence is not consistent, attention to race-related maltreatment may increase the frequency of stressor exposure and heighten stress reactivity to these events (Thoits, 2013).

More specific to the development of depression, threats to group identity may have inadvertent effects on interpersonal stress generation. Racism heightens identification with one's own group in part to promote a sense of belonging (Latrofa et al., 2012; Rudman, Dohn, & Fairchild, 2007). But studies of self-esteem compensation processes suggest that a heightened sense of belonging may be accompanied by an increase in implicit levels of antipathy towards others outside of the group (Rudman et al., 2007). Furthermore, some evidence indicates that White individuals exhibit more prejudice and potentially discriminatory behavior towards strongly identified minorities (Kaiser & Pratt-Hyatt, 2009). Further research is needed to identify and disseminate strategies that can support the development of racial identity while minimizing the potential psychosocial costs.

EFFECTS OF RACISM ON UNDERLYING COGNITIVE PROCESSES

Schemas may serve as both antecedents to, and consequences of, cognitive processes related to perception, attention, and memory that drive and maintain depressive symptoms (see the review by Joormann & Gotlib, 2010). Substantial evidence suggests that depressed individuals display deficits in cognitive control or flexibility that would enable them to turn their attention away from negative events and experience some attenuation of negative mood (see the review by Joormann & Gotlib, 2010). This sustained focus may be experienced as rumination or perseverative cognition, a key feature of depression (Nolen-Hoeksema, 1991). Further, rumination may reinforce negative schemas, maintaining depressive symptoms.

A growing body of evidence suggests that racism places a substantial burden on cognitive processes and consequently creates limitations to cognitive control. Specifically, exposure to race-based maltreatment presents a series of cognitive demands as the targeted individual must determine if the episode was a function of intentional or unintentional racial bias, and decide how to cope (Brondolo, Ver Halen, et al., 2009; Operario & Fiske, 2001). Given the potential importance of determining the motivation behind particular events, targets can devote sustained attention both to the event and to their affective response. Sustained attention to threat is known to be depressogenic (see the review by Joormann & Gotlib, 2010).

The cognitive costs of this sustained attention are beginning to be documented. Recent laboratory research suggests that when situations involve subtle versus blatant racism the cognitive demands are greater (Murphy et al., 2013). Participants showed reduced capacity on a test of working memory and cognitive flexibility after they engaged in tasks involving laboratory analogues of subtle versus blatant racism. Other experimental data reveal that hearing expressed blatant racial bias in a mixed race situation was associated with reduced cognitive flexibility on an emotional Stroop test (Bair & Steele, 2010). On a more positive note, instructions to promote positive interracial interactions were associated with improved cognitive performance on tests of working memory (Trawalter & Richeson, 2006).

Difficulties in evaluating and coping with racism and potential impairments in cognitive flexibility may lead to rumination (Brondolo, Ver Halen, et al., 2009). Several recent studies suggest that angry or brooding rumination may mediate the relation of racism to depressive symptoms (Borders & Liang, 2011; Miranda, Polanco-Roman, Tsypes, & Valderrama, 2013).

Impairments in cognitive flexibility may also contribute to depression through their effects on interpersonal stress generation. Both depression itself and other excess demands on working memory affect recognition of facial expression of emotions (Joormann & Gotlib, 2010; Phillips, Channon,

Tunstall, Hedenstrom, & Lyons, 2008). Limitations in emotion recognition may inhibit negotiation of complex social interactions or reconciliation following conflict.

This is still a very new area of research. It will be helpful to understand the degree to which the effects of racism on cognitive functioning are predictive of depressive symptoms, and if depressive symptoms worsen the effects of race-related maltreatment on cognitive functioning. Additional studies are needed to identify the aspects of exposure to racism that create the greatest cognitive demands. Studies examining moderators of these effects, including socioeconomic status, presence of social support, and other factors will be valuable.

SUMMARY AND CONCLUSIONS

Racism has substantial effects on social cognitive processes that contribute to the development of depression. Racism is associated with every type of cognitive vulnerability assessed, including negative schemas about the self and the world, and a broad range of relational schemas. The effects are particularly consistent across a wide range of schemas about the nature of relationships with other individuals (i.e., relational schemas). The data on the direct effects of racism on schemas about the self are less consistent than the findings for relational schemas and schemas about the world. However, self-schemas (i.e., self-esteem and personal control) appear to mediate the relationship of racism to depression.

Racism may increase exposure to interpersonal stressors that exacerbate the recursive nature of the relationships among schemas, interpersonal stress, and depressive symptoms. Racism itself is an interpersonal stressor, and studies document an association of racism to other types of interpersonal stress (e.g., Broudy et al., 2007). Racism may generate the development of relational schemas that undermine trust and increase hypervigilance in interpersonal relationships. Discrimination-related influences on relational schemas may heighten affective reactivity to interpersonal stress and contribute to the generation of new interpersonal stressors. Race-related threats may also trigger self-esteem compensation processes that can intensify inter-group conflict. In turn, increases in interpersonal stress may exacerbate the effects of negative schemas on depression. Ultimately, persistent depressed mood may inhibit motivation and exploration, blocking the individual's ability to develop the competencies and relationships that can support more positive schemas and improve mood (Brondolo et al., 2010).

Exposure to racism is also associated with increased burdens on cognitive functioning. The demands of evaluating episodes of maltreatment and potential responses appear to decrease cognitive flexibility. This may inhibit shifting focus away from events that evoke threat and loss. Rumination about race-related maltreatment may prolong the distress from race-related threat.

Racism intensifies aspects of racial identity, in particular racial centrality (Quintana, 2007). The evidence is inconsistent, but it has been suggested increases in identity can also increase reactivity to race-related stress (Thoits, 2013). Efforts to improve racial or ethnic pride appear to buffer the effects of racism on self-esteem, but much evidence suggests ethnic pride may be insufficient to counter racism's effects on depression (Brondolo, Ver Halen, et al., 2009). Further study of the most effective messages and contexts to support racial and ethnic identity is needed.

Ultimately, individual-level efforts at strengthening identity may prove inadequate, because the problem is not of the targeted individual's making. Even with strong ingroup belonging, gaps in full inclusion and belonging remain for individuals who are targeted for discrimination. The capacity to address these gaps and reduce race or ethnicity-related ostracism requires collaboration on the part of all involved groups. New interventions based on an application of social cognitive principles suggest that approaches to improve cross race/ethnic interactions and support health can be effective (Avery, Richeson, Hebl, & Ambady, 2009). The public health consequences of racism reinforce the importance of addressing these issues.

Mechanistic research to identify the pathways leading from racism to depression can provide new targets for interventions to reduce discrimination and ameliorate its effects on depression and other health outcomes. But the pervasive communication of negative racial stereotypes can also affect the relational schemas held by majority group members. Majority group members may also fear engaging with individuals of a different race, potentially undermining collaborative action (Richeson & Shelton, 2007).

One aim of this chapter has been to provide a vocabulary and structure for cross-race and within-race conversations about the effects of racism on mental health. We hope explicating these issues can help individuals speak the subtext necessary to clarify communication. When the communication is clearer, individuals from all groups can share in the efforts to reduce discrimination and mitigate the effects on mental health (Brondolo & Jean-Pierre, 2014).

REFERENCES

Abramson, L. Y., Metalsky, G. I., & Alloy, L. B. (1989). Hopelessness depression: A theory-based subtype of depression. *Psychological Review, 96*, 358–372. http://dx.doi.org/10.1037/0033-295X.96.2.358

Ashburn-Nardo, L., Monteith, M. J., Arthur, S. A., & Bain, A. (2007). Race and the psychological health of African Americans. *Group Processes & Intergroup Relations, 10,* 471–491. http://dx.doi.org/10.1177/1368430207081536

Avery, D. R., Richeson, J. A., Hebl, M. R., & Ambady, N. (2009). It does not have to be uncomfortable: The role of behavioral scripts in Black–White interracial interactions. *Journal of Applied Psychology, 94,* 1382–1393. http://dx.doi.org/10.1037/a0016208

Bair, A. N., & Steele, J. R. (2010). Examining the consequences of exposure to racism for the executive functioning of Black students. *Journal of Experimental Social Psychology, 46,* 127–132. http://dx.doi.org/10.1016/j.jesp.2009.08.016

Baldwin, M. W. (1992). Relational schemas and the processing of social information. *Psychological Bulletin, 112,* 461–484. http://dx.doi.org/10.1037/0033-2909.112.3.461

Beck, A. T. (1987). Cognitive models of depression. *Journal of Cognitive Psychotherapy, 1,* 5–37.

Beck, A. T. (2005). The current state of cognitive therapy: A 40-year retrospective. *Archives of General Psychiatry, 62,* 953–959. http://dx.doi.org/10.1001/archpsyc.62.9.953

Benkert, R., Peters, R. M., Clark, R., & Keves-Foster, K. (2006). Effects of perceived racism, cultural mistrust and trust in providers on satisfaction with care. *JAMA, 98,* 1532–1540.

Blair, I. V. (2002). The malleability of automatic stereotypes and prejudice. *Personality and Social Psychology Review, 6,* 242–261. http://dx.doi.org/10.1207/S15327957PSPR0603_8

Blair, I. V., Steiner, J. F., Fairclough, D. L., Hanratty, R., Price, D. W., Hirsh, H. K., . . . Havranek, E. P. (2013). Clinicians' implicit ethnic/racial bias and perceptions of care among Black and Latino patients. *Annals of Family Medicine, 11,* 43–52. http://dx.doi.org/10.1370/afm.1442

Borders, A., & Liang, C. T. H. (2011). Rumination partially mediates the associations between perceived ethnic discrimination, emotional distress, and aggression. *Cultural Diversity & Ethnic Minority Psychology, 17,* 125–133. http://dx.doi.org/10.1037/a0023357

Borton, J. L. S., Crimmins, A. E., Ashby, R. S., & Ruddiman, J. F. (2012). How do individuals with fragile high self-esteem cope with intrusive thoughts following ego threat? *Self and Identity, 11,* 16–35. http://dx.doi.org/10.1080/15298868.2010.500935

Branscombe, N. R., Schmitt, M. T., & Harvey, R. D. (1999). Perceiving pervasive discrimination among African-Americans: Implications for group identification and well-being. *Journal of Personality and Social Psychology, 77,* 135–149. http://dx.doi.org/10.1037/0022-3514.77.1.135

Brondolo, E., Beatty, D. L., Cubbin, C., Pencille, M., Saegert, S., Wellington, R., . . . Schwartz, J. (2009). Sociodemographic variations in self-reported racism in a community sample of Blacks and Latino(a)s. *Journal of Applied Social Psychology, 39,* 407–429. http://dx.doi.org/10.1111/j.1559-1816.2008.00444.x

Brondolo, E., Hausmann, L. R. M., Jhalani, J., Pencille, M., Atencio-Bacayon, J., Kumar, A., . . . Schwartz, J. (2011). Dimensions of perceived racism and self-reported health: Examination of racial/ethnic differences and potential mediators. *Annals of Behavioral Medicine, 42,* 14–28. http://dx.doi.org/10.1007/s12160-011-9265-1

Brondolo, E., & Jean-Pierre, K. L. (2014). "You said, I heard": Speaking the subtext in interracial conversations to reduce racial disparities in achievement. In A. Kalet & C. Chou (Eds.), *A midcourse correction: A framework for remediation of physician trainees/A workbook for clinical educators* (pp. 131–156). New York, NY: Springer.

Brondolo, E., Libby, D. J., Denton, E. G., Thompson, S., Beatty, D. L., Schwartz, J., . . . Gerin, W. (2008). Racism and ambulatory blood pressure in a community sample. *Psychosomatic Medicine, 70,* 49–56. http://dx.doi.org/10.1097/PSY.0b013e31815ff3bd

Brondolo, E., Libretti, M., Rivera, L., & Walsemann, K. M. (2012). Racism and social capital: The implications for social and physical well-being. *Journal of Social Issues, 68,* 358–384. http://dx.doi.org/10.1111/j.1540-4560.2012.01752.x

Brondolo, E., Ver Halen, N. B., Libby, D. J., & Pencille, M. (2010). Racism as a psychosocial stressor. In A. Baum & R. J. Contrada (Eds.), *The handbook of stress science: Psychology, medicine and health* (pp. 167–184). New York, NY: Springer.

Brondolo, E., Ver Halen, N. B., Pencille, M., Beatty, D., & Contrada, R. J. (2009). Coping with racism: A selective review of the literature and a theoretical and methodological critique. *Journal of Behavioral Medicine, 32,* 64–88. http://dx.doi.org/10.1007/s10865-008-9193-0

Broudy, R., Brondolo, E., Coakley, V., Ver Halen, N. B., Cassells, A., Tobin, J. N., & Sweeney, M. (2007). Perceived ethnic discrimination in relation to daily moods and negative social interactions. *Journal of Behavioral Medicine, 30,* 31–43. http://dx.doi.org/10.1007/s10865-006-9081-4

Burrow, A. L., & Ong, A. D. (2010). Racial identity as a moderator of daily exposure and reactivity to racial discrimination. *Self and Identity, 9,* 383–402. http://dx.doi.org/10.1080/15298860903192496

Calvete, E., Orue, I., & Hankin, B. L. (2013). Transactional relationships among cognitive vulnerabilities, stressors, and depressive symptoms in adolescence. *Journal of Abnormal Child Psychology, 41,* 399–410. http://dx.doi.org/10.1007/s10802-012-9691-y

Cassidy, C., O'Connor, R. C., Howe, C., & Warden, D. (2004). Perceived discrimination and psychological distress: The role of personal and ethnic self-esteem. *Journal of Counseling Psychology, 51,* 329–339.

Coard, S. I., Breland, A. M., & Raskin, P. (2001). Perceptions of and preferences for skin color, Black racial identity, and self-esteem among African Americans. *Journal of Applied Social Psychology, 31,* 2256–2274. http://dx.doi.org/10.1111/j.1559-1816.2001.tb00174.x

Cohen, G. L., Garcia, J., Purdie-Vaughns, V., Apfel, N., & Brzustoski, P. (2009, April 17). Recursive processes in self-affirmation: Intervening to close the minority achievement gap. *Science, 324,* 400–403. http://dx.doi.org/10.1126/science.1170769

Cole, E. R. (2009). Intersectionality and research in psychology. *American Psychologist, 64,* 170–180. http://dx.doi.org/10.1037/a0014564

Contrada, R. J., Ashmore, R. D., Gary, M. L., Coups, E., Egeth, J. D., Sewell, A., . . . Chasse, V. (2001). Measures of ethnicity-related stress: Psychometric properties, ethnic group differences, and associations with well-being. *Journal of Applied Social Psychology, 31,* 1775–1820. http://dx.doi.org/10.1111/j.1559-1816.2001.tb00205.x

Contrada, R. J., Ashmore, R. D., Gary, M. L., Coups, E., Egeth, J. D., Sewell, A., . . . Chasse, V. (2000). Ethnicity-related sources of stress and their effects on well-being. *Current Directions in Psychological Science, 9,* 136–139. http://dx.doi.org/10.1111/1467-8721.00078

Crocker, J., Luhtanen, R., Blaine, B., & Broadnax, S. (1994). Collective self-esteem and psychological well-being among White, Black, and Asian college students. *Personality and Social Psychology Bulletin, 20,* 503–513. http://dx.doi.org/10.1177/0146167294205007

Crocker, J., & Major, B. (1989). Social stigma and self-esteem: The self-protective properties of stigma. *Psychological Review, 96,* 608–630. http://dx.doi.org/10.1037/0033-295X.96.4.608

Cuddy, A. J. C., Fiske, S. T., & Glick, P. (2008). Warmth and competence as universal dimensions of social perception: The stereotype content model and the BIAS map. In M. P. Zanna (Ed.), *Advances in experimental social psychology* (pp. 61–149). San Diego, CA: Elsevier Academic Press.

Dovidio, J. F. (2009). Psychology: Racial bias, unspoken but heard. *Science, 326,* 1641–1642. http://dx.doi.org/10.1126/science.1184231

Eberhart, N. K., Auerbach, R. P., Bigda-Peyton, J., & Abela, J. R. Z. (2011). Maladaptive schemas and depression: Tests of stress generation and diathesis-stress models. *Journal of Social and Clinical Psychology, 30,* 75–104. http://dx.doi.org/10.1521/jscp.2011.30.1.75

French, S. E., & Chavez, N. R. (2010). The relationship of ethnicity-related stressors and Latino ethnic identity to well-being. *Hispanic Journal of Behavioral Sciences, 32,* 410–428. http://dx.doi.org/10.1177/0739986310374716

Gee, G. C., Ro, A., Shariff-Marco, S., & Chae, D. (2009). Racial discrimination and health among Asian Americans: Evidence, assessment, and directions for future research. *Epidemiologic Reviews, 31,* 130–151. http://dx.doi.org/10.1093/epirev/mxp009

Gray-Little, B., & Hafdahl, A. R. (2000). Factors influencing racial comparisons of self-esteem: A quantitative review. *Psychological Bulletin, 126,* 26–54.

Halvorsen, M., Wang, C. E., Richter, J., Myrland, I., Pedersen, S. K., Eisemann, M., & Waterloo, K. (2009). Early maladaptive schemas, temperament and character traits in clinically depressed and previously depressed subjects. *Clinical Psychology & Psychotherapy, 16,* 394–407. http://dx.doi.org/10.1002/cpp.618

Hammen, C. L., Krantz, S. E., & Cochran, S. D. (1981). Relationships between depression and causal attributions about stressful life events. *Cognitive Therapy and Research, 5,* 351–358. http://dx.doi.org/10.1007/BF01173686

Hatzenbuehler, M. L., Dovidio, J. F., Nolen-Hoeksema, S., & Phills, C. E. (2009). An implicit measure of anti-gay attitudes: Prospective associations with emotion regulation strategies and psychological distress. *Journal of Experimental Social Psychology, 45,* 1316–1320. http://dx.doi.org/10.1016/j.jesp.2009.08.005

Harrell, S. P. (2000). A multidimensional conceptualization of racism-related stress: Implications for the well-being of people of color. *American Journal of Orthopsychiatry, 70,* 42–57. http://dx.doi.org/10.1037/h0087722

Hunte, H. E. R., King, K., Hicken, M., Lee, H., & Lewis, T. T. (2013). Interpersonal discrimination and depressive symptomatology: Examination of several personality-related characteristics as potential confounders in a racial/ethnic heterogeneous adult sample. *BMC Public Health, 13,* 1084. http://dx.doi.org/10.1186/1471-2458-13-1084

Hurd, N. M., Sellers, R. M., Cogburn, C. D., Butler-Barnes, S. T., & Zimmerman, M. A. (2013). Racial identity and depressive symptoms among Black emerging adults: The moderating effects of neighborhood racial composition. *Developmental Psychology, 49,* 938–950. http://dx.doi.org/10.1037/a0028826

Joormann, J., & Gotlib, I. H. (2010). Emotion regulation in depression: Relation to cognitive inhibition. *Cognition and Emotion, 24,* 281–298. http://dx.doi.org/10.1080/02699930903407948

Joormann, J., & Vanderlind, W. M. (2014). Emotion regulation in depression the role of biased cognition and reduced cognitive control. *Clinical Psychological Science, 2,* 402–421. http://dx.doi.org/10.1177/2167702614536163

Jost, J. T., Banaji, M. R., & Nosek, B. A. (2004). A decade of system justification theory: Accumulated evidence of conscious and unconscious bolstering of the status quo. *Political Psychology, 25,* 881–919. http://dx.doi.org/10.1111/j.1467-9221.2004.00402.x

Kaiser, C. R., & Pratt-Hyatt, J. S. (2009). Distributing prejudice unequally: Do Whites direct their prejudice toward strongly identified minorities? *Journal of Personality and Social Psychology, 96,* 432–445. http://dx.doi.org/10.1037/a0012877

Krieger, N. (1999). Embodying inequality: a review of concepts, measures, and methods for studying health consequences of discrimination. *International Journal of Health Services: Planning, Administration, Evaluation, 29,* 295–352.

Krieger, N., Waterman, P. D., Kosheleva, A., Chen, J. T., Carney, D. R., Smith, K. W., . . . Samuel, L. (2011). Exposing racial discrimination: Implicit & explicit measures—the My Body, My Story study of 1,005 U.S.-born Black and White community health center members. *PLoS ONE, 6,* e27636. http://dx.doi.org/10.1371/journal.pone.0027636

Kwok, J., Atencio, J., Ullah, J., Crupi, R., Chen, D., Roth, A. R., . . . Brondolo, E. (2011). The perceived ethnic discrimination questionnaire—community version: Validation in a multiethnic Asian sample. *Cultural Diversity & Ethnic Minority Psychology, 17*, 271–282. http://dx.doi.org/10.1037/a0024034

Lambert, S. F., Herman, K. C., Bynum, M. S., & Ialongo, N. S. (2009). Perceptions of racism and depressive symptoms in African American adolescents: The role of perceived academic and social control. *Journal of Youth and Adolescence, 38*, 519–531. http://dx.doi.org/10.1007/s10964-009-9393-0

Latrofa, M., Vaes, J., & Cadinu, M. (2012). Self-stereotyping: The central role of an ingroup threatening identity. *The Journal of Social Psychology, 152*, 92–111. http://dx.doi.org/10.1080/00224545.2011.565382

Lee, D. L., & Ahn, S. (2013). The relation of racial identity, ethnic identity, and racial socialization to discrimination-distress: A meta-analysis of Black Americans. *Journal of Counseling Psychology, 60*, 1–14. http://dx.doi.org/10.1037/a0031275

Liang, C. T. H., & Borders, A. (2012). Beliefs in an unjust world mediate the associations between perceived ethnic discrimination and psychological functioning. *Personality and Individual Differences, 53*, 528–533. http://dx.doi.org/10.1016/j.paid.2012.04.022

Liang, C. T. H., & Fassinger, R. E. (2008). The role of collective self-esteem for Asian Americans experiencing racism-related stress: A test of moderator and mediator hypotheses. *Cultural Diversity & Ethnic Minority Psychology, 14*, 19–28. http://dx.doi.org/10.1037/1099-9809.14.1.19

Liu, R. T., & Alloy, L. B. (2010). Stress generation in depression: A systematic review of the empirical literature and recommendations for future study. *Clinical Psychology Review, 30*, 582–593. http://dx.doi.org/10.1016/j.cpr.2010.04.010

Livingston, R. W. (2002). The role of perceived negativity in the moderation of African Americans' implicit and explicit racial attitudes. *Journal of Experimental Social Psychology, 38*, 405–413. http://dx.doi.org/10.1016/S0022-1031(02)00002-1

Mallett, R. K., & Swim, J. K. (2009). Making the best of a bad situation: Proactive coping with racial discrimination. *Basic and Applied Social Psychology, 31*, 304–316. http://dx.doi.org/10.1080/01973530903316849

Markus, H. (1977). Self-schemata and processing information about the self. *Journal of Personality and Social Psychology, 35*, 63–78. http://dx.doi.org/10.1037/0022-3514.35.2.63

Mendoza-Denton, R., Downey, G., Purdie, V. J., Davis, A., & Pietrzak, J. (2002). Sensitivity to status-based rejection: Implications for African American students' college experience. *Journal of Personality and Social Psychology, 83*, 896–918. http://dx.doi.org/10.1037/0022-3514.83.4.896

Miller, G., Chen, E., & Cole, S. W. (2009). Health psychology: Developing biologically plausible models linking the social world and physical health. *Annual Review of Psychology, 60*, 501–524. http://dx.doi.org/10.1146/annurev.psych.60.110707.163551

Miranda, R., Andersen, S. M., & Edwards, T. (2013). The relational self and pre-existing depression: Implicit activation of significant-other representations exacerbates dysphoria and evokes rejection in the working self-concept. *Self and Identity, 12*, 39–57. http://dx.doi.org/10.1080/15298868.2011.636504

Miranda, R., Polanco-Roman, L., Tsypes, A., & Valderrama, J. (2013). Perceived discrimination, ruminative subtypes, and risk for depressive symptoms in emerging adulthood. *Cultural Diversity & Ethnic Minority Psychology, 19*, 395–403. http://dx.doi.org/10.1037/a0033504

Mor, N., & Inbar, M. (2009). Rejection sensitivity and schema-congruent information processing biases. *Journal of Research in Personality, 43*, 392–398. http://dx.doi.org/10.1016/j.jrp.2009.01.001

Mor, N., & Winquist, J. (2002). Self-focused attention and negative affect: A meta-analysis. *Psychological Bulletin, 128*, 638–662. http://dx.doi.org/10.1037/0033-2909.128.4.638

Moradi, B., & Hasan, N. T. (2004). Arab American persons' reported experiences of discrimination and mental health: The mediating role of personal control. *Journal of Counseling Psychology, 51*, 418–428. http://dx.doi.org/10.1037/0022-0167.51.4.418

Moradi, B., & Risco, C. (2006). Perceived discrimination experiences and mental health of Latina/o American persons. *Journal of Counseling Psychology, 53*, 411–421. http://dx.doi.org/10.1037/0022-0167.53.4.411

Murphy, M. C., Richeson, J. A., Shelton, J. N., Rheinschmidt, M. L., & Bergsieker, H. B. (2013). Cognitive costs of contemporary prejudice. *Group Processes & Intergroup Relations, 16*, 560–571. http://dx.doi.org/10.1177/1368430212468170

Nolen-Hoeksema, S. (1991). Responses to depression and their effects on the duration of depressive episodes. *Journal of Abnormal Psychology, 100*, 569–582. http://dx.doi.org/10.1037/0021-843X.100.4.569

Nuru-Jeter, A., Chae, D., Price, M., Telesford, J., Mendoza-Denton, R., & Woods-Giscombe, C. (2014, March). *Racial discrimination and inflammation among African American women: Biobehavioral and psychobiological pathways for cardiovascular health disparities.* Paper presented at the 72nd Annual Meeting of the American Psychosomatic Society, San Francisco, CA.

Operario, D., & Fiske, S. T. (2001). Ethnic identity moderates perceptions of prejudice: Judgments of personal versus group discrimination and subtle versus blatant bias. *Personality and Social Psychology Bulletin, 27*, 550–561. http://dx.doi.org/10.1177/0146167201275004

Paradies, Y. (2006). A systematic review of empirical research on self-reported racism and health. *International Journal of Epidemiology, 35*, 888–901. http://dx.doi.org/10.1093/ije/dyl056

Pascoe, E. A., & Smart Richman, L. (2009). Perceived discrimination and health: A meta-analytic review. *Psychological Bulletin, 135*, 531–554. http://dx.doi.org/10.1037/a0016059

Phillips, L. H., Channon, S., Tunstall, M., Hedenstrom, A., & Lyons, K. (2008). The role of working memory in decoding emotions. *Emotion, 8,* 184–191. http://dx.doi.org/10.1037/1528-3542.8.2.184

Pinel, E. C. (1999). Stigma consciousness: The psychological legacy of social stereotypes. *Journal of Personality and Social Psychology, 76,* 114–128. http://dx.doi.org/10.1037/0022-3514.76.1.114

Priest, N., Paradies, Y., Trenerry, B., Truong, M., Karlsen, S., & Kelly, Y. (2013). A systematic review of studies examining the relationship between reported racism and health and wellbeing for children and young people. *Social Science & Medicine, 95,* 115–127. http://dx.doi.org/10.1016/j.socscimed.2012.11.031

Quintana, S. M. (2007). Racial and ethnic identity: Developmental perspectives and research. *Journal of Counseling Psychology, 54,* 259–270. http://dx.doi.org/10.1037/0022-0167.54.3.259

Richeson, J. A., & Shelton, N. J. (2007). Negotiating interracial interactions: Costs, consequences and possibilities. *Current Directions in Psychological Science, 16,* 6316–6320. http://dx.doi.org/10.1111/j.1467-8721.2007.00528.x

Rivas-Drake, D., Seaton, E. K., Markstrom, C., Quintana, S., Syed, M., Lee, R. M., . . . The Ethnic and Racial Identity in the 21st Century Study Group. (2014). Ethnic and racial identity in adolescence: Implications for psychosocial, academic, and health outcomes. *Child Development, 85,* 40–57. http://dx.doi.org/10.1111/cdev.12200

Rudman, L. A., Dohn, M. C., & Fairchild, K. (2007). Implicit self-esteem compensation: Automatic threat defense. *Journal of Personality and Social Psychology, 93,* 798–813. http://dx.doi.org/10.1037/0022-3514.93.5.798

Ruiz, J. (2014, June). Monitoring for threats: Social vigilance as a biobehavioral pathway in racial/ethnic health disparities. In Elizabeth Brondolo (Chair), *Does stress serve as a primary pathway to explain race-related disparities in health?* Symposium conducted at the annual meeting of the Academy of Behavioral Medicine Research, Airlie, VA.

Schmader, T., & Croft, A. (2011). How stereotypes stifle performance potential. *Social and Personality Psychology Compass, 5,* 792–806. http://dx.doi.org/10.1111/j.1751-9004.2011.00390.x

Sellers, R. M., Caldwell, C. H., Schmeelk-Cone, K. H., & Zimmerman, M. A. (2003). Racial identity, racial discrimination, perceived stress, and psychological distress among African American young adults. *Journal of Health and Social Behavior, 44,* 302–317. http://dx.doi.org/10.2307/1519781

Sellers, R. M., & Shelton, J. N. (2003). The role of racial identity in perceived racial discrimination. *Journal of Personality and Social Psychology, 84,* 1079–1092. http://dx.doi.org/10.1037/0022-3514.84.5.1079

Sellers, R. M., Smith, M. A., Shelton, J. N., Rowley, S. A. J., & Chavous, T. M. (1998). Multidimensional model of racial identity: A reconceptualization of African American racial identity. *Personality and Social Psychology Review, 2,* 18–39. http://dx.doi.org/10.1207/s15327957pspr0201_2

Simons, R. L., Simons, L. G., Lei, M. K., & Landor, A. (2012). Relational schemas, hostile romantic relationships, and beliefs about marriage among young African American adults. *Journal of Social and Personal Relationships, 29*, 77–101. http://dx.doi.org/10.1177/0265407511406897

Smith, T. W. (2014, March). *Getting along and getting ahead: An interpersonal perspective on cardiovascular risk. Patricia R. Barchas award lecture.* Lecture conducted from the 72nd Annual Scientific Meeting of the American Psychosomatic Society, San Francisco, CA.

Sowislo, J. F., & Orth, U. (2013). Does low self-esteem predict depression and anxiety? A meta-analysis of longitudinal studies. *Psychological Bulletin, 139*, 213–240. http://dx.doi.org/10.1037/a0028931

Steele, C. M., & Aronson, J. (1995). Stereotype threat and the intellectual test performance of African Americans. *Journal of Personality and Social Psychology, 69*, 797–811. http://dx.doi.org/10.1037/0022-3514.69.5.797

Stein, K. F., & Corte, C. (2008). The identity impairment model: A longitudinal study of self-schemas as predictors of disordered eating behaviors. *Nursing Research, 57*, 182–190. http://dx.doi.org/10.1097/01.NNR.0000319494.21628.08

Tawa, J., Suyemoto, K. L., & Roemer, L. (2012). Implications of perceived interpersonal and structural racism for Asian Americans' self-esteem. *Basic and Applied Social Psychology, 34*, 349–358. http://dx.doi.org/10.1080/01973533.2012.693425

Thoits, P. A. (2013). Self, identity, stress, and mental health. In C. S. Aneshensel, J. C. Phelan & A. Bierman (Eds.), *Handbook of the sociology of mental health* (2nd ed., pp. 357–377). New York, NY: Springer. http://dx.doi.org/10.1007/978-94-007-4276-5_18

Trawalter, S., & Richeson, J. A. (2006). Regulatory focus and executive function after interracial interactions. *Journal of Experimental Social Psychology, 42*, 406–412. http://dx.doi.org/10.1016/j.jesp.2005.05.008

Twenge, J. M., & Crocker, J. (2002). Race and self-esteem: Meta-analyses comparing Whites, Blacks, Hispanics, Asians, and American Indians and comment on Gray-Little and Hafdahl (2000). *Psychological Bulletin, 128*, 371–408.

Umaña-Taylor, A. J., & Updegraff, K. A. (2007). Latino adolescents' mental health: Exploring the interrelations among discrimination, ethnic identity, cultural orientation, self-esteem, and depressive symptoms. *Journal of Adolescence, 30*, 549–567. http://dx.doi.org/10.1016/j.adolescence.2006.08.002

Vargas, J. H., & Kemmelmeier, M. (2013). Ethnicity and contemporary American culture: A meta-analytic investigation of horizontal–vertical individualism–collectivism. *Journal of Cross-Cultural Psychology, 44*, 195–222. http://dx.doi.org/10.1177/0022022112443733

Young, J., Klosko, J., & Weishaar, M. (2003). *Schema therapy: A practitioner's guide.* New York, NY: Guilford Press.

6

RACISM AND BEHAVIORAL OUTCOMES OVER THE LIFE COURSE

GILBERT C. GEE AND ANGIE DENISSE OTINIANO VERISSIMO

As a system of oppression, racism can influence one's life even before it begins, and can affect a person well beyond his or her legacy. In this chapter, we discuss some of the ways racism shapes behavior, focusing on three major theoretical pathways related to social stress, institutional barriers, and social norms. This chapter organized by a life course perspective (Elder & Rockwell, 1979), which suggests that an individual's biography is not merely a personal experience but also a social one that aligns in response to evolving social roles. Herein, we argue that these roles are partly influenced by racial hierarchies and contact with racialized social institutions. This dynamism recognizes that the types of racism one encounters and the behavioral responses to racism change over time (Gee, Walsemann, & Brondolo, 2012).

Our chapter begins with overviews of racism and the life course. It then reviews three theoretical pathways whereby racism can shape behaviors. Next, the chapter applies the life course perspective toward reviewing key themes

---

http://dx.doi.org/10.1037/14852-007
The Cost of Racism for People of Color: Contextualizing Experiences of Discrimination, A. N. Alvarez, C. T. H. Liang, and H. A. Neville (Editors)
Copyright © 2016 by the American Psychological Association. All rights reserved.

in the literature on racism and health behaviors. Finally, we conclude with recommendations for further study. We note that our chapter focuses specifically on racism and behavior, so some issues that have been emerging in the life course literature are not fully reviewed (e.g., racism, chronic diseases). Additional discussions on those and related issues can be found elsewhere (Acevedo-Garcia, Rosenfeld, Hardy, McArdle, & Osypuk, 2013; Gee et al., 2012; Lu & Halfon, 2003). Also, we do not comprehensively review the literature but rather illustrate major themes and examples that are promising ideas for further research.

DEFINITIONS

We adopt Feagin's (2000) concept of *systemic racism*, which focuses on the "diverse assortment of racist practices; the unjustly gained economic and political power of Whites; the continuing resource inequalities; and the White-racist ideologies, attitudes, and institutions created to preserve White advantages and power" (p. 16) This definition highlights that racism is not about random actions by individuals but is instead rooted in the day-to-day operations of social institutions and culture. Racism systematically disadvantages racial minorities and advantages Whites. These advantages and disadvantages stem from social institutions and practices that are important to maintain social hierarchies in the present and future generations. For example, although racial segregation of schools was struck down in *Brown v. Board of Education* (1954), many schools today remain segregated (Frankel & Volij, 2011; Stroub & Richards, 2013). The persistence of segregated schools contributes to systematic educational inequities that may also be related to health (Walsemann & Bell, 2010; Walsemann, Gee, & Ro, 2013).

This perspective recognizes that racism occurs at multiple levels, ranging from the individual to the institutional (Feagin, 2006; Seaton & Yip, 2009; Viruell-Fuentes, Miranda, & Abdulrahim, 2012). We find the iceberg metaphor useful for understanding these ideas (Gee, Ro, Shariff-Marco, & Chae, 2009): Individual acts of racial bias constitute the tip of the iceberg. That is, these individual actions are important and harmful, but they reflect a much larger body of racial inequities, upheld by systemic racism, that sits below the surface and is more difficult to ameliorate.

The systemic nature of racism also lends itself quite well to the *life course perspective*, which shows that people interact with different social institutions as they get older (Elder & Rockwell, 1979; Lynch & Smith, 2005; Umberson, Crosnoe, & Reczek, 2010). Hence, *age* is not simply about biological development but is also about changes in social roles, privileges, and obligations. As individuals become older, their social circles widen, they encounter new institutions, change their social roles, and obtain new rights and obligations (Umberson et al., 2010). With these changes come contact with new institutions (e.g., from schools to companies), and new opportunities to encounter discrimination (Gee et al., 2012; Yip, Gee, & Takeuchi, 2008). For example, racial discrimination in voting becomes an issue when one becomes old enough to be eligible to vote.

THREE THEORETICAL PERSPECTIVES ON RACISM AND BEHAVIOR

How might racism shape behavior? Figure 6.1 illustrates three pathways based on the literature: (a) stress and coping, (b) institutional barriers, and (c) cultural norms. These mechanisms are not mutually exclusive or meant to be a comprehensive listing of all possible mechanisms. Rather, they are a starting point for further consideration of the role of racism over the life course.

Path 1: Stress and Coping

The stress framework is often evoked in the racism and health literature (Williams & Mohammed, 2013). From this perspective, experiences of racial bias are stressors (R. Clark, Anderson, Clark, & Williams, 1999). The basic

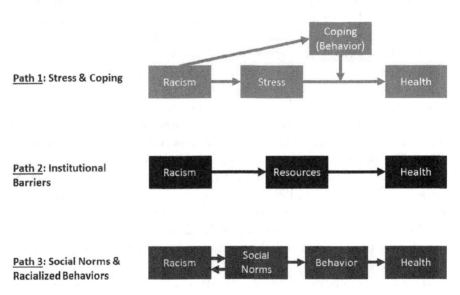

Figure 6.1. Multiple pathways for racism and health behaviors.

premise is that illness occurs when stressors exceed one's ability to cope with them (Lazarus & Folkman, 1984). Coping includes the use of diverse resources and techniques, such as the cognitive reappraisal of the stressor to make it less threatening, avoidance of the stressor, and help-seeking behavior (Alvarez & Juang, 2010; Thoits, 1995, 2010).

This framework implies two important propositions that have been widely researched. First, it denotes that a variety of personal behaviors can be used to moderate the effects of stressors (Brondolo, Brady ver Halen, Pencille, Beatty, & Contrada, 2009; Lazarus & Folkman, 1984; Thoits, 1995). For example, studies have investigated how social support (Noh & Kaspar, 2003) and religious involvement (Odom, Vernon-Feagans, & The Family Life Project Key, 2010) may protect against the effects of discrimination on mental health.

Second, this framework suggests that behaviors are themselves a consequence. Thus, studies have also examined how stressors can increase the likelihood of certain behaviors, particularly maladaptive ones, such as substance use (Brondolo et al., 2009; Lazarus & Folkman, 1984; Thoits, 1995). This perspective has been described in various frameworks, such as the tension reduction model and the self-medication hypothesis (Cappell & Herman, 1972; Khantzian, 1997). Despite subtle differences, the underlying idea is that people minimize stress through behaviors such as substance use or sex.

Path 2: Institutional Barriers

Racism can also influence personal behaviors through institutional barriers that can block or shape access to social resources (Gee & Payne-Sturges, 2004; LaVeist, 1993; Viruell-Fuentes et al., 2012; Williams & Collins, 2001). These barriers include *racial segregation*, the physical separation of racial groups (Massey & Denton, 1993). Segregation has existed at multiple levels, ranging from everyday interactions while riding a bus, to where one can live, to where one can seek medical care, to where one can seek employment, and to which nation one can emigrate. Today, de jure segregation of buses and drinking fountains have been formally outlawed; however, much de facto segregation still exists with regards to schools, neighborhoods, and even hospitals (Dimick, Ruhter, Sarrazin, & Birkmeyer, 2013; Merchant, Becker, Yang, & Groeneveld, 2011; Smith, 1998). Recently, several scholars have argued that mass incarceration has become the new form of racial segregation for many African Americans and Latinos (Alexander, 2012; Brewer & Heitzeg, 2008).

Segregation influences behavior by fundamentally altering the space for social interaction and valued resources. For example, school segregation may change the behavior of racial minorities by limiting access to good educational experiences, which then can set children into a trajectory that is less economically successful (Fiel, 2013; Goldsmith, 2009). Paradoxically, it is also possible that segregation can reduce interpersonal discrimination: If minorities live in segregated communities, they may encounter lower rates of interpersonal discrimination because of lower contact with people who discriminate against them (Borrell, Kiefe, Diez-Roux, Williams, & Gordon-Larsen, 2013). Stated another way, structural discrimination may sometimes reduce interpersonal discrimination. This does not imply that structural discrimination is better but rather highlights the complex pathways whereby discrimination at multiple levels interact.

Path 3: Social Norms

Racism can also shape behavior through cultural norms and expectations. As one example, consider norms that often emphasize Whites as the standard of beauty (Hunter, 2002). These Eurocentric beauty norms can then influence behavior by promoting cosmetic surgery, the purchasing of skin-lightening products, and similar behaviors (Glenn, 2008; Kaw, 1993; Sengupta, 2006). As a second example, consider the cultural norms related to "enemies." After the attacks of September 11, the American cultural landscape shifted dramatically to label Muslims, Sikhs, South Asians, and Middle Easterners, among others, as "terrorists" (Ahluwalia & Pellettiere, 2010; Merskin, 2004). All of these diverse religious, geographic, and nationality groups were subsumed into one generic label. The cultural shift after the attack caused many individuals from these backgrounds to experience hate crimes and other forms of discrimination (Swahn et al., 2003). In response, they did many things, among them: emigrated, prayed, hid, wrote editorials, and marched (Peña, 2007; Umbreit, Lewis, & Burns, 2003). Hence, social norms may contribute to racialized expectations of behavior and simultaneously create a climate that leads to racial animosity. At the same time, minority groups can create social movements that serve to counteract racist social norms and institutional barriers. In a sense, these social movements can be considered as the community-level equivalent to personal coping responses.

We underscore that these three pathways are not mutually exclusive but can operate simultaneously and interactively. For example, Bonilla-Silva, Goar, and Embrick (2006) discussed how racial segregation creates a *White habitus*: "a racialized uninterrupted socialization process that conditions and creates Whites' racial taste, perceptions, feelings, emotions, and views on racial matters" (p. 104). This essentially means that racial segregation helps fuel social norms related to race. These social norms, in turn, can contribute to stress. Hence, many interrelationships are across these levels of influence.

In summary, racism can cause many different kinds of behaviors as responses to personal experiences of stress and/or as reactions to living in a racialized environment. These three pathways provide some of the theoretical rationale for understanding the broad effects of systemic racism on health behavior across the life course. Our next section describes some ways that racism can influence behavior across various stages of the life course. We organize this discussion across the stages of in utero and infancy, childhood, young adulthood, adulthood, and older adulthood, but note the considerable overlap across stages.

IN UTERO/INFANCY

Fetuses and infants may be exposed to stress related to discrimination through their caregivers' experiences of discrimination. Maternal stress impacts fetal heart rate, movement, and development (Van den Bergh, 1990; Van den Bergh, Mulder, Mennes, & Glover, 2005). Similarly, infants whose mothers are exposed to stressors, such as discrimination, may be programmed to expect a stressful or negative environment in addition to a vigilant stance and state of chronic stress (Adler & Stewart, 2010). The fetal and infant stages of life are fundamental, as they set up a trajectory of health. Unfortunately, those who are exposed to discrimination and other forms of marginalization may be set up on a trajectory of poor health and poor health behaviors. One example is through the initiation of allostatic load or wear and tear on the body due to stress early on, starting from the fetal stage of life (McEwen, 1998). In fact, evidence indicates that experiencing cumulative stress in the first years of life is associated with early onset of problem drinking in adolescence and substance use disorders in early adulthood (Enoch, 2011).

Discrimination may influence fetal and infant health through maternal stress, which in general is associated with outcomes, such as elevated fetal heart rate (Van den Bergh, 1990) and low birth weight and preterm birth (Dole et al., 2003; Wadhwa, Sandman, Porto, Dunkel-Schetter, & Garite, 1993). Accordingly, stress related to discrimination may elicit a similar response. During infancy, maternal stress may interfere with breastfeeding by prohibiting initiation, minimizing exclusivity, shortening duration, and decreasing milk supply (Dewey, 2001; Lau, Hurst, Smith, & Schanler, 2007). Thus, it is plausible that discrimination may also affect outcomes, such as breastfeeding.

Moreover, discrimination may influence a child's health indirectly through parental coping behaviors. For example, everyday discrimination has been associated with maternal smoking during pregnancy (I. Bennett et al., 2010). Certainly, such smoking carries a direct harm to the developing fetus and, further, may have spillover effects, such as through fostering a family environment with more permissive views on drug use, which are in turn associated with adolescent substance use (Young-Wolff, Enoch, & Prescott, 2011).

Some of these effects are captured in the fetal origins hypothesis, which specifies that experiences during fetal development may shape health later in life (Godfrey & Barker, 2001; Lu & Halfon, 2003). Studies have shown that maternal socioeconomic status, race, and stress are predictive of birth outcomes, such as birth weight and preterm birth, which then set the stage for several adult behaviors and diseases (Lu & Halfon, 2003), specifically, coronary heart disease, stroke, hypertension, and diabetes (Barker, 2002; Godfrey & Barker, 2001). Lower birth weight has been associated with higher systolic blood pressure among children under 10 years of age and among adults in their late 30s, between 46 and 54, and between 59 and 71 (Law et al., 1993). Further, this relationship appeared to amplify over the life course, as the association became larger with increasing age (Law et al., 1993). Similarly, maternal stress in utero may also compromise one's immune system, rendering an individual more vulnerable to infection (Halfon, Larson, Lu, Tullis, & Russ, 2014; Merlot, Couret, & Otten, 2008). More troubling is that experiences in utero may not only impact an individual over their own life course but also possibly have effects across several generations (Lu & Halfon, 2003).

CHILDHOOD AND ADOLESCENCE

Awareness of race among youth in America have been well-documented. For example, studies from the 1950s have long documented how children chose dolls on the basis of skin color (K. B. Clark & Clark, 1950). At very young ages, children learn about racial labels and hierarchies, and mimic racialized adult behaviors. Van Ausdale and Feagin (2001) provided some candid accounts from their fieldwork at playgrounds. For example, they documented how 3-year-old Felicia (White) said to 3-year-old Joseph (black), "Black people are not allowed on the swing right now, especially Black boys" (p. 107). In another instance, they related how 4-year-old Renee (White) admonished 3-year-old Lingmai (Asian), "No, No. You can't pull this wagon. Only White Americans can pull this wagon" (p. 104).

It is likely that children this young do not fully realize what they are doing, but it is also evident that some children are using race as a way to construct out-groups, and as a rationale for constraining the behavior of other children. The children who are victims are hurt, like any children excluded from a swing, but further learn that their background becomes a reason for such exclusion.

Of course, children may encounter discrimination not only from peers but also from adults too. As kids enter school-age, their potential exposure to racial bias broadens. In some ways, discrimination within the school system may be particularly harmful in setting children into a trajectory of social disadvantage. This discrimination may be subtle, such as being overlooked by one's teacher, or more overt, as in the case of racial slurs (Van Ausdale & Feagin, 2001). These ideas are illustrated in recent study of youth ages 8 to 18 in Connecticut, which noted that 88% had reported experiencing some racial discrimination (Pachter, Bernstein, Szalacha, & García Coll, 2010). Further, about 36% mentioned being treated badly by their teacher because of racism, and 8% noted that they were called on less in class because of racism.

Nationally representative studies also suggest that many youth encounter racial discrimination (Sangalang, Chen, Kulis, & Yabuki, in press). For example, data from the Black Youth Culture Survey, nationally representative of Black and Latino youth ages 15 to 25, indicate that 67% report some experiences with racial discrimination (Grollman, 2012). Similarly, data from the National Survey of American Life show that more than 80% of African American and Caribbean Black youth, ages 13 to 17, reported at least one incident of discrimination within the past year (Seaton, Caldwell, Sellers, & Jackson, 2008).

These reports are related to health and behavioral outcomes. A recent systematic review found 121 empirical studies on racial discrimination and health among youth (Priest et al., 2013). The review found that discrimination was associated with numerous outcomes ranging from global feelings of lower life satisfaction; to physical health problems, such as insulin resistance, and to psychological outcomes, such as depression and suicide. The review also identified 38 articles focused on substance use, and 58 studies documenting associations with other behavioral outcomes, such as attention-deficit/hyperactivity disorder (ADHD), aggression, and other externalizing behaviors.

Racial discrimination may lead to bullying and harassment, but certainly, many children experience harassment regardless of their race. Provocatively, Russell, Sinclair, Poteat, and Koenig (2012) found that harassment based on racial bias was more strongly associated with poor outcomes than "general harassment" among school-age youth. These outcomes included a range of behaviors, including poor grades, truancy, and binge drinking. Outcomes also included damage to the youth's property and being injured with a weapon. Thus, experiences of racial bias may sometimes be more toxic than experiences of harassment that are not tied to the child's enduring characteristic of race. That is, one may grow out of childhood, but not grow out of their skin color.

Direct experiences of discrimination at young ages may be particularly harmful, and some have argued that late childhood, from ages 8 to 11, may be a critical period of development (Gibbons et al., 2007; Whitbeck, Hoyt, McMorris, Chen, & Stubben, 2001). Some hypothesize that during this period, children are developing their self-identity and ethnic identity, and are establishing their affiliation with peers whose experiences are similar to their own (Gibbons et al., 2007; Whitbeck et al., 2001). Therefore, experiences of discrimination during late childhood may prompt children to initiate substance use early on (Gibbons et al., 2007; Whitbeck et al., 2001) or engage in other delinquent behaviors (Simons, Chen, Stewart, & Brody, 2003), such as stealing or lying (Deng, Kim, Vaughan, & Li, 2010), as well as violence (Simons et al., 2006). Some behaviors, such as diet and exercise, are established in childhood (Baranowski et al., 2000; Umberson et al., 2010). Further, some behaviors in childhood escalate into disorders in adulthood, as with the example of substance use and abuse (Anthony & Petronis, 1995). Accordingly, these observations raise the provocative idea that some of the effects of discrimination in childhood may persist into adulthood, even without discrimination in adult life.

Participation in certain activities may contribute to stigma and discrimination. For example, the National School Lunch Program is designed to provide affordable or free lunches to students, but participation in the program carries stigma among some students (Bhatia, Jones, & Reicker, 2011). According to the authors, this stigma and potential for discrimination appears to have contributed to lower use of the lunch program among some students. Additionally, minority children are more likely to be labeled with problems, such as ADHD. Such labels appear to carry stigma among peers as well as teachers (Bell, Long, Garvan, & Bussing, 2011).

Additionally, discrimination may influence a child indirectly through their parents and other caregivers. For example, a study in the United Kingdom found that maternal experiences of discrimination were related several outcomes among their 5-year-old children, including increased risk for obesity and diminished nonverbal ability (Kelly, Becares, & Nazroo, 2013). Similarly, another study found that experiences of racism among caregivers were related to increased risk of childhood illnesses (e.g., respiratory infections, ear infections) among indigenous Australians (Priest, Paradies, Stevens, & Bailie, 2012). These associations might be associated with stress, which may then negatively impact parenting. For example, racism may be related to higher levels of uninvolved parenting and more punitive parenting practices (Pachter & García Coll, 2009). This stress may also lead to parental coping behaviors that spillover to their children. For example, if parents prepare comfort foods to cope with racism, then their children are likely to also consume such foods.

At the same time, some research highlights resiliency factors that may protect against discrimination. For example, recent studies show that factors such as self-esteem, ethnic identity, and cultural orientations may buffer Latino adolescents against self-reported racial discrimination (Umaña-Taylor

& Updegraff, 2007; Umaña-Taylor, Wong, Gonzales, & Dumka, 2012). Similar findings have emerged for African American and Asian American youth (Seaton, Neblett, Upton, Hammond, & Sellers, 2011; Yip et al., 2008). We caution here that the findings regarding ethnic identity and discrimination are complex, in part because of the many different types of ethnic identity (e.g., public regard, centrality).

In addition to interpersonal discrimination, institutional discrimination may shape youth outcomes. In particular, racial segregation of communities and of schools has been a long area of research. Much of this work finds that this segregation is associated with numerous poor outcomes. For example, Massey and Fisher (2000) showed that Black and Latino students growing up in racially segregated environments had poorer academic achievement in college. Their analyses suggested that this relationship was partially mediated by environmental stressors related to greater exposure to violence in their schools and neighborhoods.

Card and Rothstein (2007) showed different effects based on residential versus school segregation. They noted that increasing neighborhood segregation was related to increasing disparities in Black–White scores on the SAT exam. Yet, they also found that school segregation had no independent effect on these disparities. One possible explanation is that school segregation is partially related to neighborhood segregation.

It is interesting that Echenique, Fryer, and Kaufman (2006) noted that within-school segregation was related to lowered rates of smoking among African American and Hispanic children. Similarly, other studies have found that Black students educated in primarily minority schools are less likely to initiate smoking and report lower levels of depression compared with Black students educated in majority-White schools (Johnson & Hoffmann, 2000; Walsemann, Bell, & Maitra, 2011).

How do we reconcile these disparate findings? One potential interpretation is that residential segregation is important for generating racial inequities based on the distribution of resources across neighborhoods, with schools with higher minority composition receiving fewer resources (Frankel & Volij, 2011). In turn, these factors may contribute to poorer academic performance among minority students. At the same time, being educated within a minority school might have the benefit of fewer overt experiences of discrimination (Feagin & Imani, 1996; Walsemann et al., 2011, 2013). Minority students educated in predominantly White schools may encounter more discrimination and may be more likely to turn to smoking and similar behaviors as coping mechanisms. Although the idea is speculative, we believe that studies across multiple levels provides a promising way to more fully consider the (sometimes contradictory) effects of racial discrimination.

YOUNG ADULTHOOD

Young adulthood marks an important transition, with many new roles and expanded contact with social institutions. Adults have more rights, such as the ability to buy cigarettes, drive, and vote. Yet, adults are also more accountable for their actions, as evidenced by stronger penalties in adult versus juvenile court. New roles and expectations arise as youth leave school and potentially enter the labor force. Many things are gained, but some things are lost, such as eligibility for participation in programs like the Children's Health Insurance Program. Accordingly, young adulthood is not simply a period of personal development but is also a period that includes considerable shifts in their relationship with society, marked in ways that include their relationship with laws, policies, and institutions.

Some racial stereotypes also overlap with this life stage. For example, young men of color are often stereotyped as thugs or criminals, and young women of color are often stereotyped as overly sexual, promiscuous, and single mothers. As young adulthood has also been identified as a crucial period of development, young adults may be particularly vulnerable to poor health behaviors as a consequence of discrimination (Hatzenbuehler, Corbin, & Fromme, 2011). New forms of discrimination emerge, such as discrimination when seeking a job (Bertrand & Mullainathan, 2004).

Additionally, substance use is often initiated during early adulthood, and stress is strongly associated with alcohol consumption during this period as well (Umberson et al., 2010). Therefore, it is not surprising that the literature shows a relationship between discrimination and health behaviors, such as substance use, for young adults (Brody, Kogan, & Chen, 2012; Brook, Brook, Rubenstone, Zhang, & Finch, 2010; Hatzenbuehler et al., 2011; Otiniano Verissimo, Gee, Iguchi, Ford, & Friedman, 2013). Discrimination was associated with increases in substance use across the high school years for African Americans (Fuller-Rowell et al., 2012), Latinos (Basáñez, Unger, Soto, Crano, & Baezconde-Garbanati, 2013), and Native Americans (Galliher, Jones, & Dahl, 2011). For example, Brody et al. (2012) demonstrated that self-reported discrimination was prospectively related to increased use of alcohol, tobacco, and marijuana among African American youth living in rural areas. Similarly, Otiniano Verissimo et al. (2013) found that discrimination is related to increased use of alcohol among young Latina women and increased use of cocaine and other illicit drugs among young Latino men living in Brooklyn, New York. Gender differences in the relationship between discrimination and substance use have been documented for Latinos as well (Lorenzo-Blanco, Unger, Ritt-Olson, Soto, & Baezconde-Garbanati, 2011; Otiniano Verissimo et al., 2013). More generally, further work should be developed to consider gender variations in the relationship between discrimination and health and behavior (Liang, Alvarez, Juang, & Liang, 2007).

Further, peer relationships play an important role in health behaviors and may also be related to experiences of racism (Brondolo, Libretti, Rivera, & Walsemann, 2012). Among African American young men, the relationship between discrimination and substance use has been found to be mediated by affiliation with peers that use substances (Brody et al., 2012). The role of peers is also important when considering how peers' experiences of discrimination may also influence health behaviors. For example, having a peer who has been racially profiled may encourage individuals to remain in a vigilant state to anticipate their own experiences of discrimination. Indeed, emerging research shows that racism-related vigilance, a form of anticipatory stress, appears to be related to hypertension (Hicken, Lee, Morenoff, House, & Williams, 2014).

Young adulthood also includes newfound rights for sexual behavior, as the person is no longer a minor and subject to statutory rape regulations. Some research suggests that individuals sometimes use sex as a coping response. Accordingly, studies have found that racial bias may be related to sexual behavior (Roberts et al., 2012; Yoshikawa, Alan-David Wilson, Chae, & Cheng, 2004). For example, Stevens-Watkins, Brown-Wright, and Tyler (2011) found that race-related stress was associated with increased numbers of sexual partners among African Americans. Similarly, racial discrimination is related to HIV-risk behaviors among Black heterosexual men (Bowleg et al., 2013). A growing body of work shows that racism, homophobia, and other oppressions are related to risky behaviors, including unprotected anal intercourse, number of sexual partners, and nonuse of condoms (Choi, Hudes, & Steward, 2008; Díaz, Ayala, & Bein, 2004; Meyer & Dean, 1998; Yoshikawa et al., 2004). These associations are often aligned with stress theory, suggesting that people engage in risky behaviors as a way to cope with racial adversity.

Instructively, a qualitative study of gay Asian men provides some additional insights into reasons for some of these associations (C.-S. Han, 2008). A respondent mentioned,

> I did a small mini-experiment where in a gay chat room, I posted two profiles. They were exactly the same, except on one, I put that I was Asian and on the other, I didn't put a race. . . . Well, the guys who responded to the profile without my race started with something like, "hi" or "what's up?" The guys who responded to my profile that said "Asian" were much more aggressive. They said something like, "Do you like to be fucked?" But the most interesting thing is, the guys who didn't know I was Asian would negotiate about being a top or bottom. The guys who knew I was Asian would automatically assume I was a bottom and if I told them I wasn't, they would stop the conversation right away. (p. 8)

This qualitative research suggests an additional and complementary pathway beyond the stress paradigm, namely, that racism shapes social norms and expectations for behaviors. In this instance, Asian men are expected to behave as a "bottom" (one who receives anal penetration), a view consistent with stereotypes of Asians as being subordinate and submissive (Liang, Li, & Kim, 2004).

ADULTHOOD

As individuals age, their roles and responsibilities often increase. They have new obligations as romantic partners, parents, and caregivers for aging parents (Umberson et al., 2010). Further, the general increase in risk for chronic illnesses, such as heart disease, and a decline in some issues such as alcohol abuse (Grant et al., 2004). Moreover, it appears that many exposures in early life begin to catch up over time in the form of accumulated stressors. Examples of this theme comes from many literatures, such that related to *cumulative disadvantage*, referring to the accumulation of multiple forms of social adversity (Ferraro & Kelley-Moore, 2003; Goosby, 2013), and *allostatic load*, referring to the "wear and tear" on the body due to the accumulation of stressors (McEwen, 1998). Some health behaviors are particularly difficult to change in adulthood, especially if they become ingrained habits, or subject to constraints, such as work and family schedules (Devine et al., 2009; Umberson, 1987; Umberson et al., 2010)

Work is a particularly important part of adult life, with a very large and historic body of research on discrimination in employment and earnings (see Chapter 9, this volume). Indeed, it was the recognition of discrimination in employment that was the basis of the U.S. Equal Employment Opportunity Commission (EEOC), established as part of the 1964 Civil Rights Act. Unfortunately, such discrimination appears intact today. As one example, an "audit study" examined discrimination in receiving a callback for a job (Bertrand & Mullainathan, 2004). In this study, the investigators sent resumes in response to help-wanted advertisements placed in newspapers. Half of the surveys were randomly assigned an African-American–sounding name (e.g., Jamal, Lakisha), and the other half were assigned a White-sounding name (e.g., Greg, Emily). The resumes were otherwise identical. The investigators found that Black resumes had half of the callbacks for an interview compared with the White resumes. Other research finds that discrimination in the workplace is associated with poor health outcomes, including alcohol consumption, intentions to quit one's job, and alcohol use (de Castro, Gee, & Takeuchi, 2008; Shields & Price, 2002; Yen, Ragland, Greiner, & Fisher, 1999).

Adulthood encourages a deeper look at some of the issues that have already been discussed with earlier ages, and certainly, the basic task of examining whether discrimination is related to illness and health behaviors. Research on discrimination and health behaviors in adulthood have mirrored those at earlier ages mentioned earlier, including substance use and risky sexual behavior, as well as other issues, such as sleep, obesity, physical activity, help-seeking behavior, and diet (Crawley, Ahn, & Winkleby, 2008; Hicken, Lee, Ailshire, Burgard, & Williams, 2013; Paradies, 2006; Williams & Mohammed, 2013). However, as noted above, adulthood also encourages new questions, such as whether chronic exposures to discrimination, above and beyond discrimination at single points in time, have different effects on health (Gee et al., 2012).

Some research points to this complexity. For example, a study by Lewis, Aiello, Leurgans, Kelly, and Barnes (2010) suggests that chronic exposure to discrimination (i.e., repeated reports of unfair treatment over several years) is related to calcification of Black women's coronary arteries, whereas single reports of discrimination are not related to calcification. Similarly, Pavalko, Mossakowski, and Hamilton (2003) found that reports of discrimination at baseline (1982) and follow-up (1989) were associated with functional limitations at follow-up. However, it is interesting to note that discrimination concurrent with functional limitations (i.e., discrimination and limitations in 1982) were not associated. Similar results are found elsewhere (e.g., Gee & Walsemann, 2009). Taken together, they suggest a latency period—that is, for some outcomes, the effects of discrimination may not show up until many years later.

We welcome clarification from the literature on basic questions as to whether chronic exposure to discrimination is related to the establishment of habits. It would be instructive to learn whether the effects of some encounters with discrimination in early life become dormant, only to reactivate during times of stress, similar to the ways in which some bacteria, such as tuberculosis, behave.

OLDER ADULTHOOD

Discrimination may take its final toll in older adulthood. New issues emerge, such as retirement and new social roles as grandparents. Older adulthood can bring with it additional respect and gravitas, as well as discrimination based on age (Butler, 1969). Older adulthood sometimes corresponds with changes in residence to be closer to caretaking facilities like nursing homes.

As with schools and residences, segregation also seems to happen within nursing homes. A recent study finds that Black–White segregation of nursing homes appears to be higher than segregation of residences (dissimilarity index values of 0.70 and 0.65, respectively; Strully, 2011). Further, the data show that this segregation is related to lower chance of being personally vaccinated and of having coresidents vaccinated against influenza. Hence, segregation appears to increase the risk of influenza by both increasing one's own risk directly (i.e., not being vaccinated) and also increasing risk indirectly by reducing herd immunity (i.e., vaccination of neighbors reduces the spread of influenza within a community).

As with younger persons, self-reported discrimination is associated with health problems among older adults. For example, reports of unfair treatment are related to poor quality sleep (Lewis et al., 2013) and increased c-reactive protein—a biomarker of stress and inflammation—among older African American adults (Lewis et al., 2010). Longitudinal data from the Chicago Health and Aging project found that perceived discrimination is related to increased risk of mortality among African American and White older adults (Barnes et al., 2008).

Some of the behaviors found at earlier ages appear less prominent at older ages. For example, although older adults do use illicit substances and engage in risky sexual behavior, these risks decline with age (B. Han, Gfroerer, Colliver, & Penne, 2009; Lindau et al., 2007).

Despite not much research on racism and these behaviors at older ages, the literature on help-seeking behavior is growing. Potentially, discrimination may contribute to poor health outcomes by reducing trust in biomedicine. A qualitative study of African American older people described how distrust of doctors, in part due to race, reduced help-seeking behavior. For example, one participant reported, "To be specific, I do not trust White doctors. . . . Not any White doctor that I went to [has] really helped me with a problem" (Martin et al., 2010, p. 320). Additional evidence comes from another study that found that perceived discrimination was related to decreased likelihood to join a waitlist for a kidney transplant (Klassen, Hall, Saksvig, Curbow, & Klassen, 2002). Why would someone opt out of a waitlist because of racism? The authors suggested that "patients with greater exposure to perceived discrimination in their pasts do not want to risk new treatment situations, such as transplantation, because they have a lower expectation of successful outcomes" (Klassen et al., 2002, p. 816).

These observations suggest that experiences of racism in early life can impact behavior in late life, in part by shaping the expectations that one would have for fair and effective treatment. These findings reinforce the idea that early life experiences may influence health behaviors in late life. Therefore, studies that examine discrimination cross-sectionally, or that have very limited time frames (e.g., discrimination in the past year or past 5 years), may potentially underestimate the effects of discrimination.

CONCLUSION AND FUTURE DIRECTIONS

As documented in this chapter, racial discrimination appears to be associated with a variety of behavioral responses. Some of these behaviors are helpful, such as when religious involvement protects against depression in the face of racism (Cooper, Thayer, & Waldstein, 2013). Some of these behaviors are harmful, as with the use of alcohol to cope with racial bias (Chae et al., 2008). Much of this research comes from the stress framework, arguing that racism is a stressor that prompts a behavioral coping response (R. Clark et al., 1999). Research should continue to build this base of research.

A life course perspective also highlights the need to create measures of discrimination that are appropriate for a given life stage. Recent reviews have called for measures that are more appropriately targeted for children, adults, and older persons (Thrasher, Clay, Ford, & Stewart, 2012).

Additionally, it is critically important to consider the interconnections between events across the life course. One way to view these interconnections is via what some have called *stress proliferation* or the related idea of *chains of risk* (Lynch & Smith, 2005; Pearlin, 2010). The basic idea is that a racist incident can lead to a cascade of other events. For example, discrimination by a teacher can lead to poor academic achievement and subsequently fewer employment options. Further, this discrimination in early life may contribute to a generalized worldview of distrust that may lead to other effects in later life, such as reluctance to seek medical care (Klassen et al., 2002). As noted in our review, it would be instructive to consider the timing of various exposures of discrimination. A smaller and more circumspect literature has also shown that discrimination can establish social norms that result in further changes to behavior. Standards of beauty that define Whites as "normal and desirable" may be related to behavioral responses, such as skin lightening and cosmetic surgery (Glenn, 2008; Kaw, 1993; Sengupta, 2006). Similarly, people of color enact behavioral responses to make Whites feel more comfortable and less apt to discriminate. In a famous essay titled, "Just Walk on By: Black Men and Public Space," Staples (1986) wrote,

> I now take precautions to make myself less threatening. I move about with care, particularly late in the evening. I give a wide berth to nervous people on subway platforms during the wee hours, particularly when I have exchanged business clothes for jeans. If I happen to be entering a building behind some people who appear skittish, I may walk by, letting them clear the lobby before I return, so as not to seem to be following them. I have been calm and extremely congenial on those rare occasions when I've been pulled over by the police. And on late-evening constitutionals I employ what has proved to be an excellent tension-reducing measure: I whistle melodies from Beethoven and Vivaldi. (p. 805)

These behaviors are related to the idea of *emotional work*, referring to labor designed specifically to attend to the emotions of other people that stem from inequities in social status (Hochschild, 1979). In the case of Staples, the use of business attire, walking by, and classical music serves to reduce fear among others around him. This fear, of course, stems from racist stereotypes of Black men as violent. Accordingly, we recommend here work that further examines how racism shapes expectations of behaviors more broadly than that currently emphasized by the stress and coping literature.

Further, and perhaps more pressing, is the need to fully study how racism affects health behaviors across transitions in the entire life course. For example, one study showed how cumulative racial discrimination during adolescence was associated with less healthy eating during young adulthood (Brodish et al., 2011). Most of the literature on this topic is cross-sectional, with little consideration of age and few longitudinal studies, but most of these are also of discrete life stages (e.g., young adulthood). So, for example, research has found that discrimination is associated with increased risk of tobacco use among teenagers or among adults (G. G. Bennett, Wolin, Robinson, Fowler, & Edwards, 2005), yet it is not known how these risks change over time.

Gilman, Abrams, and Buka's (2003) study of socioeconomic status and cigarette use provides a good example of how to more comprehensively consider changes over the life course. The investigators assessed socioeconomic status (SES) in childhood and in adulthood. They found that low SES in childhood was related to initiation of smoking, progression to regular cigarette use, and lower likelihood of cessation. By contrast, low SES in adulthood was related to greater change of regular use and cessation, but not initiation. Further, Gilman et al. found variation by type of SES. For example, during childhood, parental occupation predicted smoking initiation, whereas maternal education predicted progression regular tobacco use. These findings point to divergent pathways of causality. For example, low SES occupations may make parents more likely to smoke, and children may initiate smoking to mimic their parents. But, highly educated mothers may discourage their children from continuing to smoke.

We know very little about similar pathways with regard to racial discrimination, but this example illustrates questions for future research. For example, does experiencing discrimination in childhood differ from discrimination in adulthood with regard to the initiation of smoking, progression to regular use, and cessation? Do different forms of discrimination vary in these effects? For example, does a major incident of discrimination promote smoking initiation, whereas chronic everyday discrimination promote progression?

Other important questions relate to issues of time, dosage, and latency periods. How much discrimination, and over how long a period, does it take to contribute to health outcomes? Undoubtedly, the answers to these questions will depend heavily on both the exposure and the outcomes considered. For example, the effects of discrimination on initiation of binge drinking may have a short latency period, whereas the effects of discrimination on the manifestation of heart disease may show a longer latency period.

Finally, our present task was to focus on behavioral outcomes, but it is important to recognize that behavior is interrelated with many health and social outcomes. Studies of behavior alone will tend to underestimate the potential impact of racial discrimination. The environmental affordances (EA) model provides an interesting way to simultaneously consider health behaviors, physical health, mental health, racism, and health disparities (Jackson, Knight, & Rafferty, 2010; Mezuk et al., 2010). The model begins with two astute observations. First, African Americans have worse physical health, but generally better or similar mental health, than Whites. Second, African Americans generally encounter more social adversity (e.g., racism, stress, low social class) than Whites, and this adversity is often associated with poorer physical and mental health. Accordingly, a paradox exists, whereby African Americans have better mental health than expected, given their high exposure to adversity. The EA model suggests that African Americans engage coping behaviors that protect their mental health in the short term but ultimately damage their physical health in the long term. Therefore it suggests that racism promotes behavioral responses that protect mental health in the short term but physical health in the long term; this should be a key area for future investigation.

In closing, the literature shows that racial discrimination exists at multiple levels, manifests in many ways, and appears to influence multiple behaviors over the life course. Additionally, although the nature of racism may change over the life course, it is nonetheless appears present at all stages of life. This wide breadth of influence underscores the systematic nature of racism, highlights many opportunities for future research, and also suggests that interventions to reduce its impact must be multilevel and multifaceted.

REFERENCES

Acevedo-Garcia, D., Rosenfeld, L. E., Hardy, E., McArdle, N., & Osypuk, T. L. (2013). Future directions in research on institutional and interpersonal discrimination and children's health. *American Journal of Public Health, 103*, 1754–1763. http://dx.doi.org/10.2105/AJPH.2012.300986

Adler, N. E., & Stewart, J. (2010). Health disparities across the lifespan: Meaning, methods, and mechanisms. *Annals of the New York Academy of Sciences, 1186*, 5–23. http://dx.doi.org/10.1111/j.1749-6632.2009.05337.x

Ahluwalia, M. K., & Pellettiere, L. (2010). Sikh men post-9/11: Misidentification, discrimination, and coping. *Asian American Journal of Psychology, 1*, 303–314. http://dx.doi.org/10.1037/a0022156

Alexander, M. (2012). *The new Jim Crow: Mass incarceration in the age of colorblindness.* The New York, NY: New Press.

Alvarez, A. N., & Juang, L. P. (2010). Filipino Americans and racism: A multiple mediation model of coping. *Journal of Counseling Psychology, 57,* 167–178. http://dx.doi.org/10.1037/a0019091

Anthony, J. C., & Petronis, K. R. (1995). Early-onset drug use and risk of later drug problems. *Drug and Alcohol Dependence, 40,* 9–15. http://dx.doi.org/10.1016/0376-8716(95)01194-3

Baranowski, T., Mendlein, J., Resnicow, K., Frank, E., Cullen, K. W., & Baranowski, J. (2000). Physical activity and nutrition in children and youth: An overview of obesity prevention. *Preventive Medicine, 31,* 1–10. http://dx.doi.org/10.1006/pmed.2000.0686

Barker, D. J. (2002). Fetal programming of coronary heart disease. *Trends in Endocrinology and Metabolism, 13,* 364–368. http://dx.doi.org/10.1016/S1043-2760(02)00689-6

Barnes, L. L., de Leon, C. F., Lewis, T. T., Bienias, J. L., Wilson, R. S., & Evans, D. A. (2008). Perceived discrimination and mortality in a population-based study of older adults. *American Journal of Public Health, 98,* 1241–1247. http://dx.doi.org/10.2105/AJPH.2007.114397

Basáñez, T., Unger, J. B., Soto, D., Crano, W., & Baezconde-Garbanati, L. (2013). Perceived discrimination as a risk factor for depressive symptoms and substance use among Hispanic adolescents in Los Angeles. *Ethnicity & Health, 18,* 244–261. http://dx.doi.org/10.1080/13557858.2012.713093

Bell, L., Long, S., Garvan, C., & Bussing, R. (2011). The impact of teacher credentials on ADHD stigma perceptions. *Psychology in the Schools, 48,* 184–197. http://dx.doi.org/10.1002/pits.20536

Bennett, G. G., Wolin, K. Y., Robinson, E. L., Fowler, S., & Edwards, C. L. (2005). Perceived racial/ethnic harassment and tobacco use among African American young adults. *American Journal of Public Health, 95,* pp. 238–240. http://dx.doi.org/10.2105/AJPH.2004.0378

Bennett, I. M., Culhane, J. F., Webb, D. A., Coyne, J. C., Hogan, V., Mathew, L., & Elo, I. T. (2010). Perceived discrimination and depressive symptoms, smoking, and recent alcohol use in pregnancy. *Birth: Issues in Perinatal Care, 37,* 90–97. http://dx.doi.org/10.1111/j.1523-536X.2010.00388.x

Bertrand, M., & Mullainathan, S. (2004). Are Emily and Greg more employable than Lakisha and Jamal? A field experiment on labor market discrimination. *The American Economic Review, 94,* 991–1013. http://dx.doi.org/10.1257/0002828042002561

Bhatia, R., Jones, P., & Reicker, Z. (2011). Competitive foods, discrimination, and participation in the National School Lunch Program. *American Journal of Public Health, 101,* 1380–1386. http://dx.doi.org/10.2105/AJPH.2011.300134

Bonilla-Silva, E., Goar, C., & Embrick, D. G. (2006). When Whites flock together: The social psychology of White habitus. *Critical Sociology, 32,* 229–253. http://dx.doi.org/10.1163/156916306777835268

Borrell, L. N., Kiefe, C. I., Diez-Roux, A. V., Williams, D. R., & Gordon-Larsen, P. (2013). Racial discrimination, racial/ethnic segregation, and health behaviors in the CARDIA study. *Ethnicity & Health, 18,* 227–243. http://dx.doi.org/10.1080/13557858.2012.713092

Bowleg, L., Burkholder, G. J., Massie, J. S., Wahome, R., Teti, M., Malebranche, D. J., & Tschann, J. M. (2013). Racial discrimination, social support, and sexual HIV risk among Black heterosexual men. *AIDS and Behavior, 17,* 407–418. http://dx.doi.org/10.1007/s10461-012-0179-0

Brewer, R. M., & Heitzeg, N. A. (2008). The racialization of crime and punishment: Criminal justice, color-blind racism, and the political economy of the prison industrial complex. *American Behavioral Scientist, 51,* 625–644. http://dx.doi.org/10.1177/0002764207307745

Brodish, A. B., Cogburn, C. D., Fuller-Rowell, T. E., Peck, S., Malanchuk, O., & Eccles, J. S. (2011). Perceived racial discrimination as a predictor of health behaviors: The moderating role of gender. *Race and Social Problems, 3,* 160–169. http://dx.doi.org/10.1007/s12552-011-9050-6

Brody, G. H., Kogan, S. M., & Chen, Y. F. (2012). Perceived discrimination and longitudinal increases in adolescent substance use: Gender differences and mediational pathways. *American Journal of Public Health, 102,* 1006–1011. http://dx.doi.org/10.2105/AJPH.2011.300588

Brondolo, E., Brady ver Halen, N., Pencille, M., Beatty, D., & Contrada, R. J. (2009). Coping with racism: A selective review of the literature and a theoretical and methodological critique. *Journal of Behavioral Medicine, 32,* 64–88. http://dx.doi.org/10.1007/s10865-008-9193-0

Brondolo, E., Libretti, M., Rivera, L., & Walsemann, K. M. (2012). Racism and social capital: The implications for social and physical well-being. *Journal of Social Issues, 68,* 358–384. http://dx.doi.org/10.1111/j.1540-4560.2012.01752.x

Brook, D. W., Brook, J. S., Rubenstone, E., Zhang, C., & Finch, S. J. (2010). A longitudinal study of sexual risk behavior among the adolescent children of HIV-positive and HIV-negative drug-abusing fathers. *Journal of Adolescent Health, 46,* 224–231. http://dx.doi.org/10.1016/j.jadohealth.2009.07.001

Brown v. Board of Education, 347 U.S. 483 (1954).

Butler, R. N. (1969). Age-ism: Another form of bigotry. *The Gerontologist, 9,* 243–246. http://dx.doi.org/10.1093/geront/9.4_Part_1.243

Cappell, H., & Herman, C. P. (1972). Alcohol and tension reduction. A review. *Quarterly Journal of Studies on Alcohol, 33,* 33–64.

Card, D., & Rothstein, J. (2007). Racial segregation and the Black–White test score gap. *Journal of Public Economics, 91,* 2158–2184. http://dx.doi.org/10.3386/w12078

Chae, D. H., Takeuchi, D. T., Barbeau, E. M., Bennett, G. G., Lindsey, J. C., Stoddard, A. M., & Krieger, N. (2008). Alcohol disorders among Asian Americans: Associations with unfair treatment, racial/ethnic discrimination, and ethnic identification (the national Latino and Asian Americans study, 2002–2003). *Journal of Epidemiology and Community Health, 62*, 973–979. http://dx.doi.org/10.1136/jech.2007.066811

Choi, K.-H., Hudes, E. S., & Steward, W. T. (2008). Social discrimination, concurrent sexual partnerships, and HIV risk among men who have sex with men in Shanghai, China. *AIDS and Behavior, 12*, 71–77. http://dx.doi.org/10.1007/s10461-008-9394-0

Civil Rights Act of 1964, Pub. L. 88-352, 78 Stat. 241 (1964).

Clark, K. B., & Clark, M. P. (1950). Emotional factors in racial identification and preference in Negro children. *The Journal of Negro Education, 19*, 341–350. http://dx.doi.org/10.2307/2966491

Clark, R., Anderson, N. B., Clark, V. R., & Williams, D. R. (1999). Racism as a stressor for African Americans. A biopsychosocial model. *American Psychologist, 54*, 805–816. http://dx.doi.org/10.1037/0003-066X.54.10.805

Cooper, D., Thayer, J., & Waldstein, S. (2014). Coping with racism: The impact of prayer on cardiovascular reactivity and poststress recovery in African American women. *Annals of Behavioral Medicine, 47*, 218–230. http://dx.doi.org/10.1007/s12160-013-9540-4

Crawley, L. M., Ahn, D. K., & Winkleby, M. A. (2008). Perceived medical discrimination and cancer screening behaviors of racial and ethnic minority adults. *Cancer Epidemiology, Biomarkers & Prevention, 17*, 1937–1944. http://dx.doi.org/10.1158/1055-9965.EPI-08-0005

de Castro, A. B., Gee, G. C., & Takeuchi, D. T. (2008). Workplace discrimination and health among Filipinos in the United States. *American Journal of Public Health, 98*, 520–526. http://dx.doi.org/10.2105/AJPH.2007.110163

Deng, S., Kim, S. Y., Vaughan, P. W., & Li, J. (2010). Cultural orientation as a moderator of the relationship between Chinese American adolescents' discrimination experiences and delinquent behaviors. *Journal of Youth and Adolescence, 39*, 1027–1040. http://dx.doi.org/10.1007/s10964-009-9460-6

Devine, C. M., Farrell, T. J., Blake, C. E., Jastran, M., Wethington, E., & Bisogni, C. A. (2009). Work conditions and the food choice coping strategies of employed parents. *Journal of Nutrition Education and Behavior, 41*, 365–370. http://dx.doi.org/10.1016/j.jneb.2009.01.007

Dewey, K. G. (2001). Maternal and fetal stress are associated with impaired lactogenesis in humans. *The Journal of Nutrition, 131*, 3012–3015.

Díaz, R. M., Ayala, G., & Bein, E. (2004). Sexual risk as an outcome of social oppression: data from a probability sample of Latino gay men in three U.S. cities. *Cultural Diversity and Ethnic Minority Psychology, 10*, 255–267. http://dx.doi.org/10.1037/1099-9809.10.3.255

Dimick, J., Ruhter, J., Sarrazin, M. V., & Birkmeyer, J. D. (2013). Black patients more likely than Whites to undergo surgery at low-quality hospitals in segregated regions. *Health Affairs, 32*, 1046–1053. http://dx.doi.org/10.1377/hlthaff.2011.1365

Dole, N., Savitz, D. A., Hertz-Picciotto, I., Siega-Riz, A. M., McMahon, M. J., & Buekens, P. (2003). Maternal stress and preterm birth. *American Journal of Epidemiology, 157,* 14–24. http://dx.doi.org/10.1093/aje/kwf176

Echenique, F., Fryer, R. G., & Kaufman, A. (2006). Is school segregation good or bad? *The American Economic Review, 96,* 265–269. http://dx.doi.org/10.1257/000282806777212198

Elder, G. H., & Rockwell, R. C. (1979). Life-course and human-development—Ecological perspective. *International Journal of Behavioral Development, 2,* 1–21. http://dx.doi.org/10.1177/016502547900200101

Enoch, M.-A. (2011). The role of early life stress as a predictor for alcohol and drug dependence. *Psychopharmacology, 214,* 17–31. http://dx.doi.org/10.1007/s00213-010-1916-6

Feagin, J. R. (2000). *Racist America: Roots, current realities, and future reparations.* New York, NY: Routledge.

Feagin, J. R. (2006). *Systemic racism: A theory of oppression.* New York, NY: Taylor & Francis.

Feagin, J. R., & Imani, N. (1996). *The agony of education: Black students at White colleges and universities.* New York, NY: Psychology Press.

Ferraro, K. F., & Kelley-Moore, J. A. (2003). Cumulative disadvantage and health: Long-term consequences of obesity? *American Sociological Review, 68,* 707–729. http://dx.doi.org/10.2307/1519759

Fiel, J. E. (2013). Decomposing school resegregation: Social closure, racial imbalance, and racial isolation. *American Sociological Review, 78,* 828–848. http://dx.doi.org/10.1177/0003122413496252

Frankel, D. M., & Volij, O. (2011). Measuring school segregation. *Journal of Economic Theory, 146,* 1–38. http://dx.doi.org/10.1016/j.jet.2010.10.008

Fuller-Rowell, T. E., Cogburn, C. D., Brodish, A. B., Peck, S. C., Malanchuk, O., & Eccles, J. S. (2012). Racial discrimination and substance use: Longitudinal associations and identity moderators. *Journal of Behavioral Medicine, 35,* 581–590. http://dx.doi.org/10.1007/s10865-011-9388-7

Galliher, R. V., Jones, M. D., & Dahl, A. (2011). Concurrent and longitudinal effects of ethnic identity and experiences of discrimination on psychosocial adjustment of Navajo adolescents. *Developmental Psychology, 47,* 509–526. http://dx.doi.org/10.1037/a0021061

Gee, G. C., & Payne-Sturges, D. C. (2004). Environmental health disparities: A framework integrating psychosocial and environmental concepts. *Environmental Health Perspectives, 112,* 1645–1653. http://dx.doi.org/10.1289/ehp.7074

Gee, G. C., Ro, A., Shariff-Marco, S., & Chae, D. (2009). Racial discrimination and health among Asian Americans: Evidence, assessment, and directions for future research. *Epidemiologic Reviews, 31,* 130–151. http://dx.doi.org/10.1093/epirev/mxp009

Gee, G., & Walsemann, K. (2009). Does health predict the reporting of racial discrimination or do reports of discrimination predict health? Findings from the National Longitudinal Study of Youth. *Social Science & Medicine, 68*, 1676–1684. http://dx.doi.org/10.1016/j.socscimed.2009.02.002

Gee, G. C., Walsemann, K. M., & Brondolo, E. (2012). A life course perspective on how racism may be related to health inequities. *American Journal of Public Health, 102*, 967–974. http://dx.doi.org/10.2105/AJPH.2012.300666

Gibbons, F. X., Yeh, H. C., Gerrard, M., Cleveland, M. J., Cutrona, C., Simons, R. L., & Brody, G. H. (2007). Early experience with racial discrimination and conduct disorder as predictors of subsequent drug use: A critical period hypothesis. *Drug and Alcohol Dependence, 88*, 27–37. http://dx.doi.org/10.1016/j.drugalcdep.2006.12.015

Gilman, S. E., Abrams, D. B., & Buka, S. L. (2003). Socioeconomic status over the life course and stages of cigarette use: Initiation, regular use, and cessation. *Journal of Epidemiology and Community Health, 57*, 802–808. http://dx.doi.org/10.1136/jech.57.10.802

Glenn, E. N. (2008). Yearning for lightness: Transnational circuits in the marketing and consumption of skin lighteners. *Gender & Society, 22*, 281–302. http://dx.doi.org/10.1177/0891243208316089

Godfrey, K. M., & Barker, D. J. (2001). Fetal programming and adult health. *Public Health Nutrition, 4*, 611–624. http://dx.doi.org/10.1079/PHN2001145

Goldsmith, P. R. (2009). Schools or neighborhoods or both? Race and ethnic segregation and educational attainment. *Social Forces, 87*, 1913–1941. http://dx.doi.org/10.1353/sof.0.0193

Goosby, B. J. (2013). Early life course pathways of adult depression and chronic pain. *Journal of Health and Social Behavior, 54*, 75–91. http://dx.doi.org/10.1177/0022146512475089

Grant, B. F., Dawson, D. A., Stinson, F. S., Chou, S. P., Dufour, M. C., & Pickering, R. P. (2004). The 12-month prevalence and trends in DSM–IV alcohol abuse and dependence: United States, 1991–1992 and 2001–2002. *Drug and Alcohol Dependence, 74*, 223–234. http://dx.doi.org/10.1016/j.drugalcdep.2004.02.004

Grollman, E. A. (2012). Multiple forms of perceived discrimination and health among adolescents and young adults. *Journal of Health and Social Behavior, 53*, 199–214. http://dx.doi.org/10.1177/0022146512444289

Halfon, N., Larson, K., Lu, M., Tullis, E., & Russ, S. (2014). Lifecourse health development: Past, present and future. *Maternal and Child Health Journal, 18*, 344–365. http://dx.doi.org/10.1007/s10995-013-1346-2

Han, B., Gfroerer, J. C., Colliver, J. D., & Penne, M. A. (2009). Substance use disorder among older adults in the United States in 2020. *Addiction, 104*, 88–96. http://dx.doi.org/10.1111/j.1360-0443.2008.02411.x

Han, C.-S. (2008). A qualitative exploration of the relationship between racism and unsafe sex among Asian Pacific Islander gay men. *Archives of Sexual Behavior, 37*, 827–837. http://dx.doi.org/10.1007/s10508-007-9308-7

Hatzenbuehler, M. L., Corbin, W. R., & Fromme, K. (2011). Discrimination and alcohol-related problems among college students: A prospective examination of mediating effects. *Drug and Alcohol Dependence, 115*, 213–220. http://dx.doi.org/10.1016/j.drugalcdep.2010.11.002

Hicken, M. T., Lee, H., Ailshire, J., Burgard, S. A., & Williams, D. R. (2013). "Every shut eye, ain't sleep": The role of racism-related vigilance in racial/ethnic disparities in sleep difficulty. *Race and Social Problems, 5*, 100–112. http://dx.doi.org/10.1007/s12552-013-9095-9

Hicken, M. T., Lee, H., Morenoff, J., House, J. S., & Williams, D. R. (2014). Racial/ethnic disparities in hypertension prevalence: Reconsidering the role of chronic stress. *American Journal of Public Health, 104*, 117–123. http://dx.doi.org/10.2105/AJPH.2013.301395

Hochschild, A. R. (1979). *The managed heart: The commercialization of human feeling.* Berkeley, CA: University of California Press.

Hunter, M. (2002). "If you're light you're alright": Light skin color as social capital for women of color. *Gender & Society, 16*, 175–193.

Jackson, J. S., Knight, K. M., & Rafferty, J. A. (2010). Race and unhealthy behaviors: Chronic stress, the HPA axis, and physical and mental health disparities over the life course. *American Journal of Public Health, 100*, 933–939. http://dx.doi.org/10.2105/AJPH.2008.143446

Johnson, R. A., & Hoffmann, J. P. (2000). Adolescent cigarette smoking in U.S. racial/ethnic subgroups: Findings from the National Education Longitudinal Study. *Journal of Health and Social Behavior, 41*, 392–407. http://dx.doi.org/10.2307/2676293

Kaw, E. (1993). Steven Polgar Prize Essay (1991): Medicalization of racial features: Asian American women and cosmetic surgery. *Medical Anthropology Quarterly, 7*, 74–89. http://dx.doi.org/10.1525/maq.1993.7.1.02a00050

Kelly, Y., Becares, L., & Nazroo, J. (2013). Associations between maternal experiences of racism and early child health and development: Findings from the UK Millennium Cohort Study. *Journal of Epidemiology and Community Health, 67*, 35–41. http://dx.doi.org/10.1136/jech-2011-200814

Khantzian, E. J. (1997). The self-medication hypothesis of substance use disorders: A reconsideration and recent applications. *Harvard Review of Psychiatry, 4*, 231–244. http://dx.doi.org/10.3109/10673229709030550

Klassen, A. C., Hall, A. G., Saksvig, B., Curbow, B., & Klassen, D. K. (2002). Relationship between patients' perceptions of disadvantage and discrimination and listing for kidney transplantation. *American Journal of Public Health, 92*, 811–817. http://dx.doi.org/10.2105/AJPH.92.5.811

Lau, C., Hurst, N. M., Smith, E. O., & Schanler, R. J. (2007). Ethnic/racial diversity, maternal stress, lactation and very low birthweight infants. *Journal of Perinatology, 27*, 399–408. http://dx.doi.org/10.1038/sj.jp.7211770

LaVeist, T. A. (1993). Segregation, poverty, and empowerment: Health consequences for African Americans. *The Milbank Quarterly, 71*, 41–64. http://dx.doi.org/10.2307/3350274

Law, C. M., de Swiet, M., Osmond, C., Fayers, P. M., Barker, D. J., Cruddas, A. M., & Fall, C. H. (1993). Initiation of hypertension in utero and its amplification throughout life. *BMJ, 306*, 24–27. http://dx.doi.org/10.1136/bmj.306.6869.24

Lazarus, R. S., & Folkman, S. (1984). *Stress, appraisal, and coping.* New York, NY: Springer.

Lewis, T. T., Aiello, A. E., Leurgans, S., Kelly, J., & Barnes, L. L. (2010). Self-reported experiences of everyday discrimination are associated with elevated C-reactive protein levels in older African-American adults. *Brain, Behavior, and Immunity, 24*, 438–443. http://dx.doi.org/10.1016/j.bbi.2009.11.011

Lewis, T. T., Troxel, W. M., Kravitz, H. M., Bromberger, J. T., Matthews, K. A., & Hall, M. H. (2013). Chronic exposure to everyday discrimination and sleep in a multiethnic sample of middle-aged women. *Health Psychology, 32*, 810–819. http://dx.doi.org/10.1037/a0029938

Liang, C. T. H., Alvarez, A. N., Juang, L. P., & Liang, M. X. (2007). The role of coping in the relationship between perceived racism and racism-related stress for Asian Americans: Gender differences. *Journal of Counseling Psychology, 54*, 132–141. http://dx.doi.org/10.1037/0022-0167.54.2.132

Liang, C. T. H., Li, L. C., & Kim, B. S. (2004). The Asian American racism-related stress inventory: Development, factor analysis, reliability, and validity. *Journal of Counseling Psychology, 51*, 103–114. http://dx.doi.org/10.1037/0022-0167.51.1.103

Lindau, S. T., Schumm, L. P., Laumann, E. O., Levinson, W., O'Muircheartaigh, C. A., & Waite, L. J. (2007). A study of sexuality and health among older adults in the United States. *The New England Journal of Medicine, 357*, 762–774. http://dx.doi.org/10.1056/NEJMoa067423

Lorenzo-Blanco, E. I., Unger, J. B., Ritt-Olson, A., Soto, D., & Baezconde-Garbanati, L. (2011). Acculturation, gender, depression, and cigarette smoking among U.S. Hispanic youth: The mediating role of perceived discrimination. *Journal of Youth and Adolescence, 40*, 1519–1533. http://dx.doi.org/10.1007/s10964-011-9633-y

Lu, M. C., & Halfon, N. (2003). Racial and ethnic disparities in birth outcomes: A life-course perspective. *Maternal and Child Health Journal, 7*, 13–30. http://dx.doi.org/10.1023/A:1022537516969

Lynch, J., & Smith, G. D. (2005). A life course approach to chronic disease epidemiology. *Annual Review of Public Health, 26*, 1–35. http://dx.doi.org/10.1146/annurev.publhealth.26.021304.144505

Martin, S. S., Trask, J., Peterson, T., Martin, B. C., Baldwin, C., & Knapp, M. (2010). Influence of culture and discrimination on care-seeking behavior of elderly

African Americans: A qualitative study. *Social Work in Public Health, 25,* 311–326. http://dx.doi.org/10.1080/19371910903240753

Massey, D. S., & Denton, N. A. (1993). *American apartheid: Segregation and the making of the underclass.* Cambridge, MA: Harvard University Press.

Massey, D. S., & Fischer, M. J. (2000). How segregation concentrates poverty. *Ethnic and Racial Studies, 23,* 670–691. http://dx.doi.org/10.1080/01419870050033676

McEwen, B. S. (1998). Stress, adaptation, and disease. Allostasis and allostatic load. *Annals of the New York Academy of Sciences, 840,* 33–44. http://dx.doi.org/10.1111/j.1749-6632.1998.tb09546.x

Merchant, R. M., Becker, L. B., Yang, F., & Groeneveld, P. W. (2011). Hospital racial composition: A neglected factor in cardiac arrest survival disparities. *American Heart Journal, 161,* 705–711. http://dx.doi.org/10.1016/j.ahj.2011.01.011

Merlot, E., Couret, D., & Otten, W. (2008). Prenatal stress, fetal imprinting and immunity. *Brain, Behavior, and Immunity, 22,* 42–51. http://dx.doi.org/10.1016/j.bbi.2007.05.007

Merskin, D. (2004). The construction of Arabs as enemies: Post-September 11 discourse of George W. Bush. *Mass Communication & Society, 7,* 157–175. http://dx.doi.org/10.1207/s15327825mcs0702_2

Meyer, I. H., & Dean, L. (1998). Internalized homophobia, intimacy, and sexual behavior among gay and bisexual men. In Herek, G. M. (Ed.), *Stigma and sexual orientation: Understanding prejudice against lesbians, gay men, and bisexuals* (pp. 160–186). Thousand Oaks, CA: Sage. http://dx.doi.org/10.4135/9781452243818.n8

Mezuk, B., Rafferty, J. A., Kershaw, K. N., Hudson, D., Abdou, C. M., Lee, H., . . . Jackson, J. S. (2010). Reconsidering the role of social disadvantage in physical and mental health: Stressful life events, health behaviors, race, and depression. *American Journal of Epidemiology, 172,* 1238–1249. http://dx.doi.org/10.1093/aje/kwq283

Noh, S., & Kaspar, V. (2003). Perceived discrimination and depression: Moderating effects of coping, acculturation, and ethnic support. *American Journal of Public Health, 93,* 232–238. http://dx.doi.org/10.2105/AJPH.93.2.232

Odom, E. C., Vernon-Feagans, L., & The Family Life Project Key. (2010). Buffers of racial discrimination: Links with depression among rural African American mothers. *Journal of Marriage and the Family, 72,* 346–359. http://dx.doi.org/10.1111/j.1741-3737.2010.00704.x

Otiniano Verissimo, A. D., Gee, G. C., Iguchi, M. Y., Ford, C. L., & Friedman, S. R. (2013). Discrimination, drugs, and alcohol among Latina/os in Brooklyn, New York: Differences by gender. *The International Journal on Drug Policy, 24,* 367–373. http://dx.doi.org/10.1016/j.drugpo.2013.01.010

Pachter, L. M., Bernstein, B. A., Szalacha, L. A., & García Coll, C. (2010). Perceived racism and discrimination in children and youths: An exploratory study. *Health & Social Work, 35,* 61–69. http://dx.doi.org/10.1093/hsw/35.1.61

Pachter, L. M., & García Coll, C. (2009). Racism and child health: A review of the literature and future directions. *Journal of Developmental and Behavioral Pediatrics*, 30, 255–263. http://dx.doi.org/10.1097/DBP.0b013e3181a7ed5a

Paradies, Y. (2006). A systematic review of empirical research on self-reported racism and health. *International Journal of Epidemiology*, 35, 888–901. http://dx.doi.org/10.1093/ije/dyl056

Pavalko, E. K., Mossakowski, K. N., & Hamilton, V. J. (2003). Does perceived discrimination affect health? Longitudinal relationships between work discrimination and women's physical and emotional health. *Journal of Health and Social Behavior*, 44, 18–33. http://dx.doi.org/10.2307/1519813

Pearlin, L. I. (2010). The life course and the stress process: Some conceptual comparisons. *The Journals of Gerontology: Series B. Psychological Sciences and Social Sciences*, 65B, 207–215. http://dx.doi.org/10.1093/geronb/gbp106

Peña, A. (2007). Protecting Muslim civil and human rights in America: The role of Islamic, national, and international organizations. *Journal of Muslim Minority Affairs*, 27, 387–400. http://dx.doi.org/10.1080/13602000701737236

Priest, N., Paradies, Y., Stevens, M., & Bailie, R. (2012). Exploring relationships between racism, housing and child illness in remote indigenous communities. *Journal of Epidemiology and Community Health*, 66, 440–447. http://dx.doi.org/10.1136/jech.2010.117366

Priest, N., Paradies, Y., Trenerry, B., Truong, M., Karlsen, S., & Kelly, Y. (2013). A systematic review of studies examining the relationship between reported racism and health and wellbeing for children and young people. *Social Science & Medicine*, 95, 115–127. http://dx.doi.org/10.1016/j.socscimed.2012.11.031

Roberts, M. E., Gibbons, F. X., Gerrard, M., Weng, C.-Y., Murry, V. M., Simons, L. G., . . . Lorenz, F. O. (2012). From racial discrimination to risky sex: Prospective relations involving peers and parents. *Developmental Psychology*, 48, 89–102. http://dx.doi.org/10.1037/a0025430

Russell, S. T., Sinclair, K. O., Poteat, V. P., & Koenig, B. W. (2012). Adolescent health and harassment based on discriminatory bias. *American Journal of Public Health*, 102, 493–495. http://dx.doi.org/10.2105/AJPH.2011.300430

Sangalang, C. C., Chen, A. C. C., Kulis, S., & Yabuki, S. (in press). Development and validation of a discrimination measure for Cambodian American adolescents. *Asian American Journal of Psychology*, 6, 56–65. http://dx.doi.org/10.1037/a0036706

Seaton, E. K., Caldwell, C. H., Sellers, R. M., & Jackson, J. S. (2008). The prevalence of perceived discrimination among African American and Caribbean Black youth. *Developmental Psychology*, 44, 1288–1297. http://dx.doi.org/10.1037/a0012747

Seaton, E. K., Neblett, E. W., Upton, R. D., Hammond, W. P., & Sellers, R. M. (2011). The moderating capacity of racial identity between perceived discrimination and psychological well-being over time among African American youth. *Child Development, 82,* 1850–1867. http://dx.doi.org/10.1111/j.1467-8624.2011.01651.x

Seaton, E. K., & Yip, T. (2009). School and neighborhood contexts, perceptions of racial discrimination, and psychological well-being among African American adolescents. *Journal of Youth and Adolescence, 38,* 153–163. http://dx.doi.org/10.1007/s10964-008-9356-x

Sengupta, R. (2006). Reading representations of Black, East Asian, and White women in magazines for adolescent girls. *Sex Roles, 54,* 799–808. http://dx.doi.org/10.1007/s11199-006-9047-6

Shields, M. A., & Price, S. W. (2002). Racial harassment, job satisfaction and intentions to quit: Evidence from the British nursing profession. *Economica, 69,* 295–326. http://dx.doi.org/10.1111/1468-0335.00284

Simons, R. L., Chen, Y.-F., Stewart, E. A., & Brody, G. H. (2003). Incidents of discrimination and risk for delinquency: A longitudinal test of strain theory with an African American sample. *Justice Quarterly, 20,* 827–854. http://dx.doi.org/10.1080/07418820300095711

Simons, R. L., Simons, L. G., Burt, C. H., Drummund, H., Stewart, E., Brody, G. H., . . . Cutrona, C. (2006). Supportive parenting moderates the effect of discrimination upon anger, hostile view of relationships, and violence among African American boys. *Journal of Health and Social Behavior, 47,* 373–389. http://dx.doi.org/10.1177/002214650604700405

Smith, D. B. (1998). The racial segregation of hospital care revisited: Medicare discharge patterns and their implications. *American Journal of Public Health, 88,* 461–463. http://dx.doi.org/10.2105/AJPH.88.3.461

Staples, B. (1986). Just walk on by: Black men and public space. *Ms. Magazine, 55,* 84.

Stevens-Watkins, D., Brown-Wright, L., & Tyler, K. (2011). Brief report: The number of sexual partners and race-related stress in African American adolescents. Preliminary findings. *Journal of Adolescence, 34,* 191–194. http://dx.doi.org/10.1016/j.adolescence.2010.02.003

Stroub, K. J., & Richards, M. P. (2013). From resegregation to reintegration: Trends in the racial/ethnic segregation of metropolitan public schools, 1993–2009. *American Educational Research Journal, 50,* 497–531. http://dx.doi.org/10.3102/0002831213478462

Strully, K. W. (2011). Health care segregation and race disparities in infectious disease: The case of nursing homes and seasonal influenza vaccinations. *Journal of Health and Social Behavior, 52,* 510–526. http://dx.doi.org/10.1177/0022146511423544

Swahn, M. H., Mahendra, R. R., Paulozzi, L. J., Winston, R. L., Shelley, G. A., Taliano, J., . . . Saul, J. R. (2003). Violent attacks on Middle Easterners in the United States during the month following the September 11, 2001, terrorist attacks. *Injury Prevention, 9,* 187–189. http://dx.doi.org/10.1136/ip.9.2.187

Thoits, P. A. (1995). Stress, coping, and social support processes: Where are we? What next? *Journal of Health and Social Behavior, 35*, 53–79. http://dx.doi.org/10.2307/2626957

Thoits, P. A. (2010). Stress and health: Major findings and policy implications. *Journal of Health and Social Behavior, 51*, 41–53. http://dx.doi.org/10.1177/0022146510383499

Thrasher, A. D., Clay, O. J., Ford, C. L., & Stewart, A. L. (2012). Theory-guided selection of discrimination measures for racial/ethnic health disparities research among older adults. *Journal of Aging and Health, 24*, 1018–1043. http://dx.doi.org/10.1177/0898264312440322

Umaña-Taylor, A. J., & Updegraff, K. A. (2007). Latino adolescents' mental health: Exploring the interrelations among discrimination, ethnic identity, cultural orientation, self-esteem, and depressive symptoms. *Journal of Adolescence, 30*, 549–567. http://dx.doi.org/10.1016/j.adolescence.2006.08.002

Umaña-Taylor, A. J., Wong, J. J., Gonzales, N. A., & Dumka, L. E. (2012). Ethnic identity and gender as moderators of the association between discrimination and academic adjustment among Mexican-origin adolescents. *Journal of Adolescence, 35*, 773–786. http://dx.doi.org/10.1016/j.adolescence.2011.11.003

Umberson, D. (1987). Family status and health behaviors: Social control as a dimension of social integration. *Journal of Health and Social Behavior, 28*, 306–319. http://dx.doi.org/10.2307/2136848

Umberson, D., Crosnoe, R., & Reczek, C. (2010). Social Relationships and Health Behavior Across Life Course. *Annual Review of Sociology, 36*, 139–157. http://dx.doi.org/10.1146/annurev-soc-070308-120011

Umbreit, M., Lewis, T., & Burns, H. (2003). A community response to a 9/11 hate crime: Restorative justice through dialogue. *Contemporary Justice Review, 6*, 383–391. http://dx.doi.org/10.1080/1028258032000144820

Van Ausdale, D., & Feagin, J. R. (2001). *The first R: How children learn race and racism*. Lanham, MD: Rowman & Littlefield Publishers.

Van den Bergh, B. R. H. (1990). The influence of maternal emotions during pregnancy on fetal and neonatal behavior. *Journal of Prenatal and Perinatal Psychology and Health, 5*, 119–130.

Van den Bergh, B. R. H., Mulder, E. J. H., Mennes, M., & Glover, V. (2005). Antenatal maternal anxiety and stress and the neurobehavioural development of the fetus and child: Links and possible mechanisms. A review. *Neuroscience and Biobehavioral Reviews, 29*, 237–258. http://dx.doi.org/10.1016/j.neubiorev.2004.10.007

Viruell-Fuentes, E. A., Miranda, P. Y., & Abdulrahim, S. (2012). More than culture: Structural racism, intersectionality theory, and immigrant health. *Social Science & Medicine, 75*, 2099–2106. http://dx.doi.org/10.1016/j.socscimed.2011.12.037

Wadhwa, P. D., Sandman, C. A., Porto, M., Dunkel-Schetter, C., & Garite, T. J. (1993). The association between prenatal stress and infant birth weight and gestational age at birth: A prospective investigation. *American Journal of Obstetrics and Gynecology, 169*, 858–865. http://dx.doi.org/10.1016/0002-9378(93)90016-C

Walsemann, K. M., & Bell, B. A. (2010). Integrated schools, segregated curriculum: Effects of within-school segregation on adolescent health behaviors and educational aspirations. *American Journal of Public Health, 100*, 1687–1695. http://dx.doi.org/10.2105/AJPH.2009.179424

Walsemann, K. M., Bell, B. A., & Maitra, D. (2011). The intersection of school racial composition and student race/ethnicity on adolescent depressive and somatic symptoms. *Social Science & Medicine, 72*, 1873–1883. http://dx.doi.org/10.1016/j.socscimed.2011.03.033

Walsemann, K. M., Gee, G. C., & Ro, A. (2013). Educational attainment in the context of social inequality: New directions for research on education and health. *American Behavioral Scientist, 57*, 1082–1104. http://dx.doi.org/10.1177/0002764213487346

Whitbeck, L. B., Hoyt, D. R., McMorris, B. J., Chen, X., & Stubben, J. D. (2001). Perceived discrimination and early substance abuse among American Indian children. *Journal of Health and Social Behavior, 42*, 405–424. http://dx.doi.org/10.2307/3090187

Williams, D. R., & Collins, C. (2001). Racial residential segregation: A fundamental cause of racial disparities in health. *Public Health Reports, 116*, 404–416.

Williams, D. R., & Mohammed, S. A. (2013). Racism and health: I. Pathways and scientific evidence. *American Behavioral Scientist, 57*, 1152–1173. http://dx.doi.org/10.1177/0002764213487340

Yen, I. H., Ragland, D. R., Greiner, B. A., & Fisher, J. M. (1999). Workplace discrimination and alcohol consumption: Findings from the San Francisco Muni Health and Safety Study. *Ethnicity & Disease, 9*, 70–80.

Yip, T., Gee, G. C., & Takeuchi, D. T. (2008). Racial discrimination and psychological distress: The impact of ethnic identity and age among immigrant and United States-born Asian adults. *Developmental Psychology, 44*, 787–800. http://dx.doi.org/10.1037/0012-1649.44.3.787

Yoshikawa, H., Alan-David Wilson, P., Chae, D. H., & Cheng, J.-F. (2004). Do family and friendship networks protect against the influence of discrimination on mental health and HIV risk among Asian and Pacific Islander gay men? *AIDS Education and Prevention, 16*, 84–100.

Young-Wolff, K. C., Enoch, M.-A., & Prescott, C. A. (2011). The influence of gene-environment interactions on alcohol consumption and alcohol use disorders: A comprehensive review. *Clinical Psychology Review, 31*, 800–816. http://dx.doi.org/10.1016/j.cpr.2011.03.005

7

RACISM AND PHYSICAL HEALTH DISPARITIES

JOSEPH KEAWE'AIMOKU KAHOLOKULA

Eliminating health disparities is a national public health priority in the United States (Dankwa-Mullan et al., 2010). A health disparity exists when a particular population has significantly higher rates of disease incidence, prevalence, morbidity, or mortality than the general population (Public Health Service Act, 2000). Ethnic minorities, such as American Indians, Alaska Natives, Asian and African Americans, Hispanics, and Pacific Islanders, have poorer physical health than the general population. They are at greater risks for adverse birth outcomes (Anachebe, 2006) and chronic diseases, such as diabetes and cardiovascular disease (CVD; Winston, Barr, Carrasquillo, Bertoni, & Shea, 2009). They are more likely to develop diseases at younger ages (Price, Khubchandani, McKinney, & Braun, 2013), to receive suboptimal medical care (Shavers et al., 2012), and to have shorter life expectancies (Panapasa, Mau, Williams, & McNally, 2010).

---

http://dx.doi.org/10.1037/14852-008
The Cost of Racism for People of Color: Contextualizing Experiences of Discrimination, A. N. Alvarez, C. T. H. Liang, and H. A. Neville (Editors)
Copyright © 2016 by the American Psychological Association. All rights reserved.

R. Clark, Anderson, Clark, and Williams (1999) defined *racism*, also referred to as *racial/ethnic discrimination* or *oppression*, as the beliefs, acts, or institutional measures that devalue people because of their phenotype or ethnic affiliation. It is a psychosocial stressor rooted in the very founding of the United States that threatens the physical health of ethnic minorities (Harrell, Hall, & Taliaferro, 2003). In this chapter, I discuss the impact of racism on self-reported physical health status and on hypertension (HTN), obesity, diabetes, CVD, cancer, and adverse birth outcomes, and I then provide an overview of the pathways from racism to physical health. I conclude this chapter with conceptual, methodological, and analytical considerations for future research.

RACISM AND SELF-REPORTED PHYSICAL HEALTH STATUS

Many U.S. ethnic minorities, compared with Whites and the general population, have a poorer health status across different socioeconomic conditions and the lifespan (August & Sorkin, 2010; Jang, Park, Kang, & Chiriboga, 2014). Self-reported health status is associated with morbidity and mortality (Lee et al., 2007). Studies have linked perceived racism to self-reported physical health status in different ethnic groups, independent of socioeconomic status (SES), acculturation factors, and even skin color (Borrell, Kiefe, Williams, Diez-Roux, & Gordon-Larsen, 2006; Pascoe & Smart Richman, 2009).

In African Americans, for example, Borrell et al. (2006) found that greater perceived racism was associated with a poorer physical health status, accounting for socioeconomic status and skin color. They also examined skin color as a marker of discrimination in African Americans because those of darker skin often report more discrimination than those of lighter skin (Klonoff & Landrine, 2000). However, skin color did not moderate or mediate the racism–health-status association in this study (see Chapter 4, this volume, for an explanation of moderators and mediators). Borrell et al. speculated that skin color may not matter as much now as it did in the past because African Americans are treated the same by the U.S. majority, regardless of their skin color.

In both U.S.-born and Mexico-born Mexicans, Finch, Hummer, Kol, and Vega (2001) found that greater perceived racism was associated with both poorer overall physical health status and having more self-reported chronic conditions (e.g., diabetes, HTN, heart trouble; a measure of morbidity), which held across differences in sociodemographics, SES, nativity (i.e., U.S. vs. Mexico born), acculturation-related factors (e.g., language conflict, legal status), and social support. However, depression symptoms attenuated the effects of racism on self-reported morbidity, suggesting that it serve as a mediator.

In Asian Americans, Gee, Spencer, Chen, and Takeuchi (2007) found that greater perceived racism (vs. less) was associated with a higher likelihood of self-reported cardiovascular (69%), respiratory (37%), and pain (71%) conditions, adjusting for sociodemographics, SES, and acculturation-related factors. When disaggregated, racism was associated only with cardiovascular conditions in Chinese and with respiratory and pain conditions in Vietnamese and Filipinos. In another study of Asian Americans, depression symptoms mediated the effects of racism on physical health status (Mereish, Liu, & Helms, 2012). In Filipino Americans, specifically, de Castro, Gee, and Takeuchi (2008) found that racism in the workplace was associated with more physical health complaints, adjusting for sociodemographics, SES, general discrimination, reasons for immigration to United States, and job-specific factors.

Not all studies found an association between racism and measures of general physical health status or an association in the direction expected. Paradies (2006) identified 94 studies that examined the effects of racism on self-reported measures of general physical health, of which 21% found a negative association, 17% found a positive association, and 60% found no association. Several methodological weaknesses were proposed to explain these inconsistent findings, which are elaborated on later in this chapter. However, Pascoe and Smart Richman (2009), in their meta-analysis of 36 studies of the racism–physical health relationship, found an average correlation of −.13 (95% confidence interval from −.16 to −.10), supporting the idea that racism has a modest but significant negative effect on a person's physical health status.

RACISM AND SPECIFIC PHYSICAL HEALTH OUTCOMES

Hypertension and Blood Pressure

HTN, or chronic high blood pressure (BP), is a major risk factor for CVD and stroke (Centers for Disease Control and Prevention [CDC], 2011b). HTN prevalence is greater in African Americans, at 34%; American Indians/Alaska Natives, 30%; and Native Hawaiians/Pacific Islanders, 41%—compared with Whites and the general population, at 25% (Schiller, Lucas, Ward, & Peregoy, 2012). Studies found an association between racism and HTN and BP, but with mixed results (Brondolo, Love, Pencille, Schoenthaler, & Ogedegbe, 2011; Cuffee, Hargraves, & Allison, 2012).

Earlier studies found no association between either interpersonal (Broman, 1996) or internalized racism (Tull et al., 1999) and HTN diagnosis. Chae, Nuru-Jeter, and Adler (2012), however, found that implicit racial bias—having a pro-Black versus anti-Black bias—moderates the association between racism and HTN in Blacks, adjusting for sociodemographics, SES, abdominal adiposity, and chronic medical conditions. More perceived racism was associated with a nearly 60% higher likelihood of HTN for those with an implicit anti-Black bias, but the risk was cut by half for those with an implicit pro-Black bias.

In addition to the moderating effects of implicit racial bias on the racism–HTN association, the effects of who perpetrates racism have also been examined. Din-Dzietham, Nembhard, Collins, and Davis (2004) found an association between perceived stress due to racism at work and HTN in Blacks when the perpetrator was a non-Black, after adjusting for age, gender, body mass index (BMI), and coping abilities. They found that both systolic blood pressure (SBP) and diastolic blood pressure (DBP) increased following race-based discrimination at work, whether perpetrated by another Black or by a non-Black. The magnitude of change was greater, however, when perpetrated by another Black person, albeit the effects were nonsignificant. Perhaps the tolerance for discrimination is less, at least in the short-term, when perpetuated by another person of the same race because it is either unexpected or incomprehensible. Nevertheless, experiencing discrimination from non-Blacks appears to cause more psychological distress for Blacks in the workplace.

Aside from African Americans, the racism–HTN association has been examined in Native Hawaiians. Kaholokula, Iwane, and Nacapoy (2010) found an increase likelihood of HTN for Native Hawaiians who perceived greater racism, adjusting for age, gender, education, and degree of ethnic and American identity. A stronger American identity was also independently associated with having HTN, which may be a marker of discrimination. Native Hawaiians with a higher American identity could be finding themselves marginalized by other Hawaiians for wanting to assimilate while also having difficulties being fully accepted into the American mainstream. It could also be a marker of other psychosocial stressors associated with the adoption of an American lifestyle for Native Hawaiians.

Studies that have examined the effects of perceived racism on single time-point measurements of BP yielded mixed findings. Some found no association (Barksdale, Farrug, & Harkness, 2009; Peters, 2004), whereas others found a nonlinear association (Krieger & Sidney, 1996). For example, Ryan, Gee, and Laflamme (2006) found that, among African Americans, Black immigrants, and Latinos, SBP was higher in those who reported the greatest and least racism but lower in those who reported moderate levels of racism, adjusting for sociodemographics, SES, tobacco use, exercise, BP medications, BMI, and health insurance. Krieger and Sidney (1996) also found a similar racism–SBP association in working class Blacks.

In explaining the nonlinear association between racism and HTN, Krieger and Sidney (1996) and Ryan et al. (2006) suggested that Blacks who report no experience with racism may be coping by not acknowledging its occurrence but that they are psychological or physiologically impacted in some way. Individuals of groups that often experience racism are more likely to report that other members of their group, but not themselves, are victims of racism (Krieger, Rowley, Herman, Avery, & Phillips, 1993). A member of a stigmatized group who has internalized racism may perceive themselves as "deserving," or do not interpret racist acts as such. Ryan et al. encouraged researchers to examine the functional form of racism to avoid a Type II error (failure to reject a false null hypothesis) when racism is examined only as a linear effect.

In contrast, studies that examined the effects of racism on ambulatory blood pressure (ABP), which better captures BP reactivity to daily events, are more consistent in their findings than those examining HTN status or single time-point measurements of BP. Steffen, McNeilly, Anderson, and Sherwood (2003) found that greater perceived racism was related to higher ABP during waking hours in Blacks with normal or mildly elevated BP. Brondolo et al. (2008) found that greater perceived racism was associated with higher nocturnal ABP in African Americans and Hispanics, independent of SES and the personality factors of cynicism and hostility.

Of the 79 racism-HTN/BP studies identified by Paradies (2006), only 24% found a positive association, whereas 75% found no association and 1% found a negative association. The findings of no, or a negative association, may be due to the nonlinear effects of racism on HTN and/or the failure to consider implicit racial bias (i.e., anti-Black vs. pro-Black bias) and the context (e.g., who perpetuated racist actions) and setting (e.g., workplace vs. public places) as a mediator or moderator. Although findings when HTN diagnosis and single time-point measurements of BP are used are inconsistent, the findings are much more consistent with ABP as an outcome (Brondolo et al., 2011). In comparing across studies examining the effects of racism on HTN status and BP, Dolezsar, McGrath, Herzig, and Miller (2014) conducted a meta-analysis of 44 studies. They found that perceived racism was modestly associated with HTN status (Fisher's $Z = .05$) but not with resting SBP (Fisher's $Z = .01$) or DBP (Fisher's $Z = .02$), but they also found that perceived racism was most strongly associated with nighttime ABP (Fisher's $Z = .14$), especially among Blacks.

Obesity

Obesity affects 36% of adults and 17% of children and adolescents in the United States (Ogden, Carroll, Kit, & Flegal, 2012). It is a major risk factor for HTN; CVD; diabetes; and cancer of the endometrial, breast, and colon. The adult obesity prevalence is higher in American Indians/Alaska

Natives, at 41%; African Americans, 48%; Hispanics, 43%; and Native Hawaiians/Pacific Islanders, 49%—compared with Whites, at 33% (Ogden et al., 2012). Some studies link perceived racism to obesity risk in several ethnic populations (Cozier, Wise, Palmer, & Rosenberg, 2009; McCubbin & Antonio, 2012).

In two separate studies that included people of several different ethnic groups, Shariff-Marco, Klassen, and Bowie (2010) and Hunte and Williams (2009) found a positive association between racism and overweight/obesity in Whites when compared with other ethnic populations, after adjusting for sociodemographics, SES, and other relevant factors. Both studies included African Americans and Hispanics, and the former study also included American Indians/Alaska Natives. Hunte and Williams, post hoc, divided their White sample into a non-ethnic White group and an ethnic White group, with the latter group including Irish, Italian, Jewish, and Polish Whites. They found a significant association between racism and abdominal adiposity only for the ethnic White group, noting that these ethnic Whites have, historically, been discriminated against in the United States and thus report more discrimination than do other Whites.

In women of African ancestry, studies found that internalized racism may better explain the association between racism and overweight/obesity. Vines et al. (2007) found an inverse relationship between racism and abdominal adiposity among African American women, but they hypothesized that women who perceive little or no exposure to racism may have higher internalized racism. Their hypothesis is supported by several studies of Afro-Caribbean women that found an association between internalized racism—holding a negative attitude toward Blacks—and an increase likelihood of overweight or abdominal obesity, independent of sociodemographic, SES, BMI, anxiety, and depression (Butler, Tull, Chambers, & Taylor, 2002; Chambers et al., 2004; Tull et al., 1999). Despite the role internalized racism might play, Cozier et al. (2009) found that higher levels of interpersonal racism was associated with an increase in body weight and waist circumference over an 8-year period in African American women, adjusting for age, SES, alcohol and cigarette use, physical activity, and other biological and behavioral correlates of obesity.

In Asian Americans and Pacific Islanders, Gee, Ro, Gavin, and Takeuchi (2008) found that reports of racism were associated with obesity, adjusting for sociodemographics, weight discrimination, generational status, employment, health status, and social desirability response bias. The association strengthened with increased length of time in the United States. In Native Hawaiians, specifically, McCubbin and Antonio (2012) found that greater perceived overt racism (e.g., harassed, threatened) was associated with a higher likelihood of overweight/obesity and that greater perceived covert racism (e.g., receiving poorer service) was associated with a lower likelihood, after adjusting for age, gender, SES, and years living in Hawai'i. They speculated that the counterintuitive finding of covert racism leading to less obesity may be due to the less invasive nature of covert racism as to not undermine a person's self-worth, integrity and/or identity.

The studies reviewed here support an association between racism and obesity in different ethnic groups, especially among African Americans, Asian Americans, Native Hawaiians, and ethnic Whites. However, more research is needed to sort through how racism affects obesity across these different populations and how they may differ across gender. For example, it is apparent that internalized racism is an important construct to consider in this association among Black women, but research is lacking among Black men. The idea that covert and overt racism may work differently in affecting obesity risk is also worth further investigation in other ethnic populations as they suggest differences in the degree of distress caused by, and/or type of coping strategies used to deal with, racism. Certain ethnic White populations, a group often underrepresented in racism-health research, are also affected by perceived racism, as it relates to obesity, but more studies are needed in these populations across other physical health outcomes.

Diabetes

Type 2 diabetes mellitus (DM), a risk factor for CVD and stroke, is a metabolic disease characterized by high blood glucose due to insulin resistance and relative insulin deficiency. American Indians/Alaska Natives have a higher DM prevalence, at 16%; African Americans, 13%; Hispanics, 12%; Filipinos and Native Hawaiians, 19%—compared with Asian Americans, at 8%; Whites, 10%; and the general population, 11% (CDC, 2011a). Studies have found that internalized racism is associated with DM risk in different Black populations (Butler et al., 2002; Tull & Chambers, 2001).

Among Afro-Caribbean women, Butler et al. (2002) found that those with higher levels of internalized racism (vs. those with lower levels) were two times more likely to have elevated fasting glucose, controlling for age, education, hostility, and BMI. Women with higher internalized racism had greater abdominal adiposity, adjusting for age, education, hostility, and elevated fasting glucose status. Abdominal adiposity also mediated the association between racism and fasting glucose. Similarly, Tull, Cort, Gwebu, and Gwebu (2007) found internalized racism associated with abnormal fasting glucose in women, but not men, among Blacks from Zimbabwe. In addition to racism affecting glucose levels in Black women, Chambers et al. (2004) found that Afro-Caribbean adolescent girls with higher levels of internalized racism were three times more likely to be insulin resistant than girls with less internalized racism, after adjusting for age, income, birth weight, hostility, physical activity, and family history of diabetes.

Among African Americans residing in the U.S. Virgin Islands, Tull and Chambers (2001) found an association between perceived racism and DM diagnosis. They found that those with new diagnosed DM were nearly three times more likely to report higher levels of both internalized racism and hostility than those without DM. In both groups, internalized racism and hostility were positively correlated. It appears that, even in a predominately Black-majority society, like the U.S. Virgin Islands, African Americans are still psychologically and physically impacted by racism.

Butler et al. (2002) and Tull et al. (2007) proposed that people with high internalized racism, because of the psychological distress it causes, engage in behaviors that increase their risk for abdominal obesity, such as alcohol consumption, poor diet, and physical inactivity, which in turn places them at risk for DM. Another explanation they propose is that a person with internalized racism is predisposed to "defeat" type responses to environmental stressors, which leads to dysregulations in the human stress response system. Based on the hypothesis by Björntorp, Holm, and Rosmond (1999), chronic arousal of the hypothalamic–pituitary–adrenal (HPA) axis, due to a chronic defeated response to life stressors, can cause cortisol dysregulation and metabolic abnormalities, which can lead to abnormal glucose tolerance.

Overall, there is an association between internalized racism and DM risk in women of African descent residing outside of the United States. Past research focused exclusively on the effects of internalized racism because they were conducted in areas (i.e., Caribbean, Zimbabwe) were Blacks are the majority. Interpersonal racism is believed to be less of a problem in these countries but internalized racism is presumed to exist because of past racist propaganda due to slavery (Butler et al., 2002). More studies on the effects of different forms of racism on DM risk in African Americans and other ethnic groups residing in the United States are needed.

Cardiovascular Disease

CVD, or heart disease, interferes with blood and oxygen transportation to the body and brain. It is often related to atherosclerosis—a condition that develops when plaque builds up in the walls of the arteries. CVD is the leading cause of death for African Americans (24.5%), Hispanics (20.8%), Native Hawaiians (31%), and Whites (25.1%) and the second leading cause of death for American Indians/Alaska Natives (18%) and Asians/Pacific Islanders (23%; Aluli, Reyes, & Tsark, 2007; Go et al., 2013). Paradies (2006) identified 12 studies that examined perceived racism and heart disease, with all finding no association; however, these studies were mostly done among African Americans and did not consider the effects of internalized racism. Since Paradies's review in 2006, CVD and coronary artery calcification (CAC), an early sign of coronary heart disease, has been found to be associated with perceived racism in some ethnic groups and internalized racism in African Americans, albeit the findings have not been uniform.

In New Zealand, for example, Harris et al. (2012) found that greater perceived racism was associated with self-reported CVD, as well as with self-reported overall health status, physical functioning, and smoking and drinking, in Maori, Pacific Islanders, Asians, and Europeans, adjusting for sociodemographics and SES. Although they did not analyze this association within specific ethnic groups, they found that Asians, Maori, and Pacific Islanders were about three and 10 times more likely than European New Zealanders to report having ever experienced racism and experiencing multiple types of racism (e.g., physical and verbal attacks, unfair treatment in different settings), respectively.

In examining the moderating effects of internalized racism, Chae, Lincoln, Adler, and Syme (2010) found that the experience of racism led to a higher risk of CVD among African American men who disagreed with negative beliefs about Blacks. Among those who held negative beliefs, the reporting of no experiences of racism led to a higher risk of CVD. African American men who hold negative attitudes toward their own racial group and who perceive no racism may be minimizing, discounting, or ignoring racist actions against them as a coping strategy (Williams, Neighbors, & Jackson, 2003).

When examining CAC, a risk factor for CVD, Everage, Gjelsvik, McGarvey, Linkletter, and Loucks (2012) found that greater perceived interpersonal racism was associated with a lower risk of CAC in African Americans, after adjusting for age, gender, SES, psychosocial factors, and coronary heart disease risk factors. Other studies, albeit nonsignificant, also found an inverse association between interpersonal racism and CAC (Albert et al., 2008; Lewis et al., 2006). The role of internalized racism, which was not considered in these studies, might help to explain the inverse association. As noted earlier with HTN, obesity, and DM, it could be that those who perceive no or little racism are more likely to report higher levels of internalized racism and/or to cope by not acknowledging or avoiding its occurrence, which may cause greater psychological and physiological stress than does acknowledging its presence.

Overall, studies across different ethnic groups support the notion that greater perceived racism is associated with a history of CVD. As for the inverse association found between racism and CAC in African Americans (Albert et al., 2008; Everage et al., 2012; Lewis et al., 2006), internalized racism may serve as a moderator, as it did for the association between racism and CVD diagnosis in Chae et al.'s (2010) study. More studies are needed to confirm this hypothesis in both African American men and women.

Cancer

Cancer, or malignant neoplasms, is the second leading cause of death in the United States (Heron, 2013). The incidence and survival rate of cancer differs across ethnic groups, by gender, and type of cancer (Pleis, Lucas, & Ward, 2009). Black men are more likely than White men to develop prostate cancer and are twice as likely to die from the disease. Black women are 10% less likely to develop breast cancer than White women, but 37% more likely to die from the disease. Taylor et al. (2007) examined the association between racism and breast cancer incidence in African American women. For those under 50 years of age, they found that the incidence was 48% higher in those who experienced major racial discrimination (i.e., treated unfairly on the job, in housing, by the police) than those women who did not, adjusting for age, education, BMI, and other factors related to breast cancer. Although more studies are needed to confirm these findings, and in other ethnic populations, it supports the notion that racism can increase the risk for breast cancer, a type of cancer strongly associated with obesity.

Birth Outcomes

Preterm deliveries (<37 weeks gestation), low birth weights (<2,500 g), and infant mortality rates are drastically higher in African American mothers compared with mothers of other ethnic groups (Dominguez, 2010). Preterm and low birth-weight neonates are at a greater risk for death in the first year of life. Those who survive their first year are at risk for neurological and cognitive impairments that can adversely affect their learning and lead to socioeconomic disadvantages in adulthood (Blumenshine, Egerter, Barclay, Cubbin, & Braveman, 2010).

The Black–White differences in adverse birth outcomes are only partially explained by substance use (e.g., tobacco, alcohol), use of prenatal care, genetic factors, and SES (Dominguez, Dunkel-Schetter, Glynn, Hobel, & Sandman, 2008). Dole et al. (2004) found that Black women who perceived greater racism were 80% more likely to have preterm births, but they found no such association in White women. In a sample of predominately Black and White women, Dole et al. (2003) found that women who reported more racism during pregnancy were 40% more likely to have preterm births, adjusting for BMI, SES, social support level, and depression and anxiety symptoms.

In addition to racism experienced during birth, studies have found that a lifetime experience of racism is also associated with adverse birth outcomes. For example, Mustillo et al. (2004) found that 50% of Black women who had preterm births and 62% of those who had low birth-weight babies had more lifetime experiences of racism, compared with only 5% of White women who had preterm births and 0% who had low weight babies. Overall, women who reported more racism had three times the risk of preterm delivery and nearly five times the risk of delivering a low-birth-weight baby, independent of cigarette smoking, alcohol use, depression symptoms, and SES. In another study, Collins, David, Handler, Wall, and Andes (2004) found that Black women reporting a lifetime of exposure to racism were 3 times more likely to have very low birth-weight babies than Black mothers of critically ill but normal weight babies (>2,500 gm). Other studies have also found that a lifetime of exposure to racism puts Black women, but not White women, at risk for having lower weight babies (Dominguez et al., 2008).

PATHWAYS FROM RACISM TO PHYSICAL HEALTH OUTCOMES

Adapted from Paradies et al. (2013), Figure 7.1 shows the hypothesized pathway from racism to physical health. Using the biopsychosocial model of disease risk (Engel, 1997), R. Clark, Anderson, Clark, and Williams (1999) suggested that interpreting an environmental event as racist leads

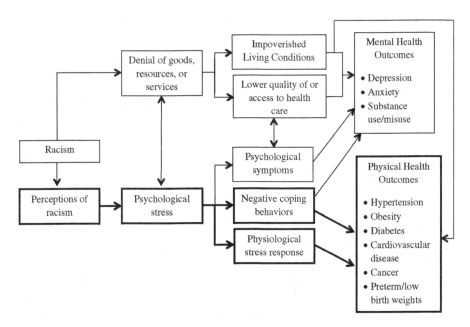

Figure 7.1. The pathways from perceived racism to physical health outcomes are depicted here. The bolded squares and arrows indicate the pathways reviewed in this chapter. From "Racism as a Determinant of Health: A Protocol for Conducting a Systematic Review and Meta-Analysis," by Y. Paradies, N. Priest, J. Ben, M. Truong, A. Gupta, A. Pieterse, . . . G. Gee, 2013, *Systematic Reviews*, p. 85. Copyright 2013 by Biomed Central Ltd. Adapted with permission.

to heightened psychological and physiological stress responses that are influenced by the interplay of sociodemographic, socioeconomic, psychosocial, and behavioral factors. Chronic activation of these stress responses leads to abnormalities of the immune, neuroendocrine, and cardiovascular systems that increase disease risk or negative medical outcomes. The pathways bolded in Figure 7.1 are the focus of this section. For more details, see Brondolo, Gallo, and Myers (2009); Harrell et al. (2003); and Pascoe and Smart Richman (2009).

Psychological Stress Response

The experience of racism affects physical health through psychological factors (Paradies et al., 2013; Williams & Mohammed, 2009). Perceived racism leads to psychological stress or distress for many people, which can manifest as depression, anxiety, emotional unrest, anger, resentment, and/or paranoia, to name a few. Vines et al. (2006) found that 41% of African American women reported very strong active emotions, such as anger, and 16% reported very strong passive emotions, such as feeling powerlessness, in response to racism. Indices of psychological distress (e.g., depression, anxiety symptoms) have been found to mediate the relationship between perceived racism and physical health outcomes in Hispanics (Todorova, Falcón, Lincoln, & Price, 2010) and Asian Americans (Mereish et al., 2012).

Many different, and often interacting, coping responses can be used by a person in response to racist acts, such as seeking social support, substance misuse, and anger suppression or expression (Brondolo et al., 2005; Gerrard et al., 2012), which can strengthen or weaken the effects of perceived racism on psychological distress. For example, a person might deal with their anger toward racist acts by misusing alcohol or with their depression by overeating (Striegel-Moore, Dohm, Pike, Wilfley, & Fairburn, 2002), which can further exacerbate anger or depression. Certain coping responses to racism, such as substance use and unhealthy eating, can put a person at risk for DM, CVD, and certain cancers.

Psychosocial and physiological factors influence, either beneficially or detrimentally, the association between racism and physical health. Among the psychological factors are racial identity (V. R. Clark, Cobb, Hopkins, & Smith, 2006), implicit racial bias (Chae et al., 2012), passive coping responses (R. Clark & Anderson, 2001), anger expression (Steffen et al., 2003), social support (R. Clark, 2003), cultural socialization (Liu & Lau, 2013), and John Henryism (i.e., the tendency to work very hard to disprove stereotypes of laziness and inability; R. Clark & Adams, 2004). Their moderating effects can differ across ethnic groups and by gender (Pascoe & Smart Richman, 2009). Heart rate variability, a physiological marker of stress vulnerability, in African American men (Utsey & Hook, 2007), and sleep disturbances in Hispanics (Steffen & Bowden, 2006) moderate the relationship between perceived racism and psychological distress.

Physiological Stress Response

Chronic activation of the physiological stress response, due to psychological or environmental stressors, can adversely affect the immune, neuroendocrine, and cardiovascular systems (Harrell et al., 2003). The effects of racism on BP, impaired fasting glucose and glucose intolerance, and on abdominal adiposity as risk factors for HTN, DM, and CVD were reviewed above. Here, I review studies that link racism to other physiological stress responses related to the inflammatory process, activation of the HPA axis, and cardiovascular reactivity.

Inflammation Biomarkers

High circulating levels of C-reactive protein (CRP), a biomarker of the inflammatory process, has been linked to CVD (Ridker, Hennekens, Buring, & Rifai, 2000), DM (Pradhan, Manson, Rifai, Buring, & Ridker, 2001), and cancer (Allin & Nordestgaard, 2011). Although Albert et al. (2008) found no direct association in Blacks, Whites, and Hispanics, the findings from other studies suggest that BMI may mediate the association between racism and CRP (Cunningham et al., 2012; Lewis, Aiello, Leurgans, Kelly, & Barnes, 2010). For instance, Cunningham et al. (2012) found that Black women who reported moderate experiences of racism had higher levels of CRP compared with Black women reporting no experiences of racism, adjusting for sociodemographics and other biological correlates. No association between racism and CRP was seen for Black women who reported high levels of racism compared with those who reported none, with the same adjustments. After adjusting for BMI and substance use, the association between racism and CRP was no longer evident in Black women. White women who reported the highest levels of racism had higher levels of CRP compared with those who reported no experiences, independent of all modifiable risk factors. No association was found in Black and White men. More research is needed to elucidate the effects of racism, especially internalized racism, on CRP levels in Blacks and other ethnic groups.

Cortisol Dysregulation

Cortisol is the main stress hormone of the HPA axis that helps the body respond to environmental or psychological stressors (Burke, Davis, Otte, & Mohr, 2005). Under acute stress, cortisol increases to prepare the body's fight or flight response, but chronic stressors can lead to lowered, flattened, or blunted cortisol responses and a delayed recovery to baseline. Cortisol dysregulation has been linked to the development of DM and CVD (Björntorp & Rosmond, 2000), and large differences in cortisol activity have been found between some ethnic minority groups and Whites (DeSantis et al., 2007). Prolonged HPA activation due to chronic psychological stress can lead to changes in cortisol homeostasis (Miller, Chen, & Zhou, 2007).

Studies have found an association between perceived racism and cortisol activity in some ethnic groups. For example, Zeiders, Doane, and Roosa (2012) found that more perceived racism was associated with greater overall cortisol output and marginally associated with a steeper cortisol awakening response (20–30 minutes after awakening in the morning) in Mexican American adolescents, adjusting for income, acculturation level, life stressors, and other correlates of cortisol activity. Among adult Native Hawaiians, Kaholokula et al. (2010) found that greater perceived racism was associated with lower diurnal cortisol output, adjusting for sociodemographics and biological and psychosocial confounders. Similarly, in adult Afro-Caribbean women, Tull, Sheu, Butler, and Cornelious (2005) also found lower cortisol levels in women with high internalized racism, which was associated with more perceived stress and a "defeated" coping style. It may be that psychological stress and maladaptive coping behaviors are linked to internalized racism, which leads to cortisol dysregulation that increases the risk of metabolic abnormalities.

Difference in the effects of perceived racism and internalized racism on cortisol activity between adolescents and adults might be indicative of chronicity. It may be that adolescents who perceive more racism have not experienced it long enough to cause wear and tear on the HPA axis that would lead to a down-regulation of hormone secretion. Adults who have experienced more racism over the course of their lives may have more wear and tear on the HPA axis. A lower, flattened, or blunted cortisol output, due to down regulation of hormone secretion, can occur after a prolonged period of HPA axis hyperactivity due to chronic stress (Fries, Hesse, Hellhammer, & Hellhammer, 2005).

Cardiovascular Reactivity and Recovery

A strong cardiovascular reactivity (i.e., the activation of the cardiovascular system to stressful stimuli) but a delayed cardiovascular recovery (i.e., the duration of cardiovascular system activation poststressor), commonly measured by BP and heart rate, is associated with risk for CVD (al'Absi, Everson, & Lovallo, 1995; Curtis & O'Keefe, 2002; Hocking Schuler & O'Brien, 1997). Fang and Myers (2001) found that Black and

White men had greater DBP reactivity to anger-provoking (but race-neutral) and racist film excerpts compared with neutral film excerpts, and a higher degree of hostility was associated with a longer recovery of SBP and DBP levels after exposure to these films. Merritt, Bennett, Williams, Edwards, and Sollers (2006) found that the interpretation of ambiguous events as racist led to elevated DBP in Black men. Lepore et al. (2006) found that Black women, compared with White women, had greater DBP reactivity to a racial stressor (vs. nonracial scenario) but had a lower heart rate during recovery afterwards. Among Black women, they found that those who explicitly made race attributions during the racial stressor had greater SBP reactivity than those who did not make racial attributions. The findings of these studies suggest that SBP and DBP can be immediately elevated when exposed to either covert or overt racism, and remain elevated long after exposure ends, especially when a person is predisposed for hostility or making racial attributions.

Conceptual, Methodological, and Analytical Considerations

Despite the plethora of studies that examined the association between perceived racism and different physical health issues, studies are still needed to unravel the inconsistencies in the findings, to explicate the interpersonal (e.g., differences between who perpetrates racism), intrapersonal (e.g., implicit racial bias, coping behaviors), and socioenvironmental (e.g., type of social support that is beneficial) factors that mediate or moderate the associations, and to better link the psychological and physiological mechanisms involved in physical health outcomes. Studies are needed to identify how and why these associations might differ between ethnic groups because of differences associated with acculturation factors (e.g., native vs. immigrant), historical relations (e.g., having been the target of overt racism and segregation vs. covert racism), and sociocultural resources (e.g., living in ethnically homogenous vs. heterogeneous communities). The review in this chapter supports the notion that the experience of racism negatively impacts the physical health of many ethnic minorities in the United States, but it also underscores the complexity of this relationship and the challenges in its evaluation.

Some of the inconsistencies (i.e., not always finding an association) and paradoxical findings (i.e., unexpected form of association) can be attributed to low statistical power to detect modest effects; to sample representativeness as to have adequate variability on constructs of interest; to geographical location (e.g., Asian Americans residing in predominately Asian communities vs. mixed ethnic communities) where study is conducted that might affect the magnitude and nature of associations; to differences in type (e.g., internalized vs. interpersonal), context (e.g., workplace vs. public settings), duration (e.g., lifetime vs. daily), and dimensions (e.g., frequency vs. intensity) of racism examined; and to issues related to self-report measures that rely on retrospective recall of racist events and health status, which are susceptible to recall bias. Future research can benefit by addressing these issues.

Aside from the apparent methodological limitations, more research is needed to examine how the setting and context in which racism is experienced (e.g., in the workplace vs. in public settings) and its perpetrator (i.e., interethnic vs. intraethnic) might influence the presence or strength of an association with specific physical health outcomes. Some of the studies reviewed here suggest that certain settings in which racist acts are committed, such as the workplace (de Castro et al., 2008; Din-Dzietham et al., 2004), might be more distressing for a person than when it occurs in other settings and thus would be more relevant to explaining certain health outcomes. Workplace racism may be more distressing because it is often unavoidable and less controllable than racism that occurs in public settings, which are avoidable and, to some degree, controllable (e.g., choosing not to shop at a particular store or eat at a particular restaurant). Who perpetrates racism, a person of the same ethnicity or another, is also important in understanding how racism affects a person. Most studies aggregated the contexts and settings in which racism was experienced into a single composite measure. Examining and comparing how the context and setting in which racism occurs might help to paint a clearer picture of how racism affects physical health.

The studies reviewed found differences in the association between racism and physical health between men and women, social classes (especially in African Americans), and between ethnic groups. The study by Gee et al. (2007) illustrates the importance of disaggregating Asians (e.g., Chinese, Filipino) and Pacific Islanders (e.g., Hawaiian, Samoan) so that important differences in the association between racism and specific physical health outcomes are not missed. The study by Krieger and Sidney (1996) illustrates the importance of examining by-gender differences within an ethnic group as well as by-social class differences in the association between racism and specific health outcomes. Ryan et al. (2006) cautioned researchers against making the assumption that the effect of racism on physical health is linear in nature.

It is important to examine the effects of internalized racism, especially with African Americans, because it has been found to moderate the association between perceived racism and physical health outcomes, which might explain the paradoxical nonlinear association found in some studies (Chae et al., 2010, 2012). More studies are needed to elucidate how internalized racism operates to negatively affect a person's physical health, especially at different levels of interpersonal racism. For example, how does internalized racism interact with other coping behaviors used to deal with racist acts as to exacerbate or negate its adverse effects on physical health? How does internalized racism lead to psychological and physiological stress?

A vast majority of the studies used cross-sectional correlational designs and used single measures of the constructs of interest and measured them at a single time point. This measurement strategy is problematic when variability is expected in a construct and in its relation with other constructs. For example, a person's BP increases when faced with a stressor and decreases when the stressor is removed. Measuring a person's BP at single time point and when the stressor of interests is not operating may, or may not, capture this association. This might explain why studies of ABP are more consistent in their findings than studies that used a single measure of BP. More studies that incorporate multiple measures of the same construct (i.e., racism), as to reduce measurement error, measures taken over multiple time periods (e.g., BP, cortisol) in real time, as to capture its variability and covariance with other constructs of interest, are needed. Longitudinal studies would be ideal so that causal inferences can be made.

CLOSING REMARKS

Collectively, good evidence indicates that interpersonal racism can negatively impact a person's overall physical health status and lead to physical health outcomes, such as HTN, obesity, DM, CVD, and adverse birth outcomes. Emerging evidence indicates an association between racism and breast cancer incidence in African American women. Racism affects the physical health of most ethnic minorities in the United States, including African Americans, Asian Americans, Hispanics, and Native Hawaiians. The racism–physical-health association has yet to be empirically examined in American Indians and Alaska Natives. Among African Americans, internalized racism appears to interact with the experience of interpersonal racism in complex ways as to impact a person's physical health. It would be worthwhile to also examine the role of internalized racism in other ethnic populations, especially native peoples, such as American Indians, Alaska Natives, and Native Hawaiians, who have also experienced overt racism for generations. Future studies would do well to elucidate the psychosocial and physiological pathways by which racism gets "under a person's skin" as to affect physical health. Many of the physical health outcomes related to racism, such as HTN, obesity, DM, CVD, and breast cancer, perhaps share common immunologic, neuroendocrine, cardiovascular, and metabolic pathways.

REFERENCES

al'Absi, M., Everson, S. A., & Lovallo, W. R. (1995). Hypertension risk factors and cardiovascular reactivity to mental stress in young men. *International Journal of Psychophysiology, 20,* 155–160. http://dx.doi.org/10.1016/0167-8760(95)00029-1

Albert, M. A., Ravenell, J., Glynn, R. J., Khera, A., Halevy, N., & de Lemos, J. A. (2008). Cardiovascular risk indicators and perceived race/ethnic discrimination in the Dallas Heart Study. *American Heart Journal, 156,* 1103–1109. http://dx.doi.org/10.1016/j.ahj.2008.07.027

Allin, K. H., & Nordestgaard, B. G. (2011). Elevated C-reactive protein in the diagnosis, prognosis, and cause of cancer. *Critical Reviews in Clinical Laboratory Sciences, 48,* 55–70. http://dx.doi.org/10.3109/10408363.2011.599831

Aluli, N. E., Reyes, P. W., & Tsark, J. (2007). Cardiovascular disease disparities in native Hawaiians. *Journal of the Cardiometabolic Syndrome, 2,* 250–253. http://dx.doi.org/10.1111/j.1559-4564.2007.07560.x

Anachebe, N. F. (2006). Racial and ethnic disparities in infant and maternal mortality. *Ethnicity & Disease, 16,* 71–76. http://dx.doi.org/10.1016/j.ajog.2009.10.864

August, K. J., & Sorkin, D. H. (2010). Racial and ethnic disparities in indicators of physical health status: Do they still exist throughout late life? *Journal of the American Geriatrics Society, 58,* 2009–2015. http://dx.doi.org/10.1111/j.1532-5415.2010.03033.x

Barksdale, D. J., Farrug, E. R., & Harkness, K. (2009). Racial discrimination and blood pressure: Perceptions, emotions, and behaviors of Black American adults. *Issues in Mental Health Nursing, 30,* 104–111. http://dx.doi.org/10.1080/01612840802597879

Björntorp, P., Holm, G., & Rosmond, R. (1999). Hypothalamic arousal, insulin resistance, and Type 2 diabetes mellitus. *Diabetic Medicine, 16,* 373–383. http://dx.doi.org/10.1046/j.1464-5491.1999.00067.x

Björntorp, P., & Rosmond, R. (2000). Obesity and cortisol. *Nutrition, 16,* 924–936. http://dx.doi.org/10.1016/S0899-9007(00)00422-6

Blumenshine, P., Egerter, S., Barclay, C. J., Cubbin, C., & Braveman, P. A. (2010). Socioeconomic disparities in adverse birth outcomes: A systematic review. *American Journal of Preventive Medicine, 39,* 263–272. http://dx.doi.org/10.1016/j.amepre.2010.05.012

Borrell, L. N., Kiefe, C. I., Williams, D. R., Diez-Roux, A. V., & Gordon-Larsen, P. (2006). Self-reported health, perceived racial discrimination, and skin color in African Americans in the CARDIA study. *Social Science & Medicine, 63,* 1415–1427. http://dx.doi.org/10.1016/j.socscimed.2006.04.008

Broman, C. L. (1996). The health consequences of racial discrimination: A study of African Americans. *Ethnicity & Disease, 6,* 148–153.

Brondolo, E., Gallo, L. C., & Myers, H. F. (2009). Race, racism and health: Disparities, mechanisms, and interventions. *Journal of Behavioral Medicine, 32,* 1–8. http://dx.doi.org/10.1007/s10865-008-9190-3

Brondolo, E., Libby, D. J., Denton, E. G., Thompson, S., Beatty, D. L., Schwartz, J., . . . Gerin, W. (2008). Racism and ambulatory blood pressure in a community sample. *Psychosomatic Medicine, 70,* 49–56. http://dx.doi.org/10.1097/PSY.0b013e31815ff3bd

Brondolo, E., Love, E. E., Pencille, M., Schoenthaler, A., & Ogedegbe, G. (2011). Racism and hypertension: A review of the empirical evidence and implications for clinical practice. *American Journal of Hypertension, 24,* 518–529. http://dx.doi.org/10.1038/ajh.2011.9

Brondolo, E., Thompson, S., Brady, N., Appel, R., Cassells, A., Tobin, J. N., & Sweeney, M. (2005). The relationship of racism to appraisals and coping in a community sample. *Ethnicity & Disease, 15,* 14–19.

Burke, H. M., Davis, M. C., Otte, C., & Mohr, D. C. (2005). Depression and cortisol responses to psychological stress: A meta-analysis. *Psychoneuroendocrinology, 30,* 846–856. http://dx.doi.org/10.1016/j.psyneuen.2005.02.010

Butler, C., Tull, E. S., Chambers, E. C., & Taylor, J. (2002). Internalized racism, body fat distribution, and abnormal fasting glucose among African-Caribbean women in Dominica, West Indies. *Journal of the National Medical Association, 94,* 143–148.

Centers for Disease Control and Prevention. (2011a). *National diabetes fact sheet: National estimates and general information on diabetes and prediabetes in the United States, 2011.* Atlanta, GA: Author.

Centers for Disease Control and Prevention. (2011b). Vital signs: Prevalence, treatment, and control of hypertension—United States, 1999–2002 and 2005–2008. *Morbidity and Mortality Weekly Report, 60,* 103–108.

Chae, D. H., Lincoln, K. D., Adler, N. E., & Syme, S. L. (2010). Do experiences of racial discrimination predict cardiovascular disease among African American men? The moderating role of internalized negative racial group attitudes. *Social Science & Medicine, 71,* 1182–1188. http://dx.doi.org/10.1016/j.socscimed.2010.05.045

Chae, D. H., Nuru-Jeter, A. M., & Adler, N. E. (2012). Implicit racial bias as a moderator of the association between racial discrimination and hypertension: A study of midlife African American men. *Psychosomatic Medicine, 74,* 961–964. http://dx.doi.org/10.1097/PSY.0b013e3182733665

Chambers, E. C., Tull, E. S., Fraser, H. S., Mutunhu, N. R., Sobers, N., & Niles, E. (2004). The relationship of internalized racism to body fat distribution and insulin resistance among African adolescent youth. *Journal of the National Medical Association, 96,* 1594–1598.

Clark, R. (2003). Self-reported racism and social support predict blood pressure reactivity in Blacks. *Annals of Behavioral Medicine, 25,* 127–136. http://dx.doi.org/10.1207/S15324796ABM2502_09

Clark, R., & Adams, J. H. (2004). Moderating effects of perceived racism on John Henryism and blood pressure reactivity in Black female college students. *Annals of Behavioral Medicine, 28,* 126–131. http://dx.doi.org/10.1207/s15324796abm2802_8

Clark, R., & Anderson, N. B. (2001). Efficacy of racism-specific coping styles as predictors of cardiovascular functioning. *Ethnicity & Disease, 11,* 286–295.

Clark, R., Anderson, N. B., Clark, V. R., & Williams, D. R. (1999). Racism as a stressor for African Americans. A biopsychosocial model. *American Psychologist, 54,* 805–816. http://dx.doi.org/10.1037/0003-066X.54.10.805

Clark, V. R., Cobb, R. E., Hopkins, R., & Smith, C. E. (2006). Black racial identity as a mediator of cardiovascular reactivity to racism in African-American college students. *Ethnicity & Disease, 16,* 108–113.

Collins, J. W., Jr., David, R. J., Handler, A., Wall, S., & Andes, S. (2004). Very low birthweight in African American infants: The role of maternal exposure to interpersonal racial discrimination. *American Journal of Public Health, 94,* 2132–2138. http://dx.doi.org/10.2105/AJPH.94.12.2132

Cozier, Y. C., Wise, L. A., Palmer, J. R., & Rosenberg, L. (2009). Perceived racism in relation to weight change in the Black women's health study. *Annals of Epidemiology, 19,* 379–387. http://dx.doi.org/10.1016/j.annepidem.2009.01.008

Cuffee, Y. L., Hargraves, J. L., & Allison, J. (2012). Exploring the association between reported discrimination and hypertension among African Americans: A systematic review. *Ethnicity & Disease, 22,* 422–431.

Cunningham, T. J., Seeman, T. E., Kawachi, I., Gortmaker, S. L., Jacobs, D. R., Kiefe, C. I., & Berkman, L. F. (2012). Racial/ethnic and gender differences in the association between self-reported experiences of racial/ethnic discrimination and inflammation in the CARDIA cohort of 4 U.S. communities. *Social Science & Medicine, 75,* 922–931. http://dx.doi.org/10.1016/j.socscimed.2012.04.027

Curtis, B. M., & O'Keefe, J. H., Jr. (2002). Autonomic tone as a cardiovascular risk factor: The dangers of chronic fight or flight. *Mayo Clinic Proceedings, 77,* 45–54. http://dx.doi.org/10.4065/77.1.45

Dankwa-Mullan, I., Rhee, K. B., Stoff, D. M., Pohlhaus, J. R., Sy, F. S., Stinson, N., Jr., & Ruffin, J. (2010). Moving toward paradigm-shifting research in health disparities through translational, transformational, and transdisciplinary approaches. *American Journal of Public Health, 100,* 19–24. http://dx.doi.org/10.2105/AJPH.2009.189167

de Castro, A. B., Gee, G. C., & Takeuchi, D. T. (2008). Workplace discrimination and health among Filipinos in the United States. *American Journal of Public Health, 98,* 520–526. http://dx.doi.org/10.2105/AJPH.2007.110163

DeSantis, A. S., Adam, E. K., Doane, L. D., Mineka, S., Zinbarg, R. E., & Craske, M. G. (2007). Racial/ethnic differences in cortisol diurnal rhythms in a community sample of adolescents. *Journal of Adolescent Health, 41,* 3–13. http://dx.doi.org/10.1016/j.jadohealth.2007.03.006

Din-Dzietham, R., Nembhard, W. N., Collins, R., & Davis, S. K. (2004). Perceived stress following race-based discrimination at work is associated with hypertension in African-Americans: The metro Atlanta heart disease study, 1999-2001. *Social Science & Medicine, 58,* 449–461. http://dx.doi.org/10.1016/S0277-9536(03)00211-9

Dole, N., Savitz, D. A., Hertz-Picciotto, I., Siega-Riz, A. M., McMahon, M. J., & Buekens, P. (2003). Maternal stress and preterm birth. *American Journal of Epidemiology, 157*, 14–24. http://dx.doi.org/10.1093/aje/kwf176

Dole, N., Savitz, D. A., Siega-Riz, A. M., Hertz-Picciotto, I., McMahon, M. J., & Buekens, P. (2004). Psychosocial factors and preterm birth among African American and White women in central North Carolina. *American Journal of Public Health, 94*, 1358–1365. http://dx.doi.org/10.2105/AJPH.94.8.1358

Dolezsar, C. M., McGrath, J. J., Herzig, A. J. M., & Miller, S. B. (2014). Perceived racial discrimination and hypertension: A comprehensive systematic review. *Health Psychology, 33*, 20–34. http://dx.doi.org/10.1037/a0033718

Dominguez, T. P. (2010). Adverse birth outcomes in African American women: The social context of persistent reproductive disadvantage. *Social Work in Public Health, 26*, 3–16. http://dx.doi.org/10.1080/10911350902986880

Dominguez, T. P., Dunkel-Schetter, C., Glynn, L. M., Hobel, C., & Sandman, C. A. (2008). Racial differences in birth outcomes: The role of general, pregnancy, and racism stress. *Health Psychology, 27*, 194–203. http://dx.doi.org/10.1037/0278-6133.27.2.194

Engel, G. L. (1997). From biomedical to biopsychosocial: 1. Being scientific in the human domain. *Psychotherapy and Psychosomatics, 66*, 57–62. http://dx.doi.org/10.1159/000289109

Everage, N. J., Gjelsvik, A., McGarvey, S. T., Linkletter, C. D., & Loucks, E. B. (2012). Inverse associations between perceived racism and coronary artery calcification. *Annals of Epidemiology, 22*, 183–190. http://dx.doi.org/10.1016/j.annepidem.2012.01.005

Fang, C. Y., & Myers, H. F. (2001). The effects of racial stressors and hostility on cardiovascular reactivity in African American and Caucasian men. *Health Psychology, 20*, 64–70. http://dx.doi.org/10.1037/0278-6133.20.1.64

Finch, B. K., Hummer, R. A., Kol, B., & Vega, W. A. (2001). The role of discrimination and acculturative stress in the physical health of Mexican-origin adults. *Hispanic Journal of Behavioral Sciences, 23*, 399–429. http://dx.doi.org/10.1177/0739986301234004

Fries, E., Hesse, J., Hellhammer, J., & Hellhammer, D. H. (2005). A new view on hypocortisolism. *Psychoneuroendocrinology, 30*, 1010–1016. http://dx.doi.org/10.1016/j.psyneuen.2005.04.006

Gee, G. C., Ro, A., Gavin, A., & Takeuchi, D. T. (2008). Disentangling the effects of racial and weight discrimination on body mass index and obesity among Asian Americans. *American Journal of Public Health, 98*, 493–500. http://dx.doi.org/10.2105/AJPH.2007.114025

Gee, G. C., Spencer, M. S., Chen, J., & Takeuchi, D. (2007). A nationwide study of discrimination and chronic health conditions among Asian Americans. *American Journal of Public Health, 97*, 1275–1282. http://dx.doi.org/10.2105/AJPH.2006.091827

Gerrard, M., Stock, M. L., Roberts, M. E., Gibbons, F. X., O'Hara, R. E., Weng, C. Y., & Wills, T. A. (2012). Coping with racial discrimination: The role of substance use. *Psychology of Addictive Behaviors, 26,* 550–560. http://dx.doi.org/10.1037/a0027711

Go, A. S., Mozaffarian, D., Roger, V. L., Benjamin, E. J., Berry, J. D., Borden, W. B., . . . Turner, M. B., & The American Heart Association Statistics Committee and Stroke Statistics Subcommittee. (2013). Heart disease and stroke statistics—2013 update: A report from the American Heart Association. *Circulation, 127,* e6–e245. http://dx.doi.org/10.1161/CIR.0b013e31828124ad (Correction published 2013, *Circulation, 127,* p. e841)

Harrell, J. P., Hall, S., & Taliaferro, J. (2003). Physiological responses to racism and discrimination: An assessment of the evidence. *American Journal of Public Health, 93,* 243–248. http://dx.doi.org/10.2105/AJPH.93.2.243

Harris, R., Cormack, D., Tobias, M., Yeh, L. C., Talamaivao, N., Minster, J., & Timutimu, R. (2012). The pervasive effects of racism: Experiences of racial discrimination in New Zealand over time and associations with multiple health domains. *Social Science & Medicine, 74,* 408–415. http://dx.doi.org/10.1016/j.socscimed.2011.11.004

Heron, M. (2013). Deaths: Leading causes for 2010. *National Vital Statistics Reports, 62,* 1–96.

Hocking Schuler, J. L., & O'Brien, W. H. (1997). Cardiovascular recovery from stress and hypertension risk factors: A meta-analytic review. *Psychophysiology, 34,* 649–659. http://dx.doi.org/10.1111/j.1469-8986.1997.tb02141.x

Hunte, H. E., & Williams, D. R. (2009). The association between perceived discrimination and obesity in a population-based multiracial and multiethnic adult sample. *American Journal of Public Health, 99,* 1285–1292. http://dx.doi.org/10.2015/AJPH.2007.128090

Jang, Y., Park, N. S., Kang, S. Y., & Chiriboga, D. A. (2014). Racial/ethnic differences in the association between symptoms of depression and self-rated mental health among older adults. *Community Mental Health Journal, 50,* 325–330. http://dx.doi.org/10.1007/s10597-013-9642-2

Kaholokula, J. K., Iwane, M. K., & Nacapoy, A. H. (2010). Effects of perceived racism and acculturation on hypertension in Native Hawaiians. *Hawaii Medical Journal, 69,* 11–15.

Klonoff, E. A., & Landrine, H. (2000). Is skin color a marker for racial discrimination? Explaining the skin color-hypertension relationship. *Journal of Behavioral Medicine, 23,* 329–338. http://dx.doi.org/10.1023/A:1005580300128

Krieger, N., Rowley, D. L., Herman, A. A., Avery, B., & Phillips, M. T. (1993). Racism, sexism, and social class: Implications for studies of health, disease, and well-being. *American Journal of Preventive Medicine, 9,* 82–122.

Krieger, N., & Sidney, S. (1996). Racial discrimination and blood pressure: The CARDIA Study of young black and white adults. *American Journal of Public Health, 86,* 1370–1378. http://dx.doi.org/10.2105/AJPH.86.10.1370

Lee, S. J., Moody-Ayers, S. Y., Landefeld, C. S., Walter, L. C., Lindquist, K., Segal, M. R., & Covinsky, K. E. (2007). The relationship between self-rated health and mortality in older black and white Americans. *Journal of the American Geriatrics Society, 55,* 1624–1629. http://dx.doi.org/10.1111/j.1532-5415.2007.01360.x

Lepore, S. J., Revenson, T. A., Weinberger, S. L., Weston, P., Frisina, P. G., Robertson, R., . . . Cross, W. (2006). Effects of social stressors on cardiovascular reactivity in Black and White women. *Annals of Behavioral Medicine, 31,* 120–127. http://dx.doi.org/10.1207/s15324796abm3102_3

Lewis, T. T., Aiello, A. E., Leurgans, S., Kelly, J., & Barnes, L. L. (2010). Self-reported experiences of everyday discrimination are associated with elevated C-reactive protein levels in older African-American adults. *Brain, Behavior, and Immunity, 24,* 438–443. http://dx.doi.org/10.1016/j.bbi.2009.11.011

Lewis, T. T., Everson-Rose, S. A., Powell, L. H., Matthews, K. A., Brown, C., Karavolos, K., . . . Wesley, D. (2006). Chronic exposure to everyday discrimination and coronary artery calcification in African-American women: The SWAN Heart Study. *Psychosomatic Medicine, 68,* 362–368. http://dx.doi.org/10.1097/01.psy.0000221360.94700.16

Liu, L. L., & Lau, A. S. (2013). Teaching about race/ethnicity and racism matters: An examination of how perceived ethnic racial socialization processes are associated with depression symptoms. *Cultural Diversity and Ethnic Minority Psychology, 19,* 383–394. http://dx.doi.org/10.1037/a0033447

McCubbin, L. D., & Antonio, M. (2012). Discrimination and obesity among Native Hawaiians. *Hawaii Journal of Medicine & Public Health, 71,* 346–352.

Mereish, E. H., Liu, M. M., & Helms, J. E. (2012). Effects of discrimination on Chinese, Pilipino, and Vietnamese Americans' mental and physical health. *Asian American Journal of Psychology, 3,* 91–103. http://dx.doi.org/10.1037/a0025876

Merritt, M. M., Bennett, G. G., Jr., Williams, R. B., Edwards, C. L., & Sollers, J. J., III. (2006). Perceived racism and cardiovascular reactivity and recovery to personally relevant stress. *Health Psychology, 25,* 364–369. http://dx.doi.org/10.1037/0278-6133.25.3.364

Miller, G. E., Chen, E., & Zhou, E. S. (2007). If it goes up, must it come down? Chronic stress and the hypothalamic–pituitary–adrenocortical axis in humans. *Psychological Bulletin, 133,* 25–45. http://dx.doi.org/10.1037/0033-2909.133.1.25

Mustillo, S., Krieger, N., Gunderson, E. P., Sidney, S., McCreath, H., & Kiefe, C. I. (2004). Self-reported experiences of racial discrimination and Black-White differences in preterm and low-birthweight deliveries: The CARDIA Study. *American Journal of Public Health, 94,* 2125–2131. http://dx.doi.org/10.2105/AJPH.94.12.2125

Ogden, C. L., Carroll, M. D., Kit, B. K., & Flegal, K. M. (2012). Prevalence of obesity in the United States, 2009–2010. *National Center for Health Statistics Data Brief, 82,* 1–8.

Panapasa, S. V., Mau, M. K., Williams, D. R., & McNally, J. W. (2010). Mortality patterns of Native Hawaiians across their life span: 1990–2000. *American Journal of Public Health, 100,* 2304–2310. http://dx.doi.org/10.2105/AJPH.2009.183541

Paradies, Y. (2006). A systematic review of empirical research on self-reported racism and health. *International Journal of Epidemiology, 35,* 888–901. http://dx.doi.org/10.1093/ije/dyl056

Paradies, Y., Priest, N., Ben, J., Truong, M., Gupta, A., Pieterse, A., . . . Gee, G. (2013). Racism as a determinant of health: A protocol for conducting a systematic review and meta-analysis. *Systematic Reviews, 2,* 85. http://dx.doi.org/10.1186/2046-4053-2-85

Pascoe, E. A., & Smart Richman, L. (2009). Perceived discrimination and health: A meta-analytic review. *Psychological Bulletin, 135,* 531–554. http://dx.doi.org/10.1037/a0016059

Peters, R. M. (2004). Racism and hypertension among African Americans. *Western Journal of Nursing Research, 26,* 612–631. http://dx.doi.org/10.1177/0193945904265816

Pleis, J. R., Lucas, J. W., & Ward, B. W. (2009). *Summary health statistics for U.S. adults: National Health Interview Survey, 2008.* Bethesda, MD: U.S. Department of Health and Human Services.

Pradhan, A. D., Manson, J. E., Rifai, N., Buring, J. E., & Ridker, P. M. (2001). C-reactive protein, interleukin 6, and risk of developing type 2 diabetes mellitus. *JAMA, 286,* 327–334. http://dx.doi.org/10.1001/jama.286.3.327

Price, J. H., Khubchandani, J., McKinney, M., & Braun, R. (2013). Racial/ethnic disparities in chronic diseases of youths and access to health care in the United States. Advance online publication. *BioMed Research International, 2013,* 787616. Retrieved from http://www.hindawi.com/journals/bmri/2013/787616/abs/

Public Health Service Act of 2000, Pub. L. No. 106-525.

Ridker, P. M., Hennekens, C. H., Buring, J. E., & Rifai, N. (2000). C-reactive protein and other markers of inflammation in the prediction of cardiovascular disease in women. *The New England Journal of Medicine, 342,* 836–843. http://dx.doi.org/10.1056/NEJM200003233421202

Ryan, A. M., Gee, G. C., & Laflamme, D. F. (2006). The association between self-reported discrimination, physical health and blood pressure: Findings from African Americans, Black immigrants, and Latino immigrants in New Hampshire. *Journal of Health Care for the Poor and Underserved, 17,* 116–132. http://dx.doi.org/10.1353/hpu.2006.0092

Shariff-Marco, S., Klassen, A. C., & Bowie, J. V. (2010). Racial/ethnic differences in self-reported racism and its association with cancer-related health behaviors. *American Journal of Public Health, 100,* 364–374. http://dx.doi.org/10.2105/AJPH.2009.163899

Schiller, J. S., Lucas, J. W., Ward, B. W., & Peregoy, J. A. (2012). Summary health statistics for U.S. adults: National Health Interview Survey, 2010. *Vital and*

Health Statistics: Series 10. Bethesda, MD: U.S. Department of Health and Human Services.

Shavers, V. L., Fagan, P., Jones, D., Klein, W. M., Boyington, J., Moten, C., & Rorie, E. (2012). The state of research on racial/ethnic discrimination in the receipt of health care. *American Journal of Public Health, 102*, 953–966. http://dx.doi.org/10.2105/AJPH.2012.300773

Steffen, P. R., & Bowden, M. (2006). Sleep disturbance mediates the relationship between perceived racism and depressive symptoms. *Ethnicity & Disease, 16*, 16–21.

Steffen, P. R., McNeilly, M., Anderson, N., & Sherwood, A. (2003). Effects of perceived racism and anger inhibition on ambulatory blood pressure in African Americans. *Psychosomatic Medicine, 65*, 746–750. http://dx.doi.org/10.1097/01.PSY.0000079380.95903.78

Striegel-Moore, R. H., Dohm, F. A., Pike, K. M., Wilfley, D. E., & Fairburn, C. G. (2002). Abuse, bullying, and discrimination as risk factors for binge eating disorder. *The American Journal of Psychiatry, 159*, 1902–1907. http://dx.doi.org/10.1176/appi.ajp.159.11.1902

Taylor, T. R., Williams, C. D., Makambi, K. H., Mouton, C., Harrell, J. P., Cozier, Y., . . . Adams-Campbell, L. L. (2007). Racial discrimination and breast cancer incidence in US Black women: The Black Women's Health Study. *American Journal of Epidemiology, 166*, 46–54. http://dx.doi.org/10.1093/aje/kwm056

Todorova, I. L., Falcón, L. M., Lincoln, A. K., & Price, L. L. (2010). Perceived discrimination, psychological distress and health. *Sociology of Health & Illness, 32*, 843–861. http://dx.doi.org/10.1111/j.1467-9566.2010.01257.x

Tull, E. S., & Chambers, E. C. (2001). Internalized racism is associated with glucose intolerance among Black Americans in the U.S. Virgin Islands. *Diabetes Care, 24*, 1498. http://dx.doi.org/10.2337/diacare.24.8.1498

Tull, E. S., Cort, M. A., Gwebu, E. T., & Gwebu, K. (2007). Internalized racism is associated with elevated fasting glucose in a sample of adult women but not men in Zimbabwe. *Ethnicity & Disease, 17*, 731–735.

Tull, E. S., Sheu, Y. T., Butler, C., & Cornelious, K. (2005). Relationships between perceived stress, coping behavior and cortisol secretion in women with high and low levels of internalized racism. *Journal of the National Medical Association, 97*, 206–212.

Tull, S. E., Wickramasuriya, T., Taylor, J., Smith-Burns, V., Brown, M., Champagnie, G., . . . Jordan, O. W. (1999). Relationship of internalized racism to abdominal obesity and blood pressure in Afro-Caribbean women. *Journal of the National Medical Association, 91*, 447–452.

Utsey, S. O., & Hook, J. N. (2007). Heart rate variability as a physiological moderator of the relationship between race-related stress and psychological distress in African Americans. *Cultural Diversity and Ethnic Minority Psychology, 13*, 250–253. http://dx.doi.org/10.1037/1099-9809.13.3.250

Vines, A. I., Baird, D. D., McNeilly, M., Hertz-Picciotto, I., Light, K. C., & Stevens, J. (2006). Social correlates of the chronic stress of perceived racism among Black women. *Ethnicity & Disease, 16*, 101–107.

Vines, A. I., Baird, D. D., Stevens, J., Hertz-Picciotto, I., Light, K. C., & McNeilly, M. (2007). Associations of abdominal fat with perceived racism and passive emotional responses to racism in African American women. *American Journal of Public Health, 97*, 526–530. http://dx.doi.org/10.2105/AJPH.2005.080663

Williams, D. R., & Mohammed, S. A. (2009). Discrimination and racial disparities in health: Evidence and needed research. *Journal of Behavioral Medicine, 32*, 20–47. http://dx.doi.org/10.1007/s10865-008-9185-0

Williams, D. R., Neighbors, H. W., & Jackson, J. S. (2003). Racial/ethnic discrimination and health: Findings from community studies. *American Journal of Public Health, 93*, 200–208. http://dx.doi.org/10.2105/AJPH.93.2.200

Winston, G. J., Barr, R. G., Carrasquillo, O., Bertoni, A. G., & Shea, S. (2009). Sex and racial/ethnic differences in cardiovascular disease risk factor treatment and control among individuals with diabetes in the Multi-Ethnic Study of Atherosclerosis (MESA). *Diabetes Care, 32*, 1467–1469. http://dx.doi.org/10.2337/dc09-0260

Zeiders, K. H., Doane, L. D., & Roosa, M. W. (2012). Perceived discrimination and diurnal cortisol: Examining relations among Mexican American adolescents. *Hormones and Behavior, 61*, 541–548. http://dx.doi.org/10.1016/j.yhbeh.2012.01.018

8

THE IMPACT OF RACISM ON EDUCATION AND THE EDUCATIONAL EXPERIENCES OF STUDENTS OF COLOR

ADRIENNE D. DIXSON, DOMINIQUE M. CLAYTON,
LEAH Q. PEOPLES, AND REMA REYNOLDS

Scholars have tried to understand the impact of race and racism on the educational experiences of African American students for several decades. Unable to make causal claims of racism as directly contributing to achievement gaps, scholars have documented inequitable access and opportunity as both a historical phenomenon (Anderson, 1988; Ladson-Billings, 2006) and a contemporary manifestation of social processes that appear to create disproportionate outcomes for African American students relative to their White peers across a number of domains. Indeed, an inference that one can draw from the qualitative and statistical data is that race does matter when it comes to the education and educational experiences of African Americans and other students of color. Overwhelmingly, the data suggest that despite making gains in terms of high school graduation and college attendance, students of color—particularly African Americans—still face schooling environments that are often racially hostile or, at the very least, places that refuse to address and acknowledge students cultural wealth (Dixson & Dodo-Seriki, 2014; Dixson, 2008).

Nearly 60 years after the landmark *Brown vs. Board of Education* (1954) decision, scholars are finding that public schools have essentially re-segregated at rates that parallel, and in some cases, exceed pre-*Brown* segregation (Orfield, Frankenberg, Ee, & Kucsera, 2014). In attempting to redress the racialized educational inequality, school districts and state and federal lawmakers have attempted to craft policies aligned with these goals. Some scholars have found that certain policy interventions have in many ways contributed to the increasing racial segregation in public schools and funding disparities that have only contributed to disparities in access and opportunity (Dixson, 2011; Dixson, Royal, & Henry, 2013).

In this chapter, we examine the educational impact of segregation as an educational policy. We believe current racial disparities in education are in large part related to the legacy of structural racism rather than the unintended consequence of race-neutral policies or individual decisions. We take a broad look at how both de jure and de facto segregation has had an impact on and shaped the educational experiences of African Americans and other students of color and the ways in which this educational policy has contributed to institutionalized disparities.

DEFINING RACISM

To discuss how racism manifests in education policy, we must first briefly define what we mean when we use the words *race* and *racism*. According to Smedley and Smedley (2005), *race* is a social construct, as opposed to a "genetically discrete, measurable and scientifically meaningful" (p. 19). The idea of race as a biological construct has been debunked. Instead, race "signifie[s] a new ideology about human difference and a new way of structuring society that had not existed in human history" (p. 19). Acknowledging the social constructions of race and racism exposes the White supremacist values embedded in American society. As Smedley and Smedley focused on the social constructions of race, Bonilla-Silva (1997) challenged the current definitions of *racism*. Bonilla-Silva argued that many definitions of *racism* focus on the idealist view of racism, which reduces it to negative attitudes and beliefs about racial groups. Bonilla-Silva highlighted the structural nature of racism, arguing it is not a disease that plagues society; instead, it is deeply ingrained into the fabric of our everyday lives.

Consistent with Bonilla-Silva's (1997) conceptualization of racism, critical race theory scholars argue that racism exists both at the structural level and in terms of ideology. Solórzano and Yosso (2001), for example, argued that racism is a construct comprising ideas such as color-blindness, objectivity, and race neutrality. The idea of color-blindness has gained traction in recent years. Simply stated, color-blindness can be described as

> a package of "postracial" understandings that claims that race no longer constitutes a significant barrier to social and economic participation. Within the discourse of color-blindness, equality is a fact of law, everyone is treated the same, and racism persists because of individual ignorance rather than because of institutional failings. (Freeman, 2005, pp. 190–191)

After World War II and through the 1960s, the United States made a formal shift from an explicit racist society to a seemingly antiracist liberal one. This marked the beginning of a color-blind, postracial era (Hairston, 2013). Largely due to the civil rights movements, gone were the days of Jim Crow, a legal system designed to overtly promulgate and protect White supremacy. By the 1980s, Jim Crow was completely replaced by a liberalism that manifests itself in society "through citizens acting more negatively and harshly towards one another; neoliberalism does this by marginalizing societal bonds and allowing individualism and competition to supersede democracy" (Hairston, 2013, p. 231). Individualism and competition offer the impression that the United States is a meritocratic society: All one has to do is work hard to attain success. Consequently, if individuals fail, they do so because they have not exerted the effort necessary for success for varied reasons.

Education reform policy is a prevalent manifestation of institutional racism. Scholars have questioned the effectiveness of education policy for years (Canfield-Davis, Anderson, & Gardiner, 2009; Freeman, 2005; Klaf & Kwan, 2010). Many critiques of educational policy focus on retention, funding, and enactment of education reform policies such as No Child Left Behind (NCLB; U.S. Department of Education, 2007) and Race to the Top. For instance, NCLB concentrated on individual achievements through high-stakes testing. Standardized tests have been used as a way to establish and maintain a baseline that appears to be race-, gender-, and class-neutral when they are far from it (Freeman, 2005). When the emphasis is on individual achievement instead of the historical and social context of the achievement gap, White supremacy is further reinforced.

SEGREGATION IN EDUCATION

Popular sentiment holds that the United States is color-blind and thus has progressed from its hostile history of segregation and White supremacy in education, and that today, more than ever, people have equal opportunities to receive a quality education despite socioeconomic status, race, gender, or address. In 1954, *Brown v. Board of Education* in Topeka overturned the *Plessy v. Ferguson* (1896) ruling, stating, "Separate educational facilities are inherently unequal." Sociologists, psychologists, and other leading experts declared that separate schooling fostered inferiority complexes and proffered lower quality materials and resources for Black children. Following the *Brown* decision, school districts were legally mandated to implement desegregation plans. As we examine contemporary segregation in this chapter, several factors that must be understood: first, how segregation is currently constructed within education; second, what causes segregation; and third, how segregation affects students.

The end of Jim Crow laws brought fewer blatant, explicit signs of racism and segregation. In other words, although the *Brown* decision eradicated de jure segregation, de facto racialized school segregation is quieter, sustained through institutional racism that includes school zoning, school choice, and accountability policies. Segregation in schools manifests in primarily two distinct systemic ways: between schools and within schools. Some scholars posit that segregation has occurred between schools in the same districts because of a racial imbalance due to the composition of the neighborhood surrounding the school. Historically, race and class served as markers for segregated neighborhoods. Even with the prominence of White flight, segregated schools existed in both urban and suburban communities (Ansalone, 2006). In the early 1990s, schools were released from the *Brown v. Board* court-ordered desegregation plans after the Supreme Court determined that such plans were not meant "to operate in perpetuity" in the *Dowell v. Board of Education of Oklahoma City Public Schools* (1991) and local control resume if schools achieved status as determined by principles from *Green v. County School Board of New Kent County* (1968). Since then, racial segregation has increased across a number of domains, but specifically in housing and education, and policy no longer stipulates direct desegregation clauses (Dixson, 2011; Fiel, 2013; Reardon, Grewal, Kalogrides, & Greenberg, 2012). Due to residential segregation and education policy, racial segregation in public schools is increasing (Clotfelter, 2001). In the year 2000, more than 70% of all Black and Latino students in the United States attended predominantly minority schools, a higher percentage than 30 years earlier. Nationally, 39% of African American students attend intensely segregated schools, where at least 90% are students of color, according to an analysis of 2007 data by the Civil Rights Project at the University of California, Los Angeles. Moreover, other racial groups are experiencing racial isolation in schools. Forty percent of Latinos are in such schools as well. The report positions Los Angeles as one of the most segregated counties in the country with 67% of Latino students attending 90% to 100% non-White schools and 56% of Black students attending 90% to 100% non-White schools.

In New York City, a majority of the White students in one district were assigned to 6 of 18 schools the district operated, while Black and Latino students were mostly assigned to the other 12 schools (Roda & Wells, 2013). School choice policies also act as an agent for de facto segregation. Vouchers, charter schools, and open enrollment are school choice implements that do not directly address desegregation and, instead, aid in the segregation of students (Roda & Wells, 2013). It is particularly important to note that despite its moniker, school choice is only a choice for families who have the resources to choose (Dixson, 2011). A family's neighborhood location, transportation, safety, time, finances, and so on, can influence school "choice." For families of color, especially low-income families of color who rely on public transportation, it can be difficult to send their students to their preferred school. In addition, in a number of large urban school districts, administrators have closed schools in neighborhoods that service students of color. This places an additional burden on low-income families and families who use public transportation. For example, since the introduction of school choice policies in metropolitan Denver, the percentage of White students enrolled in low-performing schools fell from 40% to 10%, while the enrollment for African Americans increased from 20% to 80% (Aske, Corman, & Marston, 2011). In New Orleans, the nation's first all-charter system (Layton, 2014), 76 of the 90 schools are 75% to 95% African American, one school is 58% Latino, and five schools are more than 40% White (Cowen Institute, 2013). Finally, with respect to school choice and racial segregation in New Orleans, four of the five schools that are more than 40% White are also the highest performing schools according to the state's school grade system. Although school district administrators claim that these outcomes are the result of the individual choices of families, we find that these racially segregative effects are the result of racist practices that discriminate against families of color and advantage White families (as we discuss below).

In 1954, segregation was deemed illegal because of the deleterious effects it had on students of color (*Brown v. Board of Education*). However, in the 1970s, many districts were compelled to revisit their zoning policies for equity breaches. As stated by Judge Gitelson in *Crawford v. Board of Education of the City of Los Angeles* (1970):

> The Los Angeles school board "knowingly, affirmatively and in bad faith... segregated, *de jure*, its students" and had drawn school boundaries "so as to create or perpetuate segregated schools."

In 2013, although no longer illegal, those deleterious effects reemerged along with the resegregation of schools in the 21st century. It is important to note that students of color do not perform better academically merely because they are in the presence of White students, but because students of color benefit from the resources that are often given to White and middle class students (Coleman, 1990). The negative impact of segregation is well documented in the literature. Academically, tracking (grouping students by ability) creates a restricted learning experience for students who are not labeled talented or gifted (Ansalone, 2006). These students are exposed to less rigorous curriculum, less experienced teachers, and diminished expectations. (See the discussion in the next section, Eugenics and Tracking.)

In addition to the disparity in resources, studies show a link between the individual performance of a student and the performance of his or her classmates. Ayscue (2013) found that high achievement becomes normalized when high-achieving students are in the classroom with low-achieving students. The study demonstrates the benefits of diverse student grouping in lieu of ability grouping. The separation of students or tracking can result in differing standards of achievement, which is, in effect, discrimination. It is likely that students in groups held to lower standards will also have lower achievement in comparison to students held to higher standards. Tracking is so pervasive that Assistant Secretary of Education Catherine E. Lhamon (2014) wrote a letter to school districts urging them to end the practice. According to the letter,

> While Black and Latino students represented 16 percent and 21 percent, respectively, of high school enrollment in 2011–12, they were only 8 percent and 12 percent, respectively, of the students enrolled in calculus. Black and Latino students were also underrepresented in gifted and talented programs during the 2011–12 school year. In particular, schools offering such programs had an aggregate enrollment that was 15 percent Black and 25 percent Latino, but their gifted and talented enrollment was only 9 percent Black and 17 percent Latino. (p. 4)

Thus, data compiled by the U.S. Department of Education's Office for Civil Right, shows that Black and Latino students were even underrepresented in gifted and talented programs, even in schools where their representation was fairly significant. We argue that the underrepresentation of Black and Latino students in gifted education and in higher level mathematics, science, and English courses is a form of tracking that is synonymous to racial segregation in schools.

To situate this issue in a broader context, sociologists Massey and Denton (1998) explicated additional concerns related to racial segregation:

> Under the structural conditions of segregation, it is difficult for ghetto dwellers to build self-esteem by satisfying the values and ideals of the larger society or to acquire prestige through socially accepted paths. Precisely because the ghetto residents deem themselves failures by the broader standards of society they evolve a parallel status system defined in opposition to the prevailing majority culture. As new generations are born into conditions of increasing deprivation and deepening racial

> isolation, however, the oppositional origins of the status system gradually recede and the culture of segregation becomes autonomous and independent. (p. 184)

Most studies reach the same resolution: Education policy must include intentional desegregation initiatives to address the injustices of segregation. The pervasive thought that the United States has progressed to the point where policy is color-blind only exacerbates these injustices. In addition, districts' zoning practices and allocation of land need to be regulated (Ayscue, 2013). Within segregated schools, White students suffer because they miss the rich experiences that diversity brings and are less prepared to negotiate an increasingly smaller global society. Within these same segregated schools and classrooms, students of color receive short shrift as they are denied access to resources, opportunities, and an overall quality education.

Students should not be classified as "White" and "non-White" (Black, Latino, Asian), as this erases the cultural differences between and within people of color that can be overlooked within segregated schools. Detrimentally, nuances missed when non-White students are considered a monolith can be critical when attempting to improve educational outcomes. These groups can vary in socioeconomic status, family structure, language, citizenship status, and politics. These differences indicate challenges that can be specific or inclusive of people of color. Over time, Black students' exposure to White students has decreased, while their exposure to Latino students has increased (Kucsera & Flaxman, 2012). This suggests that although students of color may have educational experiences within contexts that are diverse racially and ethnically, White students may be in schools that are more racially homogenous and therefore have limited opportunities to engage and interact with students of color. With the separation of students along racial lines, students are also separated by class, indicative of the intricate relationship between educational opportunity and earnings.

Along with zoning, and school choice policy and practice, tracking, as both a pedagogical practice and an educational policy, has had significant impact on the experiences of students of color in school and has had particular effects relative to racial segregation and disparate racialized outcomes. We offer a brief discussion that gives, what we argue, is a historical link to tracking and then briefly address tracking as a racialized practice.

Eugenics and Tracking

Eugenics is the practice of hereditary improvement of the human race by controlled selective breeding. At the turn of the century, it was a widely accepted scientific theory with negative residual effects that can be witnessed in schools and the larger society (Baker, 2002; Douthat, 2012; Rose, 2011). The case for eugenics significantly penetrated the high school biology curriculum and was supported by U.S. textbooks until 1948 (Selden, 1999). According to the theory, negative social traits run through families and are impervious to environmental influence, thus rendering desegregation efforts a moot practice. Schools are unable to rectify the alleged fact that "certain heredity types are more valuable to society and the race than others" (p. 81). Given the ubiquitous nature of eugenics as an explanatory framework for educational and achievement disparities, a number of educators were exposed to and indoctrinated by that ideology. We argue that similar to Baker's (2002) concern regarding the creation of special education, the very practices of tracking honors and advanced placement courses are in many ways the modern-day versions of 19th- and 20th-century educational eugenics policies and practices.

Tracking is also a factor that leads to racialized school segregation. Tracking was introduced shortly after the *Brown* decision (Ansalone, 2006). Today, some scholars argue that ability grouping helps students learn at an appropriate pace for them, thus helping them to learn more effectively. Others argue that ability grouping severely limits students academically. Despite the arguments for tracking as a pedagogical strategy that may increase learning and achievement, we find that at first glance, tracking can disguise schools that appear to be desegregated but upon closer examination, are segregated by classrooms. For example, special education classes are disproportionately populated with students of color, and White students tend to be overrepresented in honors and advanced placement classes. Moreover, although special education serves students with learning disabilities, language barriers, and behavioral issues, the dominant special education population, African American boys, are placed because of behavioral issues. Studies show that although African American students, regardless of gender, behave no worse than their White and Latino counterparts, they are more likely to receive disciplinary referrals and are less likely to be given warnings afforded to other classmates (U.S. Department of Justice, 2014). Findings also suggest that Black boys are perceived as less innocent, more responsible for their behavior, and more appropriate targets for police use of force compared with their White male counterparts (Goff, Jackson, Di Leone, Culotta, & DiTomasso, 2014). Sorting policies and practices like tracking and honors/advanced-placement courses can unintentionally stratify students according to race. Likewise, school discipline policies have disproportionate racially segregative effects as well.

The position taken by some teachers with regard to Black students is that they are genetically deficient and, regardless of policy, effort, and parent involvement, they require particular kinds of pedagogies and curricula (Dixson, 2008). Clark's (1965) postulation 50 years ago remains true today because some educators believe that Black students cannot achieve and thus these teachers are less enthusiastic, work less, prepare less, and respond less supportively to Black students than they do to White students. Thus, given this perception of students of color as less capable, teachers tend to recommend them to courses that are less academically rigorous.

Students for whom English is not their first language are often segregated into English as a second language (ESL) classes. After ESL services have ended, teachers often assume that the students will perform in English classrooms at the same pace as other students. Carbone and Reynolds (2012) examined the community literacies students bring to their English classes and the treatment of these literacies by their teachers. They found that instead of valuing the bilingual and sometimes trilingual abilities of their students, the teachers in the study viewed the literacies as deficits as opposed to strengths. Many times, preservice teachers are not prepared to recognize and then leverage the wealth of knowledge students bring with them to the classroom.

Recommendations for Future Research

Segregation negatively influences student achievement, identity, potential, educational opportunities, and access to resources. Segregation can exist both within a school and across a school district. Segregation manifests across both racial and economic distinctions. It is equally important for researchers to examine the spaces within schools that tend to be segregated and those that are more diverse. That is, are particular courses racially segregated beyond just the typical honors or advanced placement courses? What are those policies and informal processes that lead to or encourage racial segregation? What explicit practices and policies can policy makers, parents, and other constituents recommend and/or demand to ensure equitable educational outcomes for students of color? From a more qualitative perspective, researchers might examine how students of color experience particular courses to gain insight into what helps or hinders students of color from selecting and persisting in particular courses. Moreover, do particular pedagogies facilitate and/or frustrate the efforts and achievement for students of color? Studies that address some of these questions may help researchers to consider more effective policy interventions to address what many scholars describe as the achievement gap.

CONCLUSION

In this chapter, we briefly examined several ways that race and racism have impacted the educational experiences of students of color. We find that racialized educational segregation, as they continue to be manifested through policies—such as tracking, ability grouping, and advanced placement and honors courses, as well as special education and to a certain extent ESL programs—have disproportionate segregative effects on the educational experiences of African American students in particular and other groups of color generally. We posit that part of the reason segregation is not deliberately addressed when policymakers make decisions about school reform stems from the reluctance to discuss race and racism. Racism has long been a sore subject for people in the United States, and as mentioned earlier, citizens have opted for a color-blind rhetoric rather than an honest discussion of race and racism and their effects on schools and educational attainment. Many eagerly espouse the idea that "race has all but disappeared as a factor shaping the life chances of all Americans" (Bonilla-Silva, 2003, p. 208). However, without the critical centralization of race and racism (Solórzano, 1997) within policy discussions, we in the United States are fated to talk *around* the problems that plague our schools, ignoring the core issues, and thus continuing to perpetuate the structural, curricular, and instructional inequities students of color contend with daily as they attempt to secure a quality education.

REFERENCES

Anderson, J. (1988). *The education of Blacks in the South, 1860–1935*. Chapel Hill: University of North Carolina Press.

Ansalone, G. (2006). Tracking: A return to Jim Crow. *Race, Gender, & Class, 13*, 144–153.

Aske, D., Corman, R. R., & Marston, C. (2011). Education policy and school segregation: A study of the Denver metropolitan region. *Journal of Legal, Ethical & Regulatory Issues, 14*, 27–35.

Ayscue, J. B. (2013). *Settle for segregation or strive for diversity? A defining moment for Maryland's public schools*. Los Angeles, CA: Civil Rights Project/Proyecto Derechos Civiles. Retrieved from http://civilrightsproject.ucla.edu/research/k-12-education/integration-and-diversity/settle-for-segregation-or-strive-for-diversity-a-defining-moment-for-maryland2019s-public-schools

Baker, B. (2002). The hunt for disability: The new eugenics and the normalization of school children. *Teachers College Record, 104*, 663–703. http://dx.doi.org/10.1111/1467-9620.00175

Bonilla-Silva, E. (1997). Rethinking racism: Toward a structural interpretation. *American Sociological Review, 62*, 465–480. http://dx.doi.org/10.2307/2657316

Bonilla-Silva, E. (2003). *Racism without racists: Color-blind racism and the persistence of racial inequality in the United States*. Lanham, MD: Rowman & Littlefield.

Brown v. Board of Education, 347 U.S. 483 (1954).

Canfield-Davis, K., Anderson, K. L., & Gardiner, M. E. (2009). Urban school principals and the "No Child Left Behind" Act. *The Urban Review, 41*, 141–160. http://dx.doi.org/10.1007/s11256-008-0102-1

Carbone, P., & Reynolds, R. (2012). Considering community literacies in the secondary classroom: A collaborative teacher and researcher group. *Journal of Literacy Research, 1,* 127–145.

Clark, K. B. (1965). *Dark ghetto: Dilemmas of social power.* New York, NY: Harper & Row.

Clotfelter, C. (2001). Are Whites still fleeing? Racial patterns and enrollment shifts in urban public schools, 1987–1996. *Journal of Policy Analysis and Management, 20,* 199–221.

Coleman, J. S. (1990). *Foundations of social theory.* Cambridge, England: Belknap Press.

Cowen Institute. (2013). *New Orleans by the numbers: School enrollment and demographics, October 2013.* New Orleans, LA: The Cowen Institute.

Crawford v. Board of Education, 113 Cal.App.3d 633, 645-44, 170 Cal.Rptr. 495, 501-02 (1980).

Dixson, A. D. (2008). "Taming the beast": Race, discourse, and identity in a middle school classroom. In S. Greene (Ed.), *Literacy as a civil right: Reclaiming social justice in literacy teaching and learning* (pp. 125–149). New York, NY: Lang.

Dixson, A. D. (2011). Democracy now? Race, education, and Black self-determination. *Teachers College Record, 113,* 811–830.

Dixson, A. D., & Dodo-Seriki, V. (2014). Intersectionality and pedagogy: Teachers and the quandary of race, class and culturally relevant pedagogy. In A. D. Dixson (Ed.), *Researching race in education: Policy, practice and qualitative research* (pp. 185–218). Charlotte, NC: Information Age.

Dixson, A. D., Royal, C., & Henry, K. L. (2013). School reform and school choice in Philadelphia, Chicago, and New Orleans. In K. Lomotey & M. R. Milner (Eds.), *Handbook of urban education* (pp. 474–503). New York, NY: Routledge.

Douthat, R. (2012, June 9). Eugenics, past and present. *The New York Times,* SR12. http://www.nytimes.com/2012/06/10/opinion/sunday/douthat-eugenics-past-and-future.html?_r=0

Dowell v. Board of Education of Oklahoma City Public Schools, 498 U.S. 237 (1991).

Fiel, J. E. (2013). Decomposing school resegregation: Social closure, racial imbalance, and racial isolation. *American Sociological Review, 78,* 828–848. http://dx.doi.org/10.1177/0003122413496252

Freeman, E. (2005). No Child Left Behind and the denigration of race. *Equity & Excellence in Education, 38,* 190–199. http://dx.doi.org/10.1080/10665680591002560

Goff, P. A., Jackson, M. C., Di Leone, B. A., Culotta, C. M., & DiTomasso, N. A. (2014). The essence of innocence: Consequences of dehumanizing Black children. *Journal of Personality and Social Psychology, 106,* 526–545. http://dx.doi.org/10.1037/a0035663

Green v. County School Board of New Kent County, 391 U.S. 430 (1968).

Hairston, T. W. (2013). Continuing inequity through neoliberalism: The conveyance of White dominance in the educational policy speeches of President Barack Obama. *Interchange: A Quarterly Review of Education, 43,* 229–244.

Klaf, S., & Kwan, M. (2010). The neoliberal straitjacket and public education in the United States: Understanding contemporary education reform and its urban implications. *Urban Geography, 31,* 194–210. http://dx.doi.org/10.2747/0272-3638.31.2.194

Kucsera, J., & Flaxman, G. (September 2012). *The Western states: Profound diversity but severe segregation for Latino students.* Los Angeles, CA: Civil Rights Project/Proyecto Derechos Civiles. Retrieved from http://civilrightsproject.ucla.edu/research/k-12-education/integration-and-diversity/mlk-national/the-western-states-profound-diversity-but-severe-segregation-for-latino-students

Ladson-Billings, G. (2006). From the achievement gap to the education debt: Understanding achievement in U.S. schools. *Educational Researcher, 35,* 3–12.

Layton, L. (2014, May 28). In New Orleans, major school district closes schools for good. *The Washington Post.* Retrieved from http://www.washingtonpost.com/local/education/in-new-orleans-traditional-public-schools-close-for-good/2014/05/28/ae4f5724-e5de-11e3-8f90-73e071f3d637_story.html

Lhamon, C. E. (2014, October 1). *Resource comparability* [Letter]. Washington, DC: Office of Civil Rights, U.S. Department of Education. Retrieved from http://www2.ed.gov/about/offices/list/ocr/letters/colleague-resourcecomp-201410.pdf

Massey, D. S., & Denton, N. A. (1998). *American Apartheid: Segregation and the making of the underclass.* Cambridge, MA: Harvard University Press.

Orfield, G., Frankenberg, E., Ee, J., & Kucsera, J. (2014). *Brown at 60: Great progress a long retreat and an uncertain future.* Los Angeles: Civil Rights Project/Proyecto Derechos Civiles.

Plessy v. Ferguson, 163 U.S. 537 (1896).

Reardon, S. F., Grewal, E., Kalogrides, D., & Greenberg, E. (2012). Brown fades: The end of court-ordered school desegregation and the resegregation of American public schools. *Journal of Policy Analysis and Management, 31,* 876–904. http://dx.doi.org/10.1002/pam.21649

Roda, A., & Wells, A. S. (2013). School choice policies and racial segregation: Where White parents' good intentions, anxiety, and privilege collide. *American Journal of Education, 119,* 261–293. http://dx.doi.org/10.1086/668753

Rose, J. (2011, December 28). A brutal chapter in North Carolina's eugenics past. *National Public Radio.* Retrieved from http://www.npr.org/2011/12/28/144375339/a-brutal-chapter-in-north-carolinas-eugenics-past

Selden, S. (1999). *Inheriting shame: The story of eugenics and racism in America.* New York, NY: Teachers College Press.

Smedley, A., & Smedley, B. D. (2005). Race as biology is fiction, racism as a social problem is real: Anthropological and historical perspectives on the social construction of race. *American Psychologist, 60,* 16–26. http://dx.doi.org/10.1037/0003-066X.60.1.16

Solórzano, D. (1997). Images and words that wound: Critical race theory, racial stereotyping, and teacher education. *Teacher Education Quarterly, 24,* 5–19.

Solórzano, D. G., & Yosso, T. J. (2001). Maintaining social justice hopes within academic realities: A Freirean approach to critical race/LatCrit pedagogy. *Denver University Law Review, 78,* 595–621.

U.S. Department of Education. (2007). *No Child Left Behind.* Retrieved from http://www.ed.gov/nclb

U.S. Department of Justice. (2014). *Civil Rights data collection data snap shot: School discipline.* Washington, DC. Retrieved from http://www2.ed.gov/about/offices/list/ocr/docs/crdc-discipline-snapshot.pdf

9

THE COSTS OF RACISM ON WORKFORCE ENTRY AND WORK ADJUSTMENT

JUSTIN C. PERRY AND LELA L. PICKETT

From a historical standpoint, the role of racism in the field of career development and career counseling, also referred to as *vocational psychology*, has not garnered much scholarly interest or empirical attention. The relative absence of this topic in contemporary research and theory, unfortunately, continues to relegate racism in all of its forms to a fringe interest. Although nearly all of the major theories in the field have been examined within the context of race, such as testing propositions among people of color or comparing measures between different groups, very few studies have actually investigated racism in direct relation to their principles and constructs. Overall, the knowledge base of the costs of racism is piecemeal and isolated.

According to Fouad and Kantamneni's (2013) review of career choice and development, empirical efforts to generally understand the role of race, ethnicity, culture, and discrimination are preliminary, requiring far more research. One of their conclusions, however, seems to be at odds with

http://dx.doi.org/10.1037/14852-010
The Cost of Racism for People of Color: Contextualizing Experiences of Discrimination, A. N. Alvarez, C. T. H. Liang, and H. A. Neville (Editors)
Copyright © 2016 by the American Psychological Association. All rights reserved.

literature found in sociology, labor economics, and social psychology. In contrast to their conclusion that minimal research has been conducted on discrimination, research in other disciplines strongly indicates that issues of discrimination, including racial discrimination, can adversely affect job search processes, occupational segregation, work transitions, turnover rates, job satisfaction, hiring, promotions, productivity, and well-being. These disciplines squarely focus on issues of discrimination, affirmative action, prejudice, work climate, and racial incivility—issues that are not traditionally studied in vocational psychology. In this chapter, we address the ongoing lack of theoretical, empirical, and practical integration across disciplines, even though they often study the same work-related problems, as they apply to people of color.[1]

To be sure, the workplace is where discrimination most frequently occurs (Chou & Choi, 2011). In the United States, a national survey found that Blacks were 4 times more likely than Whites to report perceptions of discrimination in the workplace and that Hispanics were more than 3 times as likely (Avery, McKay, & Wilson, 2008), consistent with prior research evidencing similar differences between people of color and their White counterparts (Roberts, Swanson, & Murphy, 2004). Acts of workforce discrimination can be manifested through a variety of racist or prejudicial behaviors, ranging from overt actions of bullying to more subtle, covert behaviors related to discourteous comments and aspects of performance evaluations, hiring, or application screening (Khosrovani & Ward, 2011; Lalonde, 2011).

Studies of workplace discrimination have evidenced clear empirical relationships with symptoms of psychiatric disorders (e.g., depression, anxiety) and poor health conditions, such as hypertension, headaches, stomach ulcers, back problems, arthritis, asthma, and diabetes (see, e.g., de Castro, Gee, & Takeuchi, 2008). These studies are almost always published in fields outside of vocational psychology, such as public health, organizational

---

[1]Generally speaking, race is viewed as a socially constructed scheme of classifying people based on phenotypical (skin color, facial features, hair texture) and/or behavioral (language use) differences as a way to control a group that has less power (Jones, 1997). As such, the ascribed racial status is tied to multiple life consequences (e.g., money, health care, education, career, prestige), as it determines who has access to resources and how those resources are dispensed (Ridley, 1989). On the other hand, some scholars have urged the scientific community to discard the use of race in favor of ethnicity (e.g., Betancourt & Lopez, 1993). The problem with this argument, however, lies in trying to make a clear distinction between ethnicity and culture, for ethnicity is inherently grounded within the ambiguous concept of culture (Phinney, 1996). Indeed, this definitional problem was observed by the American Psychological Association's (APA; 2003) "Guidelines on Multicultural Education, Training, Research, Practice, and Organizational Change for Psychologists," concluding that *ethnicity* "does not have a commonly agreed-upon definition" (p. 380). Indeed, APA vaguely defined it as "the acceptance of the group mores and practices of one's culture of origin and the concomitant sense of belonging" (p. 380). We refer to *people of color* from the viewpoint of belonging to a race. At the same time, we recognize that racial groups are represented by different ethnicities and manifest varying cultural characteristics based on national origin and acculturative histories.

behavior, occupational health, or human resource management. As one might expect, studies consistently reveal links between workplace discrimination and adverse outcomes, such as job stress, job dissatisfaction, job burnout, and job turnover (see, e.g., Cortina, Kabat-Farr, Leskinen, Huerta, & Magley, 2013). For people of color, the majority of this research has focused on African Americans.

WORKFORCE ENTRY AND ADJUSTMENT

By virtue of their ubiquitous nature, attempts to understand job turnover, job satisfaction, job search, or reemployment defy the parameters of one discipline. These are core antecedents and outcomes of the workforce entry and adjustment process, representing vehicles for economic mobility and opportunity; it is not surprising that such mechanisms of prosperity have been examined through a variety of theories based on multiple levels of analysis, ranging from the individual person to the family, workforce organization, and society. When considering the work-related experience of people of color, we endorse an emancipatory communitarian (EC) approach (Blustein, McWhirter, & Perry, 2005) that enjoins vocational psychologists to serve the moral needs of the public good beyond the sole focus of the individual and traditional one-to-one counseling services. Against the historical backdrop of affirmative action, a rapidly diversifying and globalized workforce, and income inequalities, national concerns of equal opportunity and access in the labor market have inevitably come to the forefront of civic debate. If everyone is entitled to the pursuit of the American Dream, the costs of racism associated with preparing for work, entering work, adjusting at work, and transitioning to work must be acknowledged. For these fundamental reasons, this chapter focuses on workforce entry and work adjustment among adult populations. Readers who are interested in issues of racism and the career development of children and adolescents are referred to Perry, Cusner, and Pickett (2015).

Naturally, the psychological and behavioral processes underlying entry (or reentry) into the workforce, and then adjustment to employment, are to some extent contingent on having access, or perceiving access, to certain industries and careers within the labor market. In other words, do fair and equitable conditions exist for gaining access to a specific occupation that one might wish to pursue, devoid of societal or environmental impediments? For people of color, access to jobs may involve perceptions of equal (or unequal) representation in a career, industry, or profession on the basis of race. Workforce access and representation stand as structural issues to consider when examining the sociopolitical factors which influence job entry and work-related adjustment. On a factual level, the Bureau of Labor Statistics (e.g., 2013) unambiguously documents constant disparities and an unequal representation between people of color and Whites. Although an analysis of workforce segregation is precluded here, we highlight examples that underscore this fundamental point.

RACIAL DISPARITIES IN THE U.S. WORKFORCE

Annual employment and earnings data published by the Bureau of Labor Statistics have consistently shown the same patterns of inequity/representation that are symptomatic of other national concerns, such as trends in education and health care. In 2013, Blacks and Hispanics were more likely to be unemployed than Whites or Asians across nearly every level of education (U.S. Department of Labor, 2013). During March 2015, the unemployment rate for Black men ages 20 and older was 10.0%—more than twice as high as White men and almost three times higher than Asian men (U.S. Bureau of Labor Statistics, 2015). In 2013, Hispanics represented 26.6%, and Blacks 25.6%, of employees in service occupations (e.g., food preparation, grounds cleaning), even though they constituted 15.6% and 11.2% of the total labor force (U.S. Department of Labor, 2013).

At a more specific level, computer and mathematical occupations, for example, were represented by Whites at 70.9%, compared with Blacks (8.3%) and Hispanics (6.3%); similarly, Blacks and Hispanics were underrepresented among physicians and surgeons (6.4% and 3.8%, respectively) and architects (1.6% and 7.9%, respectively; U.S. Department of Labor, 2013). For postal service clerks (21.4%) and taxi drivers and chauffeurs (24.7%), Blacks increased by twofold in representation. And for Hispanics, they were overrepresented among maids/housekeeping cleaners (44.3%), roofers (51.2%), grounds maintenance workers (44.8%), cooks (34.0%), and cement masons (52.5%); these statistics stand in stark contrast to the 4.5% of aircraft pilots and flight engineers, 4.4% of pharmacists, 4.9% of writers/authors, and 5.5% of financial analysts represented by Hispanics (U.S. Department of Labor, 2013). In 2013, median weekly earnings of full-time workers reinforced this robust pattern of inequity: $578 for Hispanics, $629 for Blacks, $776 for Whites, and $942 for Asians (U.S. Department of Labor, 2013). Across all major occupational categories, these disparities were similar for both men and women. In 2013, the median income for families with children ages 6 to 17 was $81,664 for Whites; $80,848 for Asians; $41,153 for Blacks; and $41,134 for Hispanics (U.S. Census Bureau, 2014).

Of course, no set of trends or average annual numbers can account for every type of occupation and natural variation within races at the subgroup or individual difference level. These nuances and clarifications deserve attention. Returning to computer and mathematical occupations, for example, although Asians were overrepresented at 16.6%, they were nearly nonexistent among employed musicians, singers, and announcers, hovering at 1%, while being overrepresented among dishwashers (7.4%) and at an extraordinarily high rate of 55.1% among "personal appearance workers." Median weekly earnings further obscure poverty rates and low educational attainment that exists among Asian Americans on the basis of multiple factors, including immigrant status, English language ability, and social class. They also do not portray disparities in returns on educational investment that Asian Americans continue to face, in addition to workplace discrimination and barriers of occupational stereotyping (Weathers & Truxillo, 2008). By "returns on investment," we refer to the tendency for Asian Americans to have lower earnings or to be less likely to be promoted to higher level management/executive positions, compared with Whites with the same level of education who are employed in the same industry or occupation.

The false assumption that Asian Americans are immune to discrimination is belied by recent studies of workforce adjustment. For example, de Castro et al. (2008) investigated the relationship between racial discrimination in the workplace and health among 1,652 Filipinos, the second largest Asian American ethnic group. After controlling for everyday discrimination, general job concerns, job category, reasons for immigration, education, income, gender, and other demographic factors, the authors found that high levels of work discrimination based on being Filipino was significantly associated with poor health conditions (e.g., asthma, stroke, thyroid disease). Furthermore, such discrimination was associated with higher levels of everyday discrimination and job concerns. In a second study of 1,181 Asian immigrants, de Castro, Rue, and Takeuchi (2010) found that employment frustration predicted poor physical and mental health, even after controlling for gender, age, ethnicity, education, occupation, income, years spent in the United States.

TOWARD A NEW FRAMEWORK FOR UNDERSTANDING THE COSTS OF RACISM IN THE WORLD OF WORK

To guide our presentation of the literature in this chapter, we first offer a road map for how research can advance our collective understanding of workforce entry and adjustment. As shown in Figure 9.1, this framework of theories and research is composed of four distinct families of constructs (or boxes of variables) representing the process of job search, job selection, and outcomes of employment that can impact work as well as nonwork

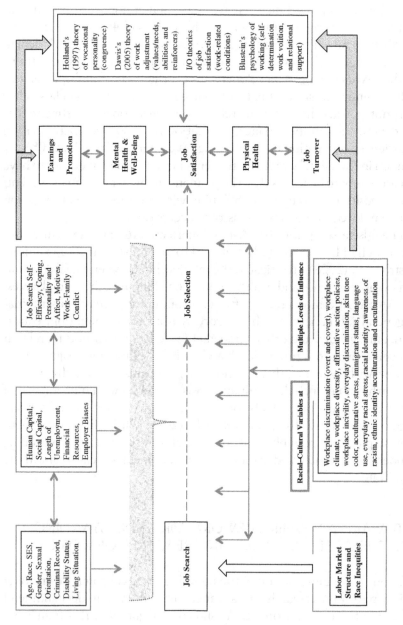

Figure 9.1. An integrative framework for examining the role of racism in the context of job search, job selection, and work adjustment.

domains: (a) the three square-shaped boxes at the top of the figure above the shaded region and (b) the rectangular-shaped box at the bottom of the figure. Located at the right of Figure 9.1 are different theories and approaches to understanding such outcomes within vocational psychology and industrial/organizational (I/O) psychology; they are tied, in turn, to the same categories of variables that interplay with each other in determining job search and selection, symbolized by the shaded region above, as well as their outcomes. At the bottom of Figure 9.1 is a larger box of variables that influence the categories of variables located at the top; these *racial–cultural variables* are conceived as informing the theoretical models and approaches on the right side. At the bottom left-hand side, the final box portrays the reality that people of color will enter their job search within a *labor market structure* that already places them at a disadvantage to the extent that industries, sectors, and occupations are underrepresented or overrepresented, as manifested by lack of equal opportunities and unequal access to education/training. Indeed, this lack of access and opportunity is maintained by the very racial–cultural variables that detrimentally impact people of color but that also can serve as protective factors if targeted and enhanced adaptively.

The complexities visually illustrated through the figure are meant to highlight several key points in undertaking an interdisciplinary approach to examining the role and costs of racism for people of color. First, it should be noted that each category of variables denoted by a square is representative of how different disciplines tend to organize their studies and address the issues, albeit, they certainly do not stand as an exhaustive list of all possible variables. Researchers in nonvocational psychology fields tend to be more interested in the two squares at the top (*demographic variables* and *sociological variables*, respectively) and the *racial–cultural variables*, whereas those in career development concentrate on the *personality and psychosocial variables* represented by the third square at the top, and to a much lesser extent on *racial–cultural variables*, broadly defined. In this respect, each family of variables/constructs consists of an open funnel that, conceptually, encourages greater synthesis with other fields of study. This framework is therefore designed to enable researchers to communicate more effectively and systematically. We do not intend for the theories/approaches we selected, however, to serve as a priori models; quite to the contrary, this new framework offers a platform for generating novel lines of research required to build new theoretical propositions, while constantly revising the use and relevance of existing theories.

As more studies of this interdisciplinary nature build on each other, the knowledge base will witness a reinvigoration of how to most accurately understand and comprehensively address the experiences of people of color in the workforce. Because of its multiple sets of variables and the fluidity of paths toward integration, operating at multiple levels, our framework provides points of entry across a variety of settings and environments for designing interventions, implementing them, and framing public policy. In the following sections, our review and critique of literature flows from the framework we propose, with a particular focus on empirical studies that have measured experiences of racism and their relationship with career or work-related outcome. We point out, however, that many of the studies do not accomplish this by measuring racism per se; rather, they tend to study racism indirectly through constructs and theories that tacitly assume that racism is responsible for giving rise to their manifestation, such as workplace incivility, ratings of job applicants, and work climate.

JOB SEARCH, JOB SELECTION, AND JOB EARNINGS

It is fitting to start with research revolving around the central artery of our framework, namely, job search and job selection. One of its core work-related outcomes of employment, job earnings and income, has received substantial empirical attention, but typically in fields outside of vocational psychology. It is also one of the most popular metrics of socioeconomic mobility and social class. The bulk of research examining the role of race during the job search and job selection process has concentrated on comparing Blacks and Whites, and to a lesser extent on Hispanics. Typically, researchers compare these two races in terms of job application ratings, job interview ratings, callback rates, frequency of interviews, and number of job offers. It is not surprising that the research has found that Whites consistently fare better than Blacks (e.g., Bertrand & Mullainathan, 2004; Quillian, 2006; Tomaskovic-Devey et al., 2006). Next, we highlight several exemplary studies.

Reflecting laboratory research conducted in university settings, Harrison and Thomas (2009) investigated how race affects the job selection of Black applicants as a function of skin tone color among a predominantly White (87.5%) and female (72.0%) sample of raters. In this particular study, the role of racism is tested via manipulating skin tone, with the assumption being that aversion to darker skinned applicants is a manifestation of prejudicial or racist attitudes. The researchers randomly assigned 240 college students to one of 12 conditions, manipulating the gender, race, qualifications, and skin tone (dark, medium, light) of mock job applicants. Although mean selection ratings given for light-skinned and medium-skinned Blacks were not significantly different, the mean ratings in both conditions were significantly higher than the ratings given for dark-skinned Blacks. The power of skin tone over other qualifications was further evidenced for male mock applicants. More specifically, light-skinned Black males with a bachelor's degree received a higher mean rating than dark-skinned Black males with a master's of business administration.

To illustrate a field-based approach, Bertrand and Mullainathan (2004) sent fictitious resumes to ads in Boston and Chicago newspapers, restricted to four general categories: sales, administrative support, clerical services, and customer services. The researchers sent resumes to over 1,300 ads, manipulating names as "distinctively African American" (e.g., Aisha, Ebony, Latoya, Darnell) or "distinctively White" (e.g., Allison, Jill, Brad, Greg). The role of racism was investigated by determining differences in callback rates (racist/prejudicial employer biases were not measured), in addition to manipulations pertaining to sex, city, and resume quality (e.g., college degree, years of experience, period of unemployment, computer skills). As one would expect, a substantial gap in callback rates was found; resumes consisting of "White-sounding" names yielded an average callback rate for every 10 ads applied to versus those with "Black-sounding" names, which had an average callback rate of every 15 ads. Higher quality resumes received more callbacks than lower quality resumes; however, African American resumes with higher quality resulted in a much lower chance to being called back compared with White resumes.

In a policy report, de Walque (2008) addressed the complex intersection between race and immigration by contrasting foreign-born and native-born individuals in the labor market. Based on Integrated Public Use Micro Data Series data for the 2000 Census, he sampled 5% of the total U.S. population, ages 25 to 65, among those classified as White, Black, Asian, and Hispanic. Among women, foreign-born individuals fared significantly worse than native-born individuals from the same race in terms of labor force participation, employment, and personal income, with the exception of Blacks, for whom the data showed that foreign-born individuals fared better. Among men, foreign-born Blacks had more favorable outcomes than native Blacks in labor force participation and employment. To explain this reversal of outcomes for native Blacks, de Walque considered citizenship, English ability, age at arrival, and time since arrival in the United States, as well as neighborhood effects. None of these variables could provide an explanation. In this study, over 70% of Black immigrants came from the Caribbean and Latin America. Overall, the findings highlighted the importance of situating the vocational impact of race within the context of immigration. Once again, racism was not a measured variable, nor was the process of acculturation.

When considering the role of racism in affecting job earnings, differences exist between scholars who tend to belong to one of two competing schools of thought: (a) status attainment or social reproduction theory, grounded in a classical sociological perspective (Blau & Duncan, 1967; Bourdieu, 1977); or (b) human capital theory, based on a free market, economic perspective

(Becker, 1964; Lang, 1994). In the first camp, the basic premise is that mechanisms of social class (parental socioeconomic status [SES], school quality, school curriculum tracking), coupled with psychosocial processes such as educational aspirations and teacher support, function as the main determinants of occupational attainment, setting in motion a constrained pathway of life chances for economic mobility and educational attainment among the disadvantaged (Hotchkiss & Borow, 1996). In the other camp, the exact opposite premise is endorsed. The assumption is that all individuals have equal access and opportunity in the labor market; consequently, the relationship is linear between the education and job training one possesses and the chances of entering a job market that demands such knowledge and skills (Becker, 1964). Accordingly, it should not matter if one is a person of color, as long as he/she can meet the qualifications for the job. We challenge the assumption that is embraced by human capital theory, but we also question the simplicity of status attainment theory. Neither perspective, in our view, offers a powerful or adequately nuanced explanation for a variety of outcomes in the world of work. Although the two studies below illustrate empirical support for both perspectives, the findings are rather modest, mixed, or fail to explain the majority of variance in a particular outcome of interest.

Drawing from status attainment or social reproduction theory, Sakura-Lemessy, Carter-Tellison, and Sakura-Lemessy (2009) found support for their prediction that racial disparities would be evidenced in educational and employment outcomes, even after controlling for prior academic achievement, on the basis of youth identified as noncollege workers from the National Educational Longitudinal Study. As expected, Blacks were significantly less likely than Whites to show significant wage growth; the same trend was revealed according to social class, with the low-SES quartile students faring the worst. The practical magnitudes of the effect sizes, however, were not very substantial, with odds ratios falling between .73 and .76. In contrast to Sakura-Lemessy et al. (2009), Baffoe-Bonnie (2009) examined the Black–White wage gap on the basis of 6,815 individuals drawn from the 1994 cohort of the National Longitudinal Study of Youth, who at the time were 29 to 36 years old. In this study, two sources of selection bias for estimating Black–White wage differentials were examined: (a) propensity to be in the labor force, as measured by variables such as work experience, education, health, marital status, age, gender, or family size; and (b) employer hiring decision practices, as measured by variables such as length of time one expects to stay on the job, local unemployment rates, or individuals who consistently reject job offers. In this study, human capital was treated as a salient construct. The results offered mixed findings for a human capital perspective. For example, although wage differentials decreased by 30.9% between Blacks and Whites when labor force participation selection bias was entered, it certainly did not disappear; when employer hiring decision practices was entered as another source of bias, the reduction in wage gaps was marginally increased to 33.6%. And even though education and work experience was positively associated with higher wages, the return on credentials was still greater for Whites than Blacks. Taken together, the results showed that human capital yields a significant effect, but it does not favor Blacks equally. In other words, more human capital can help reduce racial wage gaps, but it cannot eradicate them, as wage differentials remained intact. In both of these studies, neither one measured racism. Instead, the impact of racism can only be inferred by comparing the outcomes between races (see also Conley & Glauber, 2007).

Unemployment Research

What other factors may help further explain both risk and protective factors involved in the job search and job selection process among people of color, including those who are in the process of finding reemployment because of voluntarily or involuntarily job loss? Studies in the unemployment literature reveal a number of robust risk factors for gaining reemployment: Being an older adult, having a low income, possessing a criminal record, using passive coping strategies, and being unemployed for an extended amount of time (e.g., 6 months). Indeed, all of these factors can reduce the likelihood of retransitioning back into the workforce (Hanisch, 1999).

Other attitudinal- or personality-based factors (e.g., optimism, job search self-efficacy, extraversion, motivation, commitment) may help increase job search intensity (i.e., frequency of activities and effort put into searching for a job within a set period) but remain relatively weak predictors of reemployment and job offers (Jome & Phillips, 2013; Vansteenkiste, Verbruggen, & Sels, 2013). Moreover, an individual's access to financial resources and social support are widely supported in terms of understanding how people manage unemployment and eventually find reemployment (Blustein, Kozan, & Connors-Kellgren, 2013). Out of all of these additional sources of influence, the two most robust predictors, social capital (who you know) and human capital (what you know), are consistently linked to the odds of finding reemployment (Koen, Klehe, & Van Vianen, 2013). Collectively, the body of research on unemployment complicates the capacity to predict which people of color may have a greater chance of reemployment.

Summary

Our review suggests that race can negatively influence job search, job selection, and job earnings among people of color. Furthermore, it clearly suggests that the relationship between race and such outcomes is not straightforward, as they are subject to change on the basis of a myriad of factors with the potential to either worsen or improve the outcomes. Some of the many types of third variables have been recently examined by researchers (e.g., immigrant status, language use, SES, skin tone color), but many other variables have not (e.g., social capital, racial identity, work–family conflict). In essence, the research we discussed seems to both discount the human capital perspective proposed in economics and, at least a certain degree, support the free market assumption that education and job training/skills can function as vehicles for defying the odds and rising above one's seemingly irrevocable station in the labor market structure. As is evident in our review, unemployment research may help shed some light on the complexities involved in making such predictions and tailoring interventions to specific people of color under specific circumstances. To date, the problem of wedding these multiple facets of the job search and selection process has limited empirical progress in this much needed area of future research.

JOB TURNOVER AND JOB SATISFACTION

Similar to job earnings, mental health, and physical health, the work-related outcomes of job turnover and satisfaction have attracted widespread interest across the social sciences, as they too serve as core consequences of workforce entry and adjustment. Vocational psychologists have been traditionally concerned with trait–factor models that focus on understanding the relationship between personality traits and individual characteristics with job turnover and satisfaction. The best-known theories from this family of models are Holland's (1997) theory of RIASEC types (e.g., Realistic, Investigative, Artistic, Social, Enterprising, and Conventional) and the theory of work adjustment (TWA; Dawis, 2005; Dawis & Lofquist, 1984). These two models are briefly discussed in a later section. Outside of career development, researchers have devoted their attention primarily to the types of racial–cultural variables presented in Figure 9.1. These are precisely the variables which vocational psychologists have historically neglected. In corporate America, women (White as well as non-White) and minorities quit their jobs at higher rates than men and Whites. Hom, Roberson, and Ellis (2008), for example, found that African Americans in professional and managerial positions are disproportionately represented in high risk, short-tenure jobs (6 or fewer years of tenure) compared with Whites (as cited in Burt & Vesey, 2010); furthermore, women of color had higher turnover rates than White women. Of course, the challenge in explaining these disparities still remains, as racism, or racist attitudes in organizations, was not directly measured.

Organizational and Workplace Climate

In keeping with our focus on empirical studies that measure racism directly, we highlight several studies that examined job turnover and satisfaction using psychological measures of workplace climate and recruitment/hiring practices from a perspective of affirmative action and uncivil or prejudicial behavior. These studies are typically conducted in business and personnel management, as well as social psychology. Trait–factor constructs (e.g., personality types, work values) are rarely considered in these studies, as exemplified in the ones below. Essentially, this body of research approaches job satisfaction and turnover from a very different theoretical lens than the matching models existing in career development choice theories.

In the first illustrative study, 185 professionals of color (business school faculty) were examined to understand turnover rates (Buttner, Lowe, & Billings-Harris, 2010). In brief, to the extent to which organizational and diversity climate were met, they positively predicted perceived levels of organizational commitment, while reducing the likelihood of turnover intentions. Diversity climate fulfillment, in turn, had a stronger effect on reducing turnover intentions compared with organizational fulfillment. Of interest, faculty exhibiting higher levels of racial awareness were more likely than "color-blind" faculty to report a violation of contract (e.g., university failing to meet obligations to faculty) when their perceptions of diversity fulfillment were low, such as the input from faculty of color being considered. In contrast to Buttner et al. (2010), a less complex study of academics was conducted by Niemann and Dovidio (2005) among a sample of African American, Latino/a, and Asian faculty in psychology departments (the authors used the term *Asian* in their study). In this study, job satisfaction was predicted by perceived department climate and self-doubt; moreover, perceptions of voluntary affirmative action policies (active effort to recruit minority faculty) or involuntary policies (imposed to fill a hiring quota) were examined. The authors hypothesized faculty of color may tend to self-handicap themselves because they feel uncertain about their abilities to perform via perceptions of affirmative action, leading to lower job satisfaction. A chief finding pertained to the positive effect voluntary affirmative action had on job satisfaction, which was not significant when racial and ethnic department climate (e.g., views of minority faculty proving themselves longer than White faculty) and self-doubt (e.g., perceptions of being hindered because of affirmative action policies) were entered into the equation. Thus, more positive departmental climate views and lower self-doubt was related to higher job satisfaction.

As another way to conceptualize and study job turnover, the notion of workplace incivility is illustrated by Cortina et al. (2013), who tested the theory of selective incivility, namely, a modern form of racism "held by egalitarian-minded persons who harbor no discriminatory intent" (p. 1580). Examples of "uncivil" work behavior were noted as using a condescending tone, interrupting a colleague, or belittling one's contribution. On the basis of surveys of employees in a city government, law enforcement agency, and the U.S. military, race (dummy coded as White or minority), job tenure, and workplace incivility (but not age) were significant predictors of turnover intentions among the law enforcement sample ($n = 653$), whereas gender, race (coded as White or African American), workplace incivility, and job tenure significantly predicted turnover intentions for the military sample ($n = 15,497$). (Race was not treated as predictor of job turnover in the city government sample.) Consistent with the hypothesis of women of color experiencing double-jeopardy as targets of modern racism and sexism, a significant interaction effect was revealed among the military sample, in which African American women reported higher levels of uncivil treatment than any other group.

Moving Forward

By taking the various deficits of knowledge across all disciplines into account, which have both their areas of strength and weakness in explaining career- and work-related outcomes, we see that the integrative framework proposed in Figure 9.1 is far from being complete. To engage in the kind of paradigm shift we advocate, one that fundamentally reshapes habits of research, it will likely require a less theoretically bound agenda to break the artificial divisions set up between disciplines. Thus, the capacity and willingness to hang core theoretical assumptions at some level of suspension is necessary so that new constructs can be brought into the fold. The road map outlined in Figure 9.1 does not abandon time-honored values of self-agency and choice held within the field of career development and vocational psychology, but it provides a stimulus for this kind of deep, comprehensive theoretical and empirical integration to occur. At the same time, the limitations of career development theories appropriate to this framework still need to be critically examined to make this progress happen.

SELECTED THEORIES FOR THE PROPOSED FRAMEWORK: SUMMARY AND CRITIQUE

We briefly comment on the assumptions and tenets of each theory or perspective, which should be viewed as one of multiple ways to organize future research but certainly not the only way. The selected theories are therefore meant to serve as conceptual guides and points of reference, either in terms of emphasizing their strengths or their inherent limitations.

Holland's (1997) Theory and the Theory of Work Adjustment

Holland's (1997) theory is perhaps the least constructive for understanding the costs of racism in the workforce, or helping people overcome the hardships of racism in the workforce. Yet, the goal of helping clients finding a desirable fit with their occupation or career choices is not irrelevant to people of color. In essence, the main application of his theory is to help clients identify and explore careers/work environments that match their personality type, traditionally consisting of a two or three high-point code of scores on Realistic, Investigative, Artistic, Social, Enterprising, and Conventional interest scales on the Strong Interest Inventory, Self-Directed Search, or similar types of inventories/measures. Guided by the assumption that the stronger the match, or the more congruent the fit, is between a person's personality type (e.g., Social) and the characteristics of careers/occupations (e.g., social worker), the more satisfied the individual is predicted to be with their job or occupational choice.

The test-and-tell approach that has characterized trait–factor models such as Holland's (1997) theory could have implications for assisting people of color with understanding how their scores (e.g., low scores on Investigative, high scores on Realistic) may be the product of how they were socialized or what racist messages they may have received; in this respect, it might help clients explore how they may have foreclosed on careers or did not have opportunities to develop an interest in certain careers. Beyond these activities, however, the theory simply does not attempt to explain how racism affects job satisfaction and job tenure—the two work-related outcomes that align most naturally between the theory and the framework put forth in this chapter. When assisting clients with their career choices and decision making, this theoretical model would not be concerned with helping clients anticipate how racism might prevent them from enjoying their occupational choices or with advocating for them by identifying resources and providing information to overcome such obstacles.

Compared with Holland's (1997) theory, the TWA, which is referred to as the Minnesota theory of work adjustment (Dawis, 2005), has a more elaborate model for understanding job tenure through its propositions underlying the prediction of satisfaction and satisfactoriness. In brief, *satisfaction* is defined as the correspondence between one's needs, manifested by six work values (achievement, comfort, status, altruism, safety, and autonomy) underlying those needs and the environment's reinforcement of those needs. On the other hand, *satisfactoriness* is defined as the degree of correspondence between the individual's abilities and the environment's ability requirements. Swanson and Schneider (2013) summarized the behavioral, methodically operationalized set of propositions governing the theory:

> If an individual is both satisfied and satisfactory, then the individual and his or her environment are in state of harmonious equilibrium, and work adjustment has been achieved. If, however, the individual is dissatisfied, unsatisfactory, or both, then a state of disequilibrium exists. This disequilibrium serves as a motivational force, propelling some type of change to occur. (p. 33)

Similar to trait-factor models, TWA is heavily based on quantitative instruments to assess its core constructs: (a) work-related needs and values; (b) job satisfactoriness (completed by the work supervisor); and (c) abilities, such as those measured by the General Aptitude Test Battery. Once a client's abilities and need are assessed, they can be matched with the work environment that best fits those characteristics. Like the Strong Interest Inventory, norm-referenced reports provide information about the correspondence one's work values/needs and abilities share with different occupations, which in turn have a corresponding level of predicted satisfaction. Such an approach lends itself to finding people a good fit but does not offer much practical value in terms of helping people of color overcome racism in the workplace, or anticipate racism in the world of work, in an adaptive and realistic manner. The notion of satisfactoriness also does not devote attention to issues such as workforce climate, prejudice, or discrimination as interfering with the fair and objective use of "ability requirements." Indeed, TWA is not designed to address reasons people of color decide to quit their jobs for reasons not based on abilities or values. It also does not address a major issue of biases (explicit or implicit) held by work supervisors.

Despite its limitations, TWA remains relevant for people of color across a wide spectrum of occupations and industries. Eggerth and Flynn (2012), for example, sought complementary ground between a psychology of working (Blustein, 2006) and TWA (Dawis & Lofquist, 1984) among 10 Latino immigrant workers. By situating TWA and Blustein's (2006) perspective within Maslow's (1970) hierarchy of needs, they attempted to draw parallels between the three models. Results showed that 17 out of the 20 TWA reinforcers were identified in the interview data, with compensation and security mentioned the most frequently. (In TWA, *reinforcement* refers to how much an occupation or work environment meets the needs and values of the individual, e.g., how much the need for activity is reinforced through one's work.) The reinforcers mapped onto Maslow's level of *self-actualization* were not referred to during the interviews (creativity, moral values, and supervision-technical).

Blustein's (2006) Psychology of Working

Commenting on status attainment theory, Sharf (2013) asserted the following:

> The challenge for the counselor is to provide support and information that will help a client counter sociological processes that may interfere with making full use of her or his intellectual abilities. Status attainment theory does not explain how to do this. Rather, status attainment theory underscores the importance of making special efforts to open areas of the labor market to clients who may otherwise have considered these areas closed. (p. 72)

We contend that helping clients counter sociological processes in the counseling office, the school classroom, the community agency, and beyond, in legislative and public policy arenas, is precisely why models like status attainment theory are needed—a point that naturally falls in line with the tents of the psychology of working and its approach to vocational counseling, based on a strong social justice orientation.

The psychology of working, which Blustein (2006, 2013) called a "perspective," stands as a sweeping integration of various strands of theory located across various disciplines, including but not limited to self-determination theory, feminist theories, relational theories, psychoanalytic and psychodynamic theories, labor economics, I/O psychology, critical psychology, sociology, educational psychology, occupational health psychology, journalism, the musical arts, and world literature. In effect, Blustein (2006) fashioned an amalgamation of ideas woven together in a rich, empathic academic language that appeals to the importance of social activism as much as it does to an inclusive psychological practice of working. By that reckoning, the psychology of working also has natural connections with the framework we propose, which is a similar attempt to bring together various schools of thought from various disciplines. It also fits with the stance of taking action against racism across multiple points of intervention.

We refer readers to Blustein (2006, 2013), as well as other works that present a few core ideas pertinent to our framework. First, the construct of work volition is vital. According to Duffy, Diemer, Perry, Laurenzi, and Torrey (2012), *work volition* can be defined as "an individual's perceived capacity to make occupational choices despite constraints" (p. 400), such as financial constraints (e.g., "Due to my financial situation, I need to take any job that I can find") and social constraints (e.g., "I feel that outside forces have really limited my work and career options"). In their study, Duffy et al. validated the Work Volition Scale, a psychometric instrument designed to assess feelings of control over one's job choices, feeling able to change jobs if one wanted to, doing the work one wants to do, and similar kinds of experiences; fundamentally, it is concerned with the experience of feeling that one has some degree of choice in his/her working life, an experience that can be influenced by racism, along with other societal forces. Many people of color, for example, may not feel they have control over their career choices or working lives because of prejudicial attitudes among employers, a hostile or unwelcoming work climate, lack of diversity in certain professions, and so forth. Indeed, these are not just hypothetical deterrents/barriers, they are well documented and supported by research, some of which is illustrated in our review. Duffy et al.'s study was limited by a sample that was 85% White, where 53% of the participants were earning more than $70,000 per year. Clearly, future research will need to systematically focus on a wide range of people of color.

In addition to work volition, another key theoretical construct that is conceptualized as one of the three functions of working, *self-determination*, warrants attention. In the context of racism, self-determination theory (SDT; Deci & Ryan, 1985) offers a taxonomy for examining how people of color can find a sense of purpose and dignity in their working lives, despite social or economic barriers they might face pertaining to racism. SDT posits that people have self-regulatory styles that determine their pursuit of goals and associated behavior, ranging from a purely extrinsic motivational style (e.g., working to pay the bills) to a purely intrinsic state (e.g., working because it is fun or interesting). The power of SDT lies in its capacity to account for a large segment of the global working population, namely, people who don't necessarily like their jobs or feel intrinsically motivated to go to work but continue to persist and extract some sense of pride, purpose, and meaning because they have integrated the value and outcomes of their work with their self-concept or identity. In this respect, one can see how this notion fits naturally with the experience of many people of color across a wide spectrum of conditions and occupations, including the middle class and economically secure individuals.

Because of its conceptual versatility and breadth of coverage, scholars have begun to use a psychology of working as a perspective that is compatible with other theories/models in the field. Guerrero and Singh (2013), for example, applied the psychology of working to job preferences of Mexican American women. Based on a case study, they combined Hackman and Oldham's (1975) job characteristics theory with Blustein's (2013) work. Overall, results obtained from the 27 women, all of whom had low levels of education, revealed that salary and job security were the most important characteristics, coinciding with the need for survival and power in Blustein's (2006) model.

Industrial/Organizational Theories of Job Satisfaction

Lent (2008) conducted a selective review of both counseling–vocational and I/O models of job satisfaction, which informs our proposed framework. In the third box at the top of Figure 9.1, personality and affect are listed as salient variables; Lent's coverage of personality traits (extraversion, neuroticism, and conscientiousness) and dispositional affect (positive and negative affectivity) as significant correlates of job satisfaction lends credence to their inclusion in the framework, although their relevance to people of color (or any diverse group, for that matter) across work conditions, work transitions, social classes, occupations, and industries was not discussed. Nonetheless, organizational variables captured by perceived and objective job conditions in I/O models are worthy of attention. Perceived job conditions overlap with some of the racial–cultural variables in Figure 9.1, although they have not been traditionally concerned with discrimination or racism. Lent provided several models of how personality and organizational constructs could be combined. Without detailing how various I/O theories can be configured, it is sufficient to note that they have the promise to be complementary lenses with which to investigate job satisfaction and its various correlates.

RECOMMENDATIONS FOR FUTURE RESEARCH

The proposed framework we have laid out is designed as a starting point for sparking the next generation of research on the role of racism from the time of job search to job selection and associated outcomes of work adjustment that occur over time. The possibilities are virtually endless, leaving far more questions to be explored than propositions to be confirmed. To bring some focus to the task that lies ahead, we present recommendations that will help guide future empirical activities.

- *Recommendation 1*: When studying job search and/or job selection, select at least one variable from each box, including a construct designed to assess/explore the role of racism (past or present) experienced in the workplace and/or in other settings/situations.
- *Recommendation 2*: When studying job satisfaction, earnings and promotion, and job turnover, as well as their correlates, select at least one variable from each box, including at least one construct designed to assess/explore the role of racism (past or present) experienced in the workplace. Racism in other settings/situations may also be studied.

- *Recommendation 3*: When applying theory (or a combination of theories) to the study of job satisfaction, earnings and promotion, and job turnover, as well as their correlates, select at least one variable from each box as moderators, mediators, or alternative explanations.
- *Recommendation 4*: Drawing from Recommendations 1 through 3, researchers should compare the results of studies between different groups of people of color, including subgroups within a specific race, to test for their generalizability.
- *Recommendation 5*: Drawing from Recommendations 1 through 3, researchers should compare the results of studies between different workforce industries, sectors, and occupations among different groups of people of color, including subgroups within a specific race, to test for their generalizability.
- *Recommendation 6*: Drawing from Recommendations 1 through 3, researchers should examine job search, job selection, and work adjustment using variables that assess individual-level factors, as well as factors operating at other ecological levels of influence, including peers, family, coworkers, employers, communities, society, and the media. Studies that only look at one level of influence, whether individual or systems level, should be generally discouraged.

CONCLUSION

In this chapter, we have covered a considerable range of issues. Nonetheless, not all relevant aspects of workforce entry and work adjustment were addressed in sufficient depth, particularly with regard to the processes and vocational tasks of career development that may be more salient to a specific phase of life, such as midcareer or late-career stages (e.g., promotion and advancement, succession planning, retirement). We also recognize that more attention was devoted to theory and research than practice, including various strategies that can counteract or prevent work-related racism. These topics concerning practice are addressed in Part III of the book. Yet, it should be noted that the vast majority of this literature is not found in the field of vocational psychology; indeed, similar to other topics we discussed, diversity initiatives and diversity management in the workplace tends to be published in other disciplines, such as human resource development or I/O psychology—the very disciplines that could benefit from the contributions of career development (e.g., Wentling & Palma-Rivas, 1998). As we have suggested, Blustein's (2006) psychology of working is a theory which can bridge efforts to combat the costs of racism with concrete approaches to practice in counseling. Readers are encouraged to consult his book, which articulates implications for practice among people of color in much greater detail than what could be afforded within the space of our chapter.

Considering the broader scheme of workforce development, preschool through higher education, public assistance programs, housing segregation, affordable health care, affirmative action, and chronic poverty, we must ultimately be able to come to terms with the reality that long-term solutions to fighting the costs of racism in the world of work must be grounded in a systemic paradigm of policy and interventions. Because no single solution will solve these problems, our framework and list of recommendations cannot be divorced from the entangled effects of racism addressed by authors in other chapters in this volume. As long as people work together with a variety of stakeholders, public officials, and constituents, the "color line" we unfortunately witness in today's global economy will always have a chance of, once and for all, becoming defeated in an age of restored ideals.

REFERENCES

American Psychological Association. (2003). Guidelines on multicultural education, training, research, practice, and organizational change for psychologists. *American Psychologist, 58,* 377–402.

Avery, D. R., McKay, P. F., & Wilson, D. C. (2008). What are the odds? How demographic similarity affects the prevalence of perceived employment discrimination. *Journal of Applied Psychology, 93,* 235–249. http://dx.doi.org/10.1037/0021-9010.93.2.235

Baffoe-Bonnie, J. (2009). Black–White wage differentials in a multiple sample selection bias model. *Atlantic Economic Journal, 37,* 1–16. http://dx.doi.org/10.1007/s11293-008-9150-x

Becker, G. S. (1964). *Human capital.* New York, NY: Columbia University Press.

Bertrand, M., & Mullainathan, S. (2004). Are Emily and Greg more employable than Lakisha and Jamal? A field experiment on labor market discrimination. *The American Economic Review, 94,* 991–1013. http://dx.doi.org/10.1257/0002828042002561

Betancourt, H., & Lopez, S. R. (1993). The study of culture, ethnicity, and race in American psychology. *American Psychologist, 48,* 629–637. http://dx.doi.org/10.1037/0003-066X.48.6.629

Blau, P. M., & Duncan, O. D. (1967). *The American occupational structure.* New York, NY: Wiley.

Blustein, D. L. (2006). *The psychology of working: A new perspective for career development, counseling, and public policy.* Mahwah, NJ: Erlbaum.

Blustein, D. L. (Ed.). (2013). *The Oxford handbook of the psychology of working*. New York, NY: Oxford University Press.

Blustein, D. L., Kozan, S., & Connors-Kellgren, A. (2013). Unemployment and underemployment: A narrative analysis. *Journal of Vocational Behavior, 82*, 256–265. http://dx.doi.org/10.1016/j.jvb.2013.02.005

Blustein, D. L., McWhirter, E. H., & Perry, J. C. (2005). An emancipatory communitarian approach to vocational development theory, research, and practice. *The Counseling Psychologist, 33*, 141–179. http://dx.doi.org/10.1177/0011000004272268

Bourdieu, P. (1977). Cultural reproduction and social reproduction. In J. Karabel & A. H. Halsey (Eds.), *Power and ideology in education* (pp. 487–511). New York, NY: Oxford University Press.

Burt, W. M., & Vesey, J. T. (2010). Quit rates of women and minorities in Corporate America: Executive Summary. *The Business Journal of Hispanic Research*, 63–66.

Buttner, E. H., Lowe, K. B., & Billings-Harris, L. (2010). The impact of diversity promise fulfillment on professionals of color outcomes in the USA. *Journal of Business Ethics, 91*, 501–518. http://dx.doi.org/10.1007/s10551-009-0096-y

Chou, R. J., & Choi, N. G. (2011). Prevalence and correlates of perceived workplace discrimination among older workers in the United States of America. *Ageing and Society, 31*, 1051–1070. http://dx.doi.org/10.1017/S0144686X10001297

Conley, D., & Glauber, R. (2007). Family background, race, and labor market inequality. *The Annals of the American Academy of Political and Social Science, 609*, 134–152. http://dx.doi.org/10.1177/0002716206296090

Cortina, L. M., Kabat-Farr, D., Leskinen, E. A., Huerta, M., & Magley, V. J. (2013). Selective incivility as modern discrimination in organizations: Evidence and impact. *Journal of Management, 39*, 1579–1605. http://dx.doi.org/10.1177/0149206311418835

Dawis, R. V. (2005). The Minnesota theory of work adjustment. In S. D. Brown & R. W. Lent (Eds.), *Career development and counseling: Putting theory and research to work* (pp. 3–23). Hoboken, NJ: Wiley.

Dawis, R. V., & Lofquist, L. H. (1984). *A psychological theory of work adjustment*. Minneapolis: University of Minnesota Press.

de Castro, A. B., Gee, G. C., & Takeuchi, D. T. (2008). Workplace discrimination and health among Filipinos in the United States. *American Journal of Public Health, 98*, 520–526. http://dx.doi.org/10.2105/AJPH.2007.110163

de Castro, A. B., Rue, T., & Takeuchi, D. T. (2010). Associations of employment frustration with self-rated physical and mental health among Asian American immigrants in the U.S. Labor force. *Public Health Nursing, 27*, 492–503. http://dx.doi.org/10.1111/j.1525-1446.2010.00891.x

de Walque, D. (2008). *Race, immigration, and the U.S. labor market: Contrasting the outcomes of foreign-born and native Blacks* (Policy Research Working Paper

No. 4737). Washington, DC: The World Bank, Development Research Group. http://dx.doi.org/10.1596/1813-9450-4737

Deci, E. L., & Ryan, R. M. (1985). *Intrinsic motivation and self-determination in human behavior.* New York, NY: Plenum. http://dx.doi.org/10.1007/978-1-4899-2271-7

Duffy, R. D., Diemer, M. A., Perry, J. C., Laurenzi, C., & Torrey, C. L. (2012). The construction and initial validation of the Work Volition Scale. *Journal of Vocational Behavior, 80,* 400–411. http://dx.doi.org/10.1016/j.jvb.2011.04.002

Eggerth, D. E., & Flynn, M. A. (2012). Applying the theory of work adjustment to Latino immigrant workers: An exploratory study. *Journal of Career Development, 39,* 76–98. http://dx.doi.org/10.1177/0894845311417129

Fouad, N. A., & Kantamneni, N. (2013). The role of race and ethnicity in career choice, development and adjustment. In S. D. Brown & R. W. Lent (Eds.), *Career development and counseling: Putting theory and research to work* (2nd ed., pp. 215–244). Hoboken, NJ: Wiley.

Guerrero, L., & Singh, S. (2013). The psychology of working: A case study of Mexican American women with low educational attainment. *The Career Development Quarterly, 61,* 27–39. http://dx.doi.org/10.1002/j.2161-0045.2013.00033.x

Hackman, J. R., & Oldham, G. R. (1975). Development of the job diagnostic survey. *Journal of Applied Psychology, 60,* 159–170. http://dx.doi.org/10.1037/h0076546

Hanisch, K. A. (1999). Job loss and unemployment research from 1994 to 1998: A review and recommendations for research and intervention. *Journal of Vocational Behavior, 55,* 188–220. http://dx.doi.org/10.1006/jvbe.1999.1722

Harrison, M. S., & Thomas, K. M. (2009). The hidden prejudice in selection: A research investigation on skin color bias. *Journal of Applied Social Psychology, 39,* 134–168. http://dx.doi.org/10.1111/j.1559-1816.2008.00433.x

Holland, J. L. (1997). *Making vocational choices: A theory of vocational personalities and work environments* (3rd ed.). Odessa, FL: Psychological Assessment Resources.

Hom, P. W., Roberson, L., & Ellis, A. D. (2008). Challenging conventional wisdom about who quits: Revelations from corporate America. *Journal of Applied Psychology, 93,* 1–34. http://dx.doi.org/10.1037/0021-9010.93.1.1

Hotchkiss, L., & Borow, H. (1996). Sociological perspective on work and career development. In D. Brown & L. Brooks (Eds.), *Career choice and development* (3rd ed., pp. 281–334). San Francisco, CA: Jossey-Bass.

Jome, L. M., & Phillips, S. D. (2013). Interventions to aid job finding and choice implementation. In S. D. Brown & R. W. Lent (Eds.), *Career development and counseling: Putting theory and research to work* (2nd ed., pp. 595–620). Hoboken, NJ: Wiley.

Jones, J. M. (1997). *Prejudice and racism* (2nd ed.). New York, NY: McGraw-Hill.

Khosrovani, M., & Ward, J. W. (2011). African Americans' perceptions of access to workplace opportunities: A survey of employees in Houston, Texas. *Journal of Cultural Diversity, 18,* 134–141.

Koen, J., Klehe, U., & Van Vianen, A. E. M. (2013). Employability among the long-term unemployed: A futile quest or worth the effort. *Journal of Vocational Behavior, 82,* 37–48. http://dx.doi.org/10.1016/j.jvb.2012.11.001

Lalonde, S. (2011). Inclusivity in the workplace: Assessing the prevalence of implicit prejudiced attitudes. *The International Journal of Humanities, 8,* 185–196.

Lang, K. (1994). Does the human capital/educational sorting debate matter for development Policy? *The American Economic Review, 67,* 353–358.

Lent, R. W. (2008). Understanding and promoting work satisfaction: An integrative view. In S. D. Brown & R. W. Lent (Eds.), *Handbook of counseling psychology* (4th ed., pp. 462–482). Hoboken, NJ: Wiley.

Maslow, A. H. (1970). *Motivation and personality* (Rev. ed.). New York, NY: Harper & Row.

Niemann, Y. F., & Dovidio, J. F. (2005). Affirmative action and job satisfaction: Understanding underlying processes. *Journal of Social Issues, 61,* 507–523. http://dx.doi.org/10.1111/j.1540-4560.2005.00418.x

Perry, J. C., Cusner, A., & Pickett, L. L. (2015). Fostering adolescent work and career readiness. In C. Juntunen & J. Schwartz (Eds.), *Counseling across the lifespan: Prevention and treatment* (2nd ed., pp. 147–164). Thousand Oaks, CA: Sage.

Phinney, J. S. (1996). When we talk about American ethnic groups what do we mean? *American Psychologist, 51,* 918–927. http://dx.doi.org/10.1037/0003-066X.51.9.918

Quillian, L. (2006). New approaches to understanding racial prejudice and discrimination. *Annual Review of Sociology, 32,* 299–328. http://dx.doi.org/10.1146/annurev.soc.32.061604.123132

Ridley, C. R. (1989). Racism in counseling as an adverse behavioral process. In P. B. Pedersen, J. G. Draguns, W. J. Lonner, & J. E. Trimble (Eds.), *Counseling across cultures* (3rd ed., pp. 55–77). Honolulu: University of Hawaii Press.

Roberts, R. K., Swanson, N. G., & Murphy, L. R. (2004). Discrimination and occupational mental health. *Journal of Mental Health, 13,* 129–142. http://dx.doi.org/10.1080/09638230410001669264

Sakura-Lemessy, I., Carter-Tellison, K., & Sakura-Lemessy, D. (2009). Curriculum placement, race, class and gender differences in wage growth amongst non-college workers: Evidence from the NELS 1988–2000 data. *Journal of African American Studies, 13,* 406–430. http://dx.doi.org/10.1007/s12111-009-9093-6

Sharf, R. S. (2013). *Applying career development theory to counseling* (6th ed.). Belmont, CA: Brooks/Cole.

Swanson, J. L., & Schneider, M. (2013). Minnesota theory of work adjustment. In S. D. Brown & R. W. Lent (Eds.), *Career development and counseling: Putting theory and research to work* (2nd ed., pp. 29–54). Hoboken, NJ: Wiley.

Tomaskovic-Devey, D., Zimmer, C., Stainback, K., Robinson, C., Taylor, T., & McTague, T. (2006). Documenting desegregation: Segregation in American workplaces by race, Ethnicity, and sex, 1966–2003. *American Sociological Review, 71,* 565–588. http://dx.doi.org/10.1177/000312240607100403

U.S. Bureau of Labor Statistics. (2015). *Table A-2: Employment status of the civilian population by race, sex, and age.* Washington, DC: Author. Retrieved from http://www.bls.gov/news.release/empsit.t02.htm

U.S. Census Bureau. (2014). *Presence of related children under 18 years old—All families by total money income in 2013, type of family, work experience in 2013, race and Hispanic origin of reference person (Table FINC-03).* Washington, DC: Author. Retrieved from http://www.census.gov/hhes/www/cpstables/032014/faminc/finc03_000.htm

U.S. Department of Labor. (2013). *Labor force characteristics by race and ethnicity, 2013 (Report 1050).* Washington, DC: U.S. Bureau of Labor Statistics. Retrieved from http://www.bls.gov/opub/reports/cps/race_ethnicity_2013.pdf

Vansteenkiste, S., Verbruggen, M., & Sels, L. (2013). Being unemployed in the boundaryless career era: Does psychological mobility pay off? *Journal of Vocational Behavior, 82,* 135–143. http://dx.doi.org/10.1016/j.jvb.2012.11.007

Weathers, V. M., & Truxillo, D. M. (2008). Whites' and Asian Americans' perceptions of Asian Americans as targets of affirmative action. *Journal of Applied Social Psychology, 38,* 2737–2758. http://dx.doi.org/10.1111/j.1559-1816.2008.00412.x

Wentling, R. M., & Palma-Rivas, N. (1998). Current status and future trends of diversity initiatives in the workplace: Diversity experts' perspective. *Human Resource Development Quarterly, 9,* 235–253. http://dx.doi.org/10.1002/hrdq.3920090304

10

THE IMPACT OF RACISM ON COMMUNITIES OF COLOR: HISTORICAL CONTEXTS AND CONTEMPORARY ISSUES

AZARA L. SANTIAGO-RIVERA, HECTOR Y. ADAMES, NAYELI Y. CHAVEZ-DUEÑAS, AND GREGORY BENSON-FLÓREZ

> Our mission, therefore, is to confront ignorance with knowledge, bigotry with tolerance, and isolation with the outstretched hand of generosity. Racism can, will, and must be defeated.
> —Annan, 1999

As the United States becomes an even more multiracial, multiethnic, and multicultural society (White & Henderson, 2008), the need to revisit the history of racism and its impact on communities of color continues. The history of racism has shaped the opportunities and access to resources available to people of color in today's society, and what is done in the present to challenge the system of oppression will undoubtedly frame the future (Chavez-Dueñas, Adames, & Organista, 2014). If the field of psychology and its constituents are indeed committed to fostering a society of inclusion, respect, and well-being for communities of color, the history of racism, and its aftermath, must be known, acknowledged, and understood. Although the focus in psychology has primarily been on racism's impact at the individual level, the influence of historical and structural racism on people of color has also negatively affected communities in detrimental ways. Poverty, housing discrimination, mental health disparities, community violence, low levels of educational attainment,

---

http://dx.doi.org/10.1037/14852-011
The Cost of Racism for People of Color: Contextualizing Experiences of Discrimination, A. N. Alvarez, C. T. H. Liang, and H. A. Neville (Editors)
Copyright © 2016 by the American Psychological Association. All rights reserved.

and anti-immigrant sentiment are some ways that racism continues to impact communities of color today. This chapter offers a critical look at how histories of oppression in the United States have contributed to such disparities and provides examples of how racial inequalities continue to exist. The chapter ends with how communities come together in the aftermath of racism to collectively heal, liberate, and empower themselves.

HISTORICAL CONTEXTS AND CONTEMPORARY CHALLENGES

Understanding the context surrounding the first encounter between a powerful or dominant group and the less powerful group helps contextualize the impact of racism on communities of color. The initial contact between groups may occur through voluntary and involuntary immigration, military or political intervention (i.e., political asylum), invasion, or forced translocation from the homeland (i.e., slavery). Although an in-depth review of the history of the four main minority ethnic groups in the United States (i.e., African Americans, Latino/as, Native Americans, Asian Americans) is beyond the scope of this chapter, we use different ethnic groups as exemplars to highlight how communities of color have historically and currently been impacted by racial and structural discrimination.

Poverty and Racism

High levels of conflict resulting from a history of dehumanization, enslavement, oppression, and segregation have marked the history of African Americans in the United States. In fact, African Americans were officially granted "freedom" following the 4 years of armed conflict known as the Civil War. In 1865, the U.S. House of Representatives passed the 13th Amendment to the U.S. Constitution, which abolished slavery in the union. Despite this, freedom has never been complete for African Americans, and as a group, they continued to experience high levels of marginalization and oppression even after the passage of the 13th Amendment (Clark Hine, Hine, & Harrold, 2011; Loewen, 1995). For instance, during the Jim Crow era, which lasted from 1880 to the 1960s, most states enforced a number of laws segregating African Americans from shared public spaces (e.g., public restrooms and restrooms, housing, education, cemeteries). The struggle for equality led the African American community into the Civil Rights Movement, which sought to end segregation and gain equity in education, housing, health care, and the like. Although the Civil Rights Movement resulted in gains in greater rights, the community-level effects of Jim Crow continue to be felt.

Although the African American community is diverse with respect to socioeconomic status (SES), educational levels, and political orientation, the struggle for equality continues. For instance, poverty continues to be of major concern for many African Americans (Parham, 2012), with 38.2% children under the age of 18 living below the poverty line, compared with 12.4% of European Americans (National Poverty Center, 2010). In addition, higher levels of unemployment (11.66% African American, compared with 5.3% European American; U.S. Department of Labor, 2014) and lower levels of academic achievement (40% of European Americans have a bachelor's degree or higher, compared with 23% for African Americans; National Center for Education Statistics, 2013) are examples of disparities in education and employment. Last, African American men are 6 times more likely than European American men to be incarcerated (U.S. Bureau of Justice Statistics, 2011).

Impact of Dislocation and Relocation

Native Americans, along with Alaska Natives, indigenous Hawaiians, and some Mexican Americans, are the only native inhabitants of U.S. territory today. Thus, these groups are in fact the only ethnic/racial group who did not immigrate, were transplanted, or sought asylum into today's U.S. territory (LaFromboise, Trimble, Mohatt, & Thomason, 1993). Nevertheless, they have suffered a long history of marginalization, discrimination, and segregation that began with the invasion of their lands and their forced removal and relocation (Sue & Sue, 2013; Townsend & Nicholas, 2013).

The historical relationship between Native Americans and the U.S. government has been characterized by conflict resulting from the colonization and invasion of Native American lands. These practices were legitimized through laws (Maas, 2001; Waldman, 2006). Some of these laws included the Indian Removal Act, which required the relocation of Native Americans living in the eastern part of the United States to territories west of the Mississippi River. Another law that negatively impacted Native was the Dawes Allotment Act (Townsend & Nicholas, 2013). This law allowed the U.S. government to distribute reservation land among individual tribesmen that resulted in the weakening of the Native American social structure. As a result, the Dawes Allotment Act permitted the government to make the surplus of land available to White Americans (Townsend & Nicholas, 2013). Finally, the relocation and termination policies forced Native Americans out of their reservations and into urban areas (Townsend & Nicholas, 2013). These legitimized discriminatory practices led to the American Indian Movement that mobilized Native communities to respond to economic, sociopolitical, employment and educational inequalities. Currently, Native Americans continue to experience the legacy of discrimination and racism. For instance, they experience disproportionately high rates of poverty ($35,062 median income for a household compared with the national average of $50,046), infant mortality (614.7 deaths for every 100,000 births), unemployment, and low rates of high school completion (77% with a high school diploma or GED, compared with 86%; Centers for Disease Control and Prevention, 2008; Murphy, Xu, Kochanek, & Division of Vital Statistic, 2013; U.S. Bureau of the Census, 2011). Moreover, high rates of mortality due to alcoholism (10.3 deaths for every 100,000; Murphy et al., 2013), coupled with high rates of obesity and diabetes (National Center for Health Statistics, 2012), are common among the Native American communities.

Community Segregation

Many people of color in the United States continue to live in hypersegregated, isolated, and economically impoverished neighborhoods. Racial disparities in homeownership and residential segregation began with discriminatory practices of redlining neighborhoods. Unfair lending practices have declined; however, people of color are still directed to specific neighborhoods (Reskin, 2012). In fact, research by the U.S. Department of Housing and Urban Development (HUD) in 30 metropolitan areas in the United States revealed biases across many dimensions (Pager & Shepherd, 2008). For instance, individuals for whom their racial and or ethnic background is visibly identifiable, encounter more discrimination than those who are perceived as White (HUD, 2012). Specifically, about 12% of Latinos, 11% of African Americans, and 10% of Asian Americans who contacted agents regarding recently advertised housing units for rent were shown fewer available units than equally qualified European Americans. For homebuyers of color, less assistance was offered for financing. They were steered toward less affluent neighborhoods with higher proportions of ethnic minority residents (Pager & Shepherd, 2008). Clearly, these housing practices lead to segregated neighborhoods and contribute to inequalities in access to transportation, employment, and quality of health care and education.

More recently, the devastating impact of Hurricane Katrina in 2005 serves as an example of discrimination in housing and lending practices, where the New Orleans metropolitan area was divided along racial lines creating low socioeconomic segregated neighborhoods (Henkel, Dovidio, & Gaertner, 2006). As a result, the damage caused by the hurricane affected impoverished communities that were primarily inhabited by African Americans. Because most victims of Hurricane Katrina were African Americans, implicit racial bias played a pivotal role in the lack of immediate recovery efforts by the U.S. government (Henkel, Dovidio, & Gaertner, 2006).

Impact of Segregation on Socioeconomic Status

Racial segregation exacerbates SES disparities by concentrating poverty and other social problems that are harmful to communities of color. An example of the impact of racial segregation has been documented in St. Louis, Missouri's, "Delmar Divide" where two communities are separated by Delmar Boulevard (Goodman & Gilbert, 2013). To the south of the boulevard, 70% of the residents are European Americans and have median annual income of $47,000; have home values of $310,000; and approximately 70% have completed college. In glaring contrast, north of the boulevard, 99% of the residents are African Americans, with an annual median income of $22,000; have home values of $78,000; and approximately 5% of the residents have completed college (Goodman & Gilbert, 2013).

Impact of Segregation on Exposure to Environmental Hazards

In addition to high levels of poverty, housing segregation has also been associated with exposure to multiple environmental hazards. For instance, communities of color are typically located near toxic industrial factories and freeways, which often lead to health problems resulting from air pollutants (Morello-Frosch, Zuk, Jerrett, Shamasunder, & Kyle, 2011). Residents in segregated communities are also increasingly susceptible to obesity due to the overrepresentation of fast food restaurants and minimal access to public parks and playgrounds (Floyd, Crespo, & Sallis, 2008). Research has shown that low-income communities have access to fewer supermarkets with fresh and nutritious fruits and vegetables (Morello-Frosch et al., 2011) and have many more liquor stores per capita as compared with predominantly European American communities (LaVeist & Wallace, 2000).

Impact of Segregation on Community Violence

Higher crime rates, coupled with the disproportionate number of people of color in the criminal justice system, demonstrate the impact of structural racism. For instance, community violence has been found to be experienced at higher rates among youth of color residing in low SES, urban areas (U.S. Bureau of Justice Statistics, 2012). In addition, racial profiling and police surveillance have been found to be more common in predominantly low-income communities of color than in predominantly low-income European American communities (Zapolski, Pedersen, McCarthy, & Smith, 2014). These discriminatory practices help explain why more than two thirds of the adult inmates in U.S. prisons and jails are people of color (Sourcebook, 2010). The racial disparity in incarceration rates leads to the unfortunate breakdown of families, thus negatively impacting the stability of such communities (Parham, Ajamu, & White, 2011).

Recently, a number of events highlight how racism continues to negatively affect communities of color. For instance, in 2012 the state of Florida acquitted George Zimmerman (neighborhood watchman) for the murder of 17-year-old Trayvon Martin, an African American male. Trayvon's story is one of many examples of how men of color are stereotyped as violent and aggressive and how structural racism continues to support the actions of individuals like Zimmerman (American Psychological Association's Ethnic Minority Issues Caucus, Public Interest Caucus, Society of Counseling Psychology [Division 17], Society for the Psychological Study of Ethnic Minority Issues [Division 45], & Society for the Psychological Study of Men and Masculinity [Division 51], 2013; Toporek, 2013). As in many related circumstances, instead of justice being served for these racially provoked crimes involving people of color, the victims are often blamed. Additionally, since the events of September 11, 2001, an astounding 1,600% increase in hate crimes impacting the Middle Eastern community and those perceived as such has been reported. Unfortunately, family, friends, and community members are often left to deal with the senseless loss while many of these crimes remain unpunished.

Racism and Mental Health

Disparities in access to mental health care, including stigma associated with seeking services, are related to structural forms of racism. In fact, it is well documented that the quality of care received by clients who are of varying ethnic and racial backgrounds is significantly inferior to that received by European American clients. In addition to the typical barriers commonly associated with receiving quality mental health (e.g., cost of services), other barriers, such as mistrust, fear, discrimination, and language differences, have also been found to negatively affect such clients (Adames, Chavez-Dueñas, Fuentes, Salas, & Perez-Chavez, 2014; Barrio et al., 2008; Chavez-Dueñas, Torres, & Adames, 2011). Correlational studies have also documented high levels of social isolation and mental health concerns among members of racial groups (Hatzenbuehler, Phelan, & Link, 2013).

No one can deny that the pervasive exposure to oppression in the form of *microaggressions*, defined as everyday experiences of implicit and/or covert verbal or behavioral insults directed toward people of color (Pierce, Carew, Pierce-Gonzalez, & Willis, 1978; Sue, 2010), can contribute to learned helplessness.

Consequently, and as Sue (2010) noted, the continuous exposure to microaggressions can negatively affect psychological health and overall well-being. Moreover, overt and covert forms of discrimination, including microaggressions, have been associated with stress (Sue, 2010; Sue & Capodilupo, 2008).

Impact of Racism on Access to Education

The impact of institutional racism can be observed throughout the educational system. For instance, more than 60% of African Americans and Latino/a students attend schools that are poorly funded and do not provide quality education compared with 30% of Asians and 18% of Whites (Orfield & Lee, 2005). Besides the funding disparities, which are often based on local property taxes, the overall quality of education in lower SES communities of color is lacking. For example, teachers in schools with higher proportions of students of color often have less teaching experience and lack teaching certification (Orfield & Lee, 2005). In addition, schools located in impoverished neighborhoods are likely to be affected by community violence, which in turn likely has a negative effect on student learning (Pager & Shepherd, 2008).

Access to higher education and college completion is another example of how inequities in our educational system impacts communities of color. The National Center for Education Statistics (NCES, 2010) indicates that approximately 29% of all U.S. adults 25 years of age or older had a bachelor's degree. Asian/Pacific Islanders have the highest percentage of individuals with a postsecondary degree (52%), followed by European Americans (33%), African Americans (20%), American Indian/Alaskan Natives (15%), and Latino/as (13%). These figures underscore that students of color, with the exception of Asian/Pacific Islanders, are completing college at a lower rate than European American students. However, these figures are misleading for Asian Americans, as they do not account for within-group differences, which further perpetuate the stereotype of the "model minority." With respect to within group differences and educational attainment, significant gaps exist within the Asian population. For example, only 40% of the Hmong have completed high school and fewer than 14% of Tongon, Cambodian, Laotian, and Hmong adults have bachelor degrees (Sue & Sue, 2013).

Despite the high levels of educational attainment, many Asian American subgroups report considerably lower annual income and return investment compared with European Americans. For example, Asian Americans adults over the age of 25 who have completed a bachelor's degree reported earning a median annual salary of $46,857 compared with $48,667 for European Americans (U.S. Bureau of the Census, 2009). Asian Americans are also underrepresented in higher level administrative and managerial positions

(Zane & Song, 2007). It is important to note that a variety of factors have been identified as contributing to the lower return on investment for education among Asian Americans when compared with European Americans, such as levels of acculturation, language proficiency, and experiencing racial and ethnic discrimination (Saad, Sue, Zane, & Cho, 2012).

Despite the increase in college student enrollment for some communities of color (i.e., Latino/as), other and racial groups remain unrepresented at almost every level of the educational system (Sólorzano, Villalpando, & Oseguera, 2005). Moreover, although overt acts of racism have declined, covert racial microaggressions are still prevalent in today's schools. Such covert acts include disparaging comments made by professors or advisors referencing a student's lack of ability, as well as the exclusion specific racial/ethnic groups in campus activities. Sólorzano et al. (2005) surmised that these types of experiences are likely to affect academic self-efficacy, which in turn leads to low academic motivation.

Impact of Immigration Policies on Communities of Color

The United States has a long history of race-based immigration policies. The Chinese Exclusion Act of 1882, a piece of legislation banning immigration from China (Okihiro, 2001), and the Gentlemen's Agreement, which restricted Japanese immigration to the United States, are two historical examples of such policies (Munson, 2000). However, anti-immigrant policies affecting communities of color are still evident. For instance, in 2010 the state of Arizona passed SB1070 (see Magaña & Lee, 2013), a law later upheld by the U.S. Supreme Court, allowing the local and state police to ask for proof of residency. This law has primarily affected undocumented immigrants, increasing the fear of being deported and separated from their families. Additionally, SB1070 has led to an increase in racial profiling of individuals who are perceived to be immigrants (Archibold, 2010; National Conference of State Legislatures, 2013). In response, President Obama expressed his opposition to Arizona's immigration law by stating that SB1070 "threatened to undermine basic notions of fairness that we cherish as Americans, as well as the trust between police and their communities that is so crucial to keeping us safe" (Obama, 2010). However, by 2011, 16 states had introduced bills similar to SB1070, with five states enacting similar laws (American Civil Liberties Union, 2012). Aggressive enforcement of immigration policies, by local and state police, has a negative impact on the relationship between communities and law enforcement (Pew Hispanic Center, 2010). Moreover, these policies often create a hostile environment that encourages residents to act in a racist manner (Frymer, 2005; Prilleltensky, 2003).

Communities impacted by anti-immigrant legislations, along with civil rights leaders and activists, have responded to these damaging policies. For instance, since 2007, communities throughout the country have marched in great numbers protesting the inhumane treatment experienced by immigrants who are detained and deported as a result of these unjust practices. They have also spoken against the high numbers of individuals deported (i.e., 2,000,000 by March of 2014) during Obama's presidency (Félix, González, & Ramírez, 2008; Mexican American Legal Defense and Educational Fund, National Day Laborer Organizing Network, & National Hispanic Leadership Agenda, 2014; Pantoja, Menjívar, & Magaña, 2008). It is interesting to note that civic engagement in the Latino/a community may have increased after the passage of SB1070 (Reza, Bustamante, & Benson-Flórez, 2014). Thus, it seems that the threatening nature of these policies possibly motivated community members to come together and actively participate in events. The various responses to anti-immigrant policies demonstrate that communities can unite to raise their voices against injustice.

WORKING TOGETHER TO MOBILIZE: CONSIDERING LEVEL OF ACCULTURATION AND STAGE OF ETHNIC IDENTITY BEFORE MOBILIZING

The United States is increasingly becoming more diverse with regard to race and ethnicity, which promises a new dawn—one in which today's minority will be tomorrow's new numerical majority. However, a collective commitment to work together across racial and ethnic divides will be what determines the strength that communities of color will have at the political, economic, and social levels. Two factors need to be considered before people of color can mobilize to work together: ethnic identity (Atkinson, Morten, & Sue, 1989) and acculturation (Kohatsu, Concepción, & Perez, 2010). Both of these factors may influence the extent to which individuals commit to, and believe in, the importance of creating coalitions to address racism. For instance, individuals at the early stages of their ethnic identity are less likely to recognize the impact of racism on communities of color because during these early stages individuals consider the self as "color-blind" and the world as "raceless."

Acculturation is defined as the process through which individuals adjust to a new culture, which involves the incorporation of the new culture's beliefs, values, norms, language, and behaviors (Berry, 1990). *Ethnic identity* is

> an aspect of the self that includes a sense of acceptance and congruence regarding one's membership in a socially constructed ethnic group. Furthermore, it involves an individual's perceptions and feelings about

members of his/her own ethnic group as well as members of the dominant group. (Adames et al., 2014, p. 7)

We posit that a person's stage of ethnic identity and level of acculturation will determine his or her awareness, understanding, and commitment to working with other ethnic minority groups to better the lives of all people of color.

Despite the differences in level of acculturation and ethnic identity among people of color, they share several commonalities, including history of invisibility, rejection, poverty, disparities in health, housing discrimination, and lower levels of academic achievement—all of which can help them to work together and mobilize as a group. This is exemplified by the words of Dr. Martin Luther King Jr. in a telegram sent to, Cesar Chavez: "Our separate struggles are really one—our struggle for freedom, for dignity, and humanity" (King, 1966).

IN THE AFTERMATH OF RACISM: COLLECTIVELY HEALING, LIBERATING, AND EMPOWERING

Empowering residents of a community can heal and liberate. Speer and colleagues (e.g., Speer, Jackson, & Peterson, 2001; Speer, Peterson, Armstead, & Allen, 2013) defined *community empowerment* as having a sense of control and competence to act, coupled with a sense of awareness of how social and political processes affect one's community. Moreover, community participation is a form of psychological empowerment that can lead to greater health and well-being (Speer et al., 2013).

The psychological wellness of communities of color may be improved through social justice efforts as a way to heal from the effects of racism. Prilleltensky, Dokecki, Friden, and Ota Wang (2007) argued that what leads to social justice is the belief that one has the capacity and the opportunity to pursue a given course of action. Accordingly, helping those who have been marginalized in society to become aware of their oppression can be liberating and transformational, which is in line with the concept of *concientización*, coined by the Brazilian philosopher Paulo Freire (Abe, 2012; Freire, 2000; Prilleltensky, 2008).

With respect to specific interventions, Miller and Garran (2008) offered meaningful ways that community members can work together for positive change. Specifically, they argue that public dialogues can promote reconciliations between and within ethnic and racial groups in communities manifesting conflict. As noted earlier, misinformation and stereotypic perceptions can create misunderstandings across groups that can contribute to racist attitudes, beliefs, and behaviors. As such, structured community dialogues about race, ethnicity, and racism can reduce myths, misconceptions, and negative stereotypes, as well as promote understanding. Miller and Garran also noted that political activism, in which the leadership engages in promoting equality, is vital to the growth of a healthy community. Activism on specific issues that are of importance to the majority of community residents can facilitate the formation of coalitions that, in turn, organize and challenge institutional barriers that limit the equal representation of underserved groups. An example of this kind of activism, is the social movement created by undocumented students, known as the DREAMers, to raise awareness about the barriers they encounter because of their legal immigrant status. They advocated for the passage of the Dream Act, a legislation that would provide undocumented youth who immigrated to the United States before the age 16 a path toward legalization (Batalova & McHugh, 2010; Perez-Chavez, Cruz, & Gonzalez, 2014). Their efforts, along with the support of many communities and advocacy groups led to the Deferred Action for Childhood Arrivals (DACA), an executive order announced in 2012 by the Secretary of Homeland Security and signed by the U.S. President, Barack Hussein Obama (Perez-Chavez et al., 2014). Essentially, DACA gives DREAMers the possibility of obtaining a 2-year relief from immigration enforcement.

Community institutions, such as schools, parks and recreational facilities, libraries and community-based organizations, can provide safe public spaces for people to gather where influential leaders and stakeholders can discuss constructive ways of teasing apart racism, as well as facilitate the development of relationships and networks. In addition, validating and respecting the experiences encountered by community members of color and highlighting their strengths and contributions are ways to decrease stereotypical perceptions and increase tolerance and acceptance (Lowe, Okubo, & Reilly, 2012). In addition, faith-based organizations can play a pivotal role in educating and promoting equality and social justice by hosting community-wide gatherings in which racism is discussed. In closing, we envision a world "where many other worlds will have a place . . . the country we want to build is one where all people fit with their own languages" (Subcomandante Marcos, 1996, Section 3), their own shades of color, histories, contributions, and strength.

REFERENCES

Abe, J. (2012). A community ecology approach to cultural competence in mental health service delivery: The case of Asian Americans. *Asian American Journal of Psychology, 3*, 168–180. http://dx.doi.org/10.1037/a0029842

Adames, H. Y., Chavez-Dueñas, N. Y., Fuentes, M. A., Salas, S. P., & Perez-Chavez, J. G. (2014). Integration of Latino/a cultural values into palliative health care:

A culture-centered model. *Journal of Palliative & Supportive Care, 12,* 149–157. http://dx.doi.org/10.1017/S147895151300028X

American Civil Liberties Union. (2012). *Arizona's SB 1070 and copycat laws.* Retrieved from http://www.aclu.org/arizonas-sb-1070-and-copycat-laws

American Psychological Association's Ethnic Minority Issues Caucus, Public Interest Caucus, Society of Counseling Psychology (Division 17), Society for the Psychological Study of Ethnic Minority Issues (Division 45), & Society for the Psychological Study of Men and Masculinity (Division 51). (2013). *Taking a stand against racism: A time to act.* Retrieved from http://helenneville1.wix.com/time-to-act

Annan, K. (1999, September). A historical perspective: Getting from here to there. *World Conference against Racism.* Retrieved from http://www.un.org/WCAR/e-kit/fact2.htm

Archibold, R. (2010, April 23). Arizona enacts stringent law on immigration. *New York Times,* p. A1. Retrieved from http://www.nytimes.com/2010/04/24/us/politics/24immig.html?_r=0

Atkinson, D. R., Morten, G., & Sue, D. W. (1989). A minority identity development model. In D. R. Atkinson, G. Morten, & D. W. Sue (Eds.), *Counseling American minorities* (pp. 35–52). Dubuque, IA: Brown.

Barrio, C., Palinkas, L. A., Yamada, A. M., Fuentes, D., Criado, V., Garcia, P., & Jeste, D. V. (2008). Unmet needs for mental health services for Latino older adults: Perspectives from consumers, family members, advocates, and service providers. *Community Mental Health Journal, 44,* 57–74. http://dx.doi.org/10.1007/s10597-007-9112-9

Batalova, J., & McHugh, M. (2010). *Dream vs. reality: An analysis of potential DREAM act beneficiaries.* Washington, DC: Migration Policy Institute National Center on Immigrant Integration Policy.

Berry, J. W. (1990). Psychology of acculturation: Understanding individuals moving between cultures. In A. Brislin (Ed.), *Applied cross-cultural psychology* (pp. 232–253). Newbury Park, CA: Sage. http://dx.doi.org/10.4135/9781483325392.n11

Centers for Disease Control and Prevention. (2008, August 29). Alcohol-attributable deaths and years of potential life lost Among American Indians and Alaska Natives—United States, 2001–2005. *Morbidity and Mortality Weekly Report, 47,* 938–941. Retrieved from http://www.cdc.gov/mmwr/preview/mmwrhtml/mm5734a3.htm

Chavez-Dueñas, N. Y., Adames, H. Y., & Organista, K. C. (2014). Skin-color prejudice and within group racial discrimination: Historical and current impact on Latino/a populations. *Hispanic Journal of Behavioral Sciences, 36,* 3–26. http://dx.doi.org/10.1177/0739986313511306

Chavez-Dueñas, N. Y., Torres, H. L., & Adames, H. Y. (2011). Barriers to mental health utilization among Latinos: A contextual model and recommendations. *Journal of Counseling in Illinois, 1,* 49–58.

Clark Hine, D., Hine, W., & Harrold, S. C. (2011). *African Americans: A concise history* (4th ed.). Upper Saddle River, NJ: Pearson.

Félix, A., González, C., & Ramírez, R. (2008). Political protest, ethnic media, and Latino naturalization. *American Behavioral Scientist, 52*, 618–634. http://dx.doi.org/10.1177/0002764208324611

Floyd, M. F., Crespo, C. J., & Sallis, J. F. (2008). Active living research in diverse and disadvantaged communities stimulating dialogue and policy solutions. *American Journal of Preventive Medicine, 34*, 271–274. http://dx.doi.org/10.1016/j.amepre.2008.01.014

Freire, P. (2000). *Pedagogy of the oppressed*. New York, NY: Bloomsbury Academic.

Frymer, P. (2005). Racism revised: Courts, labor law, and the institutional construction of racial animus. *The American Political Science Review, 99*, 373–387. http://dx.doi.org/10.1017/S0003055405051725

Goodman, M. S., & Gilbert, K. L. (2013, November). Segregation: Divided cities lead to differences in health. In *For the sake of all: A Report on the health and wellbeing of African Americans in St. Louis*. St. Louis, MO: Washington University in St. Louis and St. Louis University. Retrieved from https://forthesakeofall.files.wordpress.com/2013/11/policy-brief-4.pdf

Hatzenbuehler, M. L., Phelan, J. C., & Link, B. G. (2013). Stigma as a fundamental cause of population health inequalities. *American Journal of Public Health, 103*, 813–821. http://dx.doi.org/10.2105/AJPH.2012.301069

Henkel, K. E., Dovidio, J. F., & Gaertner, S. L. (2006). Institutional discrimination, individual racism and Hurricane Katrina. *Analyses of Social Issues and Public Policy, 6*, 99–124. http://dx.doi.org/10.1111/j.1530-2415.2006.00106.x

King, M. L., Jr. (1966). *Telegram to Cesar Chavez*. Retrieved from http://www.thekingcenter.org/archive/document/telegram-mlk-cesar-chavez.pdf

Kohatsu, E. L., Concepción, W. R., & Perez, P. (2010). Incorporating levels of acculturation in counseling practice. In J. G., Ponterotto, J. M. Casas, L. A. Suzuki, & C. M. Alexander (Eds.), *Handbook of multicultural counseling* (3rd ed., pp. 343–356). Thousand Oaks, CA: Sage.

LaFromboise, T. D., Trimble, J. E., Mohatt, G. V., & Thomason, T. C. (1993). The American Indian client. In D. R. Atkinson, G. Morten, & D. W. Sue (Eds.), *Counseling American minorities: A cross-cultural perspective* (4th ed., pp. 119–191). Madison, WI: Brown & Benchmark.

LaVeist, T. A., & Wallace, J. M., Jr. (2000). Health risk and inequitable distribution of liquor stores in African American neighborhood. *Social Science & Medicine, 51*, 613–617. http://dx.doi.org/10.1016/S0277-9536(00)00004-6

Loewen, J. W. (1995). *Lies my teacher told me: Everything your American history textbook got wrong*. New York, NY: Touchstone.

Lowe, S. M., Okubo, Y., & Reilly, M. F. (2012). A qualitative inquiry into racism, trauma and coping: Implications for supporting victims of racism. *Professional Psychology: Research and Practice, 43*, 190–198. http://dx.doi.org/10.1037/a0026501

Maas, P. (2001, September 9). The broken promise: The story of how the U.S. government stole 40 million from Native Americans. *Parade Magazine*, 4–6.

Magaña, L., & Lee, E. (2013). *Latino politics and Arizona's immigration law SB 1070*. New York, NY: Springer.

Marcos, S. (1996). *The four declarations of Lacandona rainforest*. Retrieved from http://palabra.ezln.org.mx/comunicados/1996/1996_01_01_a.htm

Mexican American Legal Defense and Educational Fund, National Day Laborer Organizing Network, & National Hispanic Leadership Agenda. (2014). *Detention, deportation, and devastation: The disproportionate effect of deportations on the Latino community*. Retrieved from http://www.maldef.org/assets/pdf/DDD_050514.pdf

Miller, J., & Garran, A. M. (2008). *Racism in the United States: Implications for the healing professions*. Belmont, CA: Thomson Brooks/Cole.

Morello-Frosch, R., Zuk, M., Jerrett, M., Shamasunder, B., & Kyle, A. D. (2011). Understanding the cumulative impacts of inequalities in environmental health: Implications for policy. *Health Affairs, 30*, 879–887. http://dx.doi.org/10.1377/hlthaff.2011.0153

Munson, C. B. (2000). Japanese on the West coast. In J. Wu & M. Song (Eds.), *Asian American studies: A reader* (pp. 84–92). Piscataway, NJ: Rutgers University Press.

Murphy, S. L., Xu, J., Kochanek, K. D., & Division of Vital Statistics. (2013). Deaths: Final data for 2010. *National Vital Statistics Reports, 61*, 1–118. Retrieved from http://www.cdc.gov/nchs/data/nvsr/nvsr61/nvsr61_04.pdf

National Center for Health Statistics. (2012). *Health, United States, 2012: With special feature on emergency care*. Bethesda, MD: U.S. Department of Health and Human Services. Retrieved from http://www.cdc.gov/nchs/data/hus/hus12.pdf#045

National Conference of State Legislatures. (2013). *2013 Immigration-related laws and resolutions in the states*. http://www.ncsl.org/research/immigration/2012-immigration-related-laws-jan-december-2012.aspx

Obama, B. (2010, April 23). *Remarks by the President at naturalization ceremony for active-duty service members* [Speech]. Retrieved from http://www.whitehouse.gov/the-press-office/remarks-president-naturalization-ceremony-active-duty-service-members

Okihiro, G. Y. (2001). *The Columbia guide to Asian American history*. New York, NY: Columbia University Press.

Orfield, G., & Lee, C. (2005). *Why segregation matters: Poverty and educational inequality*. Cambridge, MA: Civil Rights Project, Harvard University.

National Center for Education Statistics. (2010). *Status and trends in the education of racial and ethnic groups*. Washington, DC: U.S. Department of Education.

National Center for Education Statistics. (2013). *Fast facts*. Retrieved from https://nces.ed.gov/fastfacts/display.asp?id=27

National Poverty Center. (2010). *Poverty in the United States*. Retrieved from http://www.npc.umich.edu/poverty/

Pager, D., & Shepherd, H. (2008). The sociology of discrimination: Racial discrimination in employment, housing, credit, and consumer markets. *Annual Review of Sociology, 34,* 181–209. http://dx.doi.org/10.1146/annurev.soc.33.040406.131740

Pantoja, A. D., Menjívar, C., & Magaña, L. (2008). The spring marches of 2006: Latinos, immigration, and political mobilization in the 21st century. *American Behavioral Scientist, 52,* 499–506. http://dx.doi.org/10.1177/0002764208324603

Parham, T. A. (2012). Delivering culturally competent therapeutic services to African American clients: The skills that distinguish between clinical intention and successful outcomes. In M. E. Gallardo, C. J. Yeh, J. E. Trimble, & T. A. Parham (Eds.), *Culturally adaptive counseling skills: Demonstrations of evidence-based practices* (pp. 23–42). Thousand Oaks, CA: Sage. http://dx.doi.org/10.4135/9781483349329.n2

Parham, T. A., Ajamu, A., & White, J. L. (2011). *The psychology of Blacks: Centering our perspectives in the African consciousness* (4th ed.). Boston, MA: Prentice Hall.

Perez-Chavez, J. G., Cruz, X., & Gonzalez, J. (2014). Dreaming about choices and access: Soñadores luchando por un mejor mañana. *Latina/o Psychology Today, 1,* 19–22.

Pew Hispanic Center. (2010). *Hispanics and Arizona's new immigration law* [Fact sheet]. Washington, DC: Pew Research Center. Retrieved from http://pewhispanic.org/files/factsheets/68.pdf

Pierce, C., Carew, J., Pierce-Gonzalez, D., & Willis, D. (1978). An experiment in racism: TV commercials. In C. Pierce (Ed.), *Television and education* (pp. 62–88). Beverly Hills, CA: Sage.

Prilleltensky, I. (2003). Understanding, resisting, and overcoming oppression: Toward psychopolitical validity. *American Journal of Community Psychology, 31,* 195–201. http://dx.doi.org/10.1023/A:1023043108210

Prilleltensky, I. (2008). The role of the power in wellness, oppression, and liberation: The promise of psychopolitical validity. *Journal of Community Psychology, 36,* 116–136. http://dx.doi.org/10.1002/jcop.20225

Prilleltensky, I., Dokecki, P., Friden, G., & Ota Wang, V. (2007). Counseling for wellness and justice: Foundations and ethical dilemmas. In E. Aldarondo (Ed.), *Advancing social justice through clinical practice* (pp. 19–42). Mahwah, NJ: Erlbaum.

Reskin, B. (2012). The race discrimination system. *Annual Review of Sociology, 38,* 17–35. http://dx.doi.org/10.1146/annurev-soc-071811-145508

Reza, E., Bustamante, A. L., & Benson-Flórez, G. (2014, October). *After SB 1070: Perceptions of social trust and civic engagement for Latinas/os in Arizona.* Poster session presented at the National Latina/o Psychological Association conference, Albuquerque, NM.

Saad, C. S., Sue, S., Zane, N., & Cho, Y. I. (2012). The relationship between education and ethnic minority factors in income among Asian Americans. *Asian American Journal of Psychology, 3,* 66–78. http://dx.doi.org/10.1037/a0026867

Sólorzano, D. G., Villalpando, O., & Oseguera, L. (2005). Educational inequities and Latina/o undergraduate students in the United States: A critical race analysis of their educational progress. *Journal of Hispanic Higher Education, 4*, 272–294. http://dx.doi.org/10.1177/1538192705276550

Sourcebook. (2010). *U.S. sentencing commissions: 2010 sourcebook of federal sentencing statistics*. Retrieved from http://www.ussc.gov/research-and-publications/annual-reports-sourcebooks/2010/sourcebook-2010

Speer, P. W., Jackson, C. B., & Peterson, N. A. (2001). The relationship between social cohesion and empowerment: Support and new implications for theory. *Health Education & Behavior, 28*, 716–732. http://dx.doi.org/10.1177/109019810102800605

Speer, P. W., Peterson, N. A., Armstead, T. L., & Allen, C. T. (2013). The influence of participation, gender and organizational sense of community on psychological empowerment: The moderating effects of income. *American Journal of Community Psychology, 51*, 103–113. http://dx.doi.org/10.1007/s10464-012-9547-1

Sue, D. W. (2010). *Microaggressions in everyday life: Race, gender, and sexual orientation*. Hoboken, NJ: Wiley.

Sue, D. W., & Capodilupo, C. M. (2008). Racial, gender, and sexual orientation microaggressions: Implications for counseling and psychotherapy. In D. W. Sue & D. Sue (Eds.), *Counseling the culturally diverse: Theory and practice* (5th ed., pp. 105–130). Hoboken, NJ: Wiley.

Sue, D. W., & Sue, D. S. (2013). *Counseling the culturally diverse: Theory and practice* (6th ed.). Hoboken, NJ: Wiley.

Toporek, R. L. (2013). Violence against individuals and communities: Reflecting on the Trayvon Martin Case—An introduction to the special issue. *Journal for Social Action in Counseling and Psychology, 5*, 1–10.

Townsend, K. W., & Nicholas, M. (2013). *First Americans: A history of Native peoples*. Upper Saddle River, NJ: Pearson.

U.S. Bureau of Justice Statistics. (2011). *Correctional populations in the United States, 2010*. Retrieved from http://www.bjs.gov/content/pub/pdf/cpus10.pdf

U.S. Bureau of Justice Statistics. (2012). *Violent crime against youth, 1994–2010*. Retrieved from http://www.bjs.gov/content/pub/pdf/vcay9410.pdf

U.S. Bureau of the Census. (2009). *Educational attainment in the U.S.: 2007*. Retrieved from http://www.census.gov/prod/2009pubs/p20-560.pdf

U.S. Bureau of the Census. (2011). *American Indian and Alaska Native Heritage Month: Facts and figures*. Retrieved from http://www.census.gov/newsroom/releases/archives/facts_for_features_special_editions/cb11-ff22.html

U.S. Department of Housing and Urban Development (HUD). (2012). *Housing discrimination against racial and ethnic minorities*. Washington, DC: U.S. Department of Housing and Urban Development.

U.S. Department of Labor. (2014). *April 2014 news release*. Retrieved from http://www.bls.gov/news.release/pdf/empsit.pdf

Waldman, C. (2006). *Encyclopedia of Native American tribes* (3rd ed.). New York, NY: Checkmark Books.

White, J. L., & Henderson, S. J. (2008). The Browning of America: Building a new multicultural, multiracial, multiethnic paradigm. In J. L. White & S. J. Henderson (Eds.), *Building multicultural competency: Development, training and practice* (pp. 17–49). New York, NY: Rowman & Littlefield.

Zane, N., & Song, A. (2007). Interpersonal effectiveness among Asian Americans: Issues of leadership, career advancement, and social competence. In F. T. L. Leong, A. Ebreo, L. Kinoshita, A. G. Inman, L. H. Yang, & M. Fu (Eds.), *Handbook of Asian American psychology* (pp. 283–301). Thousand Oaks, CA: Sage.

Zapolski, T. C., Pedersen, S. L., McCarthy, D. M., & Smith, G. T. (2014). Less drinking, yet more problems: Understanding African American drinking and related problems. *Psychological Bulletin, 140,* 188–223. http://dx.doi.org/10.1037/a0032113

III

INTERVENTIONS AND FUTURE DIRECTIONS

11

RACIAL TRAUMA RECOVERY: A RACE-INFORMED THERAPEUTIC APPROACH TO RACIAL WOUNDS

LILLIAN COMAS-DÍAZ

> It takes a thousand voices to tell a single story.
> —Native American saying

Racism continues to be a national problem in the United States. Despite the progress in the promotion of racial equality, racism still affects the lives of many people of color. The effects of racism on its victims include health problems, psychological disturbances (Ong, Fuller-Rowell, & Burrow, 2009), spiritual injuries, and nefarious effects on communities of color. Most victims of racism experience direct and/or vicarious trauma (Helms, Nicolas, & Green, 2010). Because racist attacks frequently occur on an ongoing basis, victims who experience trauma can be retraumatized (Bryant-Davis & Ocampo, 2006; Comas-Díaz, 2007). Even more, racial victimization can result in cross-generational trauma (Dunbar & Blanco, 2014).

The findings of an empirical study on the perceived racial discrimination among African Americans, Latina/os, and Asian Americans suggested that racism may be a traumatic experience (Chou, Asnaani, & Hofmann, 2012). *Racial trauma* refers to the events of danger related to real or perceived experience of racial discrimination, threats of harm and injury, and humiliating and shaming events, in addition to witnessing harm to other ethnoracial individuals because of real or perceived racism (Smith, 2010). Race-based traumatic stress trauma differs from posttraumatic stress disorder (PTSD) in that victims are exposed to constant racial microaggressions (Miller, 2009). Therefore, psychological treatment of racial trauma victims is needed. As most therapists ignore clients' racial wounds, clinicians urgently need to address these issues in treatment (Scurfield & Mackey, 2001).

In this chapter, I first discuss the effects of racial attacks on people of color. Then, I present three clinical models of treating racial trauma. Afterward, I discuss a therapeutic approach to the evaluation and treatment of racial trauma. This approach entails the assessment of clients' race-related stress and trauma, helps clients to reprocess the traumatic incidents, promotes psychological decolonization, and finally, fosters engagement in social action. I discuss a case vignette and conclude the chapter with a brief discussion of the role of prevention in working with racial wounds and trauma.

RACISM: LEGACIES AND CONTEMPORARY MANIFESTATIONS

Cultural oppression has played a central role in the development of the United States. Elementary school teachers tell their students the story of the pilgrims' settlement as a search for religious freedom. Paradoxically, a nation founded in response to religious oppression based a significant part of its development on oppressing diverse cultural groups. To illustrate, examples of people of color's legacies of cultural oppression and racial subjugation include Native American genocide; African American slavery; the United States' annexation of Mexican territories; the colonization of Philippines, Puerto Rico, and Guam; and the forced internment of Japanese Americans (Comas-Díaz, 2012).

The legacies of racial oppression are vividly present in the lives of many people of color. For instance, according to Duran (2006), Native Americans experience soul wounds, resulting from their legacy of genocide and oppression. These experiences engender unresolved and complicated bereavement, PTSD, anxiety, and depression among most Native Americans (Duran, 2006). Moreover, Duran noted that a historical trauma emerged out of these oppressive experiences and caused Native Americans to develop a cross-generational vulnerability to emotional and spiritual distress.

It is also notable that racial victimization can activate a historical racial trauma. In other words, a legacy of racial oppression, in addition to contemporary racial attacks, can result in the development of traumatic reactions among people of color (Bryant-Davis & Ocampo, 2006; Dunbar & Blanco,

2014). People of color exposed to continuing racial-based incidents frequently develop racial trauma. Although racial trauma shares the experiences of most forms of trauma, it differs from other types of trauma because victims are targeted solely on the basis of their race and ethnicity. To illustrate, Carter (2007) advanced the concept of race-based traumatic stress injury, a set of emotional reactions to racism that is similar to PTSD but that differs in that these reactions involve the victims' subjective experience of the event, with or without consensual validation. Within this conceptualization, victims' attributions of cultural meaning to the racist event influence the severity of their PTSD (Hinton & Lewis-Fernández, 2011). Moreover, perpetrators of racial trauma communicate a global message related to what they consider to be the goodness or badness of a specific racial and/or ethnic group to gain and/or maintain power over the target group (Tummala-Narra, 2005). Consequently, the racial attacks occur within the context of racial stereotypes, resulting in a societal response of blaming the victim (Craig-Henderson & Sloan, 2003).

Although overt expressions of racism are no longer publicly accepted, more subtle and insidious forms of racism have emerged, such as microaggressions (Sue, 2010). Brief behavioral and environmental indignities, *racial microaggressions* constitute messages that convey hostile, derogatory, and/or invalidating meanings to people of color (Pierce, 1995; Sue et al., 2007). Racial microaggression offenders are frequently not aware of their behaviors, which adds a level of confusion and self-doubt for the victims of microaggressions. Particularly, racial microaggressions include assumptions of inferiority, second-class citizenship, discriminatory language (e.g., racist, sexist, heterosexist, elitist), denial of reality (e.g., racial, gender, socioeconomic class issues), and environmental microaggressions—subtle messages of discrimination embedded in several systems and environments (e.g., sexualization and objectification of girls and women in the media; Sue et al., 2007). Some specific examples of racial microaggressions are

- A White European woman clerk saying to a dark-skinned Latina who spoke English without a foreign accent, "You are so articulate in your English! Where are you from?"
- A White European American lesbian saying to an African American woman, "As a lesbian, I know what is like to be discriminated due to your being a minority woman."

The above subtle forms of discrimination can be more harmful than blatant expressions of racism (Nadal, 2008; Sue, 2010). People of color who grow up in a racist society are at risk of developing internalized racism when they are exposed to racial negative media images and are victimized by educational, work, health, criminal, political, and other social systems. I have observed in my clinical experience that such risk is augmented when people of color witness racial discrimination among members of their cultural group, as such exposure results in vicarious microaggression. Moreover, internalized racism can metamorphosize into a disorder of the self, caused by severe oppressive insults to both personal and collective self-esteem (Grace, 1997).

The terms *insidious trauma, racist-incident-based trauma,* and *racism* have been used to designate race-based traumatic stress (Bryant-Davis, 2007). Race-related traumatic stress is a common indignity among many people of color. For instance, research has shown that among African Americans, race-related stress was a more powerful risk factor than stressful life events for the development of psychological distress (Utsey, Giesbrecht, Hook, & Stanard, 2008). Being a victim of discrimination, regardless of race, affects individuals' health. To illustrate, Smart Richman, Pascoe, and Bauer (2010) found that both African Americans and White European Americans who perceived being discriminated against increased their cardiovascular and affective responses in a manner that augmented their vulnerability to pathogens. However, victims of racial attacks experience reactions that are qualitatively different from those experienced following nonracially based victimization (Craig-Henderson & Sloan, 2003). For example, victims of racial microaggressions experience emotional distress expressed as shock, anger, sadness, belittlement, frustration, and alienation (Nadal & Hayes, 2012). Moreover, the cumulative effect of microaggressions can result in depression, anxiety, and trauma (Sue, 2010). Furthermore, when people of color are exposed continuous racial discrimination, they can experience insidious trauma. A form of cumulative, almost imperceptible, slights, insidious trauma reminds persons of color that they are denied the rights and privileges that dominant society members enjoy (Root, 1992). The nefarious, pervasive, and subtle nature of insidious trauma alters people of color's perception of the world, their sense of self, and the nature of their relationships. It is vital for clinicians to become aware of their clients' historical trauma and their exposure to insidious trauma and racial microaggressions. If therapists ignore these factors, they risk underdiagnosing race-related stress and racial trauma. In addition to being aware of their clients' histories, clinicians also should have awareness of their own racial life stories and resulting beliefs. Numerous therapists engage in racial microaggressions during the clinical hour (Constantine, 2007; Nadal & Hayes, 2012; Sue et al., 2007). Some examples of racial microaggressions during psychotherapy include the following:

- A Jewish male therapist saying to his Native American female client, "Like your ancestors, mine also suffered from genocide." Although the therapist wanted to express empathy to his Native American client, the Jewish genocide is not interchangeable with the Native American genocide.

- A White European American woman psychologist saying to her Latina client, "Although I don't offer this to my clients, I can see you pro bono if you cannot afford to pay for therapy." The therapist offered an unrequired "help" to her client, engaging in dysfunctional help and stereotyping her Latina client as a person who could no pay for therapy.
- A White European American male therapist saying to his Native American female client, "I understand your people have treated their trauma with alcohol." Of course, this statement needs no explanation—it is clear that instead of being empathetic, the therapist engaged in a racial microaggression.

Notwithstanding clinicians' racial unawareness and microaggressions, victims of race-related stress and trauma benefit from treatment because racism negatively affects their health and sense of well-being (see Chapters 5–10, this volume). Additionally, a pervasive exposure to racial discrimination is a form of psychosocial trauma (Martín-Baró, 1990) because both racism and psychosocial trauma result from sociopolitical and cultural repression, and both bear individual and collective effects. Racial trauma also results in cross-generational effects on families, as well as on communities. To elaborate, victims of racial trauma frequently engage in existential questioning, discontinue their faith practices, become demoralized, and lose hope (Comas-Díaz, 2007). Because many people of color use spirituality as a resilience coping mechanism, a disconnection from the sacred decreases their vitality and aliveness. Therefore, clinical treatment modalities that address race-related wounds and racial trauma need to expand their clinical focus to include clients' spiritual beliefs, meaning-making process, context, and sociopolitical factors.

CLINICAL TREATMENT OF RACE-RELATED VICTIMIZATION AND TRAUMA

Some of the healing approaches to treat trauma are feminist therapy (Brown, 2004), trauma-focused cognitive behavioral therapy (Cohen, Mannarino, & Deblinger, 2006), storytelling, spiritual development, art therapy, movement therapy (Bryant-Davis & Ocampo, 2006), and eye movement desensitization reprocessing (EMDR; Shapiro, 1995). As of now, mainstream trauma therapies have not been empirically validated for the treatment of racial trauma (Bryant-Davis & Ocampo, 2006). Consequently, clinicians and scholars have suggested the modification of mainstream psychotherapy to address the needs of victims of racial trauma (Bell, 1978; Dunbar & Blanco, 2014; Rittenhouse, 2000; Sluzki, 1993). More important, however, is that a literature on the clinical treatment of racial trauma is emerging. Indeed, some clinical models are specifically developed to treat survivors of racial trauma. For example, Dunbar (2001) advanced a treatment approach of working with victims of racism and/or gender, ethnic, and/or religious hostility. He suggested that clinicians examine survivors' level of psychological functioning, acuity of hate victimization, coping behaviors, and identity reformation. Dunbar identified five treatment phases: (a) safety, including event-containing; (b) assessment of client–incident characteristics; (c) addressing diversity issues in the therapeutic alliance; (d) acute symptom reduction; and (e) identity reformulation. In other words, the clinician establishes client safety from the perpetrators and identifies client's support and resources during the first stage. In the second stage, the clinician determines the client's history of traumatic events and assesses the client's psychological symptomatology during pre- and post-traumatic event. Afterward, the clinician examines cultural issues in the therapeutic relationship, such as cultural credibility, as well as articulates ingroup coping and resilience during the third stage. In the fourth stage, the clinician uses skills training in stress inoculation and in vivo desensitization. Finally, in the last stage, the clinician measures symptom reduction, reappraises cultural assumptions, assesses client's ingroup identity, and establishes after-care maintenance goals.

A clinical model proposed by Bryant-Davis and Ocampo (2006) focuses on the therapeutic relationship, therapeutic process, and trauma history. In this model clinicians help clients to (a) acknowledge the racist incident; (b) share their trauma within a safe environment; (c) enhance safety and self-care; (d) grieve/mourn the losses; (e) examine shame, self-blame, and internalized racism; and (f) demand equality. In a similar fashion, Comas-Díaz (2007) advanced an ethnopolitical approach to treating race-related stress and trauma, focusing on liberating and decolonizing aspects. In other words, the ethnopolitical approach aims to decolonize people of color, reformulate their ethnic identity, and promote racial reconciliation, personal transformation, and sociopolitical change. As such, it fosters healing and transformation through the development of critical consciousness and sociopolitical action. I devote the rest of this chapter to a discussion of a race-informed therapeutic model for the treatment of racial wounds and trauma. This approach expands on the ethnopolitical model and is informed by my clinical practice as a trauma therapist.

A RACE-INFORMED THERAPEUTIC APPROACH TO RACIAL WOUNDS AND TRAUMA

A race-informed approach to racial victimization is holistic, and thus, it integrates culturally adapted mainstream therapies, ethnic healing systems, and liberation psychology. A central focus in this approach is the empowerment of survivors to voice their reality, perceive themselves as s a source of authority, and develop critical consciousness to transform themselves and their circumstances. More specifically, the race informed-treatment phases includes (a) assessment and stabilization, (b) desensitization, (c) reprocessing, (d) psychological decolonization, and (e) social action. Although this therapeutic approach focuses on racial trauma, it can also be used for coping with race-related stress. Table 11.1 presents the race-informed treatment phases.

ASSESSMENT OF RACE-RELATED STRESS AND TRAUMA

An initial assessment step is to facilitate clients' ability to give voice to their race-related stress and trauma. Indeed, when survivors tell their story in a safe environment, they promote their agency and power over the traumatic incident (Sudderth, 1998). To further facilitate these goals, clinicians nurture the development of a holding environment—one in which the client feels safe, understood, and validated. Inviting clients of color to tell their trauma stories is a healing strategy that is culturally congruent (Comas-Díaz, 2012). Within this context, psychologists assess clients' perception of the severity of their experiences with racist events. To assist this process, psychologists of color developed instruments to assess racial stress and trauma. For instance, clinicians can use the Schedule of Racist Events, an 18 item self-report tool that assesses the frequency of racial discrimination (Landrine & Klonoff, 1996), in addition to a scale developed to measure gender stress with ethnically diverse individuals (Woods-Giscombé & Lobel, 2008). In this way,

TABLE 11.1
Race-Informed Therapeutic Assessment and Treatment

Phase	Goals	Method
Assessment	Racial stress/trauma	Testimony, scales
	Centrality of event	Testimony
Desensitization	Self-regulation	Ethnic healing, mind–body approaches
Reprocessing	Meaning-making	Racial stress inoculation, eye movement desensitization reprocessing
	Cultural resilience	Ethnocultural socialization and pride
Decolonization	Internalized racism challenge	Critical consciousness
	Agency, identity reformation, posttraumatic growth, personal transformation	Coloniality of power awareness
Social action	Collective agency	Storying, advocacy, activism
	Social change, racial equality	Psychoeducation, solidarity

clinicians examine the interaction of racism, sexism, oppression, and history in the lives of their clients. An assessment of the client's legacies of racial oppression further helps to place the wounds and trauma in context.

In addition to assessing the existence of racial trauma, clinicians evaluate the severity of the trauma. For example, Carter et al. (2013) developed the Race-Based Traumatic Stress Symptom Scale and suggested that clinicians ask clients to describe the three most memorable racist events they had experienced in their lives. After the identification of the racist events, clients respond to *yes/no* questions about the most memorable events covering diverse areas of trauma. Carter et al. suggested the examination of (a) depression ("I felt that life was meaningless"), (b) intrusion ("I experience mental images of the event. There are times when I feel and think as if the event is happening again"), (c) anger ("I become easily pissed-off. I tended to overeat on situations"), (d) hypervigilance ("I feel intimidated, worried, hyperactive, paranoid, etc."), (e) physical ("I experience physical reactions when something reminds me of the event"), (f) low self-esteem ("I think I am no good at all"); and (g) avoidance ("I have used alcohol or other drugs to help me sleep or to make me forget the event. I often find myself denying that the event occurred"). Both race-related stress/trauma assessment tools provide psychologists a baseline to work on their clients' racial victimization.

Besides using scales to assess clients' race-related stress and racial trauma experiences, clinicians can further evaluate the race-related incidents' context dependency, including their meaning attribution. Taking a complete trauma history can complement the assessment of racial stress and trauma. In other words, clinicians can ask clients about their coping strategies, strengths, medical psychological history, and explanatory models about the trauma (Bryant-Davis & Ocampo, 2006). Specifically, they can explore clients' centrality of the event, that is, the degree to which survivors believe that the event became a core part of their identity. Although the centrality of the event contributes to the posttraumatic distress (Boals, 2010), research found that it might also contribute to posttraumatic growth (Groleau, Calhoun, Cann, & Tedeschi, 2013). *Posttraumatic growth* refers to the extent to which individuals experience positive life changes in the aftermath of the traumatic event (Tedeschi & Calhoun, 1996). Following this analysis, psychologists working within a racial trauma recovery aim to enhance survivors' meaning-making process. For instance, people of color are the focus of a sociopolitical discourse. Such focus produces the need to create meaning out of a marginalized sociopolitical situation (Martín-Baró, 1994). Therefore, the treatment of racial wounds promotes clients' meaning making, critical consciousness of their sociopolitical reality, and transformation at personal and societal levels. In the next subsection, I discuss the treatment phases in more detail.

Desensitization

The second phase in the treatment of racial trauma is clients' desensitization. This process is necessary because when clients disclose during assessment, they relive the racial stress and trauma. Clinicians can help clients to self-regulate their trauma reactions after they voice their testimony and acknowledge their racial wounds. The goal is to help survivors to integrate their traumatic experiences (Herman, 1997). To accomplish integration, clinicians begin clients' desensitization by using the racial stress and racial trauma measurement results as a baseline. Clinicians use these findings for the desensitization phase by unfolding the survivor's hierarchy of exposure to racist incidents. Using these data, clinicians ask clients to imagine and visualize the racist events to identify their negative emotions associated with the attacks. Afterward, clinicians teach clients progressive muscle relaxation. Next, they help survivors to identify and name a positive cognition to later be used during the reprocessing inoculation process.

To enhance survivors' self-healing, clinicians can teach them EMDR techniques such as safe-place imagery, healing visualizations, body scan, butterfly hug, and self-directed eye movements (Shapiro, 1995). Additionally, psychologists can teach clients to self-regulate with mind–body strategies, such as yoga healing-light visualization, creative visualization, and cognitive behavior techniques (e.g., thought stop technique). As many people of color endorse a holistic perspective, clinicians can complement the culturally adapted mainstream therapies through the use of mind–body approaches during the desensitization phase. Because most ethnic/indigenous healing practices endorse mind–body approaches, such as relaxation techniques, guided imagery, creative visualization, and meditation, among others, a systematic desensitization is congruent with these modalities. Indeed, ethnic and indigenous healing provide a culturally relevant framework, one that validates the importance of racial, ethnic, historical, and political contexts of oppression. Moreover, these techniques promote self-healing capacities. Even more, psychologists can become familiar with indigenous forms of healing. When appropriate, they can use these culturally relevant healing approaches to complement the treatment of racial trauma. Interested readers are referred to Comas-Díaz (2012) for a discussion of several ethnic indigenous healing approaches.

Ethnic/indigenous healing approaches can be used individually and/or in combination with mainstream psychotherapy to alleviate trauma symptoms. Based on practical evolution, indigenous approaches are receptive to syncretism. For example, *espiritismo* and *Santeria* have been syncretized as *santerismo* in multicultural urban areas (Baez & Hernandez, 2001). As most individuals culturally regress under distress, ethnic and indigenous healing offers a cultural holding environment by helping survivors to recover from trauma, increase resilience, reconnect with their original culture, and foster transformation (Comas-Díaz, 2003).

Reprocessing

After desensitization and symptom relief (as measured by the racial trauma assessment tools, and/or client subjective responses), clinicians can facilitate clients' reprocessing of the racial wounds and trauma. For example, psychologists can help survivors to reprocess negative cognitions and substitute them with positive cognitions, combining an EMDR format (Shapiro, 1995) with indigenous healing. For example, Comas-Díaz (2007) discussed the use of *dichos*, or Spanish proverbs, in reprocessing a Latina's negative cognitions of feeling inadequate because of traumatic stress. Quoting the *dicho* "*El que no sabe es como el que no ve*" ("She or he who doesn't know is like she or he who doesn't see"), the therapist promoted her client's empowerment and fostered the development of critical consciousness through the psychoeducation about gendered racism. Indeed, Landrine and Klonoff (1997) reported that women who developed an understanding of the sociopolitical basis of gender discrimination, recovered sooner from gender victimization than those women who did not have such understanding. Clinicians, however, need to be careful when using reprocessing to not give clients the message of adapting to a racist oppressive situation, instead of working towards changing the oppressive situation (Troy, Shallcross, & Mauss, 2013).

A goal in the racial trauma treatment is to assist survivors to develop posttraumatic growth. Within this context, searching for meaning after experiencing race-related stress and trauma could promote both healing and posttraumatic growth. For instance, clinicians can foster clients' meaning-making processes by reframing the centrality of the event as a learning, empowering, and/or wisdom-enhancing experience. Certainly, reframing problems as life-long teachers is congruent with many people of color's worldviews. To illustrate, although most Native Americans believe adversity teaches life lessons (Mehl-Madrona, 2003), numerous Asian Americans perceive suffering as a path for enlightenment (Tan & Dong, 2000), and many Latina/os use *dichos*/proverbs to illustrate lessons in living. In addition to helping clients to enhance their self-esteem, a positive reframing facilitates clients' identity reformulation from victim to victor. Consequently, a recovery goal is to promote survivors' transformation by tapping into what Ossana et al. (1992) identified as a stagewise developmental process. Reprocessing and reframing the racial trauma enhances a developmental process toward generativity and, thus, promotes the sharing of life lessons with others.

Additionally, clinicians can invite their clients to engage in a racial stress inoculation program. Modeled after the stress inoculation method advanced by Foa, Rothbaum, Riggs, and Murdock (1991), a race-based stress inoculation offers tools to cope with race-based stress and trauma (Comas-Díaz, 2007). As such, this program facilitates critical racial stress incident management to foster empowerment and to alleviate racial wounds. Within this framework, psychologists explore clients' racial and gender socialization (or lack of) to enhance the reprocessing phase. The examination and support of cultural pride and racial socialization is a central treatment aspect because research found that these experiences correlate with less depression among African Americans adolescents (Davis & Stevenson, 2006) and among Latina/o youth (Umaña-Taylor & Updegraff, 2007). Indeed, when complemented with liberation psychological approaches (Martín-Baró, 1994), a racial stress inoculation helps disempowered individuals to enhance a personal sense of agency and mastery. Succinctly put, liberation psychological approaches enhance marginalized individuals' awareness of the oppression and structural inequality that have kept them oppressed (Martín-Baró, 1994). Following this perspective, clinicians work in context through strategies that enhance awareness of racial oppression and of the ideologies and structural inequality that have kept them victimized. During the reprocessing phase, clinicians help survivors to develop a critical analysis of racism. To illustrate, critical consciousness facilitates the reprocessing of negative cognitions into positive ones by providing a sociopolitical framework to understand the racial attacks and to initiate transformative action (Freire, 1970). Likewise, a spiritual understanding of the attacks can be of help to the survivors. For example, spiritual transformation has been documented among individuals who experienced traumatic events, such as sexual assaults, terrorist attacks, natural disasters (Schultz, Altmaier, Ali, & Tallman, 2014), and racial attacks.

Even though liberation psychology emphasizes a collective effort to transform the oppressive conditions, it also focuses on promoting personal empowerment to transform individuals' social identities. Therefore, psychologists can frame the reprocessing phase within a cultural resilience framework. *Cultural resilience*—a set of values, strengths, and practices that promote adapting coping reactions to traumatic oppression (Elsass, 1992)—is an essential concept in the recovery of racial trauma. By contextualizing clients' responses to racism as cultural resilience, clinicians help to strengthen clients' reprocessing of the racial trauma. Moreover, clinicians can engage in psychoeducation as they focus on promoting functional strategies to cope with racist attacks and, thus, initiate the psychological decolonization.

Psychological Decolonization

Many people of color have a collective history of colonization. Such a legacy frequently results in a colonized mentality. A psychological legacy of colonization, the *colonized mentality* refers to the internalization of the colonial cultural values as being superior to the colonized native ways (David & Okazaki, 2006). Racism is a form of colonization in which oppressors assign a mentality of subordination to the oppressed (Fanon, 1967). Indeed, the first African American president of the American Psychological Association, Kenneth Clark (1989), identified the experience of many African Americans as a form of colonization.

The colonized mentality generates psychological alienation, self-denial, assimilation, strong ambivalence, and cognitive distortions (Memmi, 1991). In addition to changes in the perceptions of self and others, the cognitive distortions include changes in the sense of trust, power, and safety. Further, a colonized mentality persists long after the end of the colonial political domination in the form of a *coloniality of power*, which describes how the structures of power, control, dominance, and privilege that emerged during European colonization continue to be prevalent in Latin America (Quijano, 2000). Consequently, the coloniality of power functions as a pattern of control imposing Eurocentric ideals over individuals with a history of colonization. For instance, the coloniality of power exerts Eurocentric influence in the definitions of trauma, traumatic stress, and trauma treatment (Hernández-Wolfe, 2013). To illustrate, when clinicians working within a coloniality of power context infuse individualistic values into the treatment of trauma, they separate clients' traumatic experiences from contextual, historical, and sociopolitical realities. Therefore, psychological decolonization practitioners recognize that the imposition of Eurocentric concepts on psychological practices helps to maintain systems of exploitation and domination that recreate an oppressor–oppressed pattern. Conversely, instead of engaging in methods that promote historical trauma and neocolonization, clinicians can use psychological decolonization to focus on normalizing people of color's survivalist and resilient responses to racism, as well as learning to differentiate functional from dysfunctional responses. Because internalized racism among people of color who experience racial trauma is often expressed through shame and self-blame (Bryant-Davis & Ocampo, 2006), the psychological decolonization fosters critical consciousness. I use Paulo Freire's (1970) term *conscientization*, or critical consciousness, to designate oppressed individuals' process of personal and social transformation as they author their trauma narrative in a dialectic conversation with their world. This dialectical conversation entails asking critical questions (Freire & Macedo, 2000), such as, Who benefits from racism? Against whom is racism directed? In favor of what does racism exist? To what end?

Indeed, the aim of asking critical questions is to nurture individuals' developmental journey from a noncritical stage to a liberation stage. Moreover, a therapeutic decolonization sheds light into the psychological effects of racial trauma, including the comorbidity with substance abuse. Moreover, it helps to reduce stigma and emphasizes healing approaches that restore individual and collective well-being (Hernández-Wolfe, 2013). In this way, a psychological decolonization helps individuals to recognize and validate different narratives of transformation. Consequently, a race-informed treatment of racial wounds and trauma promotes identity reformulation. As clinicians help survivors to overcome psychological decolonization, they foster their transformation from a powerless position to an empowered perspective. In this way, clinicians promote clients' involvement in social action.

Social Action

Racism is a form of ethnoviolence (Helms et al., 2010). Therefore, the race-informed therapeutic approach is anchored in liberation psychology, and thus, it promotes social and sociopolitical action. Certainly, many trauma survivors find healing through their engagement in social action. Within a race-informed therapeutic approach, social action is defined in diverse ways: for instance, giving testimony, advocacy, community involvement, psychoeducation, consultation with social change agencies, spiritual/religious engagement, and sociopolitical activities, among others, constitute examples of social action (Comas-Díaz, 2007; Duran, 2006). More specifically, clinicians aim to empower clients to choose their preferred sociopolitical actions. The sociopolitical activities range from being involved in community affairs (e.g., community education and organization), to giving testimony, and to engaging in political activism—including running for political office. Given that trauma silences survivors' voices, healing involves encouraging storying or the retelling the trauma story. Indeed, storying is a style of relating that is culturally congruent with many people of color. Moreover, it is an effective tool for remembering and retelling people's cultural memory and fostering identity reconstruction (Comas-Díaz, 2007). Without a doubt, the narration of racial trauma victimization helps the reconstruction of a historical memory. Needless to say, the development of a historical memory is an important psychosocial recovery process (Chauca-Sabroso & Fuentes-Polar, 2009). Narrating one's trauma story preserves memory and, thus, provides continuity and infuses resilience into the suffering experiencing of contemporary racial victimization. Moreover, when survivors share their trauma story with others, they promote self-healing and collective healing, communal empowerment, and racial solidarity. To illustrate, the Native American tradition of the talking stick can be used to help survivors tell their racial trauma story in a collective context. The talking stick practice refers to a stick that is passed along in a circle of people, where the individual holding the stick is allowed to talk without being interrupted until the completion of the narrative (Comas-Díaz, 2009). This practice strengthens the cohesion of a group bound by wounding and healing. In this spirit, survivors are moved to engage in social action to address societal and ecological issues. For instance, in discussing soul wounds among Native Americans, Duran (2006) suggested the inclusion of the land in the healing of people who experienced historical trauma. When survivors of racial trauma share their story with others, they promote self-healing and ecological healing, collective empowerment, and transformation. In this vein, research has documented that the combination of a holistic healing approach with a liberation framework empowers traumatized individuals, families, and communities (Cane, 2000).

Regardless of the treatment phase, the therapeutic relationship in the race-informed therapeutic approach to racial wounds and trauma is of paramount centrality. In the following section, I discuss the central role of the therapeutic relationship in the treatment of racial wounds and trauma.

THERAPEUTIC RELATIONSHIP

A significant aspect of the therapeutic relationship is the clinician's ability to earn the trust of the survivors of trauma. In this vein, clinicians need to examine and monitor their reactions to clients' disclosure of racist incidents. More specifically, clinicians avoid engaging in denial; disbelief; blaming the victim; and/or invalidation, ignoring, minimization, rationalization, and/or intellectualization of racism. As previously mentioned, if psychologists commit racial microaggressions during the clinical hour, they further traumatize their clients (Bryant-Davis & Ocampo, 2006). Instead, clinicians are advised to respond to clients' racial story with belief, empathy, support, validation, and understanding. Given the power differential inherent in the clinician–client dyad, psychologists need to prevent replicating oppressor–oppressed dynamics. These dynamics are even more relevant when the psychologist is a White European clinician and the client is a person of color. In other words, on the one hand, clinicians need to examine their internalized racism and the emergence of historical transference. On the other hand, clinicians of color need to examine their internalized oppression and, particularly, their internalized racism. Moreover, all clinicians working with racial trauma victims need to understand their own cultural identity within a racist society, identify the traumatic dynamics of racist events, recognize their amount of social power and privilege, and become aware of the trauma recovery process (Bryant-Davis & Ocampo, 2006). A power differential analysis can facilitate this process. When clinicians use a power differential analysis, they compare their own areas of privilege and oppression with those of their clients' (Worell & Remer, 2003), including internalized oppression, privilege, and racism.

Following this reasoning, clinicians are advised to monitor the emergence of racial transference and countertransference. For example, survivors working with White European American therapists may spend a longer time developing the therapeutic alliance and trust. If the clinician engages in racial microaggression within interracial dyads, survivors could react with silence, mistrust, and/or premature treatment termination. Similarly, White European American psychologists could develop countertransferential reactions of defensiveness, doubts about their cultural competence, shame, guilt, and/or helplessness. Instead, White clinicians need to recognize their own internalized privilege. For example, Jordan (2010) discussed a case vignette, where her African American woman client told her, "I seriously doubt any White woman of privilege can get that one" (p. 60). In response, Jordan acknowledged the impact of her White privilege and apologized to her client. According to Jordan, her apology cemented the therapeutic alliance. On the other hand, clients within an intra racial clinical dyad could react to their therapist with projective identification, presumed similarity, "us-and-them" mentality, ambivalence, and anger. Consider the following example of a racial transference of presumed similarity:

> Bill, an African American young man said to Carlos, a light-skinned middle age Latino therapist: "You should understand; you're not White," while narrating his history of racial wounds and trauma. Bill assumed that Carlos, although a light-skinned Latino, was able to relate to his racial trauma history. He based this assumption on his belief that as a Latino, most Whites in the United States perceive Carlos to be a man of color. In other words, Bill engaged in an intraperson of color transference with his therapist. In a similar fashion, clinicians of color could experience racial countertransferential reactions of over identification, vicarious racial traumatization, re-traumatization, guilt, anger, rescue tendencies, "us-and-them" mentality, and ambivalence, among others. In sum, clinicians need to monitor racial transference and countertransferential reactions, both within inter racial and intra racial therapeutic dyads.

Even more salient, to enhance clients' trust, clinicians need to endorse authenticity and mutuality within the therapeutic relationship. Whereas *authenticity* refers to the clinician's process of "speaking truth to power," the concept of *mutuality* relates to the clinician's commitment to mutual empathy and mutual empowerment (Jordan, 2010). The previously presented example of Jordan (2010) apologizing to her African American female client illustrates these processes. In other words, psychologists achieve authenticity and mutuality by listening with a willingness to promote change in both client and clinician (Comas-Díaz, 2012). Because participating in the growth of the client helps the clinician's well-being, a therapeutic mutuality enhances relational resilience (Jordan, 2010).

Finally, a significant aspect of managing the therapeutic relationship when working with victims of racial trauma is the expansion of the clinician's role. For example, psychologists use psychoeducation and modeling to assist survivors' engagement in social action. Notably, modeling is a clinical strategy within feminist and multicultural psychotherapies. As an illustration of modeling, clinicians can embrace an antiracism stance and engage in sociopolitical action. Within this context, psychologists implement consultation and provide outreach, advocacy, and healing services to communities of color. Even though the expansion of the therapist role goes beyond the clinical hour, psychologists can provide effective services within the context of their preferred mode of social action. Below, I present two clinical examples illustrating the application of a race-informed therapeutic approach to racial wounds and trauma.

TREATMENT OF RACIAL TRAUMA: CLINICAL ILLUSTRATIONS

Cane (2000) provided a healing program that illustrates a race-informed treatment of trauma. She used a holistic approach combined with a liberation framework in the treatment of Latin American victims of violence, including indigenous peoples, refugees, prisoners, and battered women and children. Specifically, Cane used mind–body approaches and spiritual techniques such as Tai Chi, Pal Dan Gum, acupressure, visualization, breath work, ritual, massage, labyrinth, body movement, and intuition work to promote self-healing. Additionally, she taught critical consciousness to grassroots leaders and asked them to share the knowledge with their communities. Cane's clinical findings showed that this holistic approach was effective in decreasing clients' traumatic stress and PTSD symptoms.

As another clinical illustration, I worked with Hope, a 65-year-old divorced African American woman who experienced race-related trauma reactions. The precipitant incident happened at a department store when a security guard stopped Hope and accused her of shoplifting. After searching Hope's bags, the guard apologized profusely for his error. The store manager intervened and offered Hope a store coupon. Hope refused the manager's offer. Weeks after the racist incident, Hope began to experience obsessive thoughts. Her intrusive thoughts were accompanied by feelings of humiliation, and coupled with anxiety and sleep disturbances. Hope's internist referred her to me—a Latina clinical psychologist.

"Both guard and manager were White folks," Hope said during our first session. In narrating her trauma story, Hope identified the *intersectionality*— her intersecting multiple memberships in terms of societal inequality due to hierarchies of race, gender, age, and socioeconomic status (Cole, 2009)—of her identity as her centrality event: "The guard stopped me because I am a middle-age, dark-skinned African American woman." During assessment, Hope disclosed multiple experiences of racial discrimination throughout her life. After assessing Hope's racial wounds, I suggested desensitization. I taught her relaxation techniques and creative visualization. Hope responded well to the mind–body interventions and reported that she enjoyed the guided imagery. A profoundly spiritual woman, Hope stated that she saw Jesus as her guide during the guided visualizations.

Next, we worked on a racial stress inoculation program. Hope reported positive responses to this strategy. We then worked on reprocessing the racial centrality event. During reprocessing, I suggested the reframing of the racial incident as an example of racial profiling. Although Hope agreed with the suggestion, however, she identified her passivity during the racial attack as the source of self-blame and guilt. With this in mind, we moved into the psychological decolonization phase. During this stage, I identified Hope's refusal to accept the store coupon the manager offered her as an example of cultural resilience. This cognitive reframing seemed to initiate the psychological decolonization process. Hope, who had an associate's degree, mentioned that she had heard Dr. Joy DeGruy discuss the posttraumatic slave syndrome (DeGruy, 2005), and identified this syndrome (DeGruy, 2005) as a potential source of her internalized racism. According to DeGruy (2005) this syndrome refers to the slavery legacy of physical, emotional, and spiritual effects on African Americans. Similar to the colonial mentality, a posttraumatic slave syndrome imparts racial retraumatization. Paradoxically, it also facilitates the development of strength and resilience among African Americans (DeGruy, 2005). Using psychoeducation, I helped Hope to connect the posttraumatic slave syndrome with colonial mentality and the coloniality of power. This psychoeducative intervention enhanced Grace's historical and sociopolitical perspective, in addition to preparing the ground for psychological decolonization.

During this treatment phase, Hope exhibited a racial transferential reaction: "You have lighter skin than mine, but your Spanish accent betrays you," she told me. "Have you suffered from racial discrimination?" Hope asked. The power differential analysis comparing the areas of privilege and oppression between us helped me to manage Hope's racial transference. My awareness of the similarities between us (middle-age women of color with a spiritual orientation), as well as our differences (skin color, educational background, socioeconomic class, marital status) infused mutuality into the therapeutic relationship. Simply put, I shared some of the power differential analysis findings with Hope. To illustrate, I connected with Hope's spiritual orientation, and I suggested that she try *Feeding Your Demons* (Allione, 2008), a Tibetan Buddhist psychospiritual approach. Indeed, research has demonstrated that spiritual coping decreased psychological distress among survivors of child abuse, sexual trauma, intimate partner violence, community violence, and war trauma (Bryant-Davis & Wong, 2013). My aim was to promote Hope's posttraumatic growth. Hope agreed to try a *Feeding Your Demons* exercise. This indigenous psychospiritual method addressed the transformation of Hope's racial wound (demon) into an ally through the incorporation of the negative aspect into a positive cognition. Hope identified generativity as her positive cognition during the desensitization phase. After completing the *Feeding your Demons* exercise, Hope reported being very pleased with the results of this approach.

During the final phase of treatment, Hope engaged in critical consciousness and identified her previous dysfunctional reactions to racial wounds. "As a girl, I was taught to keep my mouth shut," she recalled. Hope resolved to re-author her racial narrative. After storying her racial trauma at church, Hope decided to work with children as her social action. She designed, developed and implemented an antiracism, antisexism program at her church. "I want to help Black girls to say no to racial and gender discrimination," Hope declared during our termination session.

CONCLUSION: THE NEED FOR PREVENTION OF RACE-RELATED STRESS AND TRAUMA

A therapeutic approach to the recovery of racial trauma entails the integration of culturally adapted mainstream psychotherapies, ethnic/indigenous approaches, and a liberating psychological approach. The main phases of a race-informed therapeutic approach to racial wounds and trauma include (a) assessing historical, past, generational, and continuing racist wounds/trauma; (b) desensitizing and stabilizing; (c) reprocessing the racially traumatic event(s); (d) promoting psychological decolonization; and (e) engaging in social action. In addition to healing racial wounds, social action can help to prevent racial trauma. For example, in one of the clinical cases I discussed, Hope designed her social action program to inoculate and prevent racial trauma among African American children attending her church. In this vein, Utsey et al. (2008) identified psychological resources, such as optimism, resilience, family resources (including adaptability and cohesion), and cultural resources (e.g., as cultural and racial pride, spirituality, religion) as means of counteracting racial attacks. These valuable resources could be extended not only to communities of color but also to all communities to enhance cultural resilience, racial literacy, and racial solidarity. A public information campaign against racism, racist behaviors, racial microaggressions, and others, could prove beneficial. Because research findings demonstrated that individuals who are sexist also exhibited racist tendencies (Garaigordobil &

Aliri, 2011), such a campaign could potentially target all types of discrimination under a unified banner. This approach could generate solidarity among diverse groups of targeted groups of "others" and their allies. Needless to say, racial equality requires sociopolitical action to implement changes in society. Although people of color bear most of the brunt of racial victimization, racism affects everyone, regardless of race or ethnicity. Psychologists can play a major role in this endeavor. For example, as my client Hope did, psychologists can work toward the creation of a society with racial equality and social justice. In conclusion, psychologists are encouraged to choose their preferred mode of social action to contribute to the creation of a society with justice for all.

REFERENCES

Allione, T. (2008). *Feeding your demons: Ancient wisdom for resolving inner conflict.* New York, NY: Little, Brown and Company.

Baez, A., & Hernandez, D. (2001). Complementary spiritual beliefs in the Latino community: The interface with psychotherapy. *American Journal of Orthopsychiatry, 71,* 408–415. http://dx.doi.org/10.1037/0002-9432.71.4.408

Bell, C. C. (1978). Racism, narcissism, and integrity. *Journal of the National Medical Association, 70,* 89–92.

Boals, A. (2010). Events that have become central to identity: Gender differences in the Centrality of Events Scale for positive and negative events. *Applied Cognitive Psychology, 24,* 107–121. http://dx.doi.org/10.1002/acp.1548

Brown, L. S. (2004). Feminist paradigms of trauma treatment. *Psychotherapy: Theory, Research, Practice, Training, 41,* 464–471. http://dx.doi.org/10.1037/0033-3204.41.4.464

Bryant-Davis, T. (2007). Healing requires recognition: The case for race-based traumatic stress. *The Counseling Psychologist, 35,* 135–143. http://dx.doi.org/10.1177/0011000006295152

Bryant-Davis, T., & Ocampo, C. (2006). A therapeutic approach to the treatment of racist incident-based trauma. *Journal of Emotional Abuse, 6,* 1–22. http://dx.doi.org/10.1300/J135v06n04_01

Bryant-Davis, T., & Wong, E. C. (2013). Faith to move mountains: Religious coping, spirituality, and interpersonal trauma recovery. *American Psychologist, 68,* 675–684. http://dx.doi.org/10.1037/a0034380

Cane, P. (2000). *Trauma, healing, and transformation: Awakening a new heart with body–mind spirit practices.* Watsonville, CA: Capacitar.

Carter, R. T. (2007). Racism and psychological and emotional injury: Recognizing and Assessing race-based traumatic stress. *The Counseling Psychologist, 35,* 13–105. http://dx.doi.org/10.1177/0011000006292033

Carter, R. T., Mazzula, S., Victoria, R., Vazquez, R., Hall, S. S., Smith, S., . . . Williams, B. (2013). Initial development of the Race-Based Traumatic Stress Symptom Scale: Assessing the emotional impact of racism. *Psychological Trauma: Theory, Research, Practice, and Policy, 5*, 1–9. http://dx.doi.org/10.1037/a0025911

Chauca-Sabroso, R., & Fuentes-Polar, S. (2009). Development of historical memory as a psychosocial recovery process. In M. Montero & C. Sonn (Eds.), *Psychology of liberation: Theory and applications* (pp. 205–219). New York, NY: Springer. http://dx.doi.org/10.1007/978-0-387-85784-8_11

Chou, T., Asnaani, A., & Hofmann, S. G. (2012). Perception of racial discrimination and psychopathology across three U.S. ethnic minority groups. *Cultural Diversity & Ethnic Minority Psychology, 18*, 74–81. http://dx.doi.org/10.1037/a0025432

Clark, K. B. (1989). *Dark ghetto: Dilemmas in social power* (2nd ed.). Middletown, CT: Wesleyan University.

Cohen, J. A., Mannarino, A. P., & Deblinger, E. (2006). *Treating trauma and traumatic grief in children and adolescents*. New York, NY: Guilford Press.

Cole, E. R. (2009). Intersectionality and research in psychology. *American Psychologist, 64*, 170–180. http://dx.doi.org/10.1037/a0014564

Comas-Díaz, L. (2003). The Black Madonna: The psychospiritual feminism of Guadalupe, Kali, and Monserrat. In L. Silverstein & T. J. Goodrich (Eds.), *Feminist family: Empowerment and social context* (pp. 147–160). Washington, DC: American Psychological Association. http://dx.doi.org/10.1037/10615-011

Comas-Díaz, L. (2007). Ethnopolitical psychology: Healing and transformation. In E. Aldarondo (Ed.), *Promoting social justice in mental health practice* (pp. 91–118). Hillsdale, NJ: Erlbaum.

Comas-Díaz, L. (2009). Changing psychology: History and legacy of the Society for the Psychological Study of Ethnic Minority Issues. *Cultural Diversity & Ethnic Minority Psychology, 15*, 400–408. http://dx.doi.org/10.1037/a0016592

Comas-Díaz, L. (2012). *Multicultural care: A clinician's guide to cultural competence*. Washington, DC: American Psychological Association. http://dx.doi.org/10.1037/13491-000

Constantine, M. (2007). Racial microaggressions against African American clients in cross-racial counseling relationships. *Journal of Counseling Psychology, 54*, 1–16. http://dx.doi.org/10.1037/0022-0167.54.1.1

Craig-Henderson, K., & Sloan, K. (2003). After the hate: Helping psychologists help victims of racist hate crime. *Clinical Psychology: Science and Practice, 10*, 481–490. http://dx.doi.org/10.1093/clipsy.bpg048

David, E. J. R., & Okazaki, S. (2006). Colonial mentality: A review and recommendation for Filipino American psychology. *Cultural Diversity & Ethnic Minority Psychology, 12*, 1–16. http://dx.doi.org/10.1037/1099-9809.12.1.1

Davis, G. Y., & Stevenson, H. C. (2006). Racial socialization experiences and symptoms of depression among black youth. *Journal of Child and Family Studies, 15*, 293–307. http://dx.doi.org/10.1007/s10826-006-9039-8

DeGruy, J. (2005). *Posttraumatic slave syndrome*. Washington, DC: Author.

Dunbar, E. (2001). Counseling practices to ameliorate the effects of discrimination and hate events: Toward a systematic approach to assessment and intervention. *The Counseling Psychologist, 29*, 281–310. http://dx.doi.org/10.1177/0011000001292007

Dunbar, E., & Blanco, A. (2014). Psychological perspectives on culture, violence, and intergroup animus: Evolving traditions in the bonds that tie and hate. In. F. T. L. Leong, L. Comas-Díaz, G. C. Nagayama Hall, V. C. Mcloyd, & J. E. Trimble (Eds.), *APA handbook of multicultural psychology: Vol. 2. Applications and training* (pp. 377–399.). Washington, DC: American Psychological Association.

Duran, E. (2006). *Healing the soul wound: Counseling with American Indians and other Native people*. New York, NY: Teachers College Press.

Elsass, P. (1992). *Strategies for survival: The psychology of cultural resilience in ethnic minorities*. New York, NY: New York University Press.

Fanon, F. (1967). *Black skin, White masks*. New York, NY: Grove Press.

Foa, E. B., Rothbaum, B. O., Riggs, D. S., & Murdock, T. B. (1991). Treatment of posttraumatic stress disorder in rape victims: A comparison between cognitive–behavioral procedures and counseling. *Journal of Consulting and Clinical Psychology, 59*, 715–723. http://dx.doi.org/10.1037/0022-006X.59.5.715

Freire, P. (1970). *Pedagogy of the oppressed*. New York, NY: Seabury Press.

Freire, P., & Macedo, D. (2000). *The Paulo Freire reader*. New York, NY: Continuum.

Garaigordobil, M., & Aliri, J. (2011). *Sexismo hostil y benevolente: Relaciones con el autoconcepto, el racismo y la sensibilidad intercultural* [Hostile and benevolent sexism: Relationship with self-concept, racism, and intercultural sensitivity]. *Revista de Psicodidáctica, 16*, 331–350.

Grace, C. (1997). Clinical applications of racial identity theory. In C. Thompson & R. Carter (Eds.), *Racial identity theory: Applications to individual, group, and organizational interventions* (pp. 55–68). Hillsdale, NJ: Erlbaum.

Groleau, J. M., Calhoun, L. G., Cann, A., & Tedeschi, R. G. (2013). The role of centrality of events in posttraumatic distress and posttraumatic growth. *Psychological Trauma: Theory, Research, Practice, and Policy, 5*, 477–483. http://dx.doi.org/10.1037/a0028809

Helms, J. E., Nicolas, G., & Green, C. E. (2010). Racism and ethnoviolence as trauma: Enhancing professional training. *Traumatology, 16*, 53–62. http://dx.doi.org/10.1177/1534765610389595

Herman, J. (1997). *Trauma and recovery*. New York, NY: Basic Books.

Hernández-Wolfe, P. (2013). *A borderlands view on Latinos, Latin Americans, and decolonization: Rethinking mental health*. Lanham, MD: Jason Aronson.

Hinton, D. E., & Lewis-Fernández, R. (2011). The cross-cultural validity of posttraumatic stress disorder: Implications for DSM–5. *Depression and Anxiety, 28*, 783–801. http://dx.doi.org/10.1002/da.20753

Jordan, J. (2010). *Relational-cultural therapy*. Washington, DC: American Psychological Association.

Landrine, H., & Klonoff, E. A. (1996). The Schedule of Racist Events: A measure of racial discrimination and a study of its negative physical and mental health consequences. *The Journal of Black Psychology, 22,* 144–168. http://dx.doi.org/10.1177/00957984960222002

Landrine, H., & Klonoff, E. A. (1997). *Discrimination against women: Prevalence, consequences, and remedies.* Thousand Oaks, CA: Sage.

Martín-Baró, I. (Ed.). (1990). *Psciología social de la guerra* [Social psychology of war]. San Salvador: UCA Editores.

Martín-Baró, I. (1994). *Writings for a liberation psychology.* Cambridge, MA: Harvard University.

Mehl-Madrona, L. (2003). *Coyote healing: Miracles in Native medicine.* Rochester, VT: Bear & Company.

Memmi, A. (1991). *The colonizer and the colonized.* Boston, MA: Beacon Press.

Miller, G. H. (2009, March). Commentary: The trauma of insidious racism. *Journal of the American Academy of Psychiatry and the Law, 37,* 41–44.

Nadal, K. L. (2008). Preventing racial, ethnic, gender, sexual orientation, disability, and religious microaggressions: Recommendations for promoting positive mental health. *Counseling Psychology: Theory, Research, Practice and Training, 2,* 22–27. Retrieved from http://www.div17.org/preventionsection/Prevention_Pub_08.pdf

Nadal, K. L., & Hayes, K. (2012). The effects of sexism, gender, microaggressions, and other forms of discrimination on women's mental health and development. In P. Lundberg-Love, K. L. Nadal, & M. A. Paludi (Eds.), *Women and mental disorders: Vol. 2. Roots in abuse, crime, and sexual victimization* (pp. 87–102). Santa Barbara, CA: Praeger.

Ong, A. D., Fuller-Rowell, T., & Burrow, A. L. (2009). Racial discrimination and the stress process. *Journal of Personality and Social Psychology, 96,* 1259–1271. http://dx.doi.org/10.1037/a0015335

Ossana, S. M., Helms, J. E., & Leonard, M. M. (1992). Do "Womanist" Identity Attitudes Influence College Women's Self-Esteem and Perceptions of Environmental Bias? *Journal of counseling & development, 70*(3), 402–408.

Pierce, C. M. (1995). Stress analogs of racism and sexism: Terrorism, torture and disaster. In C. V. Willie, P. P. Reiker, & B. S. Brown (Eds.), *Mental health, racism, and sexism* (pp. 277–293). Pittsburgh, PA: University of Pittsburgh Press.

Quijano, A. (2000). Coloniality of power, Eurocentrism and Latin America. *Nepantla: Views from South, 1,* 533–580.

Smart Richman, L., Pek, J., Pascoe, E., & Bauer, D. J. (2010). The effects of perceived discrimination on ambulatory blood pressure and affective responses to interpersonal stress modeled over 24 hours. *Health Psychology, 29,* 403–411. http://dx.doi.org/10.1037/a0019045

Rittenhouse, J. (2000). Using eye movement desensitization and reprocessing to treat complex PTSD in a biracial client. *Cultural Diversity & Ethnic Minority Psychology, 6,* 399–408. http://dx.doi.org/10.1037/1099-9809.6.4.399

Root, M. P. P. (1992). Reconstructing the impact of trauma on personality. In L. S. Brown & M. Ballou (Eds.), *Personality and psychopathology: Feminist reappraisals* (pp. 229–265). New York, NY: Guilford Press.

Schultz, J. M., Altmaier, E., Ali, S., & Tallman, B. (2014). A study of posttraumatic spiritual transformation and forgiveness among victims of significant interpersonal offenses. *Mental Health, Religion & Culture, 17,* 122–135. http://dx.doi.org/10.1080/13674676.2012.755616

Scurfield, R., & Mackey, D. (2001). Racism, trauma and positive aspects of exposure to race-related experiences: Assessment and treatment implications. *Journal of Ethnic & Cultural Diversity in Social Work, 10,* 23–47. http://dx.doi.org/10.1300/J051v10n01_02

Shapiro, F. (1995). *Eye movement desensitization and reprocessing: Basic principles, protocols, and procedures.* New York, NY: Guilford Press.

Sluzki, C. E. (1993). Toward a model of family and political victimization: Implications for treatment and recovery. *Psychiatry: Interpersonal and Biological Processes, 56,* 178–187.

Smith, W. H. (2010, February 16). *The impact of racial trauma on African Americans.* Pittsburgh, PA: The Heinz Endowments. Retrieved from http://www.heinz.org/UserFiles/ImpactOfRacialTraumaOnAfricanAmericans.pdf

Sudderth, L. (1998). "It will come back right at me": The interactional context of discussing rape with others. *Violence Against Women, 4,* 572–594. http://dx.doi.org/10.1177/1077801298004005004

Sue, D. W. (2010). *Microaggression in everyday life: Race, gender, gender, and sexual orientation.* New York, NY: Wiley.

Sue, D. W., Capodilupo, C. M., Torino, G. C., Bucceri, J. M., Holder, A. M., Nadal, K. L., & Esquilin, M. (2007). Racial microaggressions in everyday life: Implications for clinical practice. *American Psychologist, 62,* 271–286. http://dx.doi.org/10.1037/0003-066X.62.4.271

Tan, S.-Y., & Dong, N. J. (2000). Psychotherapy with members of Asian American churches and spiritual traditions. In P. S. Richards & A. E. Bergin (Eds.), *Handbook of psychotherapy and religious diversity* (pp. 421–444). Washington, DC: American Psychological Association. http://dx.doi.org/10.1037/10347-017

Tedeschi, R. G., & Calhoun, L. G. (1996). The Posttraumatic Growth Inventory: Measuring the positive legacy of trauma. *Journal of Traumatic Stress, 9,* 455–471. http://dx.doi.org/10.1002/jts.2490090305

Troy, A. S., Shallcross, A. J., & Mauss, I. B. (2013). A person-by-situation approach to emotion regulation: Cognitive reappraisal can either help or hurt, depending on the context. *Psychological Science, 24,* 2505–2514. http://dx.doi.org/10.1177/0956797613496434

Tummala-Narra, P. (2005). Addressing political and racial terror in the therapeutic relationship. *American Journal of Orthopsychiatry, 75,* 19–26. http://dx.doi.org/10.1037/0002-9432.75.1.19

Umaña-Taylor, A. J., & Updegraff, K. A. (2007). Latino adolescents' mental health: Exploring the interrelations among discrimination, ethnic identity, cultural orientation, self-esteem, and depressive symptoms. *Journal of Adolescence, 30,* 549–567. http://dx.doi.org/10.1016/j.adolescence.2006.08.002

Utsey, S. O., Giesbrecht, N., Hook, J., & Stanard, P. M. (2008). Cultural, sociofamilial, and psychological resources that inhibit psychological distress in African Americans exposed to stressful life events and race-related stress. *Journal of Counseling Psychology, 55,* 49–62. http://dx.doi.org/10.1037/0022-0167.55.1.49

Woods-Giscombé, C. L., & Lobel, M. (2008). Race and gender matter: A multidimensional approach to conceptualizing and measuring stress in African American women. *Cultural Diversity & Ethnic Minority Psychology, 14,* 173–182. http://dx.doi.org/10.1037/1099-9809.14.3.173

Worell, J., & Remer, P. (2003). *Feminist perspectives in therapy* (2nd ed.). New York, NY: Wiley.

12

CRITICAL RACE, PSYCHOLOGY, AND SOCIAL POLICY: REFUSING DAMAGE, CATALOGING OPPRESSION, AND DOCUMENTING DESIRE

MICHELLE FINE AND WILLIAM E. CROSS, JR.

In his remarkable history of the 1954 U.S. Supreme Court School Desegregation Decision (*Brown vs. Board of Education*, 1954), Richard Kluger (1975) wrote that Thurgood Marshall was noticeably excited when his associate Bob Carter informed him of the existence of doll studies, conducted by the psychologist Kenneth Clark (Clark & Clark, 1950):

> "I told the staff that we had to try this case like any other one in which you would try to prove damages to your client," recounts Thurgood Marshall. "If your car ran over my client, you'd have to pay up, and my function as an attorney would be to put experts on the stand to testify to how much damage was done. We needed exactly that kind of evidence in the school cases. When Bob Carter came to me with Ken Clark's doll test, I thought it was a promising way of showing injury to these segregated youngsters. I wanted this kind of evidence on the record." (Kluger, 1975, p. 397)

http://dx.doi.org/10.1037/14852-013
The Cost of Racism for People of Color: Contextualizing Experiences of Discrimination, A. N. Alvarez, C. T. H. Liang, and H. A. Neville (Editors)
Copyright © 2016 by the American Psychological Association. All rights reserved.

In psychologizing the problem, Clark enabled the courts and the broader public to (a) individualize and pathologize the problem of segregation within the bodies of Black children, (b) slide away from an analysis of structural oppression into a diagnosis of racialized damage, and (c) obscure the Black community's deep desire for schools of quality and cultural dignity. We fear this slippage, lubricated by psychological research, enabled injustice to slip off the hook and advocated policies aimed at "fixing" the Black child while ignoring the landscape of inequality and injustice. Paradoxically, the decision reproduced privilege and deflected attention away from structural issues that, left unchecked—as history has shown—minimized the impact of the court's decision. In the logic of *Brown*, it stood to reason that the solution was not to send Black children back to their segregated, albeit inferior, schools but to, in fact, dismantle Black schools, no matter their historical relationship to the Black community itself, while leaving White schools untouched. Years later, Derrick Bell (2004) revisited the court's decision and conclude that, from a critical race theory perspective, the court did not

- require the immediate equalization of school-funding formulas;
- require the immediate change in resource distribution for all schools such that no matter where the site of their schooling, Black children would have access to adequate school buildings, up-to-date text books, advanced placement (AP) classes, school counselors, school nurses, and so on; nor
- require the immediate reshaping of methods for electing school board representatives.

To Bell (2004), the mere mixing of children was an indirect response *to* the oppressive education system within which Blacks were ensnarled and left their overall powerlessness untouched and the unjust privilege of White schools unchecked. In his analysis, the difference in school performance between White and Black children was not a function of Black children themselves—rather, their academic achievement was tied directly to the underfunding of their schools, less adequate facilities, underqualified teachers, and the political powerlessness of their community leaders in school affairs. Between 1900 and 1954, studies showed the distribution of school tax dollars was designed by law to result in the long-term disinvestment and underdevelopment of Black education, and the resulting overflow of tax dollars enabled the overfunding and thus accelerated development of White children (Anderson, 2006). As an important aside, the resistance of White lawmakers across almost all the states to school-funding equalization remains at the heart of debates on urban education that effects children of color.

The point we are making is that the psychological discourse on Black inferiority sidetracked the Supreme Court's analysis of the systemic issues at play and obscured the Black community's efforts to create schools of quality and cultural dignity. As future research would show (Cross, 1991), Clark and Clark's (1950) analysis was deeply flawed and the ordinary Black child and the everyday Black person of the times faced less a problem of self-hatred and more the predicament of unfair distribution of public educational funds and lack of educational voice due to limited voting rights, neither of which the court's decision addressed. As an important aside, Clark and Clark's failed attempt at demonstrating that the average Black person experienced racial self-hatred set the stage for future psychological research on internalized oppression. Modern psychological studies using sophisticated methodologies and psychometrically sound instruments have revealed the existence of internalized oppression; however, as a complement to the thrust of our main argument, the percentage shown to suffer such consequences is but a fraction of the group as a whole. When psychologists study internalized oppression, it is critical that their findings be accurately reported such that significant findings highlighting the blight of a fraction are not misconstrued as applying to the majority (Cross, 1991, 2003, 2012; Rosenberg & Simmons, 1971; Worrell, 2012). From our vantage point, findings that an oppressed group is psychologically resilient and thriving do not provide a basis for denial of due process and/or legally sanctioned relief:

> In discovering the unromantic depiction of black strength, people are incredulous. Where there is slavery and brutality, there must be the crushing of humanity; where there is Jim Crow, there must be self-hatred, where there is the underclass, there must be psychological implosion. When, as happened after the 1954 *Brown* desegregation decision, researchers began to entertain that racial self-hatred was *not* the starting point for the discourse on black psychological functioning, pejorativists acted as if the righteousness of the decision itself was being undermined and called into question. In the present, we find the same type of befuddled reaction to evidence showing that, with key demographic variables held constant, blacks are no more likely to turn to crime than members of any other group. Puzzlement turns to incredulity when, in the face of facts showing black males are a disproportionate fraction of all males currently incarcerated, additional evidence shows that the relationship between criminality and psychopathology is no higher for black than it is for white males. We pathologize and psychologize almost as a way of guarding against comprehending how predicaments excreted by social injustice, greed, and avarice can make normal people, ordinary people, seem odd. (Cross, 2012, p. 718)

PSYCHOLOGIZING DELINQUENCY

At an earlier period in Black history, the sociologist E. Franklin Frazier (1939) argued that Black children were vulnerable and predisposed to delinquency and crime—*a psychological argument*—because a disproportionate number of Black children came from single-parent homes. Frazier based his conclusions on the behavior of Black children living in Chicago. However, in a historical study of Chicago schools covering the period, when Frazier collected his data, Homel (1984) found that the Black community experienced unimaginable school overcrowding. Homel discovered that one of the strategies the Chicago School Board used to bring relief was to send Black students to school in shifts. Although this was true at all grade levels, more to the point, the policy saw Black adolescents spending anywhere from 20% to 40% less time in school, than their White counterparts. Homel concluded that "School overcrowding... hurt youth... by offering too many chances to get into trouble... the shift system made it easy for pupils to become truants" (p. 82). Regarding school achievement, Homel quoted a Black journalist as saying, "In such an undesirable situation reading habit, attention, concentration, and discipline are lost" (p. 82). Homel also provided a quote from the noted playwright Larraine Hansberry, who grew up in Chicago during the shift policy:

> One result is that—to this day—I cannot count properly. I do not add, subtract or multiply with ease. The mind which was able to grasp university reading material in the sixth and seventh grades had not been sufficiently exposed to elementary arithmetic to make even simple change in a grocery store. (p. 82)

The implication of Hormel's findings and Hansberry's reflections are that even if Black people at the time were paragons of mental health, the risks and temptations inherent in their predicament made it nearly impossible for Black youth to avoid delinquency. In a manner of speaking, psychologizing helped mask, rather than illuminate, history and context.

PSYCHOLOGIZING THE BLACK–WHITE ACHIEVEMENT GAP

The now deceased anthropologist John Ogbu (2003)—in psychologizing causes for the Black–White achievement gap—claimed that Black youth equated high achievement with White rather than Black culture. As a result, Black students who did achieve were often singled out by their Black associates for "acting White." Ogbu theorized that Black attitudes about acting White were part of a psychological shield Blacks developed in slavery—and carried over into freedom—reflecting Black resistance to assimilation and acculturation. Ogbu's (2003) acting-White thesis has been discredited on two fronts: historical and contemporary. We first turn to the historical record, and in a later section we review contemporary research by Galletta (2003), the results from which complicate the acting White thesis (Galletta & Cross, 2007).

From a historical perspective, Anderson (1988) and Spencer, Cross, Harpalani, and Goss (2003) have shown that the social movement for education—spearheaded by the ex-slaves immediately following emancipation and the end of the Civil War—undercuts any notion of an organic Black resistance to achievement and social mobility rooted in the slavery experience. In diaries kept by those who traveled to the South to aid in the Black transition to freedom, members of the Union Army and members of the freedman's aid societies remarked how difficult it was to keep up with the demand for education being made by the ex-slaves, a demand targeting the education not only of their children but also for adults themselves (Anderson, 1988; Butchart, 1980; Webber, 1978):

> The drive toward Black education, after the Civil War, can only be given its due if framed as a social movement—not a trend, not a drift, and not a contrivance imposed by White allies from the North. While educated free-Blacks and White allies where crucial elements, the shear scope of the educational demands and depth of these ex-slaves revealed a deep seated *achievement motivation* that had its origins in slavery itself. (Spencer et al., 2003, p. 284)

Blunting Black progress and achievement required that the Southern region use horrific state-sponsored terrorism. The lowly status of Black people entering the 20th century had little if anything to do with Black attitudes and a negative legacy of slavery and more to do with the disfranchising of Blacks, the underfunding of Black education, and when all else failed, the White use of mob rule and terror. Anderson (2006) pointed out that had there actually been separate but equal school funding, the infusion of resources into a segregated Black community, hypermotivated for achievement and acculturation, might well have resulted in a degree of achievement and social mobility paralleling the most aggressive of White ethnic groups.

Black achievement problems in the mid- to late 20th century were the product of state policies carried out throughout the South and parts of the North, as well, wherein tax dollars and resources were funneled away from Black children and their schools (i.e., disinvestment) and into the coffers of White schools so that Black schools experienced, over time, comparative underdevelopment. The same rate of growth for Black achievement as White achievement was not possible because tax dollars were not distributed in line with a separate and equal system. The predicament within which Blacks found themselves neutralized any positive attitudes that pushed Blacks toward school achievement, in the sense that such strong positive attitudes toward education were found wanting, in the face of overwhelming White resistance and furious White violence. In light of historical facts, the legacy of slavery and the pressure to act White represent a form of psychological violence against Black culture. We return to the acting-White thesis later in this chapter.

PSYCHOLOGIZING WELFARE AND PERSONAL RESPONSIBILITY

Psychologizing complements a liberal stance toward Black challenges such that institutional arrangements are not called into question. Black behavior and Black attitudes that speak to personal deficits, personal responsibility, and freedom of choice become the target, and institutional procedures and policies are masked or positioned beyond the pale, insofar as a change agenda is concerned. In the run-up to welfare reform in 1992, psychologizing about individual and personal responsibility was dramatically played out in the public discourse. In the winter of 1992, a factory closed in Perry, Florida, and USA Today ran a front-page article (Stone, 1992) on the economic ripple effects of the closure. Small photos of 11 laid-off workers, 10 of whom were White, formed the border of a full-page pictorial schematic of the community. The photos, schematic, and accompanying article explicated how lost wages cut into the economic health of the surrounding community, with fewer dollars being spent in 31 local commercial establishments (e.g., jewelry store, cable television company, bank, ice-cream shop, hairdresser, volume of advertisements for the local newspaper).

The connection between employment, individual agency, taxpayer participation, safe and affordable housing, and community vitality could not escape the average reader. No one suggested that the laid-off workers would become lazy, unmotivated, and addicted to welfare. Around the same time period, the New York Times (July 5–10, 1992) ran a series of front-page articles (Toner, 1992) on the need for welfare reform. The focus tended to be on Black people and other people of color residing in urban centers. Only nominal reference was made to the links between employment and community vitality, and the tone of the series was that Blacks had somehow positioned themselves to be on welfare, independent of economic forces. Juxtaposing the two stories, one notes that when the focus is on Whites, the social policy implication is how to create economic activity and new jobs, but when the focus is on Blacks, the implication is how to get people off welfare. In the White case, systemic forces explain worker redundancy; in the Black case, the emphasis shifts to an implied history that has resulted in a mindset or psychology that is peculiar to Black people (Cross, 2003, p. 68).

With this brief travelogue through the history of psychological collusion in policy debates about race and (in)justice, we want to frame our concern. We are worried that psychology has long provided the "science" to support racialized policy decisions that ignore the history and structures of injustice and that focus instead on individuals, foregrounding deficits and overlooking the powerful resistance movements of communities seeking educational justice.

In the remainder of this chapter, we review three contemporary research projects in which psychologists have refused to collude in the damage thesis. Instead, with broad theoretical frameworks and complex empirical design, they have

- documented the history and structures of racialized oppression,
- interrogated the social and psychological impact on communities and children of color, and
- collaborated explicitly with social movements dedicated to racial justice.

We offer these quite distinct case studies to suggest varied models for psychologists to engage with policy and organizing for racial justice in ways that are theoretically exciting, methodologically complex, and politically provocative without the need or necessity of stamping stigma or damage on the backs of low income children of color.

CASE STUDY ONE: A SYSTEMIC ANALYSIS OF THE ACHIEVEMENT GAP

Social psychologist Anne Galletta (2003, 2013a, 2013b; Galletta & Cross, 2007) interrogated Ogbu's (2003) acting-White thesis by conducting her own study of the way integration unfolded in the school system that Ogbu researched and from which he built the case for oppositional identity: Shaker Heights, Cleveland. Rooted in critical race theory and seeking to catalogue how desegregation policy has been implemented—who benefits and who continues to pay an educational price—Galletta's (2003) research was a mixed-method project that revealed how policies and programs designed with good intentions ultimately reproduce a fair amount of classroom educational segregation and inequity within otherwise integrated buildings. As in the original *Brown* decision, when implementing desegregation, historically White school districts tend not to challenge the structures and history of privilege but focus instead on attending to the "needs" and "deficits" of children of color. By preserving privilege and adding the furniture of "support" to "struggling students," desegregated schools around the nation reproduce racial stratification through testing and tracking as if these were not technologies of segregation.

Galletta (2003) found that as school systems go, Shaker Heights developed what on the surface appeared to be a very aggressive and proactive stance in favor of integration such that every school building housed an integrated school populace. However, under the guise of maintaining a color-blind quality-education experience for gifted and talented students, children were afforded the opportunity to be placed in a gifted and enriched program during the early grades, and such placement generally became a gateway for placement in upper tracks for the remainder of a child's K–12 education. So-called culture-neutral tests and teacher recommendations determined the selection of children for the various tracks:

> The key to our deconstruction: that desegregation has meant access to a privilege once enjoyed by Whites. In this since, privilege is inherently tied up with exclusion, since what has historically contributed to the school systems' privileged status is the exclusion of others by race and class. While "notions" of "equality" were explored and debated, terms like "standards" and "excellence" remained impervious to scrutiny, creating a firewall around policies and practices presumed to sustain "quality," while simultaneously replicating race and class inequalities. (Galletta & Cross, 2007, p. 21)

Galletta (2003) reported that Black children were undersubscribed in the enrichment classes, thus setting the stage for their underrepresentation thereafter. Galletta found that although it was true that every school building reflected an integrated school population, it was also true that the tracking system, said to be race neutral or color-blind, effectively racialized the core subject matter classes. Galletta interviewed White students who said that integration was a reality in the hallways, cafeteria, and at extracurricular events; however, core subject matter classes and especially AP classes were overwhelming, and sometimes totally, White. More important, White students painted a picture of continuous support by teachers and schools across their K–12 experiences, whereas Black students discussed support in episodic terms. This inconsistent support of their academic self-image caused some Black students to vacillate between self-acceptance of their academic potential and self-neglect. It is this self-neglect that might well be perceived by others as an expression of oppositional identity; however, as explained by Galletta and Cross (2007):

> As for their educational development, black students were subject to a "zigzag" pattern. At times they relied on one dimension of their split image and at times shifted back to another image. Key shifts from one identity to another were sometimes elicited by at least one teacher—sometimes

black, sometimes white—who challenged them to dig deeper onto their sometimes self-neglected or self-repressed academic sense of self. The nature of the relationship with such a teacher took on the dynamics of an academic "intervention." Thus, whereas White students depicted fairly continuous support from a broad range of teachers across all grade levels, black students told of the discovery of their academic potential through only one or a limited number of teachers. Ironically, these few supportive teachers helped black students learn to negotiate interactions with less supportive teachers so that they could maintain high achievement motivation in the face of less optimum conditions. (p. 35)

Such arrangements led to considerable frustration among the Black parents and predictable perturbation and annoyance among Black students. In her interviews with Black students, Galletta and Cross's (2007) finding of oppositionalism seemed as readily explained by the Black students' frustration with their long-standing treatment by the system than as an expression of some preexisting attitude organic to Black culture. Galletta's scholarship provides an exquisite Lewinian topography of how unjust systems are built and sustained, despite the best of intentions to "help"—but not disrupt—existing social stratifications.

We turn now to a parallel story, more current but painfully familiar, from New York City, where public policies advanced in a language of race neutrality exacerbate segregation and legitimate stratification of opportunity structures.

CASE TWO: CRITICAL ETHNOGRAPHY ON THE RACIALIZED DISPOSSESSION PROVOKED BY "RACE-NEUTRAL" POLICY

In 2009, *The New York Times* broke the story that Brandeis High School would be one among 96 public schools serving low-income children of color slated to be closed because of a history of failure:

Brandeis, with 2,251 students, is an increasingly endangered species of school—a large general-curriculum institution rich in course offerings but short on personal interaction. These big high schools, once staples of the city's educational map, have been overhauled by the Bloomberg administration, and other urban education reformers who promote more intimate learning environments as an antidote to poor performance. Opened in 1965, Brandeis is the 15th school to be marked for closing this year; others include the Bayard Rustin High School for the Humanities in Chelsea, another large high school. Since Mayor Michael R. Bloomberg took over control of the city school system in 2002, 96 schools have been ordered to close, including more than two dozen large high schools. (Hernandez, 2009, p. A27)

Brandeis was the school where the first author (Michelle Fine) conducted ethnography of dropouts/pushouts 20-odd years ago, resulting in the book *Framing Dropouts* (Fine, 1991). The official name of the school was never used, because of respect for the hard work of the educators and youth struggling in a building structurally set up to produce widespread, racialized failure, because of wide-ranging underinvestment. But now, reading the institutional obituary, Fine learned that the large school would be closed, and a complex of small schools designed in its place. *Framing Dropouts*, written almost a quarter century earlier, opens in the auditorium of the school:

> As two hundred and fifty young people walked across the stage, with flowers and corsages, cheers and the rapid lights of cameras flickering for the survivors. Mothers, aunts, fathers, siblings, grandparents gathered from the Bronx and Harlem, Puerto Rico and the DR to celebrating their babies graduating high school. (Fine, 1991, p. 3)

My field notes read,

> "I just want a moment of silence for the 500 missing." In a school of 3000, barely $1/12$ graduated. Where are the disappeared? If this were a school with middle class White students, everyone would be outraged. What we tolerate for the poor is unthinkable for elites.

At Brandeis High School, in the 1980s and certainly since, it was normative for Black and Brown bodies to drain out of public institutions, without diplomas, with few alarmed about the disposability of a substantial majority of students of color. Progressives and conservatives explained the leakage differently—racism/capitalism vs. poor motivation/inadequate intelligence/bad mothering—but too many agreed that it was inevitable.

In the late 1980s, mass incarceration was rapidly invading communities of color in New York State. State coffers were quietly realigning budgets, migrating monies and bodies of color from schools to prisons. In 1973, the state's prison population was 10,000; by 1980, it doubled to 20,000; by 1992, it more than tripled again, to almost 62,000. Gangi, Schiraldi, and Ziedenberg (2013) documented the racialized history of mass incarceration: "Since 1989, there have been more Blacks entering the prison system for drug offenses each year than there were graduating from SUNY with undergraduate, master's and doctoral degrees—combined" (p. 57).

Almost 25 years later, after generations of disinvestment and disproportionate placement of difficult-to-teach, over-age, undercredit students into the building, in the midst of a swelling inequality gap in wealth, income, real estate, and human security, and the intensive gentrification of the Upper West Side, *The New York Times* reported that a "crisis" is finally declared. The solution is to close the school and re-open it for "better" students who live in, and beyond, the district.

On the basis of test scores, graduation rates, and cumulative disregard, the New York City Board of Education decided in 2009 that Brandeis like so many other comprehensive high schools serving Black and Latino youth, would be closed. The new building would be a complex of four small schools: two "nonselective" high schools, designed late in the summer to open in the fall; one "second-chance" school; and the new Frank McCourt high school for journalism and writing, sponsored by Symphony space, adorned with the ample support of local parents and community. Ironically, in the name of Frank McCourt, the school was being designed for the newly gentrifying families of the Upper West Side.

Fine's ethnographic notes reveal that community activists and educators were deeply engaged in challenging Brandeis' makeover. Most of the community meetings were cordial and seasoned with public commitments to "diversity." But the slippery discourse of White deservingness was leaking through the doors: "I guess this school will be for 3s and 4s?" asked one parent, referencing high-stakes test score signifiers burned into the consciousness and identity of New York City youth. "If we are serious about getting these kinds of students into that building, we'll have to remove the metal detectors," explained another parent, a father of color. And a woman facilitating the discussion elaborated, "If the other schools want to keep the metal detectors, or need them, we might want to use a different entrance."

And soon, the discursive architecture of separate and unequal was flooding the room, being spoken by White and African American prospective parents. A long-term community member spoke,

> This school has betrayed central and East Harlem for at least 30 years. It would be a cruel joke to clean it up, invest in transforming the school, and then opening it for local elite children. That would, of course, constitute just another betrayal of Black and Brown students in New York. (personal communication, July 13, 2009)

At the meeting, the U.S. Department of Education (DOE) representative explained that "any child would be welcome to the school.... They will submit attendance, grades and test scores and the computer will chose those who are eligible. Then we'll interview."

"But how about a preference for the siblings—or the children—or Brandeis' graduates?" someone asked.

"No, the building will be open to children city wide, using criteria that are demographically neutral," the DOE official replied.

The formula was explained: Students who satisfy the published criteria (scoring as a 3 or 4 on standardized tests, submitting a writing sample in English, having good attendance, and obtaining a grade point average [GPA] of 3.0 in middle school) are eligible to have a parent submit their names into a lottery. The actual conduct of the lottery itself might be considered fair. But all of the preconditions are drenched in privilege. Test scores in New York are highly correlated with race and class; writing samples in English are often coached by privately paid tutors; regular attendance and GPA are of course correlated with stable homes and hard work. The imbalance skews the process to favor of parents who are savvy, informed, and entitled enough to submit their child's name into a lottery. Cloaked in a language of open access and justice, students in the lottery underrepresent the poorest of the poor, English language learners, and students in need of special education. Similar to color-blind ideology (Neville, Awad, Brooks, Flores, & Bluemel, 2013), the language of demographic neutrality shrouds economic and cultural inequality and consequent experiences of dispossession.

It is within this context of cumulative inequalities (in terms of finance equity, facilities, resources, teacher experience, distribution of high-need students, graduation rates, rigorous curriculum, science equipment, and technology) that a pronouncement of "failure" has been asserted, relying on empirical indices of deficiency and expanding reach of police surveillance. Appearing responsible, the mayor called for the school to be closed, camouflaging a long and racist history of neglect. This strategy of educational reform—segregate children by race/ethnicity, class, and academic history into varying strata of schools, police their behavior ever more intensely, measure and publicize differential outcome data, declare crisis, close school, reopen for more selective public/charter students, and then declare victory and educational miracle for corporate reform—is a national trend built into federal, state, and local policy (Fabricant & Fine, 2013). Although the intervention was presumably designed to improve education for the children who were attending the failing schools, the scant evidence available on school closings suggests something quite different.

At the time, there was a shortage of prize elementary school seats in the affluent portion of the district. Enter charter developer and director Eva Moskowitz, who advertised that she would offer a "private school quality" education for free through her public charters. Although she stated when she was eager to gain access to Brandeis that priority would be given to English language learners, siblings of students in her other Success Academies, and students citywide slated to enter failing schools, her information and recruitment sessions were held in English in the richest and Whitest section of the Upper West Side. These sessions were at the Jewish Community Center, the Westside YMCA, and in the homes of wealthy West Side residents who supported charter schools. Moskowitz's bus shelter ads and literature were in English only and imprint the image and impression that charter schools were not just for poor children of color. In 2013, after the Success Academy had been firmly established in the building, Moskowitz announced there was no more room for English language learners.

The effort to radically restructure Brandeis High School and other schools on the Upper West Side has, in turn, produced pushback. Legislators, community organizers, educators, and parents mobilized resistance. Upper West Side and Harlem activist communities organized the "Stop the Squeeze!" rally to reject the Success Academy and other colocations in public school space.

On May 3, parents of students from various BHS schools—largely but not only Frank McCourt—filed a petition against the Board of Education of the City of New York, also known as The Panel for Educational Policy, to halt the colocation of the Success Academy Charter School within the Brandeis campus. Parents were joined by then public advocate, and now mayor, Bill DeBlasio. The petition argued that the colocation plan represented a violation of policy requiring that colocation be considered if there is evidence of what was considered under-utilization, after an educational impact statement has been produced and after an extensive process of public review, at least 45 days in advance of any city board vote, with public assessment of all public comments. The petition contested the colocation on the basis of fact and procedure. Within a few days, the United Federation of Teachers and the National Association for the Advancement of Colored People filed an additional lawsuit, challenging the list of school closings and seeking to halt the co-location practice as a policy that endorses "separate and unequal" education. On June 1, a New York City judge ordered that construction be halted. As described in *The Wall Street Journal*,

> The Bloomberg administration scored a major victory in court late Thursday when a New York State Supreme Court justice ruled against the United Federation of Teachers' efforts to keep troubled schools open and prevent charter schools from moving into public buildings. The widely watched case means that the closure of 22 schools can go forward and that 15 charter schools can move into public buildings. (Martinez, 2011, p. A14)

The biography of Brandeis echoes the dynamics of Galletta's (2003) story of Shaker Heights. A series of policy decisions operate as papercuts on the fragile institutions of public education, facilitating the upward flow of opportunity to Whites and a thin patch of "talented tenth" (Du Bois, 1903) students of color, while those who have been economically and educationally marginalized sink to the bottom of the hierarchy, as if this triage were natural or inevitable. These racially distinct gravitational pulls reflect the slow violence of testing, limiting options for almost all students of color, and more dramatically as we can see from the graphic below, closing schools for

Black youth living in poverty in New York and across the nation—all enacted perversely in the name of "accountability."

We move now from psychological research that documents the slow violence of educational resegregation to a community-based participatory research crafted in collaboration with activists, designed to expose and challenge patterns and consequences of aggressive policing in communities of color and to mobilize communities and launch lawsuits on behalf of racial dignity and justice.

CASE THREE: STOP AND FRISK—CRITICAL PARTICIPATORY ACTION RESEARCH IN COLLABORATION WITH ACTIVISTS, YOUTH, ELDERS, AND LAWYERS TO DOCUMENT THE COLLATERAL EFFECTS OF AGGRESSIVE POLICING IN COMMUNITIES OF COLOR

In 2012, social psychologists Brett Stoudt and Maria Elena Torre set out to collaborate with a group of activist lawyers, youth, and mothers/grandmothers in the South Bronx to document the community toll of "stop and frisk," or aggressive policing. With a rigorous sampling frame, and a participatory survey design, they formed the Morris Justice Project (MJP), a research collective of community residents, youth, lawyers, and researchers dedicated to documenting the frequency, impact, and collateral consequence of aggressive policing in the Bronx.

Before designing the research, Stoudt and Torre, working with their community colleagues, collaborated with lawyers, residents on basketball courts, film makers, young activists, and activist mothers who had been photographing police stopping and frisking their children. They gathered local perspectives on varied forms of productive and aggressive policing, consequences, and alternatives. The team designed a robust large-scale community survey and ultimately gathered more than 1,000 surveys in the 44th precinct, notorious for overzealous policing. On Saturdays, at the local library, they would come to consensus on where to draw the borders of the neighborhood, so they could randomly sample residents; craft accessible questions to capture both positive and negative interactions with police; catalog the range and effects of stops, physical confrontation by police, and verbal assault; and with respect and complexity ascertain what community members do when they really need help and fear the very people who are being paid to protect. Over 18 months of gathering quantitative surveys from more than 1,000 residents and qualitative stories of positive and negative police interactions, the team conducted Critical Statistics workshops, again at the library, to triangulate their community surveys with secondary analyses of the New York Police

Department (NYPD) database. They confirmed local wisdom that Black youth were more likely to be stopped than others. They lifted up new empirical evidence that lesbian, gay, bisexual, and transgendered young people were also particularly vulnerable to aggressive policing. And they documented, again, that of the massive rate of stops and frisks, an outstanding 90% to 92% of those stopped were innocent. They gathered stories about public housing hallway sweeps, where youth were being ticketed or arrested by being in public housing without ID; mothers, fathers, and grandparents being told not to congregate in their court yards or doorways in groups of more than four; young people defending friends from aggressive policing and being arrested themselves for "interfering" with an arrest. MJP has mountains of data to confirm what should already be known—all communities want desperately to feel safe. As Jackie Robinson, one of the researchers, explained in a public letter to the NYPD: "Please don't get me wrong, NYPD, we don't want you to leave. We just want to be policed with dignity" (personal communication, August 13, 2012).

Across surveys and on the street interviews, the MJP systematically documented the social, criminal justice, health, educational, and trust consequences of "growing up policed" (Stoudt, Fine, & Fox, 2011). The data document the history of aggressive policing; the racial disproportionality; the educational and psychological consequences for youth who feel they have no public authority that will intervene in the event of an emergency. Youth who identify as lesbian, bisexual, gay, transsexual, gender nonconforming, or queer, particularly in communities of color, typically fear police and many of the adults to whom they should be able to turn, in schools, on the streets, and sometimes their homes.

Refusing the slide to "damage" or despair, the project was designed explicitly to (a) document the uneven landscape of dignified and aggressive policing across zip codes, boroughs, race, immigration status, gender, and sexuality in New York City but particularly in the 44th precinct; (b) empirically assess the racialized, classed, and sexualized community and individual consequences on the ground; and (c) capture the rich resilience and resistance of youth, elders, lawyers, activists, educators, journalists, and every people in the Yankee Stadium community. In turn, this remarkably diverse research team has created scholarly documents, organizing tools, and briefs for class action lawsuits.

One evening in October 2012, a community forum for participatory data analysis was held in the outdoor terrace of a set of apartment buildings near Yankee Stadium. A group of young men were drumming, and women and men were dancing in varied ethnic traditions in an open courtyard as commuters and residents gathered, and allies from downtown filed in from the subways. As the sun set and dusk was upon the crowd, the van called

The Illuminator, a vestige of the Occupy Wall Street Movement, turned on its lights, projecting a bold series of blue circled PowerPoint slides on a neighboring apartment building. The voices of the MJP researchers filled the crisp Bronx air, shouting into the microphone, cascading across the boulevard and into nearby apartment windows: "DEAR NYPD, WE ARE THE MORRIS JUSTICE PROJECT. WE LIVE HERE!" and then detailed the research and the results. The community was stunned, engaged, and soon hanging handwritten signs out windows claiming, "WE LIVE HERE." The MJP researchers alternated as they spoke aloud the sample size and the fact that in a series of more than 4,000 stops last year, the NYPD turned up eight guns, compared with a gun buyback at a local church where, within a few hours, 85 guns were retrieved. The data projected on the North-facing side of an apartment building displayed for the full community the rates of stops, innocence, the racist names the children are called when they are stopped, the social fraying of trust, the psychic effects of being assaulted by those who are supposed to protect, and in full evidence was the rich vibrant desire for justice and resistance pouring through the veins of the community.

In *The Star of Ethiopia*, W. E. B. Du Bois' (as cited in Hill & Hatch, 2005) public pageant of African American history and sociology performed in the streets, Du Bois chose to perform his sociological and historical analyses for popular education and enjoyment through community parades and theatre to perform the history and sociology of Black oppression. On that chilly evening in the fall of 2012, MJP was displaying oppression, resistance, and the collective desire for safety, dignity, and justice through a funky van, a gravelly microphone, some simple PowerPoint slides, and the soul of a community in rage and engaged. Since then, the researchers have been working at street festivals, creating public science shorts that display by the minute, across the year, how many innocent stops occur in New York City and where, leaving "black and blue" marks on the communities of most aggressive policing (see http://www.publicscienceproject.org). They are designing buttons and pressing on the spot MJP T-shirts that reproduce words from the survey, such as, "Why do I always fit the description?" and "It is not a CRIME to be WHO YOU ARE" being adorned by young boys and older men of color, young women, grandmothers, trans youth, and concerned community members.

Turning more explicitly to policy, members of the MJP research team—Stoudt, Torre, Greene, Robinson, Bracey, Shephard, and community partners—have been collaborating with the Coalition for Police Reform, sharing the data with lawyers and activists involved in the victorious stop-and-frisk lawsuit in New York City, *Floyd, et al. v. The City of New York, et al.* (2014). In addition, they have produced varied compelling documents and tools for the community to know their rights, know the patterns of aggressive policing, and know the desires for justice held by their neighbors (see Appendix 12.1).

PSYCHOLOGY'S DEBT TO RACIAL JUSTICE THROUGH PUBLIC POLICY

We conclude with a call for disciplinary reparations. Although Kenneth Clark (Clark & Clark, 1950) was undoubtedly well intentioned when he migrated psychological material into the courts to fight for racial justice, we fear that his legacy has unleashed a long line of psychological inquiry focused on scenes of injustice cropped in ways that obscure the historic and structural violence of oppression, highlighting only the "stain" (of guilt or damage) on Black bodies and minds.

We offer here three examples of critical social psychological research that have been designed to resist psychology's downward glance at the "dependent variable" and return our analytic gaze to structures and policies that produce inequity; to appreciate the complex ways in which individuals and communities respond to, resist, embody, and grow despairing and hopeful about injustice; and to collaborate with educational institutions, community based organizations, local activists, and lawyers on research for justice. With these exemplars in mind, we close with a reflection on how psychological research can avoid appropriation and instead advance racial justice through social policy. We offer up four recommendations for a critical psychology of race and racism:

1. When studying contemporary issues within communities of color, or disparities between communities, be sure to include a systematic history of the phenomenon and resist the slide to focus on individuals, and particularly the deficits in individuals. By this, we mean to suggest that psychology for too long focused on individuals rather than structures in relation with lives and has equated oppression with damage. This is a problem. Evidence of internalized oppression among a fraction may not generalize to a group as a whole. History shows people who experience oppression and structural violence nevertheless can flourish; be resilient; can laugh; and make beautiful love, music, food, literature, and babies. Their survival should not be read to mean that they were not oppressed—rather, that humans are remarkable.
2. Psychologists and researchers interested in social (in)justice have a responsibility to design research with "critical bifocality" (Weis & Fine, 2012, p. 173), documenting the history and

structures that produce injustice and also the ways in which individuals lead lives that accommodate, resist, internalize, reject, and organize in response. Consider the work on deindustrialization, unemployment and African American street life by Yasser Payne (2013); Arlene Geronimus's work on health disparities and "weathering" of Black bodies (e.g., Walsemann, Geronimus, & Gee, 2008); the empirical work on the impact of racism on African American well-being (Krieger & Sidney, 1996); or Mindi Fullilove's (2009) groundbreaking research on gentrification, urban renewal, and the mental health consequences of Root Shock for African Americans. Psychology has much to offer to those who think at the intersections of the social and the personal.
3. Catalogue the creative ways that historically oppressed communities and individuals organize for justice. Design research that seeks to capture the rich desires for justice that flourish in communities despite—perhaps because of—being denied justice.
4. Collaborate with communities under siege. Community-based research conducted in collaboration and solidarity produces knowledge enhanced by contextual validity and sustainability over time.

Psychologists have much to offer in conversations that tell a different story about injustice and policy. As a discipline, particularly for those of us working between psychology and critical race theory, we psychologists understand context and people, damage and desire, resistance and despair, struggle and possibility.

Our ancestor Kenneth Clark was invited to remake history, and the price of admission (to the Supreme Court) required that he focus solely on individual people, damage, and despair. More than 60 years later, let us correct the error of our disciplinary ways, and move forward toward a more full-bodied telling of how injustice is crafted by persons and institutions of privilege, how it seeps under the skin for people of color and people in poverty, but also how rich and radical possibilities and solidarities have been birthed from the ashes of oppression—perhaps accelerated by the insights of our most compelling research.

We close with food for thought from the brilliant writer Arundhati Roy (2003):

> [We must tell] stories that are different from the ones we're being brainwashed to believe. . . . Remember this: Another world is not only possible, she is on her way. On a quiet day, I can hear her breathing. (http://voiceseducation.org/content/arundhati-roy-war-talk)

REFERENCES

Anderson, J. D. (1988). *The education of Blacks in the South, 1860–1935*. Chapel Hill: University of North Carolina Press. http://dx.doi.org/10.5149/uncp/9780807842218

Anderson, J. D. (2006). A tale of two Browns: Constitutional equality and unequal education. *Yearbook of the National Society for the Study of Education, 105*, 14–35. http://dx.doi.org/10.1111/j.1744-7984.2006.00073.x

Bell, D. A. (2004). *Silent covenants: Brown v. Board of Education and the unfulfilled hopes for racial reform*. New York, NY: Oxford University Press.

Brown vs. Board of Education, 347, U.S. 483 (1954).

Butchart, R. E. (1980). *Northern schools, southern Blacks, and reconstruction: Freedmen's education, 1862–1875*. Westport, CT: Greenwood Press.

Clark, K. B., & Clark, M. P. (1950). Emotional factors in racial identification and preference in Negro children. *Journal of Negro Education*, 341–350.

Cross, W. E., Jr. (1991). *Shades of Black: Diversity in African-American identity*. Philadelphia, PA: Temple University Press.

Cross, W. E., Jr. (2003). Tracing the historical origins of youth delinquency and violence: Myths & realities about Black culture. *Journal of Social Issues, 59*, 67–82. http://dx.doi.org/10.1111/1540-4560.t01-1-00005

Cross, W. E., Jr. (2012). Contemporary Black identities and personalities. In H. L. Gates (Ed.), *Oxford handbook of African American citizenship* (pp. 694–721). New York, NY: Oxford University Press.

Du Bois, W. E. B. (1903). The talented tenth. In Washington, B. T. (Ed.), *The Negro problem: A series of articles by representative American Negroes of today* (pp. 33–75). New York, NY: James Pott and Company.

Fabricant, M., & Fine, M. (2013). *The changing politics of education: Privatization and the dispossessed lives left behind*. Boulder, CO: Paradigm.

Fine, M. (1991). *Framing dropouts: Notes on the politics of an urban public high school*. Albany: State University of New York Press.

Floyd, et al. v. The City of New York, et al. Nos. 13-3088-cv, 13-3123-cv, 14-2829-cv, 14-2848-cv, 14-2834-cv (2nd Cir. October 31, 2014).

Frazier, E. F. (1939). *Negro family in the United States*. Chicago, IL: University of Chicago Press.

Fullilove, M. (2009). *Root shock: How tearing up city neighborhoods hurt America*. New York, NY: Random House.

Galletta, A. (2003). *Under one roof, through many doors: understanding racial equality in an unequal world* (Unpublished doctoral dissertation). New York, NY: The Graduate School and University Center of the City University of New York.

Galletta, A. (2013a). "In the spirit of equality": Conflict, dissonance, and the potential for transformative educational change. In C. Niedt (Ed.), *Social justice in the diverse suburb: History, politics, and prospects* (pp. 73–90). Philadelphia, PA: Temple University Press.

Galletta, A. (2013b). *Mastering the semi-structured interview and beyond: From research design to analysis and publication.* New York, NY: New York University Press.

Galletta, A., & Cross, W. E., Jr. (2007). Past as present, present as past: Historicizing Black education and interrogating "integration." In A. J. Fuligni (Ed.), *Contesting stereotypes and creating identities: Social categories, social identities, and educational participation* (pp. 15–33). New York, NY: Russell Sage Foundation.

Gangi, R., Schiraldi, V., & Ziedenberg, J. (2013). New York state of mind? Higher education vs. prison funding in the empire state, 1988–1998. *Workplace: A Journal for Academic Labor, 6*, 54–59.

Hernandez, J. (2009, February 3). Giant Manhattan school to be broken up to further smaller-is-better policy. *New York Times*, p. A27.

Hill, E. G., & Hatch, J. V. (2005). *A history of African American theatre.* Cambridge, England: Cambridge University Press.

Homel, M. W. (1984). *Down from equality: Black Chicagoans and the public schools, 1920–41.* Urbana: University of Illinois Press.

Kluger, R. (1975). *Simple justice: The history of Brown v. Board of Education and Black America's struggle for equality.* New York, NY: Albert A. Knopf.

Krieger, N., & Sidney, S. (1996, October). Racial discrimination and blood pressure: The CARDIA Study of young Black and White adults. *American Journal of Public Health, 86*, 1370–1378. http://dx.doi.org/10.2105/AJPH.86.10.1370

Martinez, B. (2011, July 22). State court ruling paves way for school closings. *Wall Street Journal.* Retrieved from http://www.wsj.com/articles/SB10001424053111903554904576460831225880352

Neville, H. A., Awad, G. H., Brooks, J. E., Flores, M. P., & Bluemel, J. (2013). Color-blind racial ideology: Theory, training, and measurement implications in psychology. *American Psychologist, 68*, 455–466. http://dx.doi.org/10.1037/a0033282

Ogbu, J. U. (2003). *Black American students in an affluent suburb: A case study of academic disengagement.* Hoboken, NJ: Taylor & Francis.

Payne, Y. (2013). *The people's report.* Newark: University of Delaware. Retrieved from http://www.thepeoplesreport.com/

Rosenberg, M., & Simmons, R. G. (1971). *Black and White self-esteem: The urban school child.* Washington, DC: American Sociological Association.

Roy, A. (2003). *War talk.* Boston, MA: South End Press.

Spencer, M. B., Cross, W., Harpalani, V., & Goss, T. N. (2003). Historical and developmental perspectives on Black academic achievement. *Surmounting all odds: Education, opportunity, and society in the new millennium, 1*, 273–304.

Stone, A. (1992, February 28). We are the U.S. in microcosm. *USA Today*, p. A1.

Stoudt, B. G., Fine, M., & Fox, M. (2011). Growing up policed in the age of aggressive policing policies. *New York Law School Law Review, 56*, 1331–1370.

Toner, R. (1992, July 5). New politics of welfare focuses on its flaws. *New York Times, 141*, 16.

Walsemann, K. M., Geronimus, A. T., & Gee, G. C. (2008). Accumulating disadvantage over the life course—Evidence from a longitudinal study investigating the relationship between educational advantage in youth and health in middle age. *Research on Aging, 30*, 169–199. http://dx.doi.org/10.1177/0164027507311149

Webber, T. L. (1978). *Deep like the rivers*. New York, NY: Norton.

Weis, L., & Fine, M. (2012). Critical bifocality and circuits of privilege: Expanding critical ethnographic theory and design. *Harvard Educational Review, 82*, 173–201. http://dx.doi.org/10.17763/haer.82.2.v1jx34n441532242

Worrell, F. C. (2012). Forty years of Cross's nigrescence theory: From stages to profiles, from African Americans to all Americans. In J. Sullivan & A. M. Esmail (Eds.), *African American racial identity: An interdisciplinary exploration of racial and cultural dimensions of the Black experience* (pp. 3–28). Lanham, MD: Lexington Books.

APPENDIX 12.1

The Morris Justice Project: A Summary of Our Findings

Born of the passion of neighborhood mothers outraged at the NYPD's treatment of their sons, the Morris Justice Project has spent the last two years documenting experiences of policing in our 40-block community near Yankee stadium. Sponsored by the Public Science Project, we are a collaborative research team of neighborhood residents in the South Bronx and members of the Public Science Project, the CUNY Graduate Center, John Jay College, and Pace University Law Center. Together we conducted focus groups of local residents, and created and analyzed a comprehensive survey that we distributed corner by corner in the 40 blocks around the Morris Avenue section of the South Bronx (from Sheridan Avenue to Park & Webster, between 161st and 167th streets). 1,030 residents took our survey, sharing with us their attitudes and experiences with police. Here's what they said:

EXPERIENCES WITH POLICE

75% OF ALL COMMUNITY MEMBERS THAT TOOK OUR SURVEY SAID THEY WERE STOPPED BY POLICE IN THEIR LIFETIME.
- 89% reported being stopped for the first time when they were 25 or younger.
- 25% stopped for the first time at 13 or younger.
- 34% stopped for the first time between the ages of 14-16

BEING STOPPED HAS BECOME PART OF EVERYDAY LIFE.

89% REPORTED BEING STOPPED IN THE LAST YEAR.
- 82% were stopped MORE THAN ONCE.
- 56% were asked to show id just outside their apt. or friends/family apt.
- 37% were spoken to disrespectfully by police

52% WERE STOPPED 4 OR MORE TIMES.

60% REPORTED BEING ASKED TO MOVE BY THE POLICE IN THE LAST YEAR. HERE'S WHERE:
- 36% standing right outside of their own building (e.g. stoop or courtyard)
- 35% standing in a group
- 29% standing on a street corner
- 29% standing outside friend or family members building
- 22% in the park
- 16% inside their building (e.g. halls, stairs)
- 10% in the subway
- 8% bus station/stop
- 6% at school

50% WERE ASKED TO SHOW ID JUST OUTSIDE THEIR HOME. THERE IS NO LAW IN NY THAT SAYS YOU HAVE TO CARRY ID OR SHOW ONE TO THE POLICE.

POLICE HAVE DISRESPECTED PEOPLE WITH NAMES LIKE "B#@CH", "ANIMAL", "DIRTY SPIC", "CRACKHEAD", "F#@GGOT", "LITTLE CORNER BOY", "MISTAKE", "F%#KING DOMINICAN IMMIGRANT", "STUPID N#&GA", "HOMO", "YOU GAY?", "BLACK WH#RE", "BABY GOT BACK", "THEY SURE GROW THEM THICK" ★

54% REPORTED BEING ARRESTED OR GIVEN A TICKET/SUMMONS IN THE LAST 6 YEARS.
- 46% of the arrests were DISMISSED in court.
- 57% of the tickets/summons were DISMISSED

MANY ARE FORCED TO PLEAD GUILTY. OF THOSE WE SURVEYED WHO PLEAD GUILTY, THE MAJORITY WERE FOR LOW LEVEL MISDEMEANOR OR 'QUALITY OF LIFE' CRIMES.

FOR THOSE WHOSE CASE WAS DISMISSED:
- 52% felt depressed
- 31% missed work/school
- 19% lost property and/or property was stolen
- 8% were injured

THE COLLATERAL DAMAGE OF BEING INVOLVED WITH THE CRIMINAL JUSTICE SYSTEM ALSO INVOLVES PROBLEMS SUCH AS PEOPLE LOSING WORK, HOUSING, PARENTAL RIGHTS, AND FACING ISSUES WITH IMMIGRATION.

43% REPORTED CALLING THE POLICE FOR HELP IN THE LAST YEAR. HERE'S WHAT HAPPENED:
- 15% reported the police NEVER came
- 59% reported the police came LATE
- 42% reported that the police arrived 30 minutes or later

32% DID NOT CALL FOR HELP BECAUSE THEY THOUGHT THE POLICE WOULD MAKE IT WORSE.

YOU COULD WATCH AN ENTIRE SITCOM WHILE YOU WAIT.

WHEN THE POLICE DID COME, WHETHER ON TIME OR LATE:
they were helpful 31% • 35% they were unhelpful
they were respectful 27% • 33% they were disrespectful

91% REPORTED SEEING POLICE STOP SOMEONE IN THE LAST YEAR
- 66% saw the police stop a family member or a friend

IN 2011 THE NYPD REPORTED 4,662 STOPS IN OUR 40 BLOCK NEIGHBORHOOD. ALL FOR ONLY 8 GUNS. GUN BUY BACK PROGRAMS DO BETTER.

PEOPLE WHO SAW THE POLICE STOPPING OTHERS REPORTED FEELING:
angry 36% • 16% didn't care
unsatisfied with the police 32% • 13% satisfied with the police
worried 25% • 13% not worried
distrustful 24% • 6% trustful
less safe 17% • 14% safer
hopeless 15% • 8% hopeful

WITNESSING THE POLICE STOP YOUR FAMILY, FRIENDS, AND NEIGHBORS LEAVES A SCAR.

ATTITUDES TOWARDS POLICE

63% REPORTED FEELING TARGETED BY POLICE
- 63% of people 25 or younger reported feeling targeted because of their age
- 57% of men felt targeted because of their gender
- 53% of people of color reported feeling targeted because of their race/ethnicity
- 36% of immigrants felt targeted because of their immigrant status
- 28% who were unemployed felt targeted because of their employment status
- 23% of people who identified as LGBT felt targeted because of their sexual orientation

IT'S NOT A CRIME TO BE WHO YOU ARE.

COMMUNITY MEMBERS' ATTITUDES TOWARDS POLICE IN THEIR NEIGHBORHOOD
they abuse power 52% • 7% they use power wisely
they are unfair 39% • 11% they are fair
I have little respect for them 35% • 19% I have a lot of respect for them
they are untrustworthy 34% • 9% they are trustworthy
they are dishonest 31% • 9% they are honest
they create problems 29% • 14% they prevent problems
they do not work in our best interest 29% • 11% they do work in our best interest
I feel unsafe when the police are around 22% • 22% I feel safe when the police are around

"THIS IS OUR HOME. WE HAVE THE RIGHT TO STAND, TALK, PLAY, AND BE IN OUR NEIGHBORHOOD!"

AGGRESSIVE POLICING POLICIES ARE TEARING APART POLICE RELATIONSHIPS WITH COMMUNITIES.

IS BEING STOPPED BY THE POLICE THE PRICE WE HAVE TO PAY FOR A SAFER NEIGHBORHOOD? COMMUNITY MEMBERS WE SURVEYED SAID:
- 43% No
- 33% Yes
- 24% In the middle

WHAT DO YOU THINK?

*We find these names deeply disturbing. We include them here to validate the level of abuse our survey-takers have experienced.

www.publicscienceproject.org

(PSP) the public science project

From *The Morris Justice Project: A Summary of Our Findings*, Morris Justice: A Public Science Project. Copyright 2011 by the Public Science Project. Reprinted with permission.

13

EDUCATION INTERVENTIONS FOR REDUCING RACISM

ELIZABETH VERA, DANIEL CAMACHO,
MEGAN POLANIN, AND MANUEL SALGADO

According to the National Center for Education Statistics (2012), students of color make up more than 45% of the current prekindergarten through 12th grade (PK–12) population, whereas teachers of color make up only 17.5% of the educator workforce. Current teacher candidates, who represent the future generation of educators, also do not reflect the demographic makeup of students in PK–12 classrooms (American Association of Colleges of Teacher Education [AACTE] 2013). Specifically, 82% of current bachelor's degrees in education are awarded to White candidates (AACTE, 2013). Thus, while classrooms across the country are becoming more and more racially diverse, those charged with providing for students' educational needs are not. This potentially creates a situation in which teachers do not share the same life experiences with, or understand the impact of racism on, their students. Without an awareness of the importance of antiracism educational strategies on the part of these teachers, unintended racism may become a part of their

http://dx.doi.org/10.1037/14852-014
The Cost of Racism for People of Color: Contextualizing Experiences of Discrimination, A. N. Alvarez, C. T. H. Liang, and H. A. Neville (Editors)
Copyright © 2016 by the American Psychological Association. All rights reserved.

students' educational experiences. In essence, the challenge to today's educators is to promote antiracist education in a multiculturally affirming learning environment.

For the purposes of this chapter, we use the term *antiracist education* to refer to education that aims to eradicate racism (Vigliante, 2007) accepting that "the impetus for antiracist education is social justice and education's role in delivering it" (Vigliante, 2007, p. 107). Hence, inherent in the goals of antiracist educational strategies are educational justice for students of color, addressing structural inequities within institutions, and challenging and empowering students to work toward reconstructing a just society (Boyd & Arnold, 2000; Vigliante, 2007). Many strategies can be part of an antiracist educational agenda, but the theme that characterizes these strategies is transforming the status quo. The consequence of educational practices that are not antiracist in nature is maintaining the status quo that has led to institutionalized oppression. In fact, among the costs of racism discussed throughout this volume, educational consequences are perhaps among the most worrisome, given their long-term impact on individuals, communities, and society in general. Because the educational impact of racism is discussed at length in Chapter 8 of this volume, in this chapter we focus on what is known about effective efforts to prevent racism within educational contexts.

Can racism truly be prevented? Scholars such as Neville and Spanierman (2013) have argued that the insidious nature of racism at individual, interpersonal, and institutional levels makes it impossible to eradicate. However, as we explore in detail within this chapter, theories that explain the development of prejudice within children also contain implications for how it might be reduced and perhaps eliminated. Furthermore, a plethora of educational researchers have attempted to implement antiracist and multicultural educational programs with the goal of reducing prejudice in young children. In fact, the majority of these researchers have suggested that such efforts must be aimed at children as early as first grade (Katz, 2003).

We frame our conversation about these issues within an ecological model (Bronfenbrenner, 1979) and examine both individual- and environmental-focused interventions that attempt to reduce racism in educational settings for youths of color. In particular, we present (a) research on K–12 multicultural education interventions that attempt to prevent racism via modifying attitudes and increasing awareness; (b) higher education diversity interventions; (c) efforts to prevent racist attitudes and expectations used in the preparation of teachers, a critical component of creating racist-free learning environments for all children; and (d) research that has examined the impact of educational policy on reducing racism and promoting multiculturally inclusive education.

MULTICULTURAL EDUCATION INTERVENTIONS K–12

Multicultural education is one strategy within the broader category of antiracist education. *Multicultural education* refers to a broad set of interventions that are aimed at increasing awareness and understanding of cultural diversity with the goal of reducing bias (Kailin, 2002). Multicultural education efforts have been examined in the literature for over half a decade. Although the outcomes of these efforts have not always been sustained over time, scholars have developed the majority of their interventions based on theories that explain the emergence of discrimination and prejudice.

One of the best known of these theories, the intergroup contact theory (Allport, 1954), states that prejudice grows due to a lack of personal and positive contact among members of different groups. According to contact theory, four conditions must be met for contact to evolve into improved group relations: (a) individuals from different groups must come together on relatively equal terms, (b) groups should come together with the support of authority figures, (c) members of different groups come together to work on common goals that engender the development of their superordinate identity, and (d) individuals should interact in a structured format, for an extended period of time. Subsequent research has shown that intergroup prejudice is in fact significantly reduced by intergroup contact, even when all of these conditions are not present, and even when participants are not voluntarily involved in the contact (Pettigrew & Tropp, 2006). Meta-analytic examination of studies of intergroup contact theory have determined that "not only do attitudes toward the immediate participants usually become more favorable, but so do attitudes toward the entire outgroup, outgroup members in other situations, and even outgroups not involved in the contact" (Pettigrew & Tropp, 2006, p. 766). Hence, the apparent robustness of this theory suggests that interventions designed accordingly could be excellent models for antiracist education interventions, in particular for White students. Specifically, racial segregation and discriminatory attitudes might be reduced by applying this theory to educational settings.

Researchers have shown that positive intergroup relationships, such as interracial friendships, may be successfully promoted by altering features of the classroom environment in accordance with intergroup contact theory. Aronson and Gonzalez (1988) designed and implemented an intervention termed the "jigsaw classroom." In this intervention, classmates work together to learn and teach each other components of an academic lesson. Students are divided into intentionally diverse work groups and are asked to learn unique parts of a particular lesson. Then, groups are formed consisting of one individual from each of the original groups and students are expected to teach

each other the entire lesson in a cooperative manner. This intervention was found to improve children's intergroup relationships, increase self-esteem, and boost students' academic success. This was true for both White majority and ethnic minority students. Zirkel (2008) provided a discussion of how cooperative learning may improve intergroup relations, which included a recommendation that teachers actively work against status differentiation in groups. Thus, the impact of this intervention is maximized when groups are carefully constructed and managed to thwart students' status hierarchies and create environments that foster positive interaction between individual group members.

Educational strategies such as the jigsaw classroom do not overtly address the existing dynamics that may lead to racism and fewer interracial friendships in school settings, yet some scholars have argued that multicultural education programs that are part of an antiracist educational agenda must explicitly address stereotyping, racism, and discrimination (Ponterotto & Pederson, 1993; Short & Carrington, 1996). Antiracist education interventions should seek to provide an in-depth awareness of the history and roots of inequality, in other words. Curricula that make these issues explicit typically focus on teaching children how to recognize and confront racism at school and in the other contexts. For example, children would learn how to define the constructs of prejudice and tolerance, discuss explicitly the historical roots of racism, how it exists in our society today, and the forces that contribute to its continuation (Spencer, 1999). Although some scholars have documented positive effects of these strategies in decreasing prejudice with kids as young as 10 (London, Tierney, Buhin, Greco, & Cooper, 2002), some important developmental issues must be taken into account. For example, younger children may lack social perspective-taking abilities that are necessary for understanding group-based discrimination (Quintana & Vera, 1999). In addition, given that such programs can raise strong emotional reactions in participants of any age, researchers have pointed out that much care must be taken with this approach in that students may experience negative side effects, such as guilt, embarrassment, anger, or self-righteousness (Kehoe & Mansfield, 1993).

Another antiracist educational strategy is empathy training, which relies on children's developed perspective-taking skills and focuses on understanding one's own and others' emotions. The goal of this intervention is to create empathy toward others whom have experienced discrimination, with the hope that students will experience others' distress as if it were their own and thus act in a less biased manner (Underwood & Moore, 1982). Although some research exists in favor of this approach (Schonert-Reichl, Smith, Zaidman-Zait, & Hertzman, 2012), it is not clear that socioemotional skill building has a direct causal relationship to reducing racism. Other researchers have attempted to build empathy by simulating discrimination experiences via role playing. In a classic study that was based on Jane Elliot's blue-eyes–brown-eyes experiments, Weiner and Wright (1973) evaluated an intervention in which a teacher divided her students into either a "blue" or "orange" group by asking them to wear the appropriate colored armband and encouraging discrimination of each group for 1 day. Students in the experimental group in this all-White classroom reported that they were more likely to attend a social event with Black children. McGregor's (1993) meta-analysis of role playing interventions such as these revealed that they are effective in reducing student prejudice. However, due to the necessity of age-related cognitive skills, this type of training is likely more effective with older individuals. Children who are not able to engage in perspective taking may only be able to focus on the negative aspects of the exercise, possibly resulting in increased avoidance of the group with whom they are supposed to be empathizing.

In summary, even though multicultural education strategies have been shown to be effective, they have not yet been widely implemented. This requires a high level of commitment from educators, parents, staff, and stakeholders. At the heart of the matter is the fact that caring and positive student relationships are fundamental to student learning. Researchers need to determine which interventions ultimately aid in the reduction of racism and promote a culturally affirming school climate that will benefit society.[1]

ANTIRACISM AND DIVERSITY PROMOTION INITIATIVE IN HIGHER EDUCATION

Neville and Spanierman (2013) argued that despite the fact that college-aged students have in all likelihood already developed racial group attitudes, antiracist interventions can be implemented by capitalizing on their budding identity development. Promoting positive interracial attitudes and relationships is seen as a desirable outcome for many institutions of higher education. Yet the reality of creating and sustaining a diverse and multiculturally affirming campus continues to be elusive. Although initiatives for promoting diversity on campuses are plentiful, long-term, institutional implementation that affects the sustainability of such efforts over time is often lacking (Danowitz & Tuitt, 2011; Krutky, 2008).

---

[1]Currently, a few national organizations offer resources (e.g., handbooks, curricula, activities, and lesson plans) for teachers, administrators, students, and parents including the National Education Association (http://www.nea.org), the Teaching Tolerance program (http://www.tolerance.org), and the Anti-Defamation League (http://www.adL.org/education). These materials may also be utilized by practitioners interested in providing programming aimed at reducing and preventing prejudice in schools. Materials are generally tailored and available for elementary school students through high school students. The literature reveals a plethora of research evaluating programs designed to reduce prejudice in children.

Drawing on intergroup contact theory and other related scholarship, institutions of higher education have used the strategy of creating a diverse student body as a starting point for most antiracism and multiculturalism initiatives. In the higher education literature, diversity goals that are related to promoting racial harmony have been conceptualized in three ways: (a) increasing structural diversity, (b) increasing interactional diversity, and (c) providing coursework focused on diversity (Gurin, Dey, Hurtado, & Gurin, 2002). Structural diversity, which encompasses representation of racial minority students, staff, and faculty as well as the diversity of leadership in institutions of higher education, is particularly salient in college campuses in which affirmative action legislation has been invoked (yet also revoked) to modify admission practices. It is widely accepted, though, that simply having greater numbers of racial and ethnic minorities on campus does not automatically create multiculturally affirming learning environments. Interactional diversity speaks to the intergroup relations on campus, evidenced in dialogues inside and outside of the classroom. Finally, coursework focused on diversity involves faculty-driven efforts to teach students about cultures different than their own and to facilitate meaningful educational experiences around such knowledge.

Higher education antiracism initiatives have been targeted at all three types of diversity goals. However, the majority of the literature evaluating the outcomes of such efforts focuses on coursework and interactional diversity efforts that mirror efforts occurring with K–12 students. Additionally, some more comprehensive higher education initiatives are aimed at reducing educational disparities and supporting students of color to build academic persistence in the face of discrimination they may encounter. In the following section, we review examples of three types of interventions, diversity coursework, interactional diversity programs, and more comprehensive diversity initiatives.

Diversity Coursework

Scholars such as Gaertner and Dovidio (1986) have built theory-based arguments that group-based knowledge reduces racism by helping students to conceptualize similarities and differences between racial groups and decreasing discomfort with other racial groups. Many institutions of higher education offer courses of study that focus on specific cultural groups (e.g., Black or African Studies) and teach students about racism. To ensure that a greater number students are exposed to issues of oppression, many universities and colleges have created "diversity courses" that are taken as requirements of the university's core curriculum. In 2000, approximately 63% of colleges and universities in the United States already had or were in the process of developing a diversity requirement for their undergraduate students (Humphreys, 2000).

Research has shown that students who take these courses often exhibit some reduction in racist attitudes, whether they are taken by choice or by requirement (Cole, Case, Rios, & Curtin, 2011). Despite not having a general formula for how such courses are taught, Engberg (2004) identified several core characteristics of existing multicultural course offerings: an explicit goal of reducing racial bias; didactic instruction coupled with readings, discussion, group exercises, and writing assignments; and enlightenment of students that occurs through content-based knowledge.

Meta-analyses of the effectiveness of such studies indicate that their existence benefits the entire campus community (i.e., majority and nonmajority students/staff/faculty), but in particular, multicultural coursework may have a more profound influence on reducing racial bias in White students than in students of color (Denson, 2009). Denson's (2009) meta-analysis found that courses have a stronger impact on students when cross-race interaction is combined with the other pedagogical elements described by Engberg (2004). This suggests that requiring these courses for all students and maximizing opportunities for students from a variety of racial groups to take these courses together will maximize their efficacy.

The racial differences that have been observed in reduction of racial bias resulting from these course may be attributable to the existing personal experiences with racism that students bring to the classroom. Specifically, it may be that students of color, versus their White counterparts, are more aware of racism and also have lower levels of racial bias, such that the benefit of such education interventions is less dramatic. However, courses that alter the perceptions and actions of White students may result in greater alliances and activism by White students (Munin & Speight, 2010), who represent a powerful coalition of social justice advocates.

Fewer evaluation studies of these courses have focused on behavioral change and/or campus climate changes as a result of these education interventions. Kernahan and Davis (2007) found that White students who took a course on racism specifically reported behavioral changes such as a greater willingness to take action against racism. Nagda, Kim, and Truelove (2004) found that those students who had more exposure to diversity courses were more confident in engaging in antiracist actions than their counterparts who lacked such experience. Presumably such confidence might lead to increased activities, but few studies have examined the long-term effects of these interventions (Engberg, 2004). Even fewer have attempted to capture the impact of such experiences on outcomes, such as numbers of reported hate crimes, perceptions of campus climate by students of color, and other factors that might indicate systemic changes that can be connected to the availability of these education interventions. Despite these limitations, data suggest that diversity coursework is an important component of combating racism on college campuses.

Intergroup Dialogues

The term *intergroup dialogues* typically refers to

> face-to-face facilitated learning experiences that bring together students from different social identity groups over a sustained period of time to understand their commonalities and differences, examine the nature and impact of societal inequalities, and explore ways of working together toward greater equality and justice. (Zúñiga, Nagda, Chesler, & Cytron-Walker, 2011, p. 2)

Intergroup dialogues can be offered as standalone cocurricular activities or as part of a formal course. The core educational goals of intergroup dialogues include consciousness raising, building relationships across cultural differences and conflicts, and strengthening individual and collective capacities to promote social justice. Dialogue programs typically rely on peer-facilitated, face-to-face meetings of students from different identity groups to explore group differences, challenge stereotypes and misinformation, and address issues of intergroup conflict (Zúñiga, Nagda, & Sevig, 2002).

Unlike diversity courses per se, intergroup dialogues use interpersonal contact as the vehicle for change much more than content-based knowledge. Specifically, participant conversation on specific topics, not curricular materials, composes the content of intergroup dialogues. Group topics can include a range of issues: race, ethnicity, gender, socioeconomic status, religion, sexual orientation, international status, ableism, and White racial identity. Different versions of dialogues exist at various universities around the United States (e.g., Voices of Discovery at Illinois State University) and Canada, with varying lengths (typically five to 15 sessions), and less structured content in favor of more dialogue facilitation. Group facilitators are peers, typically undergraduate students, who are trained in dialogue communication, group building, conflict surfacing and deescalation, and social justice education.

Researchers at the University of Michigan and around the United States have extensively evaluated these programs to determine their effectiveness and have generally found that they increase participants' activism tendencies (Gurin & Nagda, 2006; Krutky, 2008; A. Lee, Poch, Shaw, & Williams, 2012; Lopez & Zúñiga, 2010). For example, Gurin et al. (2002) found that students who participated in intergroup dialogue experiences during college were more involved in campus political activities and were more likely to participate in activities to promote racial understanding after they graduated. However, no outcomes studies have examined whether intergroup dialogue experiences actually reduce racism per se on campuses. It is likely that course-based diversity activities and intergroup dialogue experiences are instrumental in helping to raise students' awareness of racism and related issues, such as privilege, which has been found to happen at the graduate level as well (Sammons & Speight, 2008).

However, which interventions might be most effective at altering campus climate as a whole or reducing experiences of racism by students of color is unknown. Although some scholars argue that intergroup dialogues have a greater impact on students' activism than does diversity coursework (A. Lee et al., 2012; Lopez & Zúñiga, 2010), it is arguable that both types of programs can play an important role in combating racism and promoting culturally affirming campus climates. One other missing aspect in the literature that evaluates the impact of intergroup dialogues among students is the extent to which other dyadic interactions, such as faculty–students or staff–students, affects the overall campus climate.

Comprehensive Diversity Initiatives

Many universities are moving toward more comprehensive models of multicultural education that not only incorporate diversity coursework and intergroup dialoguing but also address issues of equity and provide support for underrepresented students. As discussed in Chapter 12 (this volume), the effects of racism often manifest themselves in educational disparities for students of color. Scholars (e.g., Gloria & Rodriguez, 2000) have posited that students of color often have unique self-beliefs (e.g., impostor syndrome), varying levels of social support (e.g., from family if they are first-generation college students), and less comfort in the university environment (i.e., in particular, on predominantly White campuses) than do their White counterparts. As such, higher education institutions have needed to develop resources and institutional objectives to increase the retention and success of students of color, in particular those who are first-generation college students. Such programs, then, are part of an antiracist educational agenda by creating a more inclusive campus and enhancing support for racially underrepresented students to maximize their opportunities for success.

One comprehensive initiative to reduce the impact of racism for students of color (and first-generation college students) is the use of learning communities (Thompson & Phillips, 2013). *Learning communities* are groups of students who have a common interest and/or identity status who take classes together, engage in extracurricular activities, and in some cases, reside together. The support that is provided to these students is intended to offset some of the social isolation that can negatively impact students of color. Inkelas and Weisman's (2003) evaluation of a learning community intervention at one university found that African American and Latino students who participated in an academic honors learning community felt more confident in their first year transition to college in comparison with their counterparts who did not participate in the learning community.

An example of a more institution-specific initiative with successful outcomes is the creation of the Black and Latino Male Resource Center (BLMRC) at Capital Community College, Hartford, Connecticut. The BLMRC is a center for male students of color where services targeted to their success are available, such as mentoring, academic support, and counseling services. Incoming students are invited to participate in a summer bridge program that consists of accelerated developmental courses, intensive advising, and mentoring. Since its inception in fall 2006, fall-to-fall retention of male students of color has doubled, from 25% to 50%.

In terms of larger initiatives, Making Excellence Inclusive (MEI) is an effort by the Association of American Colleges and Universities (AACU) that seeks to advance an equitable vision for liberal education, emphasizing the value of such an education within and across the diverse and evolving population of students in the United States (AACU, 2011). This effort (a) focuses on student intellectual and social development, (b) enhances student learning and psycho-social development through cross-unit collaboration, (c) pays attention to cultural differences in the classroom and campus, and (d) transforms campus and community cultures to create a welcoming environment. MEI is an initiative that directs universities to high-impact, evidence-based programs that enhance academic experiences of underrepresented students, such as participating in a learning community or having increased contact with faculty by engaging in research. AACU is now attempting to evaluate the impact of this initiative in 38 colleges involving more than 25,000 students. An initial evaluation of impact (McNair, Finley, & Krivian, 2013) revealed that Hispanic and African American students demonstrate gains in engagement, personal and social development, and overall learning that are positively related to the number of programs in which they are involved. The study did not look at retention rates or overall number of underrepresented student gains.

Although these examples of more comprehensive initiatives are promising, the goal of reducing the impact of racism on college campuses is always met with the challenge of creating the necessary infrastructure for sustained change. More empirical evidence is needed to elucidate what factors are most significant in creating such infrastructure.

TEACHER PREPARATION

Students at every academic level are profoundly influenced by the relationships they have with educators. This relationship has been found to be a highly significant predictor of student achievement for half a century (Eccles & Roeser, 2009). As mentioned previously, given that projections indicate the teaching force of the present and short-term future will be composed mostly of White educators (AACTE, 2013), careful attention must be paid to the training and preparation of teachers, who as the diversity of the student body increases, must learn to educate students who are culturally and racially diverse.

Research suggests that some teachers do not feel prepared to successfully instruct students who are not White (Aguado, Ballesteros, & Malik, 2003). Aguado et al. (2003) contended that most teachers not only report having received little to no training in working with culturally diverse students but also admit they do not possess knowledge of pedagogical strategies to enable these students to academically succeed. From a survey of more than 5,000 teachers, only 32% reported feeling "very well prepared" to address the needs of students from diverse cultural backgrounds (Parsad, Lewis, & Farris, 2001). Given the present reality that too many racial and ethnic minority children are not succeeding in public schools, and many teachers report feeling underprepared to foster their academic excellence, teacher preparation that provides teachers with the tools to meet the needs of a racially and culturally diverse body of students is a pressing need.

Feeling ill-prepared to meet the needs of culturally diverse students is a clear impediment to engaging in antiracist educational practices. E. Lee (1995) noted that for antiracist pedagogy to be structurally effective in promoting racial equity in schools, it must be reflected in interactions between teachers and students. In this review of strategies used to prepare teachers for work in diverse settings, we describe efforts taken to equip teachers with the self-understandings and awareness to acknowledge the impact of race in classrooms and schools and increase their competence in interacting with students across lines of cultural and racial difference.

RACIAL IDENTITY DEVELOPMENT AS A PRECURSOR TO ANTIRACIST PEDAGOGY

For teachers to be successful at implementing antiracist strategies, they must undergo a process of understanding their own racial identity. *Racial identity* is a sense of collective identity based on one's perception of a shared common heritage with a racial group (Helms, 1990). Carter and Goodwin (1994) asserted that teachers' own levels of racial identity influences their perceptions of students of color and consequently how they interact with these students. In turn, strategies used in teacher education have sought to prepare educators to teach racially and culturally diverse students by first fostering within these teacher candidates a sense of their own racial identities. In such a process of racial identity development, teachers who predominantly come from White, middle-class backgrounds gain awareness of their Whiteness, recognize the social salience and meaning of their race, and in the end internalize a positive attitude with respect to what it means to be White (Helms, 1990).

The most common racial identity development models used to conceptualize this process are Helms's (1990) racial identity theory and Banks's (1994) typology of ethnicity. Helms's (1990) six-stage psychological model details the process by which White individuals come to abandon racism and embrace a positive White identity through extended contact and learning about Black individuals and culture, recognition of their White racial identity and associated privilege, and gradual internalization of a positive racial identity that enables continued engagement with people from other cultures. Banks's (1994) typology of ethnicity describes a process in which individuals who previously internalized stereotypes pertaining to dominant and marginalized groups begin to recognize positive and negative aspects of their own groups, and develop cross-cultural competency. Similar to our previous discussion of diversity coursework and intergroup dialogue, teacher preparation programs can use a variety of mechanisms for helping students to become aware of their own racial identities with success. For example, Lawrence and Bunche (1996) studied the influence of a multicultural education course on White education majors and found that after the course, their understanding of institutional racism and their own White privilege was enhanced, as was the development of their own racial identities.

Another strategy that requires teachers to think more profoundly about how their experiences have been shaped by their racial and cultural upbringing is a process called structured reflection (Kyles & Olafson, 2008). Structured reflection first requires teachers to recognize their own cultural and racial background's impact on their approach to teaching. The construction of a personal or cultural autobiography has been used in teacher preparation as a reflective practice that encourages preservice teachers to see themselves within the context of a culturally diverse society (Hollins, 1990). This exercise gives preservice teachers the chance to acknowledge the sociocultural context embedded in their life histories, in hopes that they will gain greater awareness of the different social contexts and realities of their students (Kyles & Olafson, 2008). Hohensee and Derman-Sparks (1992) noted that sustained reflection best occurs through support groups composed of other teachers who seek to use antiracist curriculum. Such groups also serve as ongoing support for teachers to share successes and challenges in implementing antiracist pedagogies.

Field Experiences

Field experiences (prior to student teaching), in combination with reflective practices, are widely used by teacher education programs. These experiences may consist of placements with a social service agency or community organization, tutoring roles, or various other service-learning options that require direct service to students or community members. In addition to providing the opportunity for teachers to put theory into practice and meaningfully connect university course content with pedagogy (Jacobsen, 1999), field experiences in many cases put preservice teachers in contact with student populations they will soon have the responsibility of instructing. Ideally, within these contexts teachers are able to develop an awareness and appreciation for students and community members that are culturally different and will develop antiracist attitudes in the process.

Overall, research has supported the efficacy of field-based experiences' impact on teachers' ability to engage in antiracist educational practices. For example, Brown's (2005) study of the participation of 73 secondary preservice candidates in a 1-year school-based service-learning opportunity that included various forums for critical reflection, suggested an improvement in these teachers' multicultural perceptions, cross-cultural communication skills, and social justice cognizance. According to Adams, Bondy, and Kuhel (2005), teachers who engaged in a community-based field experience that entailed one-on-one mentoring with African American children exhibited responses that reflected themes of heightened awareness, conscious openness, the importance of being culturally responsive, and insights into oppression in working with these students. Furthermore, Wiggins, Follo, and Eberly (2007) noted that teachers with extensive previous field experiences developed more positive attitudes about working in culturally diverse classrooms than preservice teachers who had spent less time in the field experience. Given that teachers have a powerful impact on their students from the first day of school, it is imperative to find ways to train teachers to engage in antiracist pedagogy before they enter the classroom.

Increased Interaction With Students' Families

In addition to the increased direct contact that field experiences offer between preservice teachers and the students they will serve, Lin, Lake, and Rice (2008) suggested home visits and inviting parents to speak in teacher education programs as two useful antiracist education strategies. Home visits, by dispelling teachers' assumptions about students' home cultures, family structures, and backgrounds, have a potentially transformative role in teachers' beliefs and attitudes towards their students. Additionally, such visits may give preservice teachers insights into linguistic or cultural differences that exist between a student's home culture and in-school learning and recognize shared educational goals between these teachers and parents (Peralta-Nash, 2003). Additionally, McIntyre, Kyle, and Moore (2001) found that in doing family visits to better inform literacy instruction, many of their cultural assumptions about students' backgrounds were diminished.

Another option to capitalize on parents' understanding of how to effectively teach their children is by having them visit teacher education programs as guest speakers (Lin et al., 2008). Such a strategy is valuable in giving preservice teachers input about specific strategies suited to the racial and cultural needs of their students. This initial process of collaboration and increased communication to generate effective strategies, according to Derman-Sparks and Ramsey (2000), would enable teacher candidates to improve their practices. Although no studies specifically investigate the effect of this strategy on outcomes related to antibias teacher attitudes or practices, parent involvement in teacher education would likely increase how much they value parent involvement once they enter the classroom.

In summary, antiracist teacher preparation requires that educators gain awareness of how race has influenced their development and empowers teachers with the cross-cultural knowledge and skills to make their classrooms environments conducive to the success of all students. In these efforts, reflection and field experiences have traditionally been used by teacher education programs to facilitate racial awareness and provide the foundation for antiracist actions, although the results of these strategies have been mixed. Home visits and parent speakers in teacher education programs provide new avenues for the development of teachers' antiracist attitudes and beliefs. However, as Ladson-Billings (2000) asserted, no single course or set of field experiences is capable of preparing preservice students to meet the needs of diverse learners. Likewise, a more comprehensive approach that encompasses a number of the antiracist strategies described above is suggested to promote the development of teachers' racial and cultural identity and their abilities to use antiracist educational approaches. It is clear that a commitment to antiracist education is a process of intrapersonal and pedagogical development most effectively facilitated by a number of strategies. Similar to conclusions that we have stated about other comprehensive efforts, it is important for educational researchers to determine what interventions are most effective for future teachers to ensure the antiracist pedagogy is present in their future classrooms.

POLICY INTERVENTIONS

Neville and Spanierman (2013), as well as Buhin and Vera (2009), are among a number of psychology of racism scholars who have urged psychologists to adopt an ecological model of conceptualizing racism that includes contributions above and beyond the individual and group level. Specifically, they challenged psychologists to change racist policies and practices that exist in organizations, institutions, and governments. In this final section of the chapter, we discuss the ways in which educational practices and/or policies can be changed to promote cultural inclusiveness and reduce culture-based discrimination.

Some of the most egregious types of educational policies that promote racism either directly or indirectly are those that attempt to ban efforts to increase diversity in educational settings or promote cultural understanding. For example, the Michigan Civil Rights Amendment, Proposal 2 (2006), was a ballot initiative that was voted into law in late 2006. The legislation was aimed at stopping "discrimination" based on race, sex, or religion in admission to colleges, jobs, and other publicly funded institutions. This law effectively banned affirmative action in the state of Michigan, not unlike efforts that were made to do so in other states, such as California. However, since its passage, several attempts have been made to reverse this law on the basis of its alleged unconstitutionality, a decision that was recently upheld by the Sixth Circuit Court of Appeals in late 2012 (*Acosta v. Huppenthal*, 2012). The Supreme Court of the United States recently heard arguments on this case to ultimately determine its fate and in April 2014, supported the ban on affirmative action (*Schuette v. Coalition to Defend Affirmative Action*, 2014).

The problem with legislation such as the Michigan Civil Rights Amendment is its acontextual presentation of "discrimination." Policies such as affirmative action were designed to specifically address societally embedded acts of racism that, although not codified by law, were institutionalized nonetheless. By presenting arguments that equate attempts to "even the playing field" with acts of discrimination per se against the majority, those who believe that anything but the status quo will potentially "disadvantage" them personally (i.e., privileged, White, middle-class college applicants) are reinforced for their beliefs.

Another example of policy that has great potential to promote racism is an Arizona law (H.B. 2281), originally passed in 2010, that prohibits schools from including any classes that advocate "ethnic solidarity" instead of "individualism" or that are "designed" for a certain ethnicity. In this case, the classes being criticized were Mexican American studies, which were presented in the bill as potentially promoting "ethnic exclusion" and blaming White people for the oppression of Mexicans in the United States. Opponents of this law, mainly educators, pointed to the fact that the inclusion of this culturally affirming type of coursework had resulted in increased graduation rates and higher student achievement rates in a group of students who were at chronically high risk for dropping out of school. Despite hopes that this law would be ruled unconstitutional, its constitutionality was upheld in early 2013 in federal court (*Arce v. Huppenthal*, 2013). Similar to the aforementioned Michigan legislation, one of the main problems with the Arizona law is its decontextualizing the presentation of culturally inclusive curriculum, or more accurately, the lack thereof, and the reframing of inclusive curriculum as anti-individualistic. The lack of culturally inclusive curriculum has been identified as a factor in why students of color find school to be racist. Thus, when educators have attempted to make the curriculum more inclusive, even by offering elective classes such as Mexican American studies courses, it has been received as an attempt to change the status quo, which is perceived as threatening to racial majority groups.

It is important for psychologists to use their advocacy skills to educate the public and politicians as to why legislation such as the aforementioned laws actually maintain racism within our schools. As was discussed in the beginning of this chapter, social injustices are the impetus for antiracist educational practices. When only one racial group's history is represented in school curricula or when universities cannot take into account the underrepresentation of specific racial groups in their attempts to create and maintain structural diversity on their campuses, then the status quo is being protected and social injustices are reinforced. Hence, legislation such as the Michigan Civil Rights Amendment, Proposal 2 (2006), and Arizona H.B. 2281 (2010) maintain racism by protecting the status quo. However, in a world where reactions to sound bites substitute for informed decision making, it is important for the historical context of policies such as affirmative action and culturally inclusive curriculum to be reintroduced to the public's debate of these issues.

Furthermore, where research exists on the benefits of policies such as these, as it does in both instances, it is imperative that psychologists individually and as an organization enter the legal debate on these issues. The American Psychological Association (Brief for the American Psychological Association, 2003) has done so by offering amicus briefs on the issue of affirmative action, and it is unfortunate that because laws continue to be passed that only serve to protect the status quo, psychologists are needed to promote policies that will reduce racism and fight against policies that protect its continuing institutionalization.

In addition to formal legislation that exists which maintains racism within society, it is also important to consider educational policies that can be influential on racist beliefs. One example of policy that can impact racism and race-relations is the educational policy toward those students for whom English is a second language (ESL). These students, often referred to as English learners (ELs), are students whose English is not yet developed enough for them to benefit from instruction in English. As a result, ELs are typically placed into one of three educational programs, depending on the laws of a given state: ESL, bilingual education, or dual language immersion. Although ESL and bilingual education have the goals of English proficiency (i.e., bilingual education does not provide native language development per se), they create a second-class citizenship status for students who are in those classes. They also stigmatize these students as deficient as learners, which creates racist perceptions from teachers, as well as from other students.

On the other hand, dual language immersion programs create a very different climate for ELs. Dual language immersion programs see the existence of multiple native languages among students as an opportunity for both monolingual English speakers and non-English speakers to acquire bilingualism and biculturalism over the course of their education. In this way, both groups serve as resources to each other in the process of learning language, which exists as an important method to reduce prejudice (Alanís & Rodríguez, 2008). These programs profit both groups of students via promotion of native language retention, academic success, and cultural appreciation (Collier & Thomas, 2004). The need for schools to make policy decisions about EL students is growing in that approximately one in every five students in the United States has a native language other than English (National Center for Educational Statistics, 2011). Altogether, this means that more than 11.2 million children who speak a language other than English at home attend U.S. schools, a statistic that has more than doubled since 1980.

The importance of paying attention to the larger political climate that surrounds the educational system is exemplified by the aforementioned laws and educational policies. Policies must be in place to support antiracist education interventions, and psychologists and educators must play a role in participating in the public debate about these issues.

SUMMARY

Education interventions represent a powerful format for combating racism given the compulsory nature of school attendance. We have identified a variety of strategies that both directly and indirectly promote reductions in racism and increase appreciation for cultural diversity including interventions that teach and those that use experiential activities to meet these goals. In particular, interventions modeled on intergroup contact theory have strong empirical support with younger students. For college students, diversity courses that contain cross-racial interactions appear to be effective for White students in particular; students of color, in particular first-generation college students, appear to benefit from campus initiatives that increase social support and access to educational resources. The good news is that throughout the K–16 educational pipeline are many opportunities for successful interventions to be implemented. However, to truly make strides in reducing racism, educational systems will need to adopt structural changes and be guided by policy that makes antiracist educational strategies the norm. Psychologists can play an important role in fostering an educational climate that promotes success in every child and with sustained efforts, the goal of such a utopia may be achievable.

REFERENCES

Acosta v. Huppenthal, A.R.S § 15–112 (2012).

Adams, A., Bondy, E., & Kuhel, K. (2005). Preservice teacher learning in an unfamiliar setting. *Teacher Education Quarterly, 32,* 41–64.

Aguado, T., Ballesteros, B., & Malik, B. (2003). Cultural diversity and school equity: A model to evaluate and develop educational practices in multicultural education contexts. *Equity & Excellence in Education, 36,* 50–63. http://dx.doi.org/10.1080/10665680303500

Alanís, I., & Rodríguez, M. A. (2008). Sustaining a dual language immersion program: Features of success. *Journal of Latinos and Education, 7,* 305–319. http://dx.doi.org/10.1080/15348430802143378

Allport, G. (1954). *The nature of prejudice.* Cambridge, MA: Addison Wesley.

American Association of Colleges of Teacher Education. (2013). *A report from AACTE's professional education data system (PEDS).* Washington, DC: Author.

Arce v. Huppenthal, Nos. 13–15657 (2013).

Arizona H. B. 2281, 49th legislature (2010).

Aronson, E., & Gonzalez, A. (1988). Desegregation, jigsaw, and the Mexican-American experience. In P. Katz & D. A. Taylor (Eds.), *Eliminating racism: Profiles in controversy. Perspectives in Social Psychology* (pp. 301–314). New York, NY: Plenum Press. http://dx.doi.org/10.1007/978-1-4899-0818-6_15

Association of American Colleges and Universities. (2011). *Making excellence inclusive.* Retrieved from http://www.aacu.org/compass/documents/MEINewsletter_Fall11.pdf

Banks, J. (1994). *Multiethnic education: Theory and practice.* Needham Heights, MA: Allyn & Bacon.

Boyd, D., & Arnold, M. (2000). Teachers' beliefs, antiracism and moral education: Problems of intersection. *Journal of Moral Education, 29,* 23–45. http://dx.doi.org/10.1080/030572400102916

Brief for the American Psychological Association as Amici Curiae supporting respondents, Grutter v. Bollinger, 539 U.S. 306, and Gratz v. Bollinger, 539 U.S. 244 (2003).

Bronfenbrenner, U. (1979). *The ecology of human development: Experiments by nature and design.* Cambridge, MA: Harvard University Press.

Brown, E. (2005). Service-learning in a one-year alternative route to teacher certification: A powerful multicultural teaching tool. *Equity & Excellence in Education, 38,* 61–74. http://dx.doi.org/10.1080/10665680590907459

Buhin, L., & Vera, E. M. (2009). Preventing racism and promoting social justice: Person-centered and environment-centered interventions. *The Journal of Primary Prevention, 30,* 43–59. http://dx.doi.org/10.1007/s10935-008-0161-9

Carter, R. T., & Goodwin, A. L. (1994). Racial identity and education. In L. Darling-Hammond (Ed.), *Review of research in education* (Vol. 20, pp. 291–336). Washington, DC: American Education Research Association.

Cole, E. R., Case, K. A., Rios, D., & Curtin, N. (2011). Understanding what students bring to the classroom: Moderators of the effects of diversity courses on student attitudes. *Cultural Diversity & Ethnic Minority Psychology, 17*, 397–405. http://dx.doi.org/10.1037/a0025433

Collier, V. P., & Thomas, W. P. (2004). The astounding effectiveness of dual language education for all. *National Association for Bilingual Education Journal of Research Practice, 2*, 1–20.

Danowitz, M. A., & Tuitt, F. (2011). Enacting inclusivity through engaged pedagogy. *Equity & Excellence in Education, 44*, 40–56. http://dx.doi.org/10.1080/10665684.2011.539474

Denson, N. (2009). Do curricular and co-curricular diversity activities influence racial bias? A meta-analysis. *Review of Educational Research, 79*, 805–838. http://dx.doi.org/10.3102/0034654309331551

Derman-Sparks, L., & Ramsey, P. (2000). A framework for relevant "multicultural" and antibias education in 21st century. In J. Roopnarine & J. Johnson (Eds.), *Approaches to early childhood education* (pp. 201–226). Upper Saddle River, NJ: Prentice Hall.

Eccles, J. S., & Roeser, R. W. (2009). Academic motivation, and stage–environment fit. In R. Lerner & L. Sternberg (Eds.), *Handbook of adolescent psychology: Vol. 1. Individual bases of adolescent development* (3rd ed., pp. 404–434). Hoboken, NJ: Wiley.

Engberg, M. E. (2004). Improving intergroup relations in higher education: A critical examination of the influence of educational interventions on racial bias. *Review of Educational Research, 74*, 473–524. http://dx.doi.org/10.3102/00346543074004473

Gaertner, S. L., & Dovidio, J. F. (1986). *The aversive form of racism*. San Diego, CA: Academic Press.

Gloria, A., & Rodriguez, E. R. (2000). Counseling Latino university students: Psychosociocultural issues for consideration. *Journal of Counseling & Development, 78*, 145–154. http://dx.doi.org/10.1002/j.1556-6676.2000.tb02572.x

Gurin, P., Dey, E. L., Hurtado, S., & Gurin, G. (2002). Diversity and higher education: Theory and impact on educational outcomes. *Harvard Educational Review, 72*, 330–367. http://dx.doi.org/10.17763/haer.72.3.01151786u134n051

Gurin, P., & Nagda, B. A. (2006). Getting to the what, how, and why of diversity on campus. *Educational Researcher, 35*, 20–24. http://dx.doi.org/10.3102/0013189X035001020

Helms, J. E. (Ed.). (1990). *Black and White racial identity: Theory, research, and practice*. New York, NY: Greenwood.

Hohensee, J., & Derman-Sparks, L. (1992). *Implementing an anti-bias curriculum in early childhood classrooms*. Urbana: University of Illinois.

Hollins, E. R. (1990). Debunking the myth of a monolithic White American culture, or moving toward cultural inclusion. *American Behavioral Scientist, 34*, 201–209. http://dx.doi.org/10.1177/0002764290034002008

Humphreys, D. (2000). National survey finds diversity requirements common around the country. *Diversity Digest, 5*, 1–2.

Inkelas, K., & Weisman, J. (2003). Different by design: An examination of student outcomes among participants in three types of living learning programs. *Journal of College Student Development, 44*, 335–368. http://dx.doi.org/10.1353/csd.2003.0027

Jacobsen, J. (1999). The creation and evolution of an elementary field-based reading course: A professor's perspective. *Education, 119*, 408–415.

Kailin, J. (2002). *Antiracist education: From theory to practice*. Lanham, MD: Rowman & Littlefield.

Katz, P. A. (2003). Racists or tolerant multiculturalists? How do they begin? *American Psychologist, 58*, 897–909.

Kehoe, J. W., & Mansfield, E. (1993). The limitations of multicultural education and anti-racist education. *Multicultural education: The state of the art national study*, 3–9.

Kernahan, C., & Davis, T. (2007). Changing perspective: How learning about racism influences student awareness and emotion. *Teaching of Psychology, 37*, 41–45. http://dx.doi.org/10.1080/00986280903425748

Krutky, J. (2008). Intercultural competency: Preparing students to be global citizens. *Effective Practices for Academic Leaders, 3*, 1–15.

Kyles, C. R., & Olafson, L. (2008). Uncovering preservice teachers' beliefs about diversity through reflective writing. *Urban Education, 43*, 500–518. http://dx.doi.org/10.1177/0042085907304963

Ladson-Billings, G. (2000). Fighting for our lives: Teachers to teach African-American students. *Journal of Teacher Education, 51*, 206–214. http://dx.doi.org/10.1177/0022487100051003008

Lawrence, S. M., & Bunche, T. (1996). Feeling and dealing: Teaching White students about racial privilege. *Teaching and Teacher Education, 12*, 531–542. http://dx.doi.org/10.1016/0742-051X(95)00054-N

Lee, A., Poch, R., Shaw, M., & Williams, R. D. (2012). *ASHE Higher Education Report: Vol. 38. Engaging diversity in undergraduate classrooms: A pedagogy for developing intercultural competence*. San Francisco, CA: Jossey-Bass.

Lee, E. (1995). Taking multicultural, anti-racist education seriously: An interview with Enid Lee. *Rethinking schools: An agenda for change*, 9–16.

Lin, M., Lake, V. E., & Rice, D. (2008). Teaching anti-bias curriculum in teacher education programs: What and how. *Teacher Education Quarterly, 35*, 187–200.

London, L., Tierney, G., Buhin, L., Greco, D., & Cooper, C. (2002). Kids' college: Enhancing children's appreciation and acceptance of cultural diversity. *Journal of Prevention & Intervention in the Community, 24*, 61–76. http://dx.doi.org/10.1300/J005v24n02_06

Lopez, G. E., & Zúñiga, X. (2010). Intergroup dialogue and democratic practice in higher education. *New Directions for Higher Education, 152*, 35–42. http://dx.doi.org/10.1002/he.410

McGregor, J. (1993). Effectiveness of role playing and antiracist teaching in reducing student prejudice. *The Journal of Educational Research, 86*, 215–226. http://dx.doi.org/10.1080/00220671.1993.9941833

McIntyre, E., Kyle, D., & Moore, G. (2001). Linking home and school through family visits. *Language Arts, 78*, 264–272.

McNair, T., Finley, A., & Krivian, A. (2013). *Assessing underserved students' engagement in high impact practices.* Washington, DC: Association of American Colleges & Universities. Retrieved from http://www.aacu.org/assessinghips

Michigan Civil Rights Amendment, Proposal 2 (2006).

Munin, A., & Speight, S. L. (2010). Factors influencing the ally development of college students. *Equity & Excellence in Education, 43*, 249–264. http://dx.doi.org/10.1080/10665681003704337

Nagda, B. A., Kim, C., & Truelove, Y. (2004). Learning about difference, learning with others, learning to transgress. *Journal of Social Issues, 60*, 195–214. http://dx.doi.org/10.1111/j.0022-4537.2004.00106.x

National Center for Education Statistics. (2012). *The condition of education in 2012* (NCES Pub. No. 2012-045). Washington, DC: U.S. Department of Education. Retrieved from http://nces.ed.gov/pubs2012/2012045.pdf

National Center for Education Statistics. (2011). *Fast facts: English language learners.* Washington DC: Institute of Education Sciences. Retrieved from http://nces.ed.gov/fastfacts/display.asp?id=96

Neville, H., & Spanierman, L. (2013). Preventing racial injuries: Promoting social justice. In E. Vera (Ed.), *Oxford handbook of prevention in counseling psychology* (pp. 476–490). New York, NY: Oxford Press.

Parsad, B., Lewis, L., & Farris, E. (2001). Teacher preparation and professional development: 2000. *Education Statistics Quarterly, 3*, 33–36.

Peralta-Nash, C. (2003). The impact of home visit in students' perception of teaching. *Teacher Education Quarterly, 30*, 111–125.

Pettigrew, T. F., & Tropp, L. R. (2006). A meta-analytic test of intergroup contact theory. *Journal of Personality and Social Psychology, 90*, 751–783.

Ponterotto, J. G., & Pederson, P. B. (1993). *Preventing prejudice: A guide for counselors and educators.* Thousand Oaks, CA: Sage.

Quintana, S., & Vera, E. M. (1999). Mexican American children's ethnic identity, understanding of ethnic prejudice, and parental ethnic socialization. *Hispanic Journal of Behavioral Sciences, 21*, 387–404. http://dx.doi.org/10.1177/0739986399214001

Sammons, C., & Speight, S. L. (2008). A qualitative investigation of graduate student changes associated with multicultural counseling courses. *The Counseling Psychologist, 36*, 814–838. http://dx.doi.org/10.1177/0011000008316036

Schonert-Reichl, K. A., Smith, V., Zaidman-Zait, A., & Hertzman, C. (2012). Promoting children's prosocial behaviors in school: Impact of the "Roots of Empathy" program on the social and emotional competence of school-aged children. *School Mental Health, 4*, 1–23. http://dx.doi.org/10.1007/s12310-011-9064-7

Schuette v. Coalition to Defend Affirmative Action, 134 S. Ct. 1623 (2014).

Short, G., & Carrington, B. (1996). Anti-racist education, multiculturalism and the new racism. *Educational Review, 48*, pp. 65–77. http://dx.doi.org/10.1080/0013191960480106

Spencer, M. B. (1999). Social and cultural influences on school adjustment: The application of an identity-focused cultural ecological perspective. *Educational Psychologist, 34*, 43–57. http://dx.doi.org/10.1207/s15326985ep3401_4

Thompson, M., & Phillips, J. (2013). Promoting college retention in first-generation college students. In E. Vera (Ed.), *Oxford handbook of prevention in counseling psychology* (pp. 330–346). New York, NY: Oxford University Press.

Underwood, N., & Moore, B. (1982). Perspective-taking and altruism. *Psychological Bulletin, 91*, 143–173. http://dx.doi.org/10.1037/0033-2909.91.1.143

Vigliante, T. (2007). Social justice through effective antiracism education: A survey of preservice teachers. *Journal of Educational Enquiry, 7*, 103–128.

Weiner, M., & Wright, F. (1973). Effects of undergoing arbitrary discrimination upon subsequent attitudes toward a minority group. *Journal of Applied Social Psychology, 3*, 94–102. http://dx.doi.org/10.1111/j.1559-1816.1973.tb01298.x

Wiggins, R. A., Follo, E. J., & Eberly, M. B. (2007). The impact of field immersion program on pre-service teachers' attitudes toward teaching in culturally diverse classrooms. *Teaching and Teacher Education, 23*, 653–663. http://dx.doi.org/10.1016/j.tate.2007.02.007

Zirkel, S. (2008). Creating more effective multiethnic schools. *Social Issues and Policy Review, 2*, 187–241. http://dx.doi.org/10.1111/j.1751-2409.2008.00015.x

Zúñiga, X., Nagda, B. A., Chesler, M., & Cytron-Walker, A. (2011). *ASHE higher education report: Vol. 32. Intergroup dialogue in higher education: Meaningful learning about social justice.* San Francisco, CA: Jossey-Bass.

Zúñiga, X., Nagda, B. R. A., & Sevig, T. D. (2002). Intergroup dialogues: An educational model for cultivating engagement across differences. *Equity & Excellence in Education, 35*, 7–17. http://dx.doi.org/10.1080/713845248

14

TOWARD A RELEVANT PSYCHOLOGY OF PREJUDICE, STEREOTYPING, AND DISCRIMINATION: LINKING SCIENCE AND PRACTICE TO DEVELOP INTERVENTIONS THAT WORK IN COMMUNITY SETTINGS

IGNACIO D. ACEVEDO-POLAKOVICH, KARA L. BECK, ERIN HAWKS, AND SARAH E. OGDIE

Racism and other forms of prejudice, stereotyping, and discrimination plague the United States in insidious ways. Research conducted on nationally representative samples suggests that almost two thirds of adult U.S. residents experience some sort of day-to-day discrimination (e.g., receiving poor service, being called names) and more than one third experience a major discriminatory event in their lifetime (e.g., being denied or fired from a job, being prevented from buying a home; Kessler, Mickelson, & Williams, 1999). On the extreme end of prejudice, more than 6,216 hate crimes involving race (46.9%), sexual orientation (20.8%), religion (19.8%), or ethnic/national origin (11.6%) were reported to the United States Department of Justice (USDOJ, 2012) during 2011. These reports are likely a gross underestimate, as hate-crime estimates derived from the National Crime Victimization Survey (NCVS)—a yearly survey of

http://dx.doi.org/10.1037/14852-015
The Cost of Racism for People of Color: Contextualizing Experiences of Discrimination, A. N. Alvarez, C. T. H. Liang, and H. A. Neville (Editors)
Copyright © 2016 by the American Psychological Association. All rights reserved.

criminal victimization in the United States conducted by the USDOJ and involving a nationally representative sample of 76,000 households comprising nearly 135,300 persons—suggest that 191,000 hate crime incidents occur each year (Rand, 2009).

Compared with victims of random crimes, victims of hate crime exhibit higher rates of delayed effects, such as depression, stress, and anger (Herek, Gillis, Cogan, & Glunt, 1997). This is not surprising, as even relatively milder daily forms of discrimination can significantly affect individuals' health and well-being. The results of a meta-analysis that included 134 independent samples identified a significant and negative effect of perceived discrimination on both mental health ($r = -.20$) and physical health ($r = -.13$; Pascoe & Smart Richman, 2009). This meta-analysis also provided evidence of specific relations between perceived discrimination and depressive symptoms, psychiatric distress, general well-being, and the probability of being diagnosed with a mental illness. Such findings poignantly underscore the harm caused by the everyday prejudice, stereotyping, and discrimination encountered by most people in the United States and disproportionately by members of ethnic or racial minority groups.

Considering the prevalence and negative impact of prejudice, stereotyping, and discrimination in the United States, it is not surprising that addressing these variables has been an important focus of both researchers (e.g., Paluck & Green, 2009) and communities in this country (e.g., National Research Council [NRC] & Institute of Medicine [IOM], 2000). In a methodological review of the prejudice reduction literature, Paluck and Green (2009) identified 985 studies on the topic, of which 72% were published. Their review included nonpublished studies to facilitate a comparison of laboratory-based research and field-based research. Paluck and Green identified six prejudice-reduction approaches supported by both laboratory and field research (i.e., cooperative learning, entertainment, peer influence, contact, value consistency, and intercultural training), two supported mostly by laboratory evidence (i.e., social categorization, and cognitive training), and four that were often addressed in the literature but lacked research support (i.e., diversity training, multicultural education, cultural competence, and conflict resolution). These authors noted that most research has been conducted in laboratory settings, with little rigorous research occurring in field settings. As they conclude:

> Those interested in creating effective prejudice-reduction programs must remain skeptical of the recommendation of laboratory experiments until they are supported by research of the same degree of rigor outside of the laboratory. (Paluck & Green, 2009, p. 351)

THE SCIENCE–PRACTICE GAP

Given the widely documented gap between research and practice across an alarming variety of domains of human behavior (Jansson, Benoit, Casey, Phillips, & Burns, 2010; Morrissey et al., 1997), Paluck and Green's (2009) findings are best understood as a specific example of this broader gap. Scholars who study the science–practice gap point out that the goals and contexts of scientists and practitioners can differ notably (Jansson et al., 2010; Morrissey et al., 1997). Practitioners are often concerned with maintaining or expanding existing services, frequently in underresourced environments; researchers are concerned with conducting rigorous studies, most often with the goal of publication. Although the ultimate aims of both practitioners and researchers may closely overlap (e.g., effective prejudice reduction), their differing concerns can present an obstacle for collaboration. For example, practitioners might perceive practices that increase methodological rigor, such as randomized assignment, as antithetical to their service principles (Acevedo-Polakovich, Kassab, & Barnett, 2012; Mason, Fleming, Thompson, Haggerty, & Snyder, 2014).

In the interest of promoting the development of effective prejudice-reduction and antiracism interventions in the communities that need them, we introduce and illustrate in this chapter some basic concepts and approaches that promote collaboration between practitioners and researchers when developing such interventions. We first discuss community–academic partnerships and their role in addressing the science–practice gap, introducing an approach to the development and maintenance of these partnerships: community-based participatory research (CBPR). After this introduction, we use existing work to illustrate two strategies for the development of research-supported community interventions: *science-to-practice* and *practice-to-science*. Although the first strategy is frequently used by scholars, it has more often than not failed to result in effective community interventions (Paluck & Green, 2009). We discuss the second, less frequently used, strategy in greater detail, as it is explicitly designed to overcome the limitations of the first strategy. We conclude the chapter by offering recommendations for future research and practice.

ADDRESSING THE SCIENCE–PRACTICE GAP THROUGH COMMUNITY–ACADEMIC PARTNERSHIPS

Overcoming the science–practice gap regarding interventions to address racism and other forms of stereotyping, prejudice, and discrimination requires careful attention to the development of partnerships between academics and community service providers (Acevedo-Polakovich et al., 2012; Jansson et al., 2010; Morrissey et al., 1997; Paluck & Green, 2009). The development of such partnerships is slow and deliberate and can require changes to the traditional approaches of both academics and communities (Acevedo-Polakovich et al., 2012). For example, community service providers who are involved in these partnerships may have to reallocate resources (e.g., time, personnel) in exchange for data that support their efforts to refine, improve, and fund their services. Similarly, scientists who are involved in these partnerships may have to share control over the focus of research, its design, and implementation. The reward for scientists who engage in these partnerships is the ability to conduct field-based research that does not suffer from the limited external validity that characterizes most prejudice reduction research (Paluck & Green, 2009).

COMMUNITY-BASED PARTICIPATORY RESEARCH

Various approaches to research exist that can guide the formation and maintenance of community–academic partnerships. These include—but are not limited to—participatory research (e.g., Cornwall & Jewkes, 1995), participatory action research (e.g., Baum, MacDougall, & Smith, 2006), emancipatory research (e.g., Rose & Glass, 2008), and CBPR (e.g., Israel, Eng, Schulz, & Parker, 2005). Although community–academic partnerships that seek to address stereotyping, prejudice, and discrimination need not be framed by formal approaches to collaboration, the approaches we have listed are particularly worthy of consideration by such partnerships, as they represent direct attempts to rectify within the research process the very conditions of inequality that foster racism and other forms of stereotyping, prejudice, and discrimination (Wallerstein & Duran, 2003).

Traditional research paradigms devalue community perspectives by reflecting the assumption that researchers are the experts who have something to offer community participants (Wallerstein & Duran, 2003). When research is focused on historically aggrieved communities, this assumption raises the risk that the manner in which research is conducted will perpetuate the injustice experienced by these communities (Wallerstein & Duran, 2003). By emphasizing equity between researchers and the communities that they study, the approaches that we have listed attempt to ensure that the social conditions leading to racism and other forms of stereotyping, prejudice, and discrimination do not exist within the research process.

The reasons to introduce CBPR as an example of formal approaches to guide community–academic partnership development and maintenance are both conceptual and pragmatic. Conceptually, CBPR is broadly inclusive, such that it is able to capture and incorporate many important elements of other approaches (Wallerstein & Duran, 2003). Pragmatically, our extensive discussion of the practice-to-science strategy uses an active line of CBPR as an illustration. Introducing CBPR facilitates a richer understanding of the practice-to-science strategy.

Rather than relying on particular methodologies or designs, CBPR occurs when researchers and community members adhere to values and principles emphasizing equity and shared control (Minkler & Wallerstein, 2003). One popular articulation of CBPR includes nine fundamental values and practices (Israel, Eng, Schulz, & Parker, 2005): (a) recognition of the community as a unit of identity, (b) a focus on building community strengths and resources, (c) incorporation of collaborative and equitable partnerships between scientists and community members in all phases of the research, (d) colearning and capacity building for all partners, (e) balance between research and action for the mutual benefit of all partners, (f) emphasis on the multiply determined nature of problems and on the crucial role of community context when understanding and addressing them, (g) the recognition that ideal solutions develop through cyclical and iterative processes that involve researchers and the researched community, (h) dissemination of findings with a focus on relevance to all partners, and (i) committed long-term partnerships that extend beyond one singularly-focused project.

SCIENCE-TO-PRACTICE

Within the context of community–academic partnerships, the science–practice gap can be addressed using one of two broad strategies. The first of these, which is widely used and can be broadly characterized as a science-to-practice strategy, guides the work of a community–academic partnership toward understanding community needs, cross referencing these with relevant scientific findings and then either developing or adapting interventions. Typically—but not always—this intervention development or adaptation is undergone in an academic or laboratory setting before interventions are disseminated into the community (Paluck & Green, 2009).

Important challenges can arise when using the science-to-practice strategy. First, interventions that are developed in laboratory settings must then be disseminated into communities. Dissemination is an active process that requires considerable resource investment and is not always successful (Wandersman et al., 2008). The challenges to dissemination result in limited community use of interventions developed in laboratory settings (Biglan, Mrazek, Carnine, & Flay, 2003). A second challenge is that interventions that are successfully implemented must then achieve long-term sustainability. As is the case with dissemination, ensuring the sustainability of an intervention is an active process requiring considerable resource investment and—as such—often does not occur (Hawkins, Shapiro, & Fagan, 2010; Spoth et al., 2011). A final, and related, challenge of interventions developed using the science-to-practice approach involves their ecological validity—the compatibility between the conditions required for the intervention to be maximally effective and the conditions in the communities in which they are to be implemented (Bernal & Saez-Santiago, 2006). Interventions that are not responsive to community conditions are—on average—a quarter as effective as interventions that are responsive to those conditions (Griner & Smith, 2006). They are also much less likely to be successfully implemented and less likely to be sustainable in community settings (Hernandez, Nesman, Mowery, Acevedo-Polakovich, & Callejas, 2009).

Although—as the work of Paluck and Green (2009) suggests—the challenges of the science-to-practice strategy have disproportionately prevented the development and implementation of useful community interventions to address racism and other forms of stereotyping, prejudice and discrimination, some community–academic partnerships have successfully used this strategy. The development of *Musekeweya* (i.e., "New Dawn"; as cited in Staub, Pearlman, Gubin, & Hagengimana, 2005), a radio-based intervention in Rwanda, is one powerful example. Although the focus of much of this chapter is on the United States, Musekeweya is an important illustration because of the nationwide scope of the intervention and the magnitude of the prejudice, stereotyping, and discrimination that it strives to address. In this regard, it provides a patent demonstration of the capacity of well-designed community interventions (Paluck & Green, 2009).

The need for Musekeweya arose from the significant and longstanding conflict between Hutu and Tutsi ethnic groups. After taking control of Rwanda away from Germany in the aftermath of World War I, the Belgian government capitalized on historical differences between these groups and enacted policies that ensured Tutsis would hold and retain positions of authority (Sadowski, 1998). This systemic disempowerment of Hutus fueled the escalation of interethnic conflict throughout the 20th century and led to several periods of extreme ethnic violence, including the killing of at least 10,000 Tutsi during a 1959 retaliation for the Tutsi attack on a Hutu leader (Sadowski, 1998); the 1972 killing of hundreds of thousands of Hutu by the Tutsi military leadership in neighboring Burundi (Lemarchand, 1998); and bloody civil war along ethnic lines during the 1990s that resulted in approximately 1,000,000 deaths (Kanyangara, Rime, Philippot, & Yzerbyt, 2007). In the aftermath of the civil war, the Tutsi-led government pursued a policy of unity, which provided the context for the development of Musekeweya (Staub, Pearlman, Weiss, & Hoek, 2008).

As a first step toward the development of an intervention to foster interethnic unity, the community–academic partnership that ultimately designed Musekeweya documented local conditions among Rwandans, including the historical context of the violence, the resulting trauma, and the reconciliation efforts already underway (Staub, 2006; Staub et al., 2005). These local conditions were then interpreted using existing scholarship on violence, trauma, healing, and reconciliation (Staub, 2006; Staub et al., 2008). In brief, the researchers interpreted the conflict between Tutsi and Hutu as fueled by social conditions leading to the dehumanization of the other, unjust societal arrangements, and the creation of a passive bystander culture (Staub, 2006). To address these factors, the academic partners collaborated with Hutu and Tutsi Rwandans in the development of a radio-based intervention, Musekeweya, which took the form of a soap opera—followed by an estimated 85% of radio listeners in Rwanda—that integrated themes important for reconciliation (Staub et al., 2008).

Musekeweya had positive effects on listeners' perceptions of social norms and on their behavior (Paluck, 2009). When compared with a control group that listened to a health education radio show, Rwandans who listened to Musekeweya were less likely to report that they would prohibit their children from marrying individuals from a different ethnic group, more likely to report that they should speak up if they disagree with someone's actions, and more likely to endorse talking about trauma (Paluck, 2009). Consistent with the belief that they would speak up when they disagree with someone's actions, participants in the intervention group were also more likely to challenge each other during discussions (Paluck, 2009).

Musekeweya's strong effects and broad dissemination powerfully illustrate the capacity of well-designed science-to-practice interventions that are intentional about addressing the challenges that this development strategy often encounters (Paluck & Green, 2009). Working collaboratively with communities from the outset of the process, the researchers involved in the development of Musekeweya were able to design an intervention with a high degree of ecological validity and a broad, sustainable dissemination.

PRACTICE-TO-SCIENCE: EVIDENCE-BASING COMMUNITY INTERVENTIONS

Musekeweya illustrates how a thoughtful implementation of the science-to-practice strategy can lead to successful community interventions to reduce racism and other forms of prejudice, stereotyping, and discrimination; however, the challenges associated with this strategy have often prevented the development of useful community interventions (Paluck & Green, 2009). In the absence of successfully scaled science-to-practice efforts, communities have frequently developed their own interventions to address racism, often focused on improving intergroup relations (NRC & IOM, 2000).

Long-standing community-driven interventions are less likely to encounter the challenges faced by interventions developed using a science-to-practice strategy (Wandersman & Florin, 2003). Dissemination—at least with a local focus—is by definition unnecessary, as these interventions are developed in the communities that need them (Glasgow, Vogt, & Boles, 1999). Sustainability is less likely to be an issue with long-standing community interventions, as they often remain in existence because they incorporate the sustainability infrastructures that science-to-practice programs are challenged to develop (Mason et al., 2014). Finally, the development and implementation of these interventions within the community usually results in a high degree of ecological validity (Barkham & Mellor-Clark, 2003). Despite these benefits of community-driven interventions, it is usually the case that limited or no efforts have been made to rigorously examine whether these interventions produce their intended effects (NRC & IOM, 2000). For this reason, community–academic partnerships attempting to address the science–practice gap may also adopt a practice-to-science approach focused on the rigorous evaluation and improvement of interventions that are long-standing within community settings (Mason et al., 2014).

Mason et al. (2014) recently described a framework to guide community–academic partnerships that pursue the practice-to-science strategy, which we summarize in Figure 14.1. The framework assumes the existence of

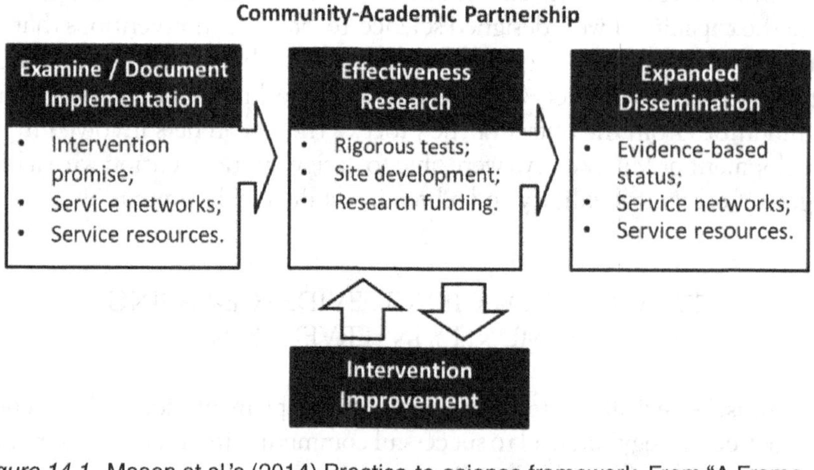

Figure 14.1. Mason et al.'s (2014) Practice-to-science framework. From "A Framework for Testing and Promoting Expanded Dissemination of Promising Preventive Interventions That Are Being Implemented in Community Settings," by W. A. Mason, C. B. Fleming, R. W. Thompson, K. P. Haggerty, and J. J. Snyder, 2014, *Prevention Science*, *15*, pp. 674–683. Copyright 2013 by Springer. Reprinted with permission.

community–academic partnerships and recognizes that their development and maintenance are effortful processes that should be guided by best practices as documented in the literature. We describe and illustrate the application of Mason et al.'s framework for the evidence-basing of community interventions to address racism and other forms of prejudice using examples from active CBPR involving ANYTOWN™, an intervention for high-school-age youth in the United States, with the goals of promoting diversity acceptance, intergroup contact, social responsibility, and community involvement. Because the practice-to-science strategy is implemented much less often than its science-to-practice alternative, we focus on providing one well-developed example of its application, and we hope that our discussion can better inform researchers and practitioners considering the application of a practice-to-science strategy in different contexts.

ANYTOWN™—the focus of our practice-to-science work—is a time-limited residential intervention typically lasting one week. For the week, youth are assigned to dormitories and discussion groups such that they are maximally exposed to peers whose background differs significantly from their own in terms of race, ethnicity, religion, gender, socioeconomic status, and sexual orientation. ANYTOWN™ includes workshops and activities on various foci of stereotyping, prejudice, and discrimination (e.g., race, sexual orientation, gender, socioeconomic status), dialogue, social responsibility, and community involvement. Along with the workshops and activities, youth participate in small dialogue groups to discuss the implications of the workshops and activities for their attitudes and their behavior.

EXAMINING AND DOCUMENTING CURRENT IMPLEMENTATION

Intervention Promise

As seen in Figure 14.1, a first step in the practice-to-science strategy is documenting current implementation efforts, specifically attending to an intervention's promise, its service provision networks, and its service provision resources (Mason et al., 2014). Examining and documenting an intervention's promise involves three important considerations, the first of which is examining whether it includes components associated with other successful interventions (Mason et al., 2014).

ANYTOWN™ was developed in the 1950s on the basis of Gordon Allport's (1954) intergroup contact theory, which at the time provided the state-of-the-science understanding of the conditions under which stereotyping, prejudice, and discrimination could be overcome. More than 60 years of research suggest that intergroup contact is among the most reliable and powerful influences on intergroup attitudes (Pettigrew & Tropp, 2006). A meta-analysis that included 713 independent samples from 515 studies conducted between 1940 and 2000 found that the average effect size of intergroup contact upon prejudice was between $r = -.20$ and $r = -.21$ (Pettigrew & Tropp, 2006). To the extent that ANYTOWN™ successfully implements intergroup contact, it appears to include at least one component that is associated with successful interventions. Cooperative learning, peer influence, contact, and value consistency—all of which were identified by Paluck and Green (2009) as components of effective interventions to decrease prejudice, stereotyping and discrimination—are also part of ANYTOWN™.

The second consideration in determining an intervention's promise is ascertaining whether it is evaluable (Mason et al., 2014). The existence of documentation of the intervention—including intervention manuals, protocols for interventionist selection and training, and tools for the monitoring of implementation fidelity—informs this consideration. The implementation of ANYTOWN™ is guided by a carefully developed curriculum; interventionists are selected and prepared according to established and documented practices; and although limited in their current form, tools exist—and can be improved—that can be used to track fidelity.

A final consideration is reviewing any preliminary evidence of an intervention's success (Mason et al., 2014). Evaluations of ANYTOWN™ published in the peer-reviewed literature document pretreatment to posttreatment changes in single-item measures of knowledge and attitudes regarding sexual orientation, gender identity, and race (Boulden, 2005, 2006) and on psychometrically derived multi-item assessments of self-concept, personal and civic responsibility, race-based prejudice, heterosexism, and gender equality (Otis & Loeffler, 2005).

Service Provision Networks

Two levels of networks are involved in the provision of ANYTOWN™. The first involves a national network associated with the dissemination of the intervention. The second involves local networks associated with ANYTOWN™'s implementation in specific communities. At the national level, ANYTOWN™ was originally developed by the National Conference of Christians and Jews (NCCJ; later renamed the National Conference for Community and Justice), an organization founded in 1927 to promote interfaith unity, which later expanded its scope to promote intergroup unity across races, social classes, genders, sexual orientations, and ability levels. Between 1927 and 2005, the NCCJ was structured as central organization with regional chapters. It was through these chapters that ANYTOWN™ was originally disseminated. Although the structure of NCCJ changed after 2005 such that regional chapters became autonomous and independent, ANYTOWN™ continues to be implemented in local communities by some of the now autonomous organizations that previously functioned as NCCJ chapters.

At the local level, the implementation of ANYTOWN™ relies on the community networks of each NCCJ chapter (or their descendant organizations). For instance, within the Tampa Bay area of Florida, the local NCCJ chapter was rebranded as Community Tampa Bay Inc. (CTB), a nonprofit organization with a mission to promote dialogue and respect among all cultures, religions, and races by cultivating leaders to change communities. The local implementation of ANYTOWN™ depends on established relations between CTB and community stakeholders—such as religious congregations, schools, civic groups, and youth-serving organizations—each of which support ANYTOWN™ by referring youth and/or providing volunteers or other tangible forms of aid (e.g., funding).

Service Provision Resources

Funding for the implementation of ANYTOWN™ in the Tampa Bay area depends on a variety of sources, including donations, grants, contracts and volunteer support. This is particularly the case as—to guarantee access to as diverse a pool of participants as possible—until 2012 the program had avoided charging participants despite per-participant costs of implementation running as high as $1,700. Reflecting national trends (Mason et al., 2014), some of the more substantial private and public grants available to CTB for the implementation of ANYTOWN™ increasingly required that the interventions they support be evidence based. This requirement both compromises the sustainability of ANYTOWN™ and heightens interest in pursuing the practice-to-science approach.

Taken together, the available evidence suggests that ANYTOWN™ is a promising intervention with strong service provision networks and resources that have enabled it to be sustainably delivered for more than 50 years nationally and for more than 20 years in the Tampa Bay area (the community that is the focus of the CBPR partnership being described in this section). At its height, the program was in existence in more than 60 communities in 22 states. Although the nationwide dissemination of the intervention has decreased—in part a result of the reduced funding of nonprofits during the recent economic downturn and the co-occurring trend among funders to primarily support evidence-based programs—CTB continues to operate ANYTOWN™ in the Tampa Bay area.

EFFECTIVENESS RESEARCH

As illustrated in Figure 14.1, through the interrelated activities of rigorous intervention testing, study site development, and pursuing research funding, the second step in Mason et al.'s (2014) practice-to-science framework is focused on establishing evidence of an intervention's effectiveness and—when indicated—modifying or improving the intervention on the basis of the research data. Our CBPR has focused on the effectiveness of ANYTOWN™ with the long-term goal of examining its eligibility for inclusion in any of several registries of empirically based programs. As Mason et al. (2014) suggested, one of the main challenges we have encountered is balancing the internal validity required of good effectiveness research with the service needs of an intervention that is well established in the community.

Rigorous Intervention Tests

Mason et al.'s (2014) consideration of the effectiveness research step in general, and its rigorous program test component in particular, is heavily focused on the difficulties that can arise in attempting to implement a randomized controlled trial (RCT), which is a best practice in efficacy/effectiveness research. Although their discussion is on point with our experience, we have found that crucial antecedent issues must be addressed. The issue of determining appropriate measures is illustrative.

Determining Appropriate Measures

Although the measurement and conceptualization of stereotypes, prejudice, and discrimination are remarkably advanced within the research literature (e.g., Olson, 2009), very little attention has been given to the conceptualization and measurement of the positive intergroup variables targeted by ANYTOWN™ (Fuertes, Sedlacek, Roger, & Mohr, 2000). Given this state of affairs—and before we formed our CBPR partnership—CTB worked closely with a researcher to examine available measures and determine their relevance. Although some existing measures were found to be relevant to the program and adopted as part of ANYTOWN™'s evaluation, no measure of positive intergroup variables was found adequate. As a result, CTB and its research partner developed a new measure, the Youth Diversity Acceptance scale (YoDA), which captured the intergroup change sought by the program (Lyons, 2005).

The YoDA was developed using standard psychometric practices and has demonstrated adequate internal validity in existing unpublished research, which has also shown that YoDA scores increase from pretreatment to posttreatment as a result of ANYTOWN™ participation (Beck,

2012; Hawks, 2010; Lyons, 2005). Consistent with the few other studies that have developed measures of positive intergroup variables (e.g., Fuertes et al., 2000)—but in contrast to the literature on stereotyping, prejudice, and discrimination (e.g., Olson, 2009)—in the YoDA behavioral, attitudinal, and cognitive indicators hold together in one factor (Lyons, 2005; Beck et al., 2014). The YoDA is thus relevant to the program, empirically sound and conceptually relevant, but not yet published in the peer-reviewed literature.

Under this state of affairs, we have implemented several complimentary strategies as we build toward a RCT. First, we have pursued the publication of expanded psychometric work supporting the YoDA (e.g., Beck et al., 2014). If successful, these efforts would allow for the YoDA to remain as one of the program's primary outcome measures in a future RCT. Second, we have examined the usefulness of several other published scales in our efforts to evaluate and/or research ANYTOWN™ (e.g., Beck, 2012; Hawks, 2010). Although none of these measures have the relevance of the YoDA, most of them have evinced pretreatment to posttreatment changes around ANYTOWN™ participation. As such, although not ideally tied to program goals, these scales are likely to make a suitable complement to the YoDA in a future RCT.

Building Toward Randomized Controlled Trials

Echoing others (e.g., Glasgow et al., 1999), Mason et al. (2014) describe the difficulties that community–academic partnerships can encounter when attempting to implement an RCT. Briefly, RCTs require significant resources and can require modifications to service delivery practices that compromise the integrity of the intervention. For these reasons, it can be necessary and useful to conduct a series of studies—beginning with designs least disruptive to the intervention—that progressively develop the infrastructure needed for an RCT along with the justification for such a design (Glasgow et al., 1999). This progressive approach can also foster site development and the procurement of research funding, two additional components of the effectiveness research step within Mason et al.'s practice-to-science framework.

In planning the work to be conducted in the effectiveness step, our CBPR partnership first estimated the cost of conducting an RCT in a manner that would not compromise the integrity of the service practices involved in the implementation of ANYTOWN™. Although procuring the resources for an RCT depended on our success attaining external funding, our available resources enabled a series of studies that could progressively strengthen the research infrastructure of our partnership and provide data to support later proposals for external funding. We began our work by designing and implementing three studies that as a group sought to build on the published pretreatment to posttreatment evaluations of ANYTOWN™.

In Study 1, we used a non-equivalent control group design and found that, compared with students enrolled in social science courses at the same high schools from which they are recruited, ANYTOWN™ participants achieved greater short-term increases in measures of knowledge regarding diversity, diversity acceptance, social competence, social responsibility, and community involvement (Acevedo-Polakovich, Lyons, Beck, Estevez, & Hawks, 2015). It is important to note that most differences between groups remained significant at a midterm follow up. In Study 2, we examined whether potential mediating variables identified through a logic modeling exercise could account for the short-term growth in ANYTOWN™ participants' scores on diversity acceptance (Acevedo-Polakovich et al., 2015). Consistent with the intergroup contact approach that underlies ANYTOWN™, results suggested that increases in the emotional closeness participants feel toward individuals who belong to socially constructed outgroups significantly mediated the increases in diversity awareness. In Study 3, we used an expert consensus methodology to identify additional potential mediators that might account for program effects (Acevedo-Polakovich et al., 2015). Results of this approach identified other potential mediators that might be explored including group categorization strategies and changes in specific cognitive processes (i.e., awareness, defusion, action).

Site Development

The key determination in site development is where and how to access study participants, which—particularly in the case of long-standing community-driven interventions, such as ANYTOWN™—must account for established service delivery practices (Mason et al., 2014). Because these service practices can be an obstacle for an RCT, methodological flexibility can be necessary (Mason et al., 2014). As previously stated, the resources required to conduct an RCT without compromising the integrity of the service practices involved in the implementation of ANYTOWN™ are at this time unavailable to our CBPR partnership without external funding. In pursuing methodological options that can strengthen the rigor of our research while fitting within our current constraints, we opted for the implementation of two additional studies, both currently active. One of these uses a wait-list control design to assess short-term effects and another involves time series data collected from a subsample of program participants during the months before and after their participation in ANYTOWN™.

Research Funding

Scientists have access to traditional research funders (e.g., the National Institutes of Health, the National Science Foundation), whereas community organizations can access national, regional, and local services funders (e.g., the U.S. Substance Use and Mental Health Service Administration, state departments of health and/or education, local foundations). Research into community interventions offers community–academic partnerships the opportunity to tie together these different funding streams (Mason et al., 2014). For instance, combining funding streams can make use of service grants to support the program evaluation component of research or, where allowable, make use of research funds to support the delivery of the intervention under study. Even with enhanced opportunities for funding, obtaining external funding is a competitive and challenging endeavor. Although our CBPR partnership includes individuals with a history of success attracting external funding from national, regional and local funders, our research activities to date have had to make creative use of our existing resources.

INTERVENTION IMPROVEMENT

Mason et al.'s (2014) practice-to-science framework directly relates the improvement of an intervention to effectiveness research. As findings emerge from research, they should guide the modification (with the goal of improvement) of the community intervention. The effects of these modifications should then be examined via follow-up research. One example from our work is illustrative. Our early research suggested that ANYTOWN™'s effects on diversity acceptance—one of its primary outcomes of interest—were associated with increases in the emotional closeness participants feel toward individuals who belong to socially constructed outgroups (Acevedo-Polakovich et al., 2015). Stated plainly, it is the quality—rather than the quantity—of intergroup relationships that seems to have an effect on attitudes. This finding led to changes in interventionist training. In the interest of expanding intergroup contact, interventionists had traditionally been trained to continuously encourage participants' active efforts to meet new people, often at the expense of spending time getting to know a few new people well. The findings regarding emotional closeness led to changes in the role of interventionists, who are now trained to facilitate the time and opportunity for participants to form close bonds with others whose backgrounds differ significantly from their own.

Mason et al.'s (2014) practice-to-science framework specifies that intervention modification can occur that is not directly guided by the findings of effectiveness research. The comparison of the intervention curriculum to those of other evidence-based interventions might reveal areas for improvement. It is also possible that an intervention might be modified to incorporate technological innovations that seem likely to enhance its effects or its reach.

This type of modification has been overlooked in our CBPR and constitutes an important direction for our future work.

EXPANDED DISSEMINATION

When research results support the effectiveness of an intervention, a community–academic partnership can move to the final step of Mason et al.'s (2014) practice-to-science framework, expanded dissemination. The three activities included in this step together support an expanded implementation of the program: establishment of evidence-based status, expansion of service networks, and expansion of service resources.

Evidence-Based Status

In the United States, several registries of evidence-based interventions exist and have come to play an important role in the promotion of interventions. As part of the trend to finance only empirically supported treatments, funders will often require that proposals seeking support for services focus only on interventions included in these registries. Given this funding climate, our CBPR into the effectiveness of ANYTOWN™ has the long-term goal of examining its eligibility for inclusion in these registries. As Mason et al. (2014) pointed out, most of these registries have a hierarchy of designations and—although it is in some cases impossible for one research team to facilitate the consideration of an intervention for the highest level designations—we have tried to develop our research agenda such that, if positive, findings would first allow for the lower level designations, with subsequent research facilitating the consideration of the program at higher designations. Inclusion at even the lowest level of the registry notably expands the funding opportunities available to ANYTOWN™ or any other community-developed intervention.

Expanded Service Networks

It is important to keep in mind that although inclusion in the registries of empirically supported programs provides the opportunity for increased dissemination of an intervention, dissemination is an active and resource-intensive process that must be carefully managed to be successful (Wandersman et al., 2008). One of the interesting challenges of our work with ANYTOWN™ is its existing dissemination across an established national network. Prevalent models for the dissemination of interventions—such as the interactive systems framework of Wandersman et al. (2008)—tend to focus on dissemination into new settings. Should our effectiveness research prove successful, we will be faced with the challenge of attempting to disseminate any innovations that have been made to the program across the existing national network. The extent to which the dissemination of innovations and/or improvements to an existing intervention parallels the dissemination of entirely new interventions is an important direction for future research.

Expanded Service Resources

We have noted that dissemination is an active and resource intensive process. Mason et al. (2014) highlight that the lack of resources to support dissemination can lead to many unrealized opportunities. To this end, they suggest that community organizations take advantage of opportunities to capitalize financially on the inclusion of the interventions they have developed into evidence-based registries.

CONCLUSIONS

Despite devoting a great deal of attention to racial and ethnic prejudice, stereotyping, and discrimination, psychologists have largely failed to provide communities with interventions to address these issues. In part, this failure reflects the broader practice of research existing independently from community needs or contexts. Successfully addressing racism and other forms of prejudice, stereotyping, and discrimination within communities requires partnerships between these communities and researchers. Community–academic partnerships can follow two broad strategies in the development of interventions to address and prevent racism. The first, science-to-practice, can lead to the development of innovative interventions with broad public impact, such as Musekeweya. The second strategy, practice-to-science, can document, improve and give broader dissemination to successful community-developed interventions, such as ANYTOWN™.

The traditional manner in which social scientists study racism and other forms of stereotyping, prejudice, and discrimination has provided few tractable solutions for the communities harmed by these social ills (Paluck & Green, 2009). The scientific understanding of racism is voluminous and growing. The human beings that suffer because of racism and other injustices do not need one more study examining one more nuance within this scientific understanding—Instead, they need solutions for the injustices that challenge their daily living. It is high time for social scientists to work alongside the communities aggrieved by the injustices that they study. To do otherwise is to be complicit with scientific obsolescence in the face of people's suffering.

REFERENCES

Acevedo-Polakovich, I. D., Kassab, V. A., & Barnett, M. L. (2012). *Las Asociaciones entre la Academia y la Comunidad como Fuente de Transformación Social Sustentable* [Community–academic partnerships as a source of sustainable social change]. In N. N. Asili (Ed.), *Vida Sustentable* [Sustainable living] (pp. 236–253). Puebla, México: Universidad de las Américas Press.

Acevedo-Polakovich, I. D., Lyons, E. M., Beck, K. L., Estevez, J., & Hawks, E. (2015). *Liberty and justice for all: The effects of a community-based youth program to promote diversity acceptance.* Unpublished manuscript, Department of Psychology, Michigan State University.

Allport, G. W. (1954). *The nature of prejudice.* Reading, MA: Addison-Wesley.

Barkham, M., & Mellor-Clark, J. (2003). Bridging evidence-based practice and practice-based evidence: Developing a rigorous and relevant knowledge for the psychological therapies. *Clinical Psychology & Psychotherapy, 10,* 319–327. http://dx.doi.org/10.1002/cpp.379

Baum, F., MacDougall, C., & Smith, D. (2006). Participatory action research. *Journal of Epidemiology and Community Health, 60*(10), 854–857. http://dx.doi.org/10.1136/jech.2004.028662

Beck, K. L. (2012). *From program evaluation to practice-based evidence: A wait-list control evaluation of the ANYTOWN program.* Unpublished master's thesis, Central Michigan University, Mount Pleasant, MI.

Beck, K. L., Acevedo-Polakovich, I. D., Sevecke, J. R., Rossman, D. L., Lyons, E., & Estevez, J. (2014). *The Youth Diversity Acceptance Scale: Development and validity.* Unpublished manuscript, Department of Psychology, Michigan State University.

Bernal, G., & Saez-Santiago, E. (2006). Culturally centered psychosocial interventions. *Journal of Community Psychology, 34,* 121–132. http://dx.doi.org/10.1002/jcop.20096

Biglan, A., Mrazek, P. J., Carnine, D., & Flay, B. R. (2003). The integration of research and practice in the prevention of youth problem behaviors. *American Psychologist, 58,* 433–440. http://dx.doi.org/10.1037/0003-066X.58.6-7.433

Boulden, W. T. (2005). Evaluation of the ANYTOWN leadership institute programming on lesbian, gay, bisexual, and transgender issues. *Journal of Gay & Lesbian Social Services, 17,* 17–38. http://dx.doi.org/10.1300/J041v17n04_02

Boulden, W. T. (2006). Youth leadership, racism, and intergroup dialogue. *Journal of Ethnic & Cultural Diversity in Social Work, 15,* 1–26. http://dx.doi.org/10.1300/J051v15n01_01

Cornwall, A., & Jewkes, R. (1995). What is participatory research? *Social Science & Medicine, 41,* 1667–1676. http://dx.doi.org/10.1016/0277-9536(95)00127-S

Fuertes, J. N., Sedlacek, W. E., Roger, P. R., & Mohr, J. J. (2000). Correlates of universal-diverse orientation among first-year university students. *Journal of the First-Year Experience & Students in Transition, 12,* 45–59.

Glasgow, R. E., Vogt, T. M., & Boles, S. M. (1999). Evaluating the public health impact of health promotion interventions: The RE-AIM framework. *American Journal of Public Health, 89*, 1322–1327. http://dx.doi.org/10.2105/AJPH.89.9.1322

Griner, D., & Smith, T. B. (2006). Culturally adapted mental health intervention: A meta-analytic review. *Psychotherapy: Theory, Research, Practice, Training, 43*, 531–548. http://dx.doi.org/10.1037/0033-3204.43.4.531

Hawkins, J. D., Shapiro, V. B., & Fagan, A. A. (2010). Disseminating effective community prevention practices: Opportunities for social work education. *Research on Social Work Practice, 20*, 518–527.

Hawks, E. M. (2010). *Bridging the science and practice of prejudice reduction: Explaining the effects of a community-based diversity acceptance program*. Unpublished master's thesis, Central Michigan University, Mount Pleasant, MI.

Herek, G. M., Gillis, J. R., Cogan, J. C., & Glunt, E. K. (1997). Hate crime victimization among lesbian, gay, and bisexual adults: Prevalence, psychological correlates, and methodological issues. *Journal of Interpersonal Violence, 12*, 195–215. http://dx.doi.org/10.1177/088626097012002003

Hernandez, M., Nesman, T., Mowery, D., Acevedo-Polakovich, I. D., & Callejas, L. M. (2009). Cultural competence: A literature review and conceptual model for mental health services. *Psychiatric Services, 60*, 1046–1050. http://dx.doi.org/10.1176/ps.2009.60.8.1046

Israel, B., Eng, E., Schulz, A. J., & Parker, E. A. (2005). *Methods in community-based participatory research for health*. San Francisco, CA: Wiley.

Jansson, S. M., Benoit, C., Casey, L., Phillips, R., & Burns, D. (2010). In for the long haul: Knowledge translation between academic and nonprofit organizations. *Qualitative Health Research, 20*, 131–143. http://dx.doi.org/10.1177/1049732309349808

Kanyangara, P., Rime, B., Philippot, P., & Yzerbyt, V. (2007). Collective rituals, emotional climate, and intergroup perception: Participation in "Gacaca" tribunals and assimilation of the Rwandan genocide. *Journal of Social Issues, 63*, 387–403. http://dx.doi.org/10.1111/j.1540-4560.2007.00515.x

Kessler, R. C., Mickelson, K. D., & Williams, D. R. (1999). The prevalence, distribution, and mental health correlates of perceived discrimination in the United States. *Journal of Health and Social Behavior, 40*, 208–230. http://dx.doi.org/10.2307/2676349

Lemarchand, R. (1998). Genocide in the Great Lakes. Which genocide? Whose genocide? *African Studies Review, 41*, 3–16. http://dx.doi.org/10.2307/524678

Lyons, E. M. (2005). *The effects of a leadership and diversity awareness program on adolescents' attitudes and behaviors*. Unpublished doctoral dissertation, University of South Florida, Tampa, FL.

Mason, W. A., Fleming, C. B., Thompson, R. W., Haggerty, K. P., & Snyder, J. J. (2014). A framework for testing and promoting expanded dissemination of promising preventive interventions that are being implemented in community settings. *Prevention Science, 15*, 674–683. http://dx.doi.org/10.1007/s11121-013-0409-3

Minkler, M., & Wallerstein, N. (2003). *Community-based participatory research for health*. San Francisco, CA: Jossey-Bass.

Morrissey, E., Wandersman, A., Seybolt, D., Nation, M., Crusto, C., & Davino, K. (1997). Toward a framework for bridging the gap between science and practice in prevention: A focus on evaluator and practitioner perspective. *Evaluation and Program Planning, 20*, 367–377. http://dx.doi.org/10.1016/S0149-7189(97)00016-5

National Research Council and Institute of Medicine. (2000). *Improving intergroup relations among youth: Summary of a research workshop*. Washington, DC: National Academies Press.

Olson, M. A. (2009). Measures of prejudice. In T. D. Nelson (Ed.), *Handbook of prejudice, stereotyping, and discrimination* (pp. 367–386). New York, NY: Psychology Press.

Otis, M. D., & Loeffler, D. N. (2005). Changing youths' attitudes toward difference: A community-based model that works. *Journal of Social Work with Groups, 28*, 41–64. http://dx.doi.org/10.1300/J009v28n01_04

Paluck, E. L. (2009). Reducing intergroup prejudice and conflict using the media: A field experiment in Rwanda. *Journal of Personality and Social Psychology, 96*, 574–587. http://dx.doi.org/10.1037/a0011989

Paluck, E. L., & Green, D. P. (2009). Prejudice reduction: What works? A review and assessment of research and practice. *Annual Review of Psychology, 60*, 339–367. http://dx.doi.org/10.1146/annurev.psych.60.110707.163607

Pascoe, E. A., & Smart Richman, L. (2009). Perceived discrimination and health: A meta-analytic review. *Psychological Bulletin, 135*, 531–554. http://dx.doi.org/10.1037/a0016059

Pettigrew, T. F., & Tropp, L. R. (2006). A meta-analytic test of intergroup contact theory. *Journal of Personality and Social Psychology, 90*, 751–783. http://dx.doi.org/10.1037/0022-3514.90.5.751

Rand, M. R. (2009, September). National Crime Victimization Survey: Criminal victimization in 2008. *Bureau of Justice Statistics Bulletin*, 1–8. Retrieved from http://www.bjs.gov/content/pub/pdf/cv08.pdf

Rose, J., & Glass, N. (2008). The importance of emancipatory research to contemporary nursing practice. *Contemporary Nurse, 29*, 8–22. http://dx.doi.org/10.5172/conu.673.29.1.8

Sadowski, Y. (1998). Ethnic conflict. *Foreign Policy, 111*, 12–23. http://dx.doi.org/10.2307/1149375

Spoth, R., Redmond, C., Clair, S., Shin, C., Greenberg, M., & Feinberg, M. (2011). Preventing substance misuse through community–university partnerships: Randomized controlled trial outcomes 4½ years past baseline. *American Journal of Preventive Medicine, 40*, 440–447. http://dx.doi.org/10.1016/j.amepre.2010.12.012

Staub, E. (2006). Reconciliation after genocide, mass killing, or intractable conflict: Understanding the roots of violence, psychological recovery, and steps toward a general theory. *Political Psychology*, 27, 867–894. http://dx.doi.org/10.1111/j.1467-9221.2006.00541.x

Staub, E., Pearlman, L. A., Gubin, A., & Hagengimana, A. (2005). Healing, reconciliation, forgiving and the prevention of violence after genocide or mass killing: An intervention and its experimental evaluation in Rwanda. *Journal of Social and Clinical Psychology*, 24, 297–334. http://dx.doi.org/10.1521/jscp.24.3.297.65617

Staub, E., Pearlman, L. A., Weiss, G., & Hoek, A. (2008). *Public education through radio to prevent violence, promote trauma healing and reconciliation, and build peace in Rwanda and the Congo.* Unpublished manuscript. Retrieved from http://people.umass.edu/estaub/radio%20article%20--January%202008.pdf

U.S. Department of Justice. (2012, October). *Uniform crime reports: Hate crime statistics, 2011.* Washington, DC: Federal Bureau of Investigation. Criminal Justice. Information Services Division. Retrieved from http://www.fbi.gov/about-us/cjis/ucr/hate-crime/2011/narratives/incidents-and-offenses

Wallerstein, N., & Duran, B. (2003). The conceptual, historical, and practice roots of community-based participatory research and related participatory traditions. In M. Winkler & N. Wallerstein (Eds.), *Community-based participatory research for health* (pp. 27–52). San Francisco, CA: Jossey-Bass.

Wandersman, A., & Florin, P. (2003). Community interventions and effective prevention. *American Psychologist*, 58, 441–448. http://dx.doi.org/10.1037/0003-066X.58.6-7.441

Wandersman, A., Duffy, J., Flaspohler, P., Noonan, R., Lubell, K., Stillman, L., . . . Saul, J. (2008). Bridging the gap between prevention research and practice: The interactive systems framework for dissemination and implementation. *American Journal of Community Psychology*, 41, 171–181. http://dx.doi.org/10.1007/s10464-008-9174-z

INDEX

AACU (Association of American Colleges and Universities), 304
Abdominal adiposity, 169
Abdullah, T., 89
Ability grouping (education), 196
ABP (ambulatory blood pressure), 167
Abrams, D. B., 149
Academic achievement, 142
Acculturation, 237–238, 277
Acosta v. Huppenthal, 309
Acting-White thesis, 276–277, 279
Activism, 33
Acupressure, 264
Acute racism reactions model, 12, 19
Adams, A., 307
Additive approach to perceived racism, 34, 36
ADHD (attention-deficit/hyperactivity disorder), 141
Adler, N. E., 165–166, 171
Adolescence
　eating habits in, 149
　experiences of racism in, 139–142
Adulthood, 145–146
　older, 146–147
　young, 142–145
Affirmative action, 14, 204, 205, 215, 300
African Americans
　and adolescent resilience, 142
　and biopsychosocial model of racism, 17
　blood pressure reactivity in, 73
　and colonization, 260
　C-reactive proteins in, 147
　depression in, 15, 64, 91
　educational access of, 235
　educational segregation of.
　　See Educational segregation
　history of, 230–231
　and housing discrimination, 232
　individualism amongst, 116
　and job earnings, 212–213
　and job selection, 210–211
　and learning communities, 303–304
　one-stage discrimination assessment with, 70
　online discrimination toward, 60
　and overrepresentation in criminal justice system, 16
　physiological effects of racism on, 164–172, 175–177
　racial trauma of, 249, 250, 252
　rates of disease and death in, 55
　religion as coping skill for, 89
　research on racism based on, 23
　and self-esteem, 116–117
　stress exposure in, 74
　and substance use during young adulthood, 143, 144
　unemployment rates of, 206
Afro-Caribbean populations, 176
Ageism, 94
Aguado, T., 305
Aiello, A. E., 146
Ajrouch, K. J., 91
Albert, M. A., 175
Alcohol use, 15, 16. *See also* Substance use
Allostatic load, 145
Altschul, D. B., 16
Alvarez, A. N., 35
Ambulatory blood pressure (ABP), 167
American Indians/Alaska Natives
　diabetes prevalence in, 169
　dislocation of, 231–232
　educational access of, 235
　historical trauma of, 59
　intergenerational trauma with, 17
　need for future research on racism toward, 23–24
　physiological effects of racism on, 55, 165, 167–168
　racial trauma of, 250
　stereotyping of, 13
　and storytelling, 261
　and substance use, 15, 143, 232
American Psychological Association, 310
Anchoring vignettes, 67–68
Anderson, J. D., 277
Anderson, N., 167
Anderson, N. B., 163, 173
Andes, S., 173

Anger, 174
Annan, K., 229
Anticipatory racism reactions, 19
Anticipatory stress, 62–64
Antiracist education, 296, 318. *See also* Education interventions for reducing racism
Antonio, M., 168
Anxiety, 60, 63, 94, 250
ANYTOWN intervention, 325–333
Apfel, N., 112
Appraisal support, 90
Arab Americans, 59, 137
Arce v. Huppenthal, 309
Arizona law, 309
Aronson, E., 297
Arrington, E. G., 98
Art therapy, 253
Asian Americans
 and adolescent resilience, 142
 careers held by, 207
 coping skills of, 88
 educational access of, 235–236
 growing research on racism toward, 23
 and housing discrimination, 232
 physiological effects of racism on, 165, 168–171
 racial trauma of, 249
 racism-related stress in, 35
 tobacco use by, 71
 unemployment rates of, 206
Association of American Colleges and Universities (AACU), 304
Attention-deficit/hyperactivity disorder (ADHD), 141
Authenticity (therapeutic relationship), 263
Avoidant coping, 37
Awad, G., 47
Ayscue, J. B., 194

Baffoe-Bonnie, J., 212
Baker, B., 196
Balsam, K. F., 41–42
Banks, J., 306
Barnes, L. L., 146
Bauer, D. J., 252
Beadnell, B., 41–42
Beal, F., 36
Beatty, D., 87–88

Beauty norms, 137, 148
Belief in a just world (BJW), 94–95
Belief in an unjust world (BUW), 94–95, 117
Bell, D. A., 274
Bell, Derrick, 274
Bennett, G. G., 61
Bennett, G. G., Jr., 177
Bertrand, M., 211
Biko, Steve, 22
Biomarkers, 175
Biopsychosocial model of disease risk, 173
Biopsychosocial model of racism, 12, 17
Birth outcomes, 139, 163, 172–173
BJW (belief in a just world), 94–95
Black and Latino Male Resource Center (BLMRC), 304
Black consciousness movement, 22
Black feminism, 33, 38, 40
Black Feminist Thought (Patricia Hill Collins), 33
Black populations. *See* African Americans
Black-white achievement gap, 276–281
Black Youth Culture Survey, 140
BLMRC (Black and Latino Male Resource Center), 304
Blood pressure (BP). *See also* Diastolic blood pressure; Systolic blood pressure
 chronic high. *See* Hypertension
 and perceived racism, 73
 physiological effects of racism on, 56, 165–167, 179
Blustein, D. L., 218–220, 222–223
Bobo, L. D., 72
Body movement, 264
Bondy, E., 307
Bonilla-Silva, E., 137, 190
Borders, A., 94
Bowie, J. V., 168
Bowleg, L., 41, 42, 44, 45, 91–92
BP. *See* Blood pressure
Brady ver Halen, N., 87–88
Brandeis High School (New York City), 281–286
Brave Heart, M. Y., 16
Breastfeeding, 138
Breath work, 264
Brittian, A. S., 91

Brody, G. H., 143
Brondolo, E., 87–88
Brooding, 93
Brooks, K., 41
Brosschot, J. F., 63
Brown, E., 307
Brown, T. L., 89
Brown v. Board of Education, 134, 190, 192, 196, 273–275
Brown-Wright, L., 144
Bryant-Davis, T., 254
Brzustoski, P., 112
Buhin, L., 308
Buka, S. L., 149
Bunche, T., 306
Butler, C., 169, 170, 176
Buttner, E. H., 215
BUW (belief in an unjust world), 94–95, 117

CAC (coronary artery calcification), 56, 171
California Health Interview Survey, 71
Cancer, 172
Cane, P., 264
Capitalism, 12
Carbone, P., 197
Card, D., 142
Cardiovascular disease, 163, 170–171
  and cortisol dysregulation, 176
  and C-reactive protein, 175
  reactivity and recovery with, 176–177
  risk factors for, 165
Career-related racism, 203–222
  future directions for research on, 221–222
  integrative framework for understanding costs of, 207–210, 216
  in job search, selection, and earnings, 210–214
  and job turnover/job satisfaction, 214–218
  prevalence of, 204
  and racial disparities in workforce, 206–207
  theories relevant to, 216–221
Carrera, S., 91
Carter, Bob, 274
Carter, R. T., 18, 63, 251, 256, 305

Carter-Tellison, K., 212
Caucasian (White) heritage, 12
CBPR (community-based participatory research), 319–321. *See also* Community interventions
Chae, D. H., 165–166, 171
Chambers, E. C., 169, 170
Chao, R. C., 91
Charter schools, 284–285
Chase, J., 16
Chavez, Cesar, 238
Chávez, N. R., 97
Cheng, W. J., 88
Chen, J., 165
Chicago Community Adult Health Study, 74
Chicago School Board, 276
Childhood
  eating habits in, 149
  experiences of racism in, 139–142
Children's Health Insurance Program, 143
Chinese Exclusion Act, 236
Chithambo, T. P., 93
Christianity, 89–90
Chronic stressors, 57–58
Civil Rights Movement, 191, 230
Civil Rights Project, 192
Civil War, 230
Clark, K. B., 196, 275
Clark, Kenneth, 260, 273–274, 289, 290
Clark, M. P., 275
Clark, R., 18, 64, 163, 173
Clark, V. R., 163, 173
Class. *See* Social class; Socioeconomic status
Classism, 39
Cognitive control, 122
Cognitive flexibility, 112, 122–123
Cognitive impairment, 56, 172
Cognitive processes, 92–95
Cognitive vulnerabilities, 110, 112
Cohen, G. L., 112
Cokley, K., 47
Cole, E. R., 35–36, 38, 39
Collective healing, 238–239
Collective Self-Esteem Scale, 48
College-level education, 236
Collins, J. W., Jr., 173
Collins, Patricia Hill, 33

Collins, R., 166
Colonialism, 12, 250
Coloniality of power, 260
Color-blind racism
 in educational segregation, 191, 195
 overview, 13–14
Comas-Díaz, L., 254, 257, 258
Combahee River Collective, 40
Communities of color, 229–239
 and acculturation, 237–238
 collective healing and empowerment in, 238–239
 education access in, 235–236
 impact of dislocation and relocation in, 231–232
 impact of immigration policies on, 236–237
 incarceration of, 282
 mental health issues in, 234–235
 poverty and racism in, 230–231
 segregation in, 232–234
Community-based participatory research (CBPR), 319–321. *See also* Community interventions
Community interventions, 317–333
 dissemination of, 332–333
 examination and documentation of, 325–327
 improvement of, 331–332
 participatory research on, 319–321, 325, 327, 328
 practice-to-science strategy for, 319, 323–325
 research on effectiveness of, 328–330
 and science-practice gap, 319–320
 science-to-practice strategy for, 319, 321–323
 sustainability of, 324
Comparative approach to perceived racism, 34–36
Computer occupations, 206
Confusion, racism-related, 19
Conscientization, 260
Consciousness raising, 22–23
Contrada, R. J., 87–88
COPE Inventory, 89
Coping
 avoidant, 37
 defined, 87

 and life course perspective of racism, 135–136
 maladaptive, 19
 as moderator and mediator in perceived racism, 86–90
 and physiological effects of racism, 174
 types of, 21
Cornelious, K., 176
Coronary artery calcification (CAC), 56, 171
Cortina, L. M., 215–216
Cortisol dysregulation, 175–176
Cort, M. A., 169
Cozier, Y. C., 168
Crawford v. Board of Education of the City of Los Angeles, 193
Crenshaw, Kimberlé Williams, 32
Criminal justice system, 16
Critical psychology, 219
Critical race theory (CRT)
 color-blind racism in, 13–14
 conceptualizations of racism in, 190–191
 intersectionality in, 32
 and social policy, 279
Critical social psychological research, 273–290
 accurate reporting in, 275
 on black-white achievement gap, 276–281
 on delinquency, 276
 on race-neutral policies, 281–286
 and racial justice, 289–290
 on stop and frisk, 286–289
 on welfare and personal responsibility, 278–279
Crocker, J., 116
Cross-cultural competency, 306
Cross, W., 277
Cross, W. E., Jr., 280–281
CRPs. *See* C-reactive proteins
CRT. *See* Critical race theory
Cultural paranoia, 63
Cultural racism. *See also* Institutional/structural racism
 defined, 13
 effects of, 14
Cultural resilience, 259

Cultural socialization, 96
Cumulative disadvantage, 145
Cunningham, T. J., 175
CVD. *See* Cardiovascular disease

DACA (Deferred Action for Childhood Arrivals), 239
Dang, P., 38
Darwinian ideology, 12
DAS (Detroit Area Study), 63–64
David, R. J., 173
Davis, S. K., 166
Davis, T., 301
Dawes Allotment Act, 231
DBP (diastolic blood pressure), 167, 176–177
DeBlaere, C., 41
de Castro, A. B., 165, 207
De facto segregation, 190
Deferred Action for Childhood Arrivals (DACA), 239
De jure segregation, 190
Delinquency, 276
Denson, N., 301
Denton, N. A., 194–195
Depression, 109–124
    Black-White disparity in, 64
    cognitive processes in, 93
    and coping, 174
    correlation between racism and, 15
    identity's role in, 121
    and internalized oppression, 16
    and interpersonal stress, 119–120
    measures of, 48
    mediators of effects of racism to, 113
    as moderator between racism and health, 19
    and physiological effects of racism, 164
    and racial trauma recovery, 250
    and racism's effect on cognitive processes, 122
    relational schemas in, 118–120
    schemas about the self in, 114–117
    schemas about the world in, 117–118
    social cognitive models of racism and, 110–113
    and social support, 91
    and trauma, 60
    and within-school segregation, 142
Derman-Sparks, L., 306, 308
Desensitization (racial trauma recovery), 257–258
Detroit Area Study (DAS), 63–64
De Walque, D., 211
Diabetes mellitus (DM), 163, 169–170, 176, 232
Diastolic blood pressure (DBP), 167, 176–177
Diemer, M. A., 219
Dill, B. T., 38
Din-Dzietham, R., 166
Discrimination, perceived. *See* Perceived discrimination
Dislocation, 231–232
Distal variables, 47–48
Diversity coursework, 300–301
DM. *See* Diabetes mellitus
Doane, L. D., 176
Dobbins, C. J., 93
Doctor-patient relationships, 147
Dokecki, P., 238
Dolan, P., 68
Dole, N., 172
Dolezsar, C. M., 167
Doll studies, 273–274
"Double jeopardy" (racism and sexism), 36. *See also* Additive approach to perceived racism
Douroux, A., 38
Dovidio, J. F., 215, 300
Dowd, J. B., 68
Dowell v. Board of Education in Oklahoma City Public Schools, 192
Dream Act, 239
Dual language immersion programs, 311
Du Bois, W. E. B., 11, 288
Duffy, R. D., 219
Dumka, L. E., 91
Dunbar, E., 254
Duran, E., 250, 262

EA (environmental affordances) model, 150
Eating behaviors, 19, 149
Eberly, M. B., 307

EC (emancipatory communitarian) approach, 205
Echenique, F., 142
Ecological model, 296
Educational psychology, 219
Educational segregation, 189–198, 273–274
   causes of, 192–197
   and definitions of racism, 190–191
   effects of, 194–195
   and eugenics, 195–197
   future directions for research on, 197
   history of, 191–192
   modern-day, 134, 136
   research on, 142
   and tracking, 195–197
Education interventions for reducing racism, 295–311
   ecological model for, 296
   in higher education, 299–304
   in K–12 settings, 297–299
   and policy, 308–311
   racial identity development in, 305–308
   teacher preparation for, 304–305
Education level, 21
Education policy, 194–195
Edwards, C. L., 61, 177
EEOC (U.S. Equal Employment Opportunity Commission), 145
Egalitarianism, 96, 98–99
Eggerth, D. E., 218
Elkins, J., 16
Elliott, Jane, 299
Emancipatory communitarian (EC) approach, 205
Embrick, D. G., 137
EMDR (eye movement desensitization reprocessing), 253, 257
Emotional support, 90
Emotional work, 149
Empathy training, 298–299
Employment and racism. *See* Career-related racism
Empowerment, 21–22, 238–239, 262
Enacted support, 91
Engberg, M. E., 301
English as a second language (ESL) classes, 197, 310

Environmental affordances (EA) model, 150
Espiritismo, 257
Essed, Philomena, 37
Ethnic/indigenous healing, 257–258
Ethnic prejudice, 110–111
Ethnic socialization, 96–99
Ethnography, 47
Eugenics, 195–197
Eurocentrism, 137, 260
Everyday Discrimination Scale, 58, 63
Expansionism, 12
Experiences of Discrimination scale, 57
Externalizing behaviors, 91
External validity, 47
Eye movement desensitization reprocessing (EMDR), 253, 257

Factorial analysis of variance, 48
Fang, C. Y., 176–177
Fann, M., 38
Fatigue, 19
Feagin, J. R., 134
Feeding Your Demons treatment approach, 265–266
Feminism, 33, 38, 40, 219
Feminist therapy, 253
Fetal origins hypothesis, 139
Field experiences (education interventions), 306–307
Filipinos, 165, 169, 250
Financial stressors, 73
Fine, M., 47, 282–283
Fischer, M. J., 142
Floyd, et. al. v. The City of New York, et. al., 288–289
Flynn, M. A., 218
Foa, E. B., 259
Folkman, S., 86–87
Follo, E. J., 307
Forbearance, 88
Ford, C. L., 14
Foster, M. D., 88
Fouad, N. A., 203
Fowler, S., 61
Framing Dropouts (M. Fine), 282
Frazier, E. Franklin, 276
Frazier, P. A., 86

Freire, Paulo, 238, 260
French, S. B., 97
Friden, G., 238
Fryer, R. G., 142
Fujii-Doe, W., 35
Fullilove, Mindi, 290

Gaertner, S. L., 300
Galleta, Anne, 277, 279–281, 285
Gangi, R., 282
Garcia, J., 112
Garran, A. M., 14, 238–239
Gavin, A., 168
Gee, G. C., 14, 165, 166, 168, 178
Gender
   and effects of racism, 21
   in intersectional approaches, 34–39
   and racial trauma recovery, 258, 259
   and substance use, 143–144
Gendered Racial Microaggressions Scale (GRMS), 37
Gendered racism, 37–38
Genocide, 59
Gentlemen's Agreement, 236
Gerin, W., 63
Geronimus, Arlene, 290
Gibbons, F. X., 93
Gilman, S. E., 149
Glucose intolerance, 16
Goar, C., 137
Gomez, J. P., 71
Gone, J. P., 17
Gonzales, N. A., 91
Gonzalez, A., 297
Gonzalez, R., 93
Goodwin, A. L., 305
Goss, T. N., 277
Green, D. P., 317, 318, 322
Greene, Beverly, 40
Green v. County School Board of New Kent County, 192
GRMS (Gendered Racial Microaggressions Scale), 37
Grounded theory, 47
Grzanka, P. R., 32, 33
Guerrero, L., 220
Gurin, P., 302
Gwebu, E. T., 169
Gwebu, K., 169

Hackman, J. R., 220
Hall, R. L., 47
Hamilton, V. J., 146
Hancock, A.-M., 44
Handler, A., 173
Harnois, C. E., 49
Harpalani, V., 277
Harrell, S. P., 18
Harris-Britt, A., 98
Harrison, M. S., 210
Hate crimes, 317–318
Health outcomes of racism. *See* Physiological effects of racism
Heart disease. *See* Cardiovascular disease
Heart rate variability, 174–175
Helms, J. E., 306
Herzig, A. J. M., 167
Heterosexism, 41–42. *See also* Sexual orientation
Higher education, 299–304
Hispanic/Latino populations
   and academic achievement, 142
   and adolescent resilience, 141
   anticipatory discrimination in, 63
   deportation of, 237
   depression in, 15
   educational access of, 235
   and educational segregation, 192–195
   and housing discrimination, 232
   and learning communities, 303–304
   microaggressions directed toward, 35
   and overrepresentation in criminal justice system, 16
   physiological effects of racism on, 55, 166, 168–169, 175
   racial trauma of, 249
   in research on racism, 23
   stress exposure in, 74
   and substance use during young adulthood, 143
   unemployment rates of, 206
Historical trauma. *See also* Racial trauma recovery
   defined, 16
   intergenerational effects of, 59
   overview, 16–17
HIV-risk behaviors, 144
Hmong populations, 235

Hohensee, J., 306
Holland, J. L., 214, 217–218
Holocaust, 59
Homel, M. W., 276
Hostility, 117
HTN. *See* Hypertension
HUD (U.S. Department of Housing and Urban Development), 232
Hughes, D., 96
Huguley, J. P., 97
Human capital theory, 211–213
Hunte, H. E., 168
Hurricane Katrina, 232–233
Hutu ethnic group, 322–323
Hypertension (HTN), 19, 64, 165–167

IAT (Implicit Association Test), 66
Identity, 121, 140–141
Ideology, 190–191
Ifatunji, M., 49
Immigration policies, 236–237
Immune system effects of racism, 139
Implicit Association Test (IAT), 66
Implicit racial bias, 174
Incarceration, 282
Index of Race-Related Stress, 49, 57, 59
Indigenous healing, 257–258
Individualism, 116, 191
Individual racism
 as central in psychological models of racism, 20
 defined, 13
 media attention on, 14
 as one level of racial bias, 134
Industrial/organizational (I/O) psychology, 209, 219, 221
Infancy, 138–139
Inflammation biomarkers, 175
Influenza vaccine, 147
Insidious trauma, 252
Institutional/structural racism. *See also specific headings, e.g.* Educational segregation
 in adolescence and childhood, 142
 and critical social psychological research, 274–275, 289
 defined, 13
 and definitions of racism, 190–191
 effects of, 14
 in life course perspective, 136–137
 as one level of racial bias, 134
 and schemas in depression, 118
 web of, 14
Instrumental support, 90
Interactional approach to perceived racism, 34, 36
Intergenerational trauma, 16–17
Intergroup contact theory, 297, 300
Intergroup dialogues, 302–303
Internalized racism and oppression
 and cortisol levels, 176
 and cultural racism, 14
 effects of, 20
 lack of research on, 16
 and physiological effects of racism, 168–171
 and racial trauma recovery, 251–252
 research on, 275
Internal validity, 47
Interpersonal discrimination, 14, 139–142. *See also* Perceived discrimination
Interpersonal stress, 119–120
Intersectional approaches to perceived racism, 31–50
 checklist for, 43–44
 and coping, 88
 definitions, 32–34
 gender in, 34–39
 methodological frameworks for analysis in, 42–49
 and racial trauma recovery, 264
 sexual orientation in, 40–42
 social class in, 39–40
Intragroup racism, 114–115
Intuition work, 264
I/O psychology. *See* Industrial/organizational psychology
Ismail, A., 91
Isolation, 16

Jaakkola, M., 91
Jackson Heart Study, 62
Jagers, R. J., 22
Japanese Americans, 88
Jasinkaja-Lahti, I., 91
"Jigsaw classroom" intervention, 297–298

Jim Crow laws, 191, 192, 230
Job earnings, 210–214
Job satisfaction, 214–218
Job search and selection, 210–214
Job turnover, 214–216
Jones, C., 37
Jones, J. M., 14
Jordan, J., 263
Journalism, 219
Juang, L. P., 35
"Just Walk on By: Black Men and Public Space" (B. Staples), 148

K–12 school settings, 297–299
Kaholokula, J. K., 176
Kantamneni, N., 203
Kaspar, V., 88
Kaufman, A., 142
Kavetsos, G., 68
Kelly, J., 146
Kernahan, C., 301
Kim, C., 301
King, Martin Luther, Jr., 238
Klassen, A. C., 168
Klonoff, E. A., 258
Klor de Alva, J., 11
Kluger, Richard, 273
Koenig, B. W., 140
Kohlman, M. H., 38
Korean Canadians, 88–89
Krieger, N., 22, 166
Kuhel, K., 307
Kurtz-Costes, B., 98
Kyle, D., 307

Labor economics, 219
Labyrinth techniques, 264
Ladson-Billings, G., 308
Laflamme, D. F., 166
Lake, V. E., 307
Landrine, H., 258
Latino populations. *See* Hispanic/Latino populations
Lau, A. S., 97
Lauderdale, D. S., 59
Laurenzi, C., 219
Lavizzo-Mourey, R., 63
Lawrence, S. M., 306
Lazarus, R. S., 86–87

Learned helplessness, 234–235
Learning communities, 303–304
Lee, E., 305
Lent, R. W., 221
Lepore, S. J., 177
Lerner, M. J., 94
Lesbian, gay, bisexual, transgender, and queer (LGBTQ) people of color, 40–42, 287
Leurgans, S., 146
Lewis, J. A., 19, 37
Lewis, T. T., 56, 73, 146
LGBTQ (lesbian, gay, bisexual, transgender, and queer) people of color, 40–42, 287
LGBTQ People of Color Microaggressions Scale, 41–42
Lhamon, Catherine E., 194
Liang, C. T. H., 35, 38, 94
Liang, M. X., 35
Liberation psychology, 259, 262
Liebkind, K., 91
Life course experiences of racism, 133–150
    in adulthood, 145–146
    in childhood and adolescence, 139–142
    future directions for research on, 148–150
    in older adulthood, 146–147
    terminology, 134–135
    and theoretical perspectives, 135–138
    in utero/infancy, 138–139
    in young adulthood, 142–145
Lim, S., 91
Lincoln, K. D., 171
Lindström, M., 63
Lin, M., 307
Lin, N., 90
Liu, L. L., 97
Lorde, Audre, 40
Lott, B., 39

Macrostressors, 58
Major depressive disorder. *See* Depression
Major Experiences of Discrimination scale, 57

Major life events (perceived discrimination), 57
Making Excellence Inclusive (MEI), 304
Mao, S., 39
Marshall, Thurgood, 274
Martin, Trayvon, 234
Maslow, A., 218
Mason, W. A., 324, 328, 331–332
Massage, 264
Massey, D. S., 142, 194–195
Mathematical occupations, 206
Mazzula, S. L., 35
McCourt, Frank, 285
McCubbin, L. D., 168
McGrath, J. J., 167
McGregor, J., 299
McIntyre, E., 307
McNeilly, M., 167
Measurement of perceived discrimination, 55–74
 and capturing all types of discrimination, 57–60
 improvement of, 60–62
 minimizing bias in, 64–72
 and other stressors, 72–74
 vigilance and anticipatory stress measurement in, 62–64
Mediators in perceived racism. See Moderators and mediators in perceived racism
MEI (Making Excellence Inclusive), 304
Mental health
 in communities of color, 234–235
 and interpersonal racism, 14
 overview of racism's effects on, 15
Merritt, M. M., 177
Mexican populations, 91, 176, 220, 309
Meyers, H. F., 176–177
Michigan Civil Rights Amendment, 309, 310
Microaggressions
 defined, 251
 and learned helplessness, 234–235
 media attention on, 14
 by therapists, 252–253
 toward LGBTQ people of color, 41–42
Midlife in the United States (MIDUS) study, 62, 69

Miller, D. T., 94
Miller, H., 38
Miller, J., 14, 238–239
Miller, S. B., 167
Mind-body self-regulation, 257, 264
Minimization bias, 65–67
Minnesota theory of work adjustment, 217–218
Miranda, R., 93
MJP (Morris Justice Project), 286–289, 294
Moderators and mediators in perceived racism, 85–100
 cognitive processes, 92–95
 coping, 86–90
 ethnic/racial socialization, 96–99
 overview, 86
 social support, 90–92
Molina, Y., 41–42
Moore, G., 307
Moradi, B., 36, 115
Morris Justice Project (MJP), 286–289, 294
Mortality rates, 16, 56
Moskowitz, Eva, 284
Mossakowski, K. N., 146
Movement therapy, 253
Mullainathan, S., 211
Multicultural education interventions, 297–299
Multidimensional model of racism-related stress, 18
Murdock, T. B., 259
Musekeweya (radio-based intervention), 322–323
Musical arts, 219
Mustillo, S., 172
Mutuality (therapeutic relationship), 263

Nadal, K. L., 35
Nagata, D. K., 88
Nagda, B. A., 301
Narrative analysis, 47
Nathwani, A., 38
National Center for Education Statistics (NCES), 235, 295
National Conference of Christians and Jews (NCCJ), 326–327

National Crime Victimization Survey (NCVS), 317
National Education Association, 299n1
National origin, 317
National Survey of American Life, 69, 140
Native Americans. *See* American Indians/Alaska Natives
Native Hawaiians/Pacific Islanders
　educational access of, 235
　physiological effects of racism on, 55, 165, 166, 168–171, 176
NCCJ (National Conference of Christians and Jews), 326–327
NCES (National Center for Education Statistics), 235, 295
NCVS (National Crime Victimization Survey), 317
Nembhard, W. N., 166
Neuroimaging research on perceived racism, 72
Neurological impairments, 172
Neville, H. A., 19, 37, 296, 299, 308
New Orleans, 232–233
New York Police Department (NYPD), 286–289
New York Times, 278, 281, 282
Niemann, Y. F., 215
No Child Left Behind Act, 191
Noh, S., 88
Nolen-Hoeksama, S., 93
Nursing home segregation, 146–147
Nuru-Jeter, A. M., 165–166
NYPD (New York Police Department), 286–289

Obama, Barack, 236, 239
Obesity, 167–169, 232, 233
Objectivity, 191
Ocampo, C., 254
Occupational health psychology, 219
Ogbu, John, 276–277
Older adulthood, 146–147
Oldham, G. R., 220
One-stage approach to discrimination assessment, 70
Optimism, 97
Ota Wang, V., 238
Otiniano Verissimo, A. D., 143

Pacific Islanders. *See* Native Hawaiians/Pacific Islanders
Pal Da Gum techniques, 264
Paluck, E. L., 317, 318, 322
Paradies, Y., 3, 167, 173
Parents, 96–97
Pascoe, E., 252
Pascoe, E. A., 165
Pavalko, E. K., 146
Payne, Yasser, 290
Payton, Carolyn, 8
Pearlin, L. I., 73, 92
Peer relationships, 144
Pencille, M., 87–88
Perceived racism. *See specific headings*
Perceived Racism Scale, 58
Perceived support, 90
"Perceptions of control," 93
Perry, J. C., 219
Personal control, 116
Personality, 21
Personality traits, 214, 217, 221
Personal responsibility, 278–279
Perspective taking, 298–299
Pessimism, 97
Phillips, C. M., 89
Physiological effects of racism, 163–179. *See also* Health disparities; Psychosocial model of racism and health
　birth outcomes, 139, 163, 172–173
　cancer, 172
　cardiovascular disease, 163, 170–171
　diabetes, 163, 169–170
　factors in, 16
　hypertension and blood pressure, 165–167
　with interpersonal racism, 14
　obesity, 167–169
　overview, 15, 16
　pathways in, 173–179
　with self-reported health status, 164–165
Pieterse, A. L., 19
Plessy v. Ferguson, 192
Policy, 194–195, 279, 308–311
Political ideology, 21
Ponterotto, J. G., 49
Positive marginality, 47

Positivist research paradigms, 44–45
Posttraumatic growth, 256
Posttraumatic stress disorder (PTSD), 18, 60, 61, 250. *See also* Racial trauma recovery
Poteat, V. P., 140
Poverty. *See also* Socioeconomic status
   in communities of color, 230–231
   and health care, 16
Power differential analysis, 262–263
Practice-to-science strategy, 319, 323–325
Prilleltensky, I., 238
Promotion of mistrust, 96
Proximal variables, 47–48
Psychoanalytic theories, 219
Psychological decolonization, 259–261
Psychological rumination, 93–94
Psychosocial model of racism and health, 18–19
Psychosocial model of racism and resistance, 19–20
PTSD. *See* Posttraumatic stress disorder
Public regard, 120
Purdie-Vaughns, V., 112
Pyke, K. D., 16

Qualitative methodology, 44–47, 189, 197
Quantitative methodology, 44–47

Race, as social construct, 12, 190, 204n1
Race-based rejection sensitivity, 119, 120
Race-based traumatic stress, 250, 251. *See also* Racial trauma recovery
Race-based traumatic stress model (RBTSM), 12, 18
Race-informed therapeutic approach (racial trauma recovery), 254–255
Race neutrality, 191, 281–286
Race to the Top, 191
Racial bias, 96, 301
Racial identity, 174
Racial identity development, 305–308
Racial identity theory, 306
Racial justice, 289–290
Racial prejudice, 110–111

Racial segregation
   in communities of color, 232–234
   effects of, 136–137
   and intergroup contact theory, 297
   in nursing homes, 146–147
   residential, 142, 192
   in school. *See* Educational segregation
Racial socialization, 96–99, 116
Racial trauma recovery, 249–267
   assessment of stress and trauma in, 255–256
   clinical illustrations, 264–266
   clinical treatment for, 253–254
   desensitization in, 257–258
   and legacies of oppression, 250–253
   and prevention of trauma, 266–267
   psychological decolonization in, 259–261
   race-informed therapeutic approach for, 254–255
   reprocessing in, 258–259
   social action in, 261–262
   therapeutic relationship in, 262–264
Racism. *See also specific headings*
   defined, 109, 190–191
   intragroup, 114–115
Racism and Life Experiences scale, 57
Racism and racial discrimination, 11–24
   definition of, 13
   evidence for consequences of, 3
   future directions for research on, 22–24
   history of, 12–13
   overview of adverse impacts of, 14–17
   pathways of, 13–14
   theoretical models for impact of, 17–22
Racism-related stress
   coping techniques for, 89
   in employment, 145
   measurement of, 60–64
   multidimensional model of, 18
   physiological effects of, 173–177. *See also* Physiological effects of racism
   and social support, 92
   in utero and infancy, 138
Racist-incident-based trauma, 252
Ramsey, P., 308

RBTSM (race-based traumatic stress model), 12, 18
Reactions to Race module, 61–62
Redington, R. M., 40
Reflective pondering, 93
Reisine, S., 91
Relational schemas, 118–120
Relational theories, 219
Religion, 89–90, 239, 317
Religious discrimination, 94
Relocation, 231–232
Reprocessing (racial trauma recovery), 258–259
Residential segregation, 21
Resilience
    adolescent, 141–142
    cultural, 259
Resistance to racism, 21–22
Reuter, A., 91
Reynolds, R., 197
RIASEC (Realistic, Investigative, Artistic, Social, Enterprising, and Conventional) types, 214, 217
Rice, D., 307
Riggs, D. S., 259
Risco, C., 115
Ritual techniques, 264
Ritz, S. F., 41
Rivera, A., 38
Rivera, D. P., 35
Ro, A., 168
Robertson, J., 89
Robinson, E. L., 61
Roosa, M. W., 176
Rothbaum, B. O., 259
Rothstein, J., 142
Rowley, S. J., 98
Roy, Arundhati, 290
Rue, T., 207
Rumination, 93–94
Russell, S. T., 140
Rwanda, 322–323
Ryan, A. M., 166

Sakura-Lemessy, D., 212
Sakura-Lemessy, I., 212
Salcedo, J., 38
Santerismo, 257
Saxon, S., 39

SBP (systolic blood pressure), 167, 177
Schedule of Racist Events, 57, 255
Schemas
    about the self, 114–117
    about the world, 117–118
    relational, 118–120
    in social cognitive models, 110, 112
Schiraldi, V., 282
School segregation. See Educational segregation
Schuette v. Coalition to Defend Affirmative Action, 309
Schwing, A. E., 38
Science-practice gap, 319–320
Science-to-practice strategy, 319, 321–323
SCWM (social class worldview model), 40
SDT (self-determination theory), 219, 220
Segregation. See Racial segregation
Self-actualization, 218
Self-control, 93, 116
Self-determination theory (SDT), 219, 220
Self-esteem, 16, 115–117
Self-focused attention, 119
Self-medication hypothesis of substance use, 136
Self-reported discrimination. See Perceived discrimination
Self schemas, 114–117
SES. See Socioeconomic status
Sexism. See also Gender
    and belief in a just world, 94
    joint impacts of racism and, 21
Sexual behavior, 144
Sexual orientation, 40–42, 317
Sharf, R. S., 219
Shariff-Marco, S., 168
Sherwood, A., 167
Sheu, Y. T., 176
Shields, S. A., 44, 45
Shorris, E., 11
Shorter-Gooden, K., 21, 37
Sidney, S., 22, 166
Simoni, J., 41–42
Sinclair, K. O., 140
Singh, S., 220

Single-axis approach to perceived racism, 34–35
Skin tone, 210–211
Slavery, 276–277
Sleep problems, 56
Smart Richman, L., 165, 252
Smedley, A., 190
Smedley, B. D., 190
Smith, Barbara, 40
Smith, L., 39, 40
Smith, S., 93
Smoking, 71, 138–139, 142, 149
Social action, 96–99, 116, 261–262
Social capital, 213
Social class worldview model (SCWM), 40
Social cognitive models of racism and depression, 110–113. *See also* Depression
Social cognitive theory, 92
Socialization
  cultural, 96
  ethnic, 96–99
  and physiological effects of racism, 174
Social norms, 137–138
Social reproduction theory, 211–212
Social support
  defined, 90
  and life course perspective of racism, 136
  as moderator and mediator of discrimination, 90–92
Socioeconomic status (SES)
  in African American communities, 231
  and birth outcomes, 139
  and discrimination, 67
  and health care, 56
  impact of segregation on, 233
  in intersectional approaches to perceived racism, 39–40
  and job earnings, 212
  overview, 21
  and physiological effects of racism, 164, 165, 171
  and tobacco use, 149
Sociology, 219

Sohn, W., 91
Sollers, J. J., III, 177
Solórzano, D. G., 190–191
South African Stress and Health study, 69
Spanierman, L. B., 19, 296, 299, 308
Special education, 196
Spencer, M. B., 98, 277
Spencer, M. S., 165
Spiritual development, 253, 257–258
Standardized testing, 191
Staples, B., 148–149
The Star of Ethiopia (W. E. B. Du Bois), 288
Status attainment theory, 211–212, 219
Steffen, P. R., 167
Stereotype confirmation concern, 118, 298
Stereotypes
  and community interventions, 317
  in intersectionality research, 49
  of Native Americans, 13
  of "welfare queens," 40
Stereotype threat, 121
Stevenson, E. G., 98
Stevens-Watkins, D., 144
Stigma consciousness, 119
Stop and frisk policing, 286–289, 294
Storytelling (clinical technique), 253, 261
Stoudt, Brett, 286
Stress, 112, 119–120, 135–136. *See* Racism-related stress
Stress inoculation method, 258–259
Stress proliferation, 148
Stress theory, 144
Stroke, 165
Strong intersectionality, 38
Structural diversity, 300
Structural racism. *See* Institutional/structural racism
Subich, L. M., 36
Substance use
  birth outcomes related to maternal, 172
  and dislocation, 232
  in early adulthood, 143–144
  and racism during adolescence, 141

Success Academy, 284–285
Suh, S. A., 72
Su, J. C., 91
Syme, S. L., 171
Systemic racism, 134. *See also* Institutional/structural racism
Systolic blood pressure (SBP), 167, 177

Tai Chi, 264
Takeuchi, D., 165
Takeuchi, D. T., 165, 168, 207
Taylor, T. R., 172
Teacher preparation (education interventions for reducing racism), 304–305
Thayer, J. F., 63
Therapeutic relationship, 262–264
Thirteenth Amendment, 230
Thomas, A. J., 37
Thomas, K. M., 210
Tobacco use. *See* Smoking
Todd, M., 68
Toomey, R. B., 91
Torre, Maria Elena, 286
Torrey, C. L., 219
Tracking (educational segregation), 195–197
Trait-factor models, 214–217
Trauma
    defined, 57
    historical. *See* Historical trauma
    recovery from racial. *See* Racial trauma recovery
    symptoms in response to, 60
Trauma-focused cognitive behavioral therapy, 253
Traumatic Life Events Questionnaire, 62
Treynor, W., 93
Trierweiler, S., 71
Tripartite model of racism/racial discrimination, 14
"Triple jeopardy" (racism, sexism, and sexual discrimination), 40
Truelove, Y., 301
Tull, E. S., 169, 170, 176
Tutsi ethnic group, 322–323
Twenge, J. M., 116
Tyler, K., 144

Unemployment rates, 206, 213
Unfair treatment, 72
United States Department of Justice (USDOJ), 317
USA Today, 278
U.S. Bureau of Labor Statistics, 206
U.S. Department of Education, 194, 283
U.S. Department of Housing and Urban Development (HUD), 232
U.S. Equal Employment Opportunity Commission (EEOC), 145
Utsey, S. O., 19, 49, 266

Valrie, C. R., 98
Van Ausdale, Feagin, 139
Vera, E. M., 308
Vigilance
    bias linked to, 65
    measurement of, 62–64
Vines, A. I., 168, 174
Vinson, E., 89
Violence, 233–234
Visualization techniques, 257, 264, 265
Vocational psychology, 204, 205, 209
Voting rights, 135

Wall, S., 173
Wallston, B. S., 93
Wallston, K. A., 93
Walters, K., 41–42
Wandersman, A., 332
Wang, M. T., 97
Warren, R. C., 63
Watts, R. J., 22
Weak intersectionality, 38
Wei, M., 91
Weiner, M., 299
Welfare, 278–279
West, C., 11
White flight, 192
White privilege, 12
"Who Must Do the Hard Things" (Carolyn Payton), 8
Wiggins, R. A., 307
Williams, D. R., 63, 70, 163, 168, 173
Williams, N. C., 22

Williams, R. B., 177
Wolin, K. Y., 61
Wong, Y. J., 38
Workforce entry and work adjustment. *See* Career-related racism
Workplace discrimination, 204–205
Workplace stress, 41
Work volition, 219–220
Work Volition Scale, 219
World literature, 219
Wright, F., 299

Yeh, C. J., 91
Yosso, T. J., 190–191
Young adulthood, 142–145
Youth Diversity Acceptance scale (YoDA), 328–329

Zeiders, K. H., 176
Ziedenberg, J., 282
Zimmerman, George, 234
Zirkel, S., 298
Zoning laws, 195

ABOUT THE EDITORS

Alvin N. Alvarez, PhD, is dean of the College of Health and Social Sciences and professor of counseling at San Francisco State University. He completed his undergraduate degree at the University of California–Irvine in biological sciences and psychology and received his doctorate in counseling psychology from the University of Maryland. His scholarship focuses on Asian Americans, racial identity, and the psychological impact of racism. Dr. Alvarez is the coauthor, with Nita Tewari, of *Asian American Psychology: Current Perspectives*. His scholarship has been supported by the National Institute of Mental Health, and he has been awarded the Janet E. Helms Award for Mentoring and Scholarship, the Asian Pacific American Network Research Award from the American College Personnel Association, the Best Paper for 2011 from the *Asian American Journal of Psychology*, and the American Psychological Association Tanaka Memorial Dissertation Award. He has also been awarded the Lifetime Achievement in Mentoring Award from the Society of Counseling Psychology. He is a former president of the Asian American Psychological Association, from which he received the Early Career Award for Distinguished Contributions and the Distinguished Contributions Award. His proudest achievements are his two daughters—Sabrina (7) and Sophie (4)—who are convinced they are smart and funny girls with even more important things to accomplish!

Christopher T. H. Liang, PhD, is an associate professor of counseling psychology at Lehigh University. He is a former president of the Society for the Psychological Study of Men and Masculinity (Division 51) of the American Psychological Association. His research interests center on how perceived racism and masculinity ideologies are associated with academic, psychological and physiological health, and health-related behaviors of ethnic minority boys and men. Dr. Liang also examines the role of coping, psychological rumination, and just-world beliefs in the associations between perceived racism and health outcomes for people of color. His work has been published in a number of peer-reviewed journals. The purpose of his research lines is to determine effective individual-level, systems-level, and policy-oriented interventions. For instance, Dr. Liang has worked with school districts, universities, departments of health and human services, as well as not-for-profit community organizations, to strengthen their capacity to serve diverse children, youth, and families. Dr. Liang currently serves on the editorial boards of *The Counseling Psychologist* and the *Psychology of Men and Masculinity*.

Helen A. Neville, PhD, is a professor of educational psychology and African American Studies at the University of Illinois at Urbana–Champaign. She is a past associate editor of *The Counseling Psychologist* and the *Journal of Black Psychology*. Her research on race, racism, and color-blind racial ideology has appeared in a wide range of peer-reviewed journals. Dr. Neville has been recognized for her research and mentoring efforts, including receiving the American Psychological Association (APA) Graduate Students Kenneth and Mamie Clark Award, the APA Division 45 Charles and Shirley Thomas Award for mentoring/contributions to African American students/community, and the APA MFP Dalmas Taylor Award for Research. She was honored with the Association of Black Psychologists' Distinguished Psychologist of the Year award and the Winter Roundtable Janet E. Helms Mentoring Award.